150.195
Y84w

Young-Bruehl, Elizabeth
Where do we fall when we fall in love?

DATE DUE

Where Do We Fall When We Fall in Love?

Where Do We Fall When We Fall in Love?

Elisabeth Young-Bruehl

IVCCD Libraries
MCC B. J. Harrison Library
Marshalltown, Iowa 50158

OTHER

Other Press
New York

Copyright © 2003 Elisabeth Young-Bruehl

Eight essays in this book appeared previously in the following journals and are reprinted with permission:

"Cherishment Culture," coauthored with Faith Bethelard, in *American Imago*, vol. 55 no. 4, 1998.

"The Hidden History of the Ego Instincts," coauthored with Faith Bethelard, in *Psychoanalytic Review*, vol. 56 no. 6, Dec. 1999.

"The Wise Baby as the Voice of the True Self," coauthored with Faith Bethelard, in *Psychoanalytic Quarterly*, LXVIII, 1999, pp. 585–610.

"A Visit to the Budapest School," in *Psychoanalytic Study of the Child*, vol. 57, November, 2002.

"Reflections on Women and Psychoanalysis," in *Psychoanalysis and Psychotherapy*, vol. 18 no. 1, Spring, 2001.

"Are All Human Beings 'By Nature' Bisexual?" in *Studies in Gender and Sexuality*, vol. 2 no. 3, 2001.

"Beyond 'The Female Homosexual'," in *Studies in Gender and Sexuality*, vol. 1 no. 1, 2000.

"Homophobia: A Diagnostic and Political Manual," in *Constellations*, vol. 9 no. 2, June, 2002.

Production Editor: Robert D. Hack

This book was set in 11 pt. Goudy by Alpha Graphics of Pittsfield, New Hampshire.

10 9 8 7 6 5 4 3 2 1

All rights reserved. No part of this publication may be reproduced or transmitted in any form or by any means, electronic or mechanical, including photocopying, recording, or by any information storage and retrieval system without written permission from Other Press LLC, except in the case of brief quotations in reviews for inclusion in a magazine, newspaper, or broadcast. Printed in the United States of America on acid-free paper. For information write to Other Press LLC, 307 Seventh Avenue, Suite 1807, New York, NY 10001. Or visit our website: www.otherpress.com.

Library of Congress Cataloging-in-Publication Data

Young-Bruehl, Elisabeth.
  Where do we fall when we fall in love? / by Elisabeth Young-Bruehl.
    p. cm.
  Many of the essays in this book appeared previously in various journals between 1998 and 2002.
    Includes bibliographical references and index.
    ISBN 1-59051-068-2 (alk. paper)
    Psychoanalysis. 2. Freud, Sigmund, 1856-1939. I. Title.
BF173 .Y68 2003
150.19'5—dc21   2003005494

For Lois and Ernest Sutton,
my cherishing parents,
to celebrate their 80th birthdays

Contents

Preface ix

Part I
Cherishment Psychology

1. Where Do We Fall When We Fall in Love? 3

2. Cherishment Culture 23
   (*coauthored with Faith Bethelard*)

3. The Hidden History of the Ego Instincts 45
   (*coauthored with Faith Bethelard*)

4. The Wise Baby as the Voice of the True Self 75
   (*coauthored with Faith Bethelard*)

5. A Developmental Matrix for the Ego Ideal 99

6. A Visit to the Budapest School 129

Part II
Sexual and Gender Identity

7. Reflections on Women and Psychoanalysis 157

8. Are Human Beings "By Nature" Bisexual? 179

9. Beyond "The Female Homosexual" 213

Part III
Character Theory and Its Applications

10. The Characters of Violence 249

11. Homophobias: A Diagnostic and Political Manual 271

12. Psychoanalysis and Characterology 285

13. *Amae* in Ancient Greece 311
    (*coauthored with Joseph Russo*)

Index 329

Preface

My earliest essays, collected in *Mind and the Body Politic*, 1989, were composed when I was a young university professor in a Humanities program, writing in the *Habilitationschrift* style for which my Ph.D. in Philosophy, bestowed by German émigré professors, had prepared me. Erudition was my ideal. But I was also, in those days, Hannah Arendt's biographer and preparing to be Anna Freud's biographer, a person struggling to find a voice worthy of general, nonscholarly readers. So my second, more memoiristic essay collection, *Subject to Biography: Psychoanalysis, Feminism, and Writing Women's Lives*, 1999, was full of reflections on being a biographer, on biography writing, and on the history of biography, particularly of women. Being true to my subjects and myself was my ideal then, and, not surprisingly, I was transitioning into training to be a psychoanalyst. This third collection, named after its opening essay, *Where Do We Fall When We Fall in Love?*, is entirely the work of my years practicing as a psychoanalyst. Clinical experience shaped it, and my ideal became to work with other people, to be receptive.

Philosopher. Biographer. Psychoanalyst. About a decade in each role. Like serial marriages—and, in fact, each decade was organized around a "significant other" (as the term goes) as well as around a significant mode of working, thinking, writing. By the standards for Love and Work of some crusty old-time Freudians, my movement from one "other" to another and my career changes would look like neurotic inconstancy or at least immaturity—something a good analysis might cure. But, in my more modern Freudian training analysis, I came to think of this course of mine as something seasonal, the patterns of which taught me a great deal while I worked to understand them and change them where they needed changing. And it also became clear to me that through all the seasons I have been asking questions about the conditions of change, the creative possibilities change can signal, and the characterological blocks that make change impossible. Constantly, I was considering the ways in which change can—even if painful, full of mourning—renew, mark new beginnings. The essays in this collection reflect my questions as they have played out in clinical work and its therapeutic action. They celebrate (and theorize about) the Growth Principle.

That term, "the Growth Principle," comes from a book that I began writing in 1995 with my friend and colleague Faith Bethelard. The result of our collaboration, *Cherishment: A Psychology of the Heart*, published in 2000, is the matrix in which all the essays in this collection germinated, especially those in the first part, three of which are joint productions with Faith Bethelard, direct spin-offs of our book.

Because *Cherishment* is a discursive, meandering, conversational book, not a treatise on theory or clinical technique—we thought of it as a double memoir—the contribution we hoped to make to psychoanalytic theory is nowhere summarized or distilled in it. There is no overview in these essays either, although all presume the *Cherishment* ideas and each of the first six essays charts a dimension of our contribution, an angle of it, a consequence of it. Several years ago I did, however, write a set of notes that we used to keep our thoughts organized when we were lecturing or doing workshops in connection with *Cherishment*. To frame all the essays, and especially those in Part I, I want to present that text.

NOTES FOR PSYCHOANALYTIC AUDIENCES

1. Among many contemporary psychoanalytic theorists, speaking about instinctual drives is regarded as retrograde or naïve, but we nonetheless find it theoretically and clinically useful—not to mention respectful of our biological, embodied existence—to say that there are two main groups of human instinctual drives: the ones originally posited by Freud (1910–1913), which he designated the self-preservative *ego instincts* and the species-preservative *sexual instincts*. (Freud initially also used the terms "the affectionate current" and "the sensual current," which reflect better his concern for energy or drive, *Trieb*, rather than the "instinct" animal biologists refer to. But Freud later confusingly described "the affectionate current" not as an independent instinctual current manifesting itself earlier than the sensual current, but as a precipitant in adolescence out of "the sensual current," a remnant, the implication being that seeking affection is a sublimation or transformation of seeking sexual pleasure.) The manifestations of the two drives coming into relation to objects were named *ego interests* and libidinal investments or *libidinal cathexes*.

2. Nowhere in all his writings did Freud discuss the ego instincts with any specificity. But, following those in Ferenczi's school, chiefly Michael Balint, we believe the ego instincts are object-related from birth—from before birth. They are first expressed as needs for the first objects, the first caregivers, to give food, warmth, safety, care, and (crucially) cherishing affection, which includes empathic attunement; later they are expressed or represented mentally as conscious wishes, narrative and declarative memories, and hopes (eventually ideals). Gradually, a child's emergent ego is able to direct its instinctual energy more consciously, intentionally toward objects. That is, the ego instincts' evolving relations to objects actually bring the ego into power, structure it, differentiate it as the relational agency of the mind and body.

3. Being object-related is, for the emergent ego, being preserved, for the objects the emergent ego seeks preserve it while it is helpless and dependent. It may be, as Freud said, that satisfying hunger is the prototypical ego instinct aim, but an infant also seeks to preserve itself in the emotional sense—it seeks soul food, cherishment as well as nourishment. In emotional terms, the ego instincts are (to use the terms of the Japanese psychoanalyst Takeo Doi) "the expectation to be sweetly

and indulgently loved." Or, to put the closeness of hunger and emotional hunger in mythological terms: everyone seeks "the land of milk and honey"—not just milk but sweetness. While the emergent ego seeks care, the caregivers seek to give care *as the child wants it*, that is, in response to the child, in reciprocity, and in attunement to the child's need for care. Our very first conversations are cherishment exchanges.

4. The sexual instincts are originally directed primarily at the child's own body; they are autoerotic. Sonograms show fetuses handling their genitals in utero, exciting themselves, playing. The infant's autoerotic condition is what Freud called *primary narcissism*, that is, libido is held within the emergent ego. The primary narcissistic libidinal condition slowly diminishes as the child discovers the erotic pleasures and excitements of other people's bodies, primarily the (usually) maternal caregiver's. As Freud noted, the sexual instincts flowing outward follow initially the paths or the evaluations and interests of the ego instincts, which are not primarily narcissistic. This means that the child's first erotic object is the breast, which feeds the child, which is care, nourishment. (Note that it has been an assumption—an incorrect one, we think—among psychoanalysts that an "object relations theory" requires rejecting Freud's notion of primary narcissism, as Melanie Klein, among others did; we are arguing that the primary narcissism notion should pertain to the sexual instincts, not the ego instincts.)

5. As Freud argued, the sexual instincts, which follow the *Pleasure Principle*, seeking pleasurable increase and release of tension and excitement, are tempered and shaped by the *Reality Principle*, which reflects, fundamentally, the physical conditions and limitations of life, but which also reflects—and more and more importantly as a child grows—familial and cultural conditions. We believe that the ego instincts follow what can be called the *Growth Principle*, which means that they seek to fulfill an inborn maturational thrust (and much child study work has been done to show that this thrust is a program) for development while they seek the safe care and cultivation that make growth possible. The ego instincts, like the sexual instincts, are tempered and shaped by the Reality Principle, but the Reality Principle in relation to the Growth Principle of the ego instincts refers fundamentally to the biological limits upon growth and development and also to the limits of growth-sponsorship into which the child is born—that is, each child is subject to the conditions of its cherishment. A child cannot have sex

with its parents for reasons of biological immaturity and social restriction (the incest taboo); a child can only develop in certain ways and at certain rates for reasons of biological program and the fact that perfect care and cherishment are beyond the means of any caregiver. The Reality Principle limitations upon sex and those upon growth-promoting or self-preserving cherishing love are different, although overlapping; similarly, the types of frustrations are different.

6. In certain periods of development, the ego instinctual drive usually predominates over the sexual. These are (a) the first year of life, when physical growth is more rapid than at any other time after gestation, and the child's dependency needs are greatest; (b) the latency period, when a child is so involved with sociality and the discovery of cherishing people other than those in the immediate family; and (c) in later adulthood, especially after the sexual shift of menopause in women and its equivalents in men. On an individual basis, people usually have other periods of ego instinctual predominance throughout adulthood, and those who have lacked cherishment in childhood tend to the extremes of always seeking predominately affection rather than sex, or of denying their needs for affection and often pursing sexual aims instead.

Similarly, there are periods when the sexual instincts predominate over the ego instincts: (a) in the anal and phallic-genital libidinal stages or during the years of the Oedipus complex; (b) in prepuberty and early adolescence; (c) during adulthood (with much, much individual variation and combination). Adolescence, which is a time of both "sexual efflorescence" (in Freud's phrase) and enormous growth in both physical and emotional object-relational terms, is a period of rapid interplay of ego instinctual and sexual instinctual expressions, and this interplay is a key ingredient of adolescence's often noted "storm and stress." Generally, the ego instincts and the sexual instincts rise and fall, oscillate, in relation to each other. Usually, the sexual instincts initially follow upon the first evaluations or interests and object relations of the ego instincts—so the infant's relation with its first caregiver is a template for the sexual instincts, and when this is not the case, the sexual instincts, without guidance, can remain very autoerotically organized and narcissistic, or they may unfold chaotically, inconstantly.

7. People generally develop ideals in relation to their instinctual drives. They will idealize, for example, harmony between the satisfied

instincts as happiness or contentment. Many people have an ideal object who is imagined as the source for them of both affection and sexual pleasure, as they have a romantic or romance ideal of how sex and affection should relate. But there are also ideals that elevate affection over sex or vice versa, splitting the two in some way.

8. In the history of psychoanalysis, a distinction was slowly made between the preoedipal and the oedipal periods in developmental terms but also in terms of transference in the analytic situation. It was recognized that experiences and elements of the two periods appeared in the transference differently. There are certainly sexual instinctual derivatives from the preoedipal that appear in the transference, but it is usually the ego instinctual interests and frustrations from the preoedipal that form the kernel or *the core of the transference*. They appear as efforts—to use the Japanese verb—to *amaeru* (presume upon someone's love, coax or cuddle up for love).

9. As the ego grows it comes into accord with the Reality Principle by means of two types of structuring. With respect to the Pleasure Principle, it is structured as the *superego*, which is made up of indentifications with and internalizations of the first sexual objects, primarily the parents, but also others in its early environment (like siblings). The superego is the voice of the past in individuals, like a Greek chorus, an agency of warning about limits, constraint, control, punishment, warning, "no." With respect to the Growth Principle, the ego is structured by the *ego ideal*. This is made up of the child's identifications with and internalizations of the cherishment it has been given, so it is the child's capacity for self-cherishment, or for promotion of its own growth. Initiallly, the ego ideal is a bodily ideal, a sense of being safely in one's own skin, boundaried, and then, after a number of developmental stages out of this matrix, the ego ideal is more a matter of identity-feeling ("this is the me I wish to be") and spiritual values. The ego ideal is a future-oriented agency of encouragement, disciplining (not punishing) vision, "yes."

10. A person whose ego instinctual drive has been frustrated, who has not been well preserved, which means cared for and cherished, becomes aggressive in response. This *aggression* is different in quality from the aggression that results when the sexual instincts are frustrated. The uncherished child becomes aggressive against relationships; it cuts itself off from relationships. The first step in such a cutting off is an internal

splitting: the ego divides into an ego still expecting cherishment and one that has given up angrily. The angry ego's state is, fundamentally, *envy*. All other people seem to have the relationships it lacks; it envies all means and modes of relationship (and both sexes envy the opposite sex's but also everyone's organs *as organs of relatedness*, so that there is general penis envy, breast envy, womb envy). The splitting of the ego may mean fragmentation or breakdown, especially when the thwarting of the expectation to be loved has been extremely traumatic. Such a person has the "all bad" mental world of the borderline (into which outbreaks of expectation to be loved by "all good" objects sometimes burst) or the all-attacking mental world of the paranoid. But more often, the angry ego aggressively nourishes its own cut-off state, its grudge, and becomes self-sufficient or self-enclosed, unreceptive, rigid, cynical, so that what is left of the expectation to be loved is covered over, hidden. The person whose sexual instinctual drives have been frustrated aggressively goes in pursuit or works to get pursued (with sadism and masochism as characteristic of these modes). In life and in therapy, most people show a great mixture of the two types of aggression stemming from ego instinctual frustrations and sexual instinctual frustrations.

11. Metapsychologically, it is not necessary to assume a "death instinct" as the foundation for aggression if aggression is understood as frustration of these two basic intertwined sorts. The phenomena that led Freud to his death instinct hypothesis—compulsions to repeat traumatizing experiences, masochistic acts, negative therapeutic reactions—can be interpreted as ways of trying to overcome loss of love and relatedness. In the case of compulsion to repeat, an effort to deny the incredible fact that love and relatedness have been refused or destroyed operates. A person who cannot summon such an effort is depressed; incredulity—the "I do not believe that I am not loved!"—is the core of the depression.

12. The psychoanalytic theory of the *mechanisms of defense* that was developed with respect to the sexual instincts and, later, to aggression, can be adapted to explore the mechanisms by which the ego instinctual drives are controlled and channeled. Studying ego and superego control of the sexual instincts, the early Freudians noted that the defenses most characteristic of hysteria are repression, regression, reversal into the opposite, while the defenses most characteristic of obsessional neurosis are the "intellectual" ones: intellectualization or

rationalization, doing and undoing, isolation (especially of affect). The defenses that preponderate when it is predominantly the ego instinctual drive that has been frustrated are the ones that can be described as creating or re-creating an object to relate to: introjection, projection and projective identification. Reaction formation can be understood as re-creating a hated person as a loved person in order to be loving rather than aggressive toward him or her. Similarly, denial can be interpreted as re-creating an object as loving rather than as hating or not cherishing, and, by extension, re-creating situations, scenes, experiences, as loving, not hurting.

13. Similarly, psychoanalytic theory of character can be adapted to recognize that there are ego instinctual ingredients of character—not just the sexual instinctual ingredients that were key to Freud's early theory of oral, anal, and genital characters. The character types (not called such) proposed by theorists of attachment, for example, are in this domain.

The last few notes—especially the very last—point to topics that I have taken up in the essays in Parts II and III of this collection, which focus on sex and gender identity (a domain our *Cherishment* book did not really approach, but a long-standing interest of mine) and on character. I have written about character in two other books, *Creative Characters* and (at greater length) *The Anatomy of Prejudices*, which provides the framework for the essay included here under the title "The Characters of Violence." But only in the next-to-last essay here, "Psychoanalysis and Characterology," published for the first time, have I ever tried to step back and reflect psychoanalytically on characterology as a way of thinking and organizing clinical work.

Finally, I am pleased to include as the last chapter in this volume an essay that was coauthored with my dear friend Joseph Russo, Professor of Classics at Haverford College, a scholar of many interests and a distinguished commentator on Homer's *Odyssey*. We teamed up to try to show that in ancient Greek there is an extensive system of words that express the ego instinctual drive for cherishment. We don't have such a vocabulary in modern English, and this is certainly one reason why it has taken English and American psychoanalysts a long time to revise Freud's work in the direction of recognizing an instinctual drive for object relatedness. This essay was written for an audience of classical scholars, but we hope that it will be of interest to a broader readership, including clinicians.

The essays in this collection were all delivered, whole or in sections, as lectures before they came into their final forms, so I am grateful to many people, many audiences, for their responses and thus their collaboration. For their hospitality, too, I am indebted to colleagues at Austen Riggs, the Chicago Psychoanalytic Society, the National Psychological Association for Psychoanalysis, the New York Psychoanalytic Society, the New York University Postdoctoral Program, APT in Philadelphia and the Philadelphia Society for Psychoanalytic Psychology, the Pittsburgh Psychoanalytic Society, the Post-Graduate Center for Mental Health, the University of Pennsylvania Humanities Center, the Washington DC branch of the New York Freudian Society, the New Directions program of the Washington Psychoanalytic Society, the William A. White Institute, and the Western New England Psychoanalytic Society in New Haven. Good copy editing work was done at the journals where some of the essays first appeared: *American Imago, Psychoanalytic Review, Psychoanalytic Quarterly, The Psychoanalytic Study of the Child, Psychoanalysis and Psychotherapy*, and *Studies in Gender and Sexuality* (where I am honored to be a contributing editor and to have benefited from Virginia Goldner's and Ken Corbett's editing).

PART I

CHERISHMENT PSYCHOLOGY

1

Where Do We Fall When We Fall in Love?

FREE FALL AND FALL TO EARTH

In recent years, evolutionary psychologists have been counting the ways in which people love one another. With their new techniques for revealing our biochemical and neurophysiological selves, a group of the contemporary Darwinians have had no trouble taking the mystery out of romantic love. They tell us that when we fall in love we are falling into a stream of naturally occurring amphetamines running through the emotional centers of our very own brains. That is why we feel exhilarated, manic, powerful, creative, suddenly grown-up if we are young and suddenly rejuvenated if we are older. The ecstasy of love is located in our nerves; we get high; we speed. Eventually, our nerves being what they are, their endings become amphetamine immune or exhausted, and the delirium of our free fall abates. We come down to earth.

The very same evolutionists who have explained passion as an amphetamine rush have seen in the fall to the quotidian of love the appearance of endorphins, those natural, morphine-like agents of calm. After periods of wildness, we human beings settle into attachment—if we do not crash or break up on the way down. The fall after the fall is into daily routine, child-rearing, going to work in the morning, participating in community life—all the attachment actions that you cannot do if you are tripping on amphetamines. The endorphins are our attachment regulators. But, these evolutionists go on to claim, receptor sites in the brain can become desensitized to endorphins as well. Even the calm of love's earthbound maturity phase—love's depressive position—must come to an end, and people, then, are ready once more for passion: they separate, divorce, commit adultery, cruise, add another concubine to their collection, go in for serial monogamy, or in some way move along to another amphetamine high. To one degree or another, everyone is, if I may use a fashionable phrase, a love addict, an alleged neurophysiological fact that would be perfectly obvious if we did not have all kinds of institutions, like marriage, to protect from view the deterioration of love's calmer forms and the reappearance of the infatuation high.

So, this is one current sociobiological imaginary for explaining love's old roller coaster. The scientific merits of such an evolutionary theory and its appeal to the alleged facts of natural amphetamine processes are certainly debatable, but the fashionableness of its imagery is attested to by the commercial success of Helen Fisher's *Anatomy of Love*, which can be read without even high school chemistry. Why would such an evolutionary theory be so fashionable now?[1] I think that the current state of love relations in America, where these theories are proliferating, is so distressing to so many people that there is tremendous appeal in an approach that explains—in one giant sweep—how we are hard-wired for passion, for attachment or marriage, and for divorce. It makes all of the above natural. Thus, among those who are worrying

---

1. In the version of evolutionary theory I am citing, the explanation for our move toward attachment is this (for men only): "For primitive man two aspects of relating to the opposite sex were important for survival as a species. The first was to have males and females become attracted to each other for long enough to have sex and reproduce. The second was for the males to become strongly attached to the females so that they stayed around while the females were raising their young and helped to gather food, find shelter, fight off marauders and teach the kids certain skills" (Fisher 1992, p. 164).

about "family values," a familiar old enemy is reaffirmed: it is our nature, in the form now of natural amphetamines, that must be fought. We must mount a war on our body's drugs. Just say no. Even the troubling matter of homosexuality can be at once denounced as an aberration because it does not promote reproduction, and forgiven if a homosexual will only, like any heterosexual adulterer, put a check of prayer or psychotherapy on his or her natural amphetamines.

But I think that explanations like these neo-Darwinian ones, which can support or substitute for religious fundamentalism, also serve to obscure psychological phenomena that are distressing for less moral-political reasons. Specifically, they obscure what it is in sexual passion that so often leads not to attachment but to impossibilities of attachment, whether tragic or comic or tragicomic. And they obscure what it is in attachment that is so frightening to us human beings and so frighteningly difficult, with the result that we as often fall away from love as we fall into its earthbound attachment forms. These are the topics I want to take up in this essay, while considering in my terms the old roller coaster of love—the tension between passion and attachment—that the neo-Darwinians have tried to explain in their terms.

My terms will presuppose the instinct theory that Sigmund Freud developed in the decade before the First World War. In that period of his work, Freud was elaborating psychologically the central Darwinian idea, adapted by the contemporary neo-Darwinists, that there are two instinct systems: the sexual instincts, which serve reproduction or preservation of the species, and the ego instincts, which serve self-preservation. He was exploring the interrelations of "the sensual current" and "the affectionate current." "Love and Hunger are the forces that rule the world," Freud said, borrowing a line from the poet Schiller's "Die Weltweisen."

But, although I am going to consider the sexual instincts and the ego instincts, I am going to develop his duality differently than Freud did because I think that Freud was just as conventional in his ideas about the sexual instincts and the ego instincts as the evolutionists were in his day and are again in our day. He thought of the aim of sexuality as pleasure, which he defined very narrowly as tension reduction, and he thought of species preservation in only one way: making of children. On the other hand, he never explored the aim of the ego instincts at all, finding it sufficient to think of self-preservation in only one narrow way: as avoidance of death from, for example, hunger, or from any other failure of biological function. But it seems to me that in human beings the fundamental aim of sexuality would better be defined as "taking pleasure in another version of yourself," and child production is only one such version. Similarly, the fundamental aim of the ego instincts is "growing," or "developing," which not only *requires* relatedness rather than aloneness, but *is* relatedness.

ON THE SEXUAL INSTINCTUAL AND THE EGO INSTINCTUAL, NARCISSISTIC OBJECTS AND ANACLITIC OBJECTS

To speak about sexual passion and about attachment or about sexual instincts and ego instincts without acknowledging the evolutionary and psychoanalytic strands of our modern tradition would be impossible. But I am going to begin my exploration by turning to a period in our historical tradition that precedes the infusion into it of Jewish and Christian ideas about the importance of ruling and taming our untamed and unruly sexual nature. The ancient Greeks, who, as Freud once astutely noted, were more interested in the sexual instinct itself—eros—than in stipulating which objects of desire in this world (or the next) were to be deemed worthy, created an image of the trouble with sexual passion that does not dwell on how it goes wild and wreaks havoc.[2] The Greeks did advise aphoristically "nothing too much," but their preoccupation was not with control; rather, they explained that our human trouble is that when we fall in love we fall in love with ourselves.

The image that the Greeks gave us for this insight is, of course, of a beautiful adolescent, Narcissus by name, who has recently spurned the nymph Echo and then rejected the handsome youth Amenius. Neither

---

2. To this statement there are obvious exceptions, particularly in parts of the Platonic corpus, which were later so attractive to Christian philosophers. Note Freud's (1905) observation: "The most striking distinction between the erotic life of antiquity and our own no doubt lies in the fact that the ancients laid stress on the instinct itself, whereas we emphasize its object. The ancients glorified the instinct and were prepared on its behalf to honor even an inferior object, while we despise the instinctual activity in itself, and find excuses for it only in the merits of the object" (p. 143, n. 1).

a female nor a male allures him—or perhaps it is that neither a female alone nor a male alone allures this androgyne. Now he is lying by a reflecting pool where the huntress goddess Artemis—quite androgynous herself—is punishing him with the condition named after him: he has fallen in love with his own image. He has fallen into a rapturous but unconsummatable love.

As Dante knew so well, the Greek gods and goddesses specialized in punishments for mortals that did unto them what they had done unto others. So Artemis made Narcissus suffer an unconsummated love and then commit suicide, as Amenius had done when Narcissus refused his suit. The blood that spurted onto the earth as Narcissus plunged a dagger into his own heart seeded white narcissi with red coronas by the side of the still pool. The nymph Echo, unforgiving in her unrequited love, but also cursed with being able to speak only other people's words, looked on as Narcissus died, sighing, "Alas! Alas!" while he sighed, "Alas! Alas!"

This extraordinarily complex image has had tremendous power for centuries, I think, because we all understand unconsciously that when we fall in love, we take off from a narcissistic state. "Primary narcissism" may well be the original condition of the sexual instincts, as Freud argued, and we also draw back our love, more or less, from the female and male caregivers of our infancy to train it on ourselves. When we launch into love in and from our self-investment or self-preoccupation, we are like adolescents, who, as psychoanalytic theorists of adolescence have told us, elaborating on the Greek wisdom in these matters, are fixed upon themselves. They are fixed on their own egos and thus full of grandiose fantasies about themselves and their power over others; or they are fixed on their own superegos and thus full of fantasies about how grandly they suffer and must bear the suffering of the world; or they are fixed upon their own bodies in the manner of hypochondriacs.[3]

But there is, I think, more to be said about the general condition of self-preoccupation, this narcissistic state. The exterior presentation of the self-preoccupation often takes harsh, callous forms because the lover is demanding of the beloved: Be like me! Do things as I do them! Love as I love! Love on my terms! This demand may be issued in a form

---

3. See Anna Freud's classic 1958 summary in "On Adolescence" (A. Freud 1974).

that disguises its desire. It may come forth as: I am humbly in your service, I will do anything for you! I will lay down my life for you! There is nothing that I would not do for you! But this hope to be of service is, I think, strong in proportion to the strength of the wish that fuels it, which is that the beloved confirm the lover's love and conform to its terms. The lover, making the beloved into a version of himself or herself, is reproducing himself or herself. That is, the sexual instincts are initially not species reproductive but self-reproductive. The beloved produced is like a baby, a brand-new version of the self who can be shaped and molded, and who, then, is a reflecting pool, a mirror. If an actual baby is also produced—when a couple does reproduce the species—that baby, too, is initially a mirror.

The Greeks, such uninhibited explorers of the sexual realm, had a very subtle understanding that the narcissist's beloved mirrors him in basically two different ways, each dangerous. First, the beloved is an Echo who simply repeats what the narcissist says, and who becomes enraged in that condition. Echo cannot be herself; the narcissist cannot allow her to have a self. Or, second, the beloved can be an Amenius, who gets erased, as Amenius was, eventually by his own hand. An Amenius despairs, unable to get any attention from Narcissus, in complete frustration.

This, it seems to me, is the fundamental dynamic—thrilling and terrible—of the sexual instincts. They aim at pleasure, as Freud said, which is initially, in childhood, the pleasure we take in our own bodies; it is self-touching, autoerotic, and tension reduction is its most obvious part. In childhood, orgasm is a pleasure you take in yourself. And if, as you become physically capable of sex with another, you want orgasm to be a pleasure you also take in and with another—in relation to another, not just in using the other as an instrument of your pleasure, as a means to pleasure yourself—you have to travel beyond the narcissistic state, not just fall into its pond. The sexual instincts can eventually have as their object another, but only after the fall, or beyond the fall, does that other become more than a mirror or a means. Something more is needed for the other to become really an *other*, that is, not just a constant object but someone with his or her own self.

But this invocation of going beyond the pleasure principle, beyond narcissism, brings us to the second half of the story. There are also the ego instincts. In the upheaval and free fall of sexual pleasure, sexual self-reproduction, something else can happen. Sexual passion alone can only satisfy a narcissist, and then only for a time, as it is—so Narcissus learned—unconsummatable *as a relationship*. Fundamentally, it is not a relationship. But it can open the way for a relationship, for what the evolutionists call an attachment. How does this happen?

Freud contributed to our understanding of love the great insight that when we lose a loved one our mourning instates the lost one in our inner world, in our ego; we internalize, we identify, holding the loved one *in memoriam* as part of our self. By contrast, when we lose the other as a version of ourselves or an expansion of ourselves, we can make the discovery that no relationship is possible with a narcissistically produced other. This is a discovery that such a narcissistically constructed other cannot give us love, but can only reflect our love. Feeling the want of love receivable, we can rediscover that prior to our sexual quest—and still—we wanted to be receivers of love, and for this a real other is needed.

Those in the Freudian tradition who developed Freud's ideas on mourning and melancholia—chiefly Abraham, Klein, and Riviere among the early circle—noted that mania follows mourning if the inner world disturbed by loss can be rebuilt, restored to order. (Manic defense is a desperate effort to bring this result about, or to leap over the painful mourning process.) In falling in love, it seems to me, mourning follows the mania of reproducing oneself in one's inner world, and the mourning says, in effect, this manic self-making, so hot, finally leaves me cold, it does not fulfill my expectation of being loved. Sometimes anger flashes; always frustration. As the illlusionless Greco-Roman theorists of narcissism famously summarized: *Omnia animalum post coitum triste* (after sex, all animals feel sad). In such a sadness, however, the ego instinctual domain can open.

The ego instinctual dynamic is not to make the beloved a baby, but to be a baby. In love, we are first adolescents and then babies. That is, when we fall past passion, we can fall into—return to—an infant state of our own in which we allow ourselves to be receptive, in which we expect love from another, who, as a real person, can give it And specifically babies have an inborn "expectation to be sweetly and indulgently loved," which is the phrase used by the Japanese psychoanalyst Takeo Doi to translate the Japanese word *amae*. In the *amae* state we say: I wish that your only wishes were to sweetly, indulgently love me and to receive my sweet and indulgent love! Cherish me, and I will cherish you! In the *amae* state we desire relationship, reciprocity, interplay—the paradigm of all play. The little lover feels the caregiver's love as such, as cherishing, caretaking; solicits its continuance; and gives in turn what he or she has felt.

This expectation for receiving and thus giving sweet and indulgent love is, Doi argued, and I agree with him, the essential manifestation of those instincts that Freud called ego instincts. When the baby, born helpless into the world, totally dependent on its caregiver's care, feels hunger, the baby's wish is to be given not just food but all the emotional nourishment that can travel into its mouth as it grasps the breast or bottle. The baby craves all the feelings of warmth, security, concentrated attention that D. W. Winnicott summed up in the phrase "primary maternal preoccupation." And this desire for the caregiver, whom Freud called the "anaclitic object," stressing our dependency, is more elemental than the sexual desire that flows from the sexual instincts. Originally—in our first infancy—this desire also prepared the way for sexual desire, and even guided it to the breast that first served to assuage hunger.[4]

---

4. The key text is Freud's (1912) "On the Universal Tendency to Debasement in the Sphere of Love," where he has been associating the sexual instincts with "the sensual current" of love and the ego instincts with "the affectionate current":

> The affectionate current is [older than the sensual current]. It springs from the earliest years of childhood; it is formed on the basis of the interests of the self-preservative instinct and is directed to the members of the family and those who look after the child. From the very beginning it carries along with it contributions from the sexual instincts—components of erotic interest—which can already be seen more or less clearly even in childhood and in any event are uncovered in neurotics by psychoanalysis later on. It corresponds to the child's primary object choice. We learn in this way that the sexual instincts find their first objects by attaching themselves to the evaluations made by the ego-instincts, precisely in the way in which the first sexual satisfactions are experienced in attachment to bodily functions necessary for the preservation of life. The "affection" shown by the child's parents and those who look after him, which seldom fails to betray its erotic nature ("the child is an erotic plaything"), does a very great deal to raise the contributions made by erotism to the cathexes of his ego-instincts, and to increase them to an amount which is bound to play a part in his later development, especially when certain other circumstances lend their support. [p. 180]

The ego instincts get sexualized as the sexual instincts intertwine with them and as caregivers stimulate children, arousing them. But it is crucial to recognize that the model

Inevitably, even in the most secure of situations, the baby will eventually be frustrated—as will the caregiver. The breast or bottle is not always ready to hand; the caregiver's attention is not always concentrated upon the baby; there are always people and conditions that emerge as rivals to love, as obstacles; and, in less than secure situations, there are traumas of negligence, abuse, abandonment, loss of love, intrusion of parental psychopathology. When we fall in love, we allow ourselves to feel again the expectation that was characteristic of our helplessness, and that we have covered over ever since with lattices of defense, because the frustration of that expectation was painful, often excruciatingly painful. We fear a repetition as much as we desire a return. And much Euro-American psychological theory reinforces our fear by urging us to think of anaclitic object choice and early dependency as something to be avoided, by telling us it is primitive, immature, babyish, and not appropriate in adult love. Dependency is shameful. Much contemporary New Age psychology makes the situation worse by claiming that there is such a thing as "unconditional love." Both the great prejudice against dependence and in favor of independence and also the illusion that love can be unconditional easily become woven into individuals' defenses against expressions of their expectation to be loved as cherishingly as possible.

So, what I am portraying here is an intra-instinctual dynamism that can be harmonious, although it is initially—and often remains—conflictual. The sexual instincts and the ego instincts are in conflict in the sense that the sexual instincts are, initially and fundamentally, not related to an *other*, but only to the self or to the other experienced as a reproduction of the self. The ego instincts, although their function is to preserve the self, do so in relationships; they are tied to others from the start, object-related—worldly—from the start of the ego's emergence in infancy. But the sexual instincts and the ego instincts are also potentially harmonious. Sexual passion can prepare the way for attach-

---

type of object choice is the one Freud (1905) called "anaclitic" (*Anlehningstypus der Objektwahl*): "children learn to feel for other people who help them in their helplessness and satisfy their needs a love that is on the model of, and a continuation of, their relation as sucklings to their nursing mother" (p. 222). Dependent love lays down the pathways that sexual love will later flow into.

ment, as attachment in infancy originally prepared the way for adult sexual passion. Throughout our lives, I think, we oscillate, one or the other of the instincts dominating.

We also, I want to suggest, create an internal gyroscope for ourselves in the form of what I will call a romantic ideal. It seems to me that everyone operates with an image of how sexual passion and attachment, or narcissistic love and anaclitic love, can be, ideally, combined. A romantic ideal is a combinatory of sex and love, passion and attachment, pleasure and security, upheaval and serenity, the pull to repeat past excitement and the pull of the future. As we follow our ideal, hope triumphs over experience, to use Samuel Johnson's well-known phrase; giving up this romantic hope is one way to define melancholia or depression.

People who can do so communicate their romantic ideals in poems, but everyone can and does put them forth in casual talk, or in therapy, where I frequently hear such versions as, "I want my lover to be my best friend." Some romantic ideals are really conducive to harmony between the sexual instinctual and the ego instinctual, and some are not. Generally speaking, I think, a romantic ideal is conducive to harmony if it promotes growth beyond narcissism, that is, if it is founded on acknowledgment or recognition of the expectation to be loved and of the loved and loving other as a person with his or her own wishes.

Another way to say the same thing is to say that a romantic ideal is conducive to harmony if it points toward reciprocity or mutuality in love, toward adult (that is, equalized) versions of the infant–caregiver interplay or playfulness. If we go again to the Greco-Roman tradition in search of an image that shows how this ego instinctual domain opens (as clearly as the Narcissus image shows how the sexual instinctual domain can become sealed off), we could go right to the scene of Odysseus' return to his faithful Penelope in the *The Odyssey*. But the most intricately developed image of this sort is to be found in the eighth book of Ovid's (1955) *Metamorphoses*. There, an old man, Lelex, tells a story of a long and harmonious companionate marriage—something for which the extremely patriarchal conditions of Augustan Rome certainly gave little support, so the story would have been understood as visionary, ideal. It is a story of simplicity and piety, in which pleasure is taken not in sex but in cooking and cheerful friendliness.

Jupiter and his son Mercury, so the story goes, came to earth disguised as mortals and wandered in the Phrygian Hills, expecting to be received hospitably, which is the social equivalent of expecting to be sweetly and indulgently loved. At house after house, they were turned away, until they came to the cottage where an old couple, Baucis and Philemon, unhesitatingly, without inquiring who they were, took them in, laid out bedding on a willow couch, set about preparing them simple but delicious food, and engaged them in conversation while the meal was heating.

> *Interea medias fallunt sermonibus horas*
> *sentirique moram prohibent*

> Then they wiled away the waiting time with talk
> so no delay was felt. (VIII, 651–2)

The old couple do the hospitality tasks together. Not only are there no servants in their house, but neither is servant to the other. And they do not make themselves servants to their guests—they talk with them, showing them friendship as equals.

> *. . . super omnia uultus*
> *accessere boni nec iners pauperque uoluntas.*

> . . . above them all goodness
> looked on, and willingness neither slack nor mean. (VIII, 677–8)

When the gods reveal their identities and power by destroying with a flood all the houses of the inhospitable Phrygian neighbors, they also want to reward Baucis and Philemon by granting them any wish. The two old people consult with each other, again as equals, and say they would like to become the guardians of the magnificent temple into which Jupiter has converted their cottage. Further, they would like, when the time comes for them to die, to share the moment, so that neither will have to live without the other. When that day does come, the story ends, the old woman is turned into a linden tree and the old man into an oak, and they grow together so closely in the temple garden that they seem to be one trunk. The implication is that, although as different as oak and linden, they had become united over the course of their long life together; so their metamorphosis reveals—as all the metamorphoses in Ovid's poem do—what they in essence were. Worshipers come to visit them, leaving wreaths, and Lelex, too, has left an offering:

> . . . *equidem pendentia uidi*
> *serta super ramos ponesque recentia dixi:*
> *cura deum di sint, et qui coluere colantur.*

> . . . I have myself seen garlands
> hanging in their branches, and left a fresh one saying:
> Gods be those who care for gods; cherished be the cherishers. (VIII, 723–5)

ON BEING UNABLE TO NOT BE NARCISSUS: TWO ROMANTIC IDEALS

Most of us are neither purely sexual instinctual beings in love nor purely ego instinctual. Neither Narcissus nor Baucis or Philemon. We and our ideals, too, are mixes, combinatories. But I do think that we all have in common that we are unhappy in love if we cannot move beyond narcissism into a balance of sexual instinctual and ego instinctual aims. Those who maintain their mental health—more or less—in the built-in conflict and oscillation of the sexual and the ego instinctual drives and object choices are the ones who do not swing too much into narcissistic self-enclosure—inventing the beloved—or mount too much defense against the expectation to be loved that underlies attachment. We have many studies in psychoanalysis of people who are too narcissistic for love, but not of how narcissism is related to sealing over the original expectation of love with defenses, so that the expectation is unable even to speak its name.

But we meet in therapy all the time people who expect rejection and recall the expectation to be loved—if they can bear to recall it at all—only as a terrible feeling of vulnerability to loss. Their attachment style is to be clingy, hypersensitive to any slight, and so alert to the possibility of rejection that they bring it about by being controlling, dictatorial, hard. The person who expects rejection cannot even really take a plunge into sexual passion and its pleasures. I am going to present first a male patient who is like this—expecting rejection—and then a woman who, in her narcissism, is unable to feel her own expectation to be loved. The two also represent different romantic ideals, neither of which is conducive to instinctual harmony. He declares, with religious fervor: First love, then sex—there ought to be no sex without love. She insists: Love will follow upon sex as the night the day, no problem.

Not long ago, the man, a divorcé in his forties, came in so excited that he could hardly contain himself. He had, he gushed, given a sonnet by Shakespeare to the woman with whom he has recently fallen head over heels in love. Neatly printed out from his word processor in dainty Gothic script, the sonnet—number 105—was placed in her lovely hands on their two-month anniversary, along with a brief declaration of his love in his own "sort of poetic" words. He had brought a copy of the sonnet for me, too, printed out just like hers, so that it was, in the transference, also meant for me.

> Let not my love be called idolatry,
> Nor my beloved as an idol show,
> Since all alike my songs and praises be
> To one, of one, still such, and ever so.
> Kind is my love today, tomorrow kind,
> Still constant in a wondrous excellence,
> Therefore my verse, to constancy confin'd,
> One thing expressing, leaves out difference.
> "Fair," "kind," and "true" is all my argument
> "Fair," "kind," and "true" varying to other words,
> And in this change is my invention spent,
> Three times in one, which wondrous scope affords.
> "Fair," "kind," and "true" have often liv'd alone,
> Which three till now never kept seat in one.

My patient took the whole session to tell me how thrilled he had been giving this cultivated and romantic gift. His beloved had been pleased, but also baffled; the complex syntax of the poem stymied her and she had asked him, candidly, to tell her what the poem meant. He admitted that explicating the text was no joke, but he had, nonetheless, loved being the professor, that is, telling her what to think. By the next session, however, he was disturbed. He had reread the sonnet to remind himself of her—of his beloved, fair, kind, and true as she is, he hopes—and to reexperience the gift-giving pleasure. But during the rereading he had realized that the "kind is my love" (of line 5) could be not the beloved (of line 2) but the lover's loving (of line 1). The sonnet could be saying that *his own loving* is fair, kind, and true, and thus it could be saying about him just what he, in fact, wants desperately to hear from her: that *he* is fair, kind, and true, and more so than any man she has ever known, more so than she had ever thought a man could be. He asked me imploringly, "Am I narcissistic, or what?"

And I thought to myself, well, yes, you are a narcissist, *mon semblable, mon frère*. And you also have stumbled upon the mystery of Shakespeare's sonnets. In them, there are two beloveds, a female Echo and a male Amenius, a woman who is kept in thrall and a gentleman who is kept at a distance. Neither have real identities. Neither the dark lady nor the patron can, really, be identified as themselves—to the frustration of generations of Shakespeare scholars. They are as the sonneteer makes them in his complex lines. And he knows this, as he says in many of the sonnets, including, for example, sonnet 62, which begins thus:

> Sin or self-love possesseth all mine eye,
> And all my soul, and all my every part;
> And for this sin there is no remedy,
> It is so grounded inward in my heart.
> Methinks no face so gracious is as mine,
> No shape so true, no truth of such account;
> And for myself mine own words do define,
> As I all others in all worths surmount . . .

Yes, my patient is a narcissist, like any other person grandiosely surmounting all others by falling in love—like Shakespeare's sonneteer, or Shakespeare the sonneteer. But his upheaval, in which he is always losing her as he gains her, because she is not real to him, not a person but his creation, has opened him to his own inner world in which his ancient expectation of being sweetly and indulgently loved by another (chiefly by his mother) was so often thwarted. His hungry child self is usually obscured behind his image of himself as a generous giver of love and rescuer of ladies in distress. But sometimes he allows himself to feel his expectation to be sweetly and indulgently loved, and lies content in his beloved's arms, like a baby, falling asleep with his head on her breast. These moments do not last, however, nor do they promote receptivity in him. For some reason, he tells me, even when he is having a wonderful time with her, something frightens him. He wants to run away before he gets hurt, he says; he has panic attacks, feeling that her rejection is imminent. Once an image of himself stabbing her flashed before his eyes and terrified him. He is enraged when she doesn't kiss him goodbye in the morning. Sometimes he hates her. If only she would tell him more frequently that she loves him, if only she would reassure him more. "Why can't she," he asked me angrily, "think to do something like send me a poem? Why do I always have to be the one who takes the initiative?" He wants her to do unto him precisely as he has done unto her; he wants her to be *him* to him. Why can't a woman be more like a man—this man?

What is happening? He wants to rescue this woman, he is aware; he would do anything for her. The melancholy in her appeals to him. She is like his mother, whom he had tried so hard to rescue from his overbearing and critical father. But he fears that at any moment she is going to cast him out, tell him he is too overbearing, too demanding in his rescue. After all, in order to raise her up, he has to keep her down, as well, even using some of his father's harsh tactics. She will get tired of his controlling behavior—won't she? He begs me to tell him it will not be so. But, then, it's terrible that he asks me this, terrible that he burdens me with all his craziness and doubts—won't he injure me, and won't I tell him that I, too, find him not fair, kind, and true, but needy, imploring, and imperfect?

When he gave his beloved the sonnet, my patient's narcissistic inflation of himself was ending, and he was becoming aware of his ancient expectation to be loved. He might have grown receptive to her. But he could not do this. His distrust is too great. So he struggled instead to make his beloved—and me, too, in the transference—into even more of an idealized being. He uses the current culturally idealized vocabulary of "unconditional love." She must *never* leave him. "I want to be like joined at the hip with her," he tells me. And he has a romantic ideal that helps keep this narcissistic mode of loving firmly in place; the ideal does not draw him toward cherishing or being cherished. "Sex," he told me very sanctimoniously and with much borrowing from Christian sources, "should come only after a couple has made a life commitment." He could not see the fear of being rejected in his chastity. And when he violated the rule, taking his lady to bed and then suffering great guilt for his sin, he could only get out of his jam by declaring that maybe the rule was not so important because neither one of them was a virgin.

Now, at the opposite end of the spectrum of romantic ideals from my patient the Shakespeare scholar is a bright, articulate, vibrant divorcée, whom I will present more briefly. She, also a fortysomething, came to see me because she was having trouble managing her early teenager, to whom she has assigned the task of being more beautiful than she herself is, even though the girl's beauty makes her envious. The daughter, understandably, feels in a double bind and is rebelling. As we talked about the girl, my patient was excited to tell me the history of her love relationships, starting when she was fourteen and fell for a handsome foreigner twice her age. As the story unfolded, it became clear that all her lovers have been in some way exotic, extraordinarily beautiful, culturally nonconformist, creatively unemployed. Each had much in common with her dashing father, but each also had some distinguishing characteristic that allowed him to escape being an incestuous object. All of the men had the capacity to make her feel sexy and attractive. She seduced them as quickly as possible and got right to "mad, passionate love-making." All the other things that matter in a relationship, she said, like enjoying each other's minds, sharing interests and tastes, holding common beliefs, maybe having a child, would just take care of themselves; what mattered to her most was this thrill at the beginning, this "some enchanted evening in bed."

She told me all this exuberantly, and a little competitively, and then got pensive. "But with me," she said, "there is maybe some kind of disconnect between the sex and the love-love, you know, the for the long haul. When the haul starts, I lose interest, the sex goes flat, and I don't get excited anymore. Some kind of disconnect." She doesn't know whether she wants to settle down. "I like the idea of companionship, making a home, but, on the other hand, it seems dull." And then, abruptly, she added, "it seems fat, like I would be fat as a wife."

This woman, who was twelve when her parents came bursting with a loud divorce out of their uptight 1950s and right into the "Make Love not War" era holds fast to an ideal of romance that says, "if the sex is great, love will follow." But she recognizes that her relationships have all fallen away from this ideal. Because there is some kind of disconnect; love does not follow. So, in this moment of mourning for the self her narcissism has produced, she stands ready to examine the romantic ideal. It turns out, as we look into it, that the initial seduction that she stage-manages has a clear purpose: it is to silence her anxiety that she is not beautiful, not sexy or skinny enough. And not-skinny means not lovable to her mother or to her father, as it means not as lovable as her brother, who was—not surprisingly—exotic, extraordinarily handsome, thin. Many of her boyfriends, she realizes, have been friends of her brother's. The seductions, she realizes, are "like a trick—I trick them into sex."

It is a wonder that my patient does not have an eating disorder, but she knows her seductress achievement is precarious. She asks me if I'm familiar with a formulation from the world of business psychology—"the success impostor." "That's me," she says, "I pose as the most successful sexy lady—and they go for it! Really, men are so foolish." All men have been good for has been to play their part, mirroring back to her her fantasy of herself as beautiful, herself as her brother, herself as lovable to her parents; any desires of their own that do not support the role have no place. Men are not allowed to love her or she to receive love, and this keeps her ancient expectation to be loved almost completely buried. There are, however, two ways that the expectation speaks currently. One is through her shame at being—so she feels—not really lovable; and the other is that she so wants me to understand this shame and love her anyway.

ON THE SUPEREGO AND THE EGO IDEAL

In concluding, I want to return for a moment to the theoretical plane. A romantic ideal is, I think, a precipitant of the interplay of the sexual and ego instinctual drives; it is an idealized portrait of that interplay. It evolves with the structuration—or, to use a less technical term—the psychic habit-formation of both the sexual instincts and the ego instincts as they interact, as they seek sexual objects and ego objects and interests. The structuring legacy of sexual object search was given the name *the superego* by Freud and it has, of course, been the subject of voluminous discussion ever since. The ego instincts' object relational story and its legacy were, I think, what Freud was gesturing toward with the name *the ego ideal*. But he never really pursued the ego ideal after he initially proposed it and tried to differentiate it from the superego. Questions about how the superego and the ego ideal are related or different then stayed very muddy and unresolved among psychoanalytic theoreticians because the instinct theory on which Freud's initial formulations rested disappeared into the later duality of "the life instincts" and "the death instinct."

So psychoanalytic theory does not help us much to understand a feature of the old roller coaster of love that I highlighted in these vignettes and would like now to single out briefly. Falling in love seems to me to involve two quite different kinds of idealization, which have two quite different functions. There is, on the one hand, narcissistic idealization, which I presented as rooted in the sexual instincts and which, I would now like to suggest, chiefly functions to assuage the superego's guilt for oedipal trespass or oedipal triumph. On the other hand, there is idealization stemming from the expectation to be loved, the essential ego instinctual manifestation, which functions to protect us from the frustrations and disappointments of attachment. This idealization regulates our good feeling about ourselves, our self-esteem, which grows initially in the context of cherishing love.

Almost everyone (masochists excepted) idealizes the person with whom they fall in love. And I was suggesting earlier that what this means initially is that we idealize the beloved along narcissistic lines; when we fall in love we fall into narcissistic idealization. The beloved is a more perfect version of ourselves—ourselves as we have been, as we hope we presently are, or as we imagine ourselves for the future. One of the consequences of the idealizing is that in the rush of passion— the "amphetamine high" of the evolutionists—old loves, including, most powerfully, oedipal loves, are stirred into action again in our inner world and there is a thrill in winging with the new love right past or right by all that is forbidden in those old loves. The narcissistic idealization means, in effect, this is not your mother, your father, and not your siblings whom you love—it is you. With guilt, with its strong "no, you must not," the superego controls this ignoring of the incest taboo and the family rules, this unrestrained pursuit of pleasure. But in the rush of passion the superego is often unable to be very effective, as it was often unable to be very effective in the narcissistic aggrandizement of adolescence. There are people who, when they fall in love, fall right into a crime of passion.

On the other hand, ego instinctually rooted idealizations of loved ones and of their cherishing love can function to protect us from any feeling we have that we are unlovable, which is a source of shame. The ego ideals people develop are, I think, their internal vision of how they might be cherished and cherishing. It pulls forward, it represents a developmental course, with its strong affirmative "yes, go that way!" Every religion has a communal version of this ego ideal, which is not its credo—the content of belief recommended—but its affective core. The ego ideal is the state of feeling demonstrated to the young not by catechism but by the example of its sages' words and deeds. By their example, the sages will show how the ego instinctual, the original and developing relational desire, can guide the sexual instinctual beyond narcissism and back to receptivity.

REFERENCES

Doi, T. (1971). *The Anatomy of Dependence.* New York: Kodansha, 1973.

Fisher, H. (1992). *The Anatomy of Love: The Natural History of Monogamy, Adultery and Divorce.* New York: Simon & Schuster.

Freud, A. (1974). On adolescence. In *The Writings of Anna Freud*, volume 5, pp. 136–166. New York: International Universities Press.

Freud, S. (1905). Three essays on the theory of sexuality. *Standard Edition* 7:123–245.

——— (1912). On the universal tendency to debasement in the sphere of love." *Standard Edition* 11:177–190.

Graves, R. (1955). *The Greek Myths.* London: Penguin, 1974.

Ovid (1955). *Metamorphoses,* trans. by R. Humphries. Bloomington, IN: Indiana University Press.

Shakespeare, W. (1936). *The Complete Works of William Shakespeare,* ed. by G. Kittredge. New York: Ginn.

2

Cherishment Culture

INTRODUCTION

Since the beginning of the nineteenth century—since Goethe in his Weimar old age—prophets in the West have had a sense of impending catastrophe, for the West, but also, in consequence, for all humankind. From European travelers like Stendhal, de Tocqueville, Burckhardt, from lonely philosophers like Kierkegaard and Nietzsche, from anticipators of salvation through catastrophe like Marx, and from the preeminent diagnostician, Freud, have come historical conceptions of a profound caesura separating modern people from their ancestors. The prophets have recognized that the world's great traditions, stemming from distinct origins in Europe and North Africa, in China, in India, were coming to a common end in a planetary condition of manmadeness, an age of all-embracing technology, and in a political condition of worldwide interdependence and ambition—eventually of *world* war, *global* trade and communications. In the period since the end of the Second World War, which to date has been the nadir of humankind as an actually existent unit, as a unit of technologically and politically common destiny, thoughtful individuals from all regions of the earth have come forth to join their hopes and fears into a conversation about humankind's possibilities.

To this conversation, the followers of Freud bring a particular perspective and experience. We, like all reflective people, can consider the *condition humaine* currently from the evidence of interactions we observe and read about, media images we receive, travels we undertake, but we can also attend to, attune to, the streams of our own and our patients' associations—to conduits from the unconscious, like oracles from Delphi, as each is a "navel of the universe." Each patient we work with needs, of course, a cure for an illness or malaise, but each, as well, needs help with a condition not peculiar to her or him but common to all of us as contemporaries, relatively well or relatively ill; a civilizational condition. The world historical thinking of a psychoanalyst is a therapeutics.

In this essay,[1] we would like to reconsider Freud's analysis of the modern civilizational condition: to appreciate it, and to build upon it as therapists working half a century after his death, half a century further into the world crisis he analyzed while it was still in its turn-of-the-century form. To put the theme we want to explore introductorily, in a very abbreviated way: what Freud analyzed, particularly in "Civilization and Its Discontents," was what might be termed the active and oedipal level of the modern civilizational condition, while the level that has been revealed since is receptive and preoedipal. Psychoanalytic theory has shifted accordingly since Freud's time. But we feel that it has not made this shift clearly or broadly enough, and that it has not developed from its new thinking a new cultural analysis or ideal. We want to invoke such an ideal—"cherishment culture" we call it.

Further, we want to argue that psychoanalysis has not come to any new cultural vision because it made its post-Freudian shift in a specifically Western way, one that reflects a specifically Western view of the

---

1. This essay was first delivered as a lecture at the March 15, 1997, celebration of the New York Psychoanalytic Society's 85th anniversary, a symposium on "Psychoanalysis and Culture." We wish to thank the organizers, particularly the late Dr. Albert Solnit, a great cherisher, and participants in that symposium for their reception of it.

civilizational condition as a crisis in human activity or productivity, not in human receptivity. From the East, by contrast, there has come a contemporary psychoanalytic revision—not fully developed, but very suggestive—that illuminates the post-Freudian direction. Its author is Takeo Doi of Japan, although Doi has been supported—unconsciously—by a tradition of Eastern philosophizing that goes back at least to the period of Confucianism and Taoism in China, the Chinese civilizational originary moment. The "cherishment culture" we want to invoke in this essay is very Chinese.

THE LOST THREAD IN FREUDIAN THEORY

The main theme of Sigmund Freud's "Civilization and Its Discontents" is, as his translator James Strachey succinctly introduced it, "the irremediable antagonism between the demands of instinct and the restrictions of civilization." But this summary, of course, requires qualification, as its stark adjective "irremediable" requires inquiry: Which demands of what instinct? Which restrictions of what civilization?

We need to put Freud's theme in context. Tentatively, speculatively, Freud had offered his dual instinct theory to his followers in the 1920 essay "Beyond the Pleasure Principle." As you know, he was replacing a distinction between ego instincts and sexual instincts that he had made many years before and discussed most thoroughly in the "On Narcissism" essay of 1914. In the post-1920 dual instinct theory, the ego instincts and the sexual instincts were merged under the rubric of "the life instinct," which was then contrasted to "the death instinct." But what the first step, the merge into "the life instinct," meant, in fact, was that Freud stopped exploring the ego instincts. The ego instincts became, in effect, features of the sexual instinct, which he then understood as "egoistical." As a consequence of the merger, the elaboration of the ego instincts that his newly formulated structural theory of id/ego/superego would otherwise have required was short-circuited.

Even among those Freudian followers who specialized in considering the ego's development—those usually called Ego Psychologists—there has since been no elaboration of ego instincts, but only elaboration of ego functions. Heinz Hartmann conjured up a "primary ego energy," but he generally spoke only of energy from the sexual instincts

26 / *Cherishment Psychology*

made available to the ego by a process of neutralization.[2] Others since have stressed the ego's search for safety and security as features of its aim of self-preservation, but, again, without a concept of ego instincts.

So, in "Civilization and Its Discontents," Freud studied how civilization tries to curb the sexual instinct on the one hand, and on the other hand, how it tries to curb aggression. As far as the sexual instinct is concerned, the main civilizing effort is directed at getting it to expand beyond egoistical pleasure-seeking with one other person to the making of aim-inhibited units, like friendships, and on to larger and larger social units. The social unit "humankind" would, theoretically, be one in which aggression was also curbed, for it is a basic feature of aggression that it seeks an outlet onto some others, outside the group. Indicating why he disagreed with the Marxist notion that eliminating private property would eliminate aggression, Freud (1930) claimed that aggression: "reigned almost without limit in primitive times, when property was very scanty, and it already shows itself in the nursery almost before property has given up its primal, anal form; it forms the basis of every relation of affection and love among people (with the single exception, perhaps, of the mother's relation to her male child)" (p. 113). At the end of his argument for the primordiality of aggression, Freud rhetorically calls upon Eros to renew its struggle with aggression by describing the specifically contemporary technological means for aggressing that have been remarked by each of the modern prophets of catastrophe:

> Men have gained control over the forces of nature to such an extent that with their help they would have no difficulty in exterminating one another to the last man. They know this, and hence comes a large part of their current unrest, their unhappiness and their mood of anxiety. And now it is to be expected that the other of the two "Heavenly Powers," eternal Eros, will make an effort to assert himself in the struggle with his equally immortal adversary. But who can foresee with what success and what result? [p. 145]

Freud, as many commentators have noted, thought in dualisms, in dualistic conflicts. Before 1920, it was the self-preservative instinct, or

---

2. Heinz Hartmann (1964, pp. 236 and 240) considers the idea that there is "primary ego energy" but says that it cannot be proved (see also pp. xiv and 227).

the ego instinct, that he contrasted to the sexual instinct with its species preservative or reproductive goal. There was Hunger, and there was Sex. Or, more complexly, there was an instinct underlying *affection* and an instinct underlying sensual or sexual love. As he considered "the affectionate current," Freud sometimes simply stressed the infant's tie to the maternal breast—the satisfier of Hunger; but in passages like the one following, from the 1912 essay "On the Universal Tendency to Debasement in the Sphere of Love," his thought was far more rich:

> The affectionate current is [older than the sensual current]. It springs from the earliest years of childhood; it is formed on the basis of the interests of the self-preservative instinct and is directed to the members of the family and those who look after the child. From the very beginning it carries along with it contributions from the sexual instincts—components of erotic interest—which can already be seen more or less clearly even in childhood and in any event are uncovered in neurotics by psychoanalysis later on. It corresponds to the child's primary object choice. We learn in this way that the sexual instincts find their first objects by attaching themselves to the evaluations made by the ego-instincts, precisely in the way in which the first sexual satisfactions are experienced in attachment to bodily functions necessary for the preservation of life. The "affection" shown by the child's parents and those who look after him, which seldom fails to betray its erotic nature ("the child is an erotic plaything"), does a very great deal to raise the contributions made by erotism to the cathexes of his ego-instincts, and to increase them to an amount which is bound to play a part in his later development, especially when certain other circumstances lend their support. [p. 180]

Freud claims here that the first object choices are ego instinctual and self-preservative, not sexual, and that they are plural—they include all caregivers, not just the mother. Secondly he claims that the evaluations of the affectionate current and the first object choices guide the sensual current and later object choices. Finally he observes that parental erotic interest in the child can disturb the normal interplay between affectionate and sensual currents by increasing the child's eroticism, and thus the sensual current—and he might also have observed that parental lack of affection can have the same effect.

But Freud did not explore further this affectionate current, the ego instinctual love, and when it disappeared from his view in the dual instinct theory, it also largely disappeared from psychoanalysis. He fell back on the idea that affection is aim-inhibited sexuality, and he developed a theory that there are two anxieties—anxiety signaling danger to the ego, especially from loss of love, and anxiety from frustration of libido. The new anxiety theory was very forcefully presented in "Civilization and Its Discontents," where Freud claimed that the *primary* anxiety in human beings is loss of love—although this love was not specified as to whether it is affectionate or sensual-sexual because that distinction had become so muted after the ego instincts disappeared.

Affection does make an appearance in "Civilization and Its Discontents," although presented not as an originary ego instinctual current but only as a result—rarely attained—of aim-inhibited sexuality.[3] Freud had come to judge sensual or erotic love as "the prototype of all happiness," which was the role once played by affectionate love, especially between mother and child:

> [Man's] discovery that sexual (genital) love afforded him the strongest experiences of satisfaction, and in fact provided him with the prototype of all happiness, must have suggested to him that he should continue to seek the satisfaction of happiness in his life along the path of sexual relations and that he should make genital erotism the central point of his life . . . [In] doing so he made himself dependent in the most dangerous way on a portion of the external world, namely, his chosen love object, and exposed himself to extreme suffering if he should be rejected by that object or should lose it through unfaithfulness or death. For that reason the wise men of every age have warned us most emphatically against this

---

3. This idea drastically simplifies—we think impoverishes—reflections prior to 1920 on how the affectionate current of love, which is prior to the Oedipus complex, is superseded in two ways. First, normally, people subsume the affectionate current in the sensual current during adolescence, when they become physically capable of genital sexuality. Secondly, abnormally, they split the affectionate current off from the sensual, so that it stays attached to its original objects (or substitutes) while the sensual goes off in other directions. Men taking this second route continue to love chastely their mothers or maternal substitutes while they love erotically a woman whom they imagine as debased, merely erotic. But even in these reflections, Freud did not invoke his 1912 idea, noted before, that affectionate love might healthily and normally continue on in all people as the foundation of and the guide for their sexual love. Affection was always to be subsumed or outgrown, if not repressed or split off.

way of life; but in spite of this it has not lost its attraction for a great number of people.

A small minority are enabled by their constitution to find happiness, in spite of everything, along the path of love. But far-reaching mental changes in the function of love are necessary before this can happen. These people make themselves independent of their object's acquiescence by displacing what they mainly value from being loved onto loving; they protect themselves against the loss of the object by directing their love, not to single objects but to all men alike; and they avoid the uncertainties and disappointments of genital love by turning away from its sexual aims and transforming the instinct into an impulse with an inhibited aim. What they bring about in themselves in this way is a state of evenly suspended, steadfast, affectionate feeling, which has little external resemblance anymore to the stormy agitations of genital love, from which it is nevertheless derived. Perhaps St. Francis of Assisi went furthest in thus exploiting love for the benefit of an inner feeling of happiness. [1930, pp. 101–102]

When exceptional people are able to inhibit themselves to achieve affectionate love, they can reach a great civilizational height; indeed, Freud argues, all friendship depends upon a capacity to self-inhibit erotism. But most of the inhibition upon sensual love that exists among people comes not from within but from without, from civilization itself. For example, civilization commands larger and larger units of human bonding, but erotism is exclusive and aims at family-making, that is, reproduction and family attachments in small units. In Freud's estimation, it is women who "represent the interests of the family and sexual life," while "the work of civilization has become increasingly the business of men" (1930, p. 103). As men rise to the occasion of civilization they become more and more able to "carry out instinctual sublimations of which women are little capable" (p. 103).

Thus did Freud back himself into a sexist view of breeder women as the undertow of civilization. But the constriction upon his thought was much more general. As these passages show, the possibilities Freud had once envisioned for affectionate love—for example, that it extends to all caregivers, and is not exclusive to the mother, and might thus be an *instinctual* foundation for love of humankind in women and men— have been squeezed out. He cannot think that the ego instincts might not be antagonistic to civilization as the sexual instincts are. There is no sense that affection might offer the sexual instincts evaluation and guidance in object choice, and that this might be the normal developmental course. Freud could not call upon the preoedipal love current, the pre-rivalrous love current, the nonexclusive love current, because it had disappeared from his view.

But, of course "primary object choice" did not disappear from psychoanalysis. It was explored, first by Sándor Ferenczi and then by all the psychoanalysts who trained with Ferenczi, from Melanie Klein to Michael Balint, and then from these to the so-called Object Relations theorists. They spoke of a primary *libidinal* object choice, however, not an ego instinctually based affectional choice.[4] Further, both Klein and Balint stressed the infant's relationship to the maternal breast and breast representation as its primary relationship, leaving behind Freud's notion that affectionate love is more general, embracing all caregivers. They also went on to make an argument, against Freud, that there is no such thing as "primary narcissism" preceding the affectional current, because the infant's natal condition is relatedness—but this was also an argument about the primacy of *libidinal* object choice.[5] Psychoanalysis since has been burdened with a dispute over whether there is such a thing as primary narcissism, a dispute we think would be completely unnecessary if a clear distinction had been articulated between sexual instincts, which are primarily narcissistic, and ego instincts, which are

---

4. W. R. D. Fairbairn is the object relations theorist of the Kleinian generation who attributed all object relations to the developing ego, but his position entailed a full rejection of Freud's instinctual drive theory—he simply located libido in the ego and dropped the id from his picture. As he wrote in a 1944 essay collected in *Psychoanalytic Studies of the Personality* (1952): "The basic conception which I advanced . . . is to the effect that libido is primarily object-seeking (rather than pleasure-seeking as in the classical theory), and that it is to disturbances in the object-relationships of the developing ego that we must look for the ultimate origin of all psychopathological conditions" (p. 82).

5. As we note in the text, we think that primary narcissism is a concept that makes much sense theoretically and nosologically for the sexual instinct—but not for the ego instinct *amae*. Object constancy of the sexual instinct or what Freud called alloerotism is only achieved when the ego is developed enough to retain clear, whole-object representations; but ego-relatedness, understood as receptivity in the way we are suggesting here, is possible as the ego develops, differentiates, structures, or, more accurately, it *is* the ego's development.

originally related. Such a distinction might, then, have informed contemporary infant research, which has made it so empirically clear that infants are very complexly related to their caregivers during the first weeks of life

It is with and from this post-Ferenczian line of psychoanalytic development that the shift in attention from the Oedipus complex over to the preoedipal has taken place, and with it a shift in attention from the oedipal triangle of father-mother-child to the preoedipal dyad mother–child (and its implications for the analyst–analysand dyad). But this shift, we are suggesting, has taken place by means of—not in argument against—the disappearance of the ego instinctual, affectional current of love. And the same could be said for the way in which psychoanalytic infant research on primary relatedness, from René Spitz and Margaret Mahler on through Daniel Stern, has been concerned with primary object choice but without any distinction between libidinal and ego instinctual choice. It is not surprising, therefore, that in contemporary psychoanalysis, the commonest vision of the discontent of civilization is like Freud's except that the instincts constricted by civilization, still understood as the sexual and the aggressive instincts, are manifested further back on the human developmental line. This social vision can be adopted, as well, by those analysts for whom instinct theory has become less and less central, including those for whom what D. W. Winnicott called "good enough mothering" in preoedipal childhood is the civilizational provision without which development is impossible. It is ultimately dyadic, preoedipally rooted sexuality and aggression that civilization frustrates if it makes good enough mothering impossible.

THE EGO INSTINCT *AMAE*—THE GROWTH PRINCIPLE

Within the psychoanalytic community, there is now a good deal of awareness about this historical shift in psychoanalysis, but it has not been reflected in any revision of the "civilization and its discontents" diagnosis. What we think is needed for such a vision—as well as for psychoanalysis itself, as a theory and a practice—is precisely the reconsideration of the ego instincts Freud did not undertake: the road not taken in his post-1920 dual instinct theory.

32 / *Cherishment Psychology*

Takeo Doi of Japan is the only psychoanalyst we know of who has proposed that the infant begins in a condition of relatedness that is predominantly ego instinctual, not predominantly aggressive, or libidinal.[6] The relation that Freud thought existed only between a mother and her male child is, in Doi's view, the norm. Japanese has an everyday noun for the basis of this relation in the child's ego instinct, *amae*, which Doi translated as "the expectation to be indulgently loved." Similarly, it has an everyday intransitive verb, *amaeru*, for the infant's love-imbibing, its cuddling up, cooing, calling forth for itself of love and for its receptivity to love called forth, expected. Because English does not have a similarly everyday *amae* lexicon, we use the word "cherishment" to capture what the infant instinctually seeks.

Infants want cherishing, and caregivers, if they are cherishers, read the infant's preverbal signals and cherish them. The infant stretches out to the caregivers, in order to receive; the caregivers receive, hold, literally and intrapsychically, the infant and her needs, in order to give. They are a circuitry, like the symbol of infinity. Cherishment is the elemental form of reciprocity. Or, if we translated this description into the philosophical language of Confucianism, which has had such an influence on both Chinese and Japanese thought, establishing the cul-

---

6. Doi's main book, *The Anatomy of Dependence*, was first issued in 1971, but he did not speak of *amae* as an ego instinct until later editions (see the appendix "Amae Reconsidered" in the 1981 edition) and essays like "Japanese Psychology, Dependency Need, and Mental Health" (1969). John Bowlby, of course, emphasized the primacy of what he called attachment. He was arguing for an instinctual basis to object relations, but his point of view allows no affective dimension and nothing distinctively human or species specific about this instinctual basis—that is, he does not speak of ego instincts. Arnold Modell (1975), in an essay called "The Ego and the Id: Fifty Years Later," suggested returning to Freud's distinction between the ego instincts and the sexual instincts, but as far as we can tell from reading his subsequent articles and his *Other Times, Other Realities* (1990), he did not develop his suggestion. Eric A. Plaut reviewed the literature on ego instincts since Freud and made a call for reinstating the concept in "Ego Instincts: A Concept Whose Time Has Come" (1984). But Plaut does not connect the concept to object relations: he rather focuses on the manifestations of ego instincts in play and creativity. Among cultural Freudians, Karen Horney (1937) focused attention on a neurotic need to be loved (one in which anxiety dominates the need) that she thought was characteristic of "the neurotic personality of our time," and Theodor Reik took up this line of thought in *The Need to Be Loved* (1963).

tural background of Doi's thought, we would say that the defining human characteristic, *jen*, human-heartedness, is indistinguishable from the basic human way of being, *shu*, reciprocity, relatedness.

Elaborating beyond Doi's suggestion, we understand the self-preservative instinct as an instinct aiming for provision of elementary food and shelter and safety or security needs, but also as an instinct for provision of a need to be loved. Self-preservation is a relational concept and an aim not satisfiable in isolation. Unlike Freud, who thought that an infant's helplessness and dependency at birth *give rise to* a need to be loved, and ultimately give rise to the Oedipus complex, Doi was assuming that a need to be loved is constitutional—it *is* the emergent ego at birth.[7] We assume, going further, that the infant's ego, being originally receptive in the time of dependency is—as it were—invisible to a theory that stresses activity and agency and executive capacity in its definition of the ego and that sees dependency as a condition that needs overcoming. Their very helplessness keeps human infants receptive to the preservative and cherishing attention they expect. We think of the ego's receptivity to the world and to its caregivers' care as what we call the growth principle of the ego, analogous to the pleasure principle of the id. The id aims at pleasure and release of tension, and it is tempered in this aim by reality—or such realities as the intermittence of satisfaction—and later by the ego itself; the ego aims at growth and is met by cherishment or cherishment's lack—good enough or not good enough cherishers. The ego is tropic—it is turned to what nourishes it. As Freud said, the ego is first a body ego; but also first a receptive body ego—the heliotropic plant in children and also in adults. We could put the matter from another angle by saying that the id—the pleasure principle—is the push or thrust in people, while the receptive ego—the growth principle—is the pull, with the aim of maturation, development, and with the object the caregiver's cherishment.

---

7. See Freud (1926) in "Inhibitions, Symptoms and Anxiety": "The biological factor is the long period of time during which the young of the human species is in a condition of helplessness and dependence. . . . The biological factor, then, establishes the earliest situations of danger and creates the need to be loved which will accompany the child through the rest of its life" (pp. 154–155).

34 / Cherishment Psychology

We think that human beings from birth wish to receive cherishing from their caregivers so that they may grow and develop, especially through the first year of life, in which physical growth and especially brain growth is so rapid, and again through the first years of puberty, in which physical growth is again so rapid. Human infants say, to put this claim in dramatic form, "Grow me!" The long period of helplessness, which is unique among the animals to humans, is a long period of receptivity, as is the period of early puberty, in which the infant helplessness and rapid growth are replayed through new forms of vulnerability or sensitivity.[8] It follows, too, that the affectionate current of love of which Freud spoke is a current of receptivity, unlike sexual love, which is—in both males and females, Freud to the contrary notwithstanding—active, pursuing, and unlike aggression, which is also active, pursuing. Trying to describe the receptive affectionate current in its distinctness, people in various cultures and eras have spoken of the innocence or innate goodness of children, but this is mythologization of the growth principle.

What we are suggesting, then, is that Freud was quite right in seeing the sexual-aggressive instinctual drives in their conflict with each other and both in conflict with civilization, which calls for regulation of sexuality to prevent incest and to bind people into larger and larger social units, and which calls for regulation of aggression to keep people from attacking each other directly or with the tools they make to exercise control over nature. These conflicts are, however, although

---

8. As libido and aggression have hormonal components, especially those—estrogen, progesterone, testosterone—involved in sexual and reproductive development, one might think that the ego instincts have among their components the hormones involved in growth (like HGH), metabolic regulation, and thyroid stimulation. But the ego instincts seem also to have a source in the perceptual-motor system, as Plaut (see note 6) has suggested, because they are manifest in motility, play: the infant's pleasure in exercising its "body ego." Psychoanalytic theorists of adolescence (Peter Blos, for example) have noted that the onset of puberty is a time of regression to the preoedipal mother, which adolescents react against strenuously—boys often becoming girl-haters and going in all-boy groups, girls lunging into heterosexuality or going in all-girl groups. But this period of preoedipalness has not, we think, been recognized as an affective growth spurt or a reactivation of the need to be loved or expectation of love, the receptivity to love, that we are here calling an ego instinct.

rooted in preoedipal development, most forcefully manifest at the oedipal level, in sexual rivalries and aggressive group formations.[9]

Further, we want to suggest that these oedipally manifest conflicts do not constitute the central discontent of mid-twentieth-century civilization—the emergent world civilization, the civilization of humankind. Behind these conflicts lies what we might call the *amae* core—the receptive instinctual drive—which is obscured by, or crusted over by, the battles Freud analyzed. This is a core lost to a psychoanalytic theory that sees dependency exclusively as a condition to be overcome, not as the first form of the human capacity for receptivity. Or, to put the matter more generally, this *amae* core is lost to a worldview that denies altogether that a need to be loved is the foundation of receptivity to love, without which the capacity to love, and to guide sexuality and aggression, withers. It is this *amae*, cherishment core, that is exposed in a civilizational condition that widely renders cherishing child care impossible, or, to say the same thing, that widely thwarts the expectation to be loved.

THE EMERGENT WORLD CIVILIZATION AND ITS DISCONTENTS

We think that the forms of civilization peculiar to the mid-twentieth century, and unprecedented in world history—first, the novel political form called totalitarianism and second, all technological forms that can be qualified as nature-destroying rather than nature-extending—entail, in their essences, assaults upon the conditions of good caregiving and concern for "the best interests of the child." To put the same large historical claim another way, we can say these mid-

---

9. At the level where Freud was focused, his statement in "Civilization and Its Discontents" (1930) follows: "The derivation of religious needs from the infant's helplessness and the longing for the father *aroused by it* [italics added] seems to me incontrovertible, especially since the feeling is not simply prolonged from childhood days, but is permanently sustained by fear of the superior power of Fate. I cannot think of any need in childhood as strong as the need for a father's protection" (p. 72). But from the point of view we are taking, a need for protection—paternal or maternal—is derivative; it arises when a need for love (and love's safety) has been thwarted.

twentieth-century phenomena marked the end—the traducing—of the modern, post-Enlightenment era, which was decisively defined in relational terms by the institutional condition Philippe Aries (1962) has called "the centering of the family around the child." Centering the family around the child led to the ethical-legal principle "in the best interests of children" being articulated for post-Enlightenment humankind by psychoanalysis, although the articulation was really a rearticulation from a much earlier era.

Child-centeredness had not been definitive of civilizations or understood as the sine qua non of a fully *human* society since the originary era of the world's great civilizations—the period named by the philosopher Karl Jaspers (1953) "The Axial Age," about 800–500 B.C.E. in China, India, Greece, Persia, and Palestine. This was the founding era of philosophy and art produced for the education of young citizens and princelings, produced explicitly to transmit wisdom to the young. Culture, then, was cultivating of the young—those Homer called in the agricultural metaphors typical of the time "green shoots," scions.

Such child-centeredness was lost and found episodically in the histories of these traditions, but in the West it emerged again as the defining human value in the course of the nineteenth century, only to be swept away in Europe by counterforces, by totalitarianism, and by destructive technologization, making world wars possible. It is the global aftermath of this assault upon the child-centeredness phenomenon, we think, that centrally challenges humankind now, and thus challenges psychoanalysis and its principle, "in the best interests of the child."

Drawing on Hannah Arendt's *The Origins of Totalitarianism* (1951), we can restate this claim in broad political theoretical terms by defining totalitarianism as government dedicated to eugenics and replacement of the family by the government; it dictates that the only conception and care of infants that is to be allowed is for the totalitarian movement and the master race, class, or culture it furthers. We can, secondly, define antinatural technologization as a process with two fundamental dictates: it says, first, that nature is totally at the service of human beings, and, second, that there need be no nature without human scientific-technical intervention and fabrication. When human artifice seeks to replace nature, it is totalitarian. In this view, even human infants—from their inception as genetic combinations—are not part of nature, they are part of human artifice, engineerable, serving only the purposes of human artifice.

Looking, in Freudian terms, at how these "civilized" forms constrain, we can say that totalitarianism is the imposition of an ideology by means of terrorization; it is social engineering—without restraint—aimed at putting reproductive sexuality and aggression at the service of a government and eliminating all human spontaneity. Antinatural technologization is a process of making living beings, in all their spontaneity, new beginnings, dynamism, growth, unpredictability, and proliferation, strictly predictable, usable, dominatable, in the service of human enterprise. Ceaseless activity, ceaseless activism, is required to keep up these ways of imposing and controlling.

Since the collapse of the mid-twentieth-century totalitarianisms in Europe, in the Soviet Union, and in China, which had repercussions in all regions of the earth where these three main forms of totalitarianism had offshoots and influence—including America, which was influenced by totalitarianism in its battles against all three of the main forms during the Second World War, the Cold War, and the Vietnam War—thoughtful people everywhere have realized that the civilizational crisis these regimes expressed had to be addressed, in its specificity, its historicity. Similarly, the way in which antinatural technologization has been destroying the earth and its natural resources has been decried everywhere, especially after the ultimate contradiction of this technologization was clear: that it imitates natural forces—as nuclear weapons do—only to threaten nature with termination. Voicing these realizations, two genuinely global movements arose in the upheaval generated in the 1960s by the anti-technological moral fervor of the international student movement and by the antitotalitarian political struggles of various national liberation movements. These movements were feminism and environmentalism. We can, again, put the meanings of these movements in declarative form. The feminist movement says, fundamentally, and put in terms that come from the East: Show respect for The Female Principle, in women and in men, which is a principle of receptivity and devotion to living beings. Environmentalism says: Human beings are part of nature and must show respect for that of which they are only a part—lest they destroy their home.

Feminism and environmentalism have since grown in a global context marked by ever-new forms of anti-natural technologization and also by post-totalitarian political and social confusion. Politically, the present context is characterized not so much by terroristic imposition of total order on populations as by anarchistic shifts of direction, contradictoriness. Not terror and secrecy so much as power for power's sake, activity for activity's sake. Information and communications explosions detrimental to reflective, unhectic, receptive thought flourish in regimes given not to total planning but to total lack of vision; this lack of vision is apparent in the lives of ordinary citizens as a sense of inhuman pace and pressure, lack of time and resources for thoughtfulness, carefulness, considerateness, kindness. Consequently needs for these show everywhere—outside of political institutions. Theodore Zeldin, a social historian from Oxford, has been the great cataloger of the present clamoring of what we would call self-preservative *amae* needs. He shows in his *An Intimate History of Humanity* (1994) how people around the world are trying to rediscover *human* beings, what it is to be human:

> The age of discovery has hardly begun. So far individuals have spent more time trying to understand themselves than discovering others. But now curiosity is expanding as never before. Even those who have never set foot outside the land of their birth are, in their minds, perpetual migrants. To know someone in every country in the world, and someone in every walk of life, may soon be a minimum demand of people who want to experience fully what it means to be alive.... The rise of Christianity and other religious movements in the Roman Empire is an example of a new gossamer spreading over a rotting civilization; though outwardly emperors and armies continued to give orders as though nothing had changed, individuals, feeling that official institutions were ceasing to be relevant to their needs, sought their consolations from each other. Today, a similar switch in attention is happening: the earth is in the early stages of being criss-crossed afresh by invisible threads uniting individuals who differ by all conventional criteria, but who are finding that they have aspirations in common. When nations were formed, all the threads were designed to meet in a central point; now there is no centre any more; people are free to meet whomever they wish. [p. 466]

Zeldin is here looking beyond the surface of the civilizations that reached a crisis point in the middle of the twentieth century and for a generation after. He is looking beneath the social and political institutions that today are challenged by global immigrations of economic and war refugees, widespread homelessness, civil and border and cultural strife, rising tides of impoverishment (flowing around fantastical concentrations of wealth), urban ghettoization of the poor, famine, deteriorating mental health and disruptions of family life, the internationalization of disease transmission and of traffic in drugs, arms, and pollutants. All of these are conditions that can make cherishing child rearing not a topic of ideological planning and social engineering, but, simply, an impossibility. He sees that there is a revolt against this impossibility, a clamoring for cherishment—Zeldin's gossamer of communicativeness.

CHERISHMENT CULTURE

Today, humanity's growth principle—the interaction of all individuals' growth principles—must be framed and lived against the conditions that make cherishing child rearing impossible. To put such a principle in a maxim: So order your society that no children go uncherished, and no adult will either. A mode of understanding and therapeutic work that truly stresses in this way—as Takeo Doi began to do—the idea that the central discontent of contemporary civilization is its neglect of the infant's, and thus the adult's, expectation to be loved, has a deep affinity with the Axial Age tradition that claims:

> Affection as the essential principle of relatedness is of the greatest importance in all relationships in the world. For the union of heaven and earth is the origin of the whole of nature. Among human beings likewise, spontaneous affection is the all-inclusive principle of union. [*I Ching*, 1967, p. 14]

This philosophical statement, from the *I Ching: The Book of Changes*, was central to Chinese civilization in the Axial Age. It was expressed in even the oldest historical layer of the *I Ching*, which was traditionally attributed to King Wen, patriarch of the Chou dynasty, who assembled the existing system of hexagrams into the book in about 1150 B.C.E., some six hundred years before other additions and commentaries were prepared by Confucius and his school and by the early Taoists.

King Wen, the Chinese cultural founding figure, lived his adult life under arrest in the court of the last Shang emperor. He was understood by his heirs to have been able to maintain his creativity and particularly his receptivity in the face of the Shang tyrant's persecution, the hyperactivity of a regime as totalitarian as possible in the ancient world. In his model of integrity and tranquillity, King Wen imagined the cosmos and himself as a microcosmos to be composed of the complementaries (not oppositions): The Creative and The Receptive, Heaven and Earth, Yang and Yin, The Masculine Principle and The Feminine Principle. The affectionate relationship of The Creative and The Receptive, he said, is always changing, as night follows day, as month follows month, season follows season. The wisdom of the sage is to be able to appreciate the changes in the cosmos and in himself or herself as these correlate; to act rightly on the basis of that appreciation; to do with perfect timing what is called for in nature and with other people, in any of all the situations the hexagrams of the *I Ching* describe. "Man achieves the height of wisdom when all that he does is as self-evident as what nature does" (p. 144).

The *I Ching* is a book for self-cultivation, for the cultivation of the family—"the family is the society in embryo"—and for the exercise of political rulership by cultivated men. The institutions the *I Ching* supports are strictly patriarchal, like those of all the ancient state-building civilizations of this period, but, on a deeper level, The Masculine Principle and The Feminine Principle are not sex specific. The qualities of character the *I Ching* recommends for all people depend upon both Masculine and Feminine principles in their relatedness, as summed up by the word for ideal human relating, *jen*, which means "human-heartedness" or "kindliness." The *I Ching* instructs, for example, that neither a king nor a father should do anything "to make himself feared; on the contrary, the whole family [or state] can trust him because love governs their intercourse" (p. 15). This is a vision of what we call Cherishment Culture.

All relationships are brought about by the presence of The Receptive, the female *principle*. In a human being, The Receptive is the receptive ego: it gives form to The Creative, which is like the inchoate, powerful, persevering energy of the id. But The Receptive is not an executive agency, a controller or a ruler over the energy of The Creative; it does not lead, it works by being devoted, steadfast. In this

Chinese tradition, the form-giver is not the ruler, but the holder—as it were, the facilitating internal and external environment. Metaphorically: "the earth is able to carry and preserve all things that live and move upon it. The earth in its devotion carries all things, good and evil, without exception" (p. 186).

Translated into the terms we have been developing, what is recognized here is that The Receptive—the ego instinctual—sustains human life, guides it, holds it. Constriction of The Receptive is as harmful as—and less necessary than—the constriction of the sexual and aggressive that Freud imagined as the discontent of civilization. In this Chinese way of thinking, unhappiness or discontent comes fundamentally when people are not growing in relatedness, or when they have created institutions that do not sponsor growth, the unfolding of each person's potentialities. The primary focus is not on conflict, for conflict is thought to follow from lack of relatedness and lack of reciprocity.

We have been looking at the discontent of contemporary civilization with Chinese concepts, but it emerges similarly if the view is globally historical, as it is in Zeldin's *An Intimate History of Humanity* (1994), which is as much a sign of the times as a record of the times. Zeldin has seen the hopefulness of the present moment to lie in a general turning of human attention away from active conquest and onto the underlying receptivity in people and to the way this is expressed now, globally, in longing for relatedness, for travel, meeting people, growing, discovering, encountering:

> The originality of our time is that attention is turning away from conflict to information. The new ambition is to prevent disasters, illnesses and crimes before they occur and to treat the globe as a single whole; women's entry into the political sphere is reinforcing the challenge to the tradition that conquest is the supreme goal of existence; more attention is being given to understanding other people's emotions than to making and unmaking institutions. [p. 16]

What Zeldin is pointing to in both of the passages from his book that we have just quoted is a shift from understanding people only in terms of their conflicts to understanding them in terms of their longings, their elemental longings—what we call their cherishment needs. In adults, these needs are manifest most strongly in desires for conversation, for being warmly listened to and listening, and for emotional attunement—what we as therapists know as therapeutic attunement. As the *I Ching* says in the hexagram "The Well," which focuses on the place in a village where people gather, their forum:

> Thus the well is the symbol of that social structure which, evolved by mankind in meeting its most primitive needs, is independent of all political forms. Political structures change, as do nations, but the life of man with its needs remains eternally the same—this cannot be changed. . . . We must go down to the very foundations of life. For any merely superficial ordering of life that leaves its deepest needs unsatisfied is as ineffectual as if no attempt at ordering had ever been made. . . . [p. 186]

The Chinese sages whose wisdom is reflected centuries later in Doi's attitude toward infant helplessness and receptivity did not, like Freud and the Western analysts of civilization, have a tragic sense or a sense of unique historicity. For them, the cosmos and human microcosmos are always changing and cycling through days and months and seasons; there are no caesuras in history, no definitive breaks and no apocalypses. Renewal is always possible, as decline is always imminent. There is no "irremediable antagonism" between human instincts and civilization in their view; there are only distortions, imbalances, which will eventually change. So they are not the thinkers with whom to explore a world crisis in terms of the irreversibility the Western prophets have described. But, on the other hand, their sense for the interplay in the world and in people of The Creative and The Receptive, which we are equating here with the sexual and aggressive and the ego instinctual—and specifically their understanding of and appreciation of The Receptive, the ego instinctual—is lacking in the West. And, we have been suggesting, this lack makes the Freud-influenced Western assessment of the present historical moment of crisis incomplete.

REFERENCES

Arendt, H. (1951). *The Origins of Totalitarianism*. New York: Meridian, 1958.
Aries, P. (1962). *Centuries of Childhood*. New York: Knopf.
Doi, T. (1969). Japanese psychology, dependency need, and mental

health. In *Mental Health Research in Asia and the Pacific*, ed. W. Caudill and T.-Y. Lin, pp. 335–341. Honolulu: East-West Center.

——— (1971). *The Anatomy of Dependence*. New York: Kodansha, 1981.

Fairbairn, W. R. D. (1952). *Psychoanalytic Studies of the Personality*. London: Tavistock.

Freud, S. (1912). On the universal tendency to debasement in the sphere of love. *Standard Edition* 11:177–190.

——— (1926). Inhibitions, symptoms and anxiety. *Standard Edition* 20:75–172.

——— (1930). Civilization and its discontents. *Standard Edition* 21:57–146.

Hartmann, H. (1964). On the theory of sublimation. In *Essays on Ego Psychology*, pp. 215–240. New York: International Universities Press.

Horney, K. (1937). *The Neurotic Personality of Our Time*. New York: Norton.

I Ching: The Book of Changes. (1967). Trans. into German R. Wilhelm and into English C. F. Baynes. Princeton, NJ: Bollingen, Princeton University Press.

Jaspers, K. (1953). *The Origin and Goal of History*. Trans. M. Bullock. London: Routledge & Kegan Paul.

Modell, A. (1975). The ego and the id: fifty years later. *International Journal of Psycho-Analysis* 56:57–67.

——— (1990). *Other Times, Other Realities*. Cambridge, MA: Harvard University Press.

Plaut, E. A. (1984). Ego instincts: a concept whose time has come. *Psychoanalytic Study of the Child* 39:235–255.

Reik, T. (1963). *The Need to Be Loved*. New York: Farrar, Straus & Giroux.

Zeldin, T. (1994). *An Intimate History of Humanity*. New York: Oxford University Press.

3

The Hidden History of the Ego Instincts

INTRODUCTION

All the theoretical and technical disputes among psychoanalysts—during Freud's lifetime and since—have had as their key battleground The Libido Theory. The major schisms have opened over The Libido Theory; but critics have also set up opposition parties within the psychoanalytic parliaments to push for their views of the inadequacies of The Libido Theory.

Again and again, both by schismatics and by dissidents within the psychoanalytic movement, it has been said either that Freud placed too much emphasis on the sexual instinctual drives to the neglect of something else, or that he failed to ground them in something nonsexual or presexual. That is, he was either monomaniacal about his Theory, or he was superficial; too focused, or not deep enough. As Robert Waelder (1960) noted forty years ago, there have been critics who were heirs to Adler and critics who were heirs to Jung.

In the present complicated moment in the history of psychoanalysis, The Libido Theory has defenders but they are on the defensive, as various exponents of object relations theory, interpersonalism, intrasubjectivism, Self Psychology, and so on have come forth to catalog what has been missing or denied in Freudianism during the reign of The Libido Theory. Even though the critics and criticisms are diverse, we think that a general indictment can be drawn up—provided that the last version of Freud's instinct theory in which a death instinct is opposed to the life (including libidinal) instincts is left aside as too complicating. In its simple form, the indictment has four counts:

First, The Libido Theory presents human beings as aiming, fundamentally, at tension reduction or tension discharge, which is how the Theory defines pleasure. The Pleasure Principle rules until the Reality Principle modifies it. Critics ask, "Is this what human beings want?" and "Isn't the aim too normative, too prescriptive?" before going on to propose many different kinds of alternatives as well as revisions of the timing of libidinal stages. Other critics note that the discharge model is deeply indebted to nineteenth-century Helmholtzian mechanistic conceptions of how the body works.

Second, The Libido Theory does not acknowledge that human beings are related to others—attached, in the fullest sense now given to that verb—from their births. It presents them as having to overcome an autistic or narcissistic condition in order to come into relatedness, and it begins the story of object relations with the achievement of sexual "object constancy" and not with object need. Within the large concept "related to others from their births," there are, however, many different visions housed: some speak of "primary object relations" and some imagine an initial condition of merger or symbiosis for which human beings always feel nostalgia.

Third, The Libido Theory, focused on sexual instinctual drives, makes it impossible to appreciate the ego in its social and cultural context or its interpersonal field. A human being viewed under the aegis of The Libido Theory is a monad.

Fourth, The Libido Theory underlies visions of "the therapeutic action" that are "one person," not "two person" in their scope; the relation between analysand and psychoanalyst is presented as one in which the analyst releases fixated or regressed or arrested libido or libidinal development, making ego be where id was. Freud did not, thus, really explore the therapeutic dyad, the interaction of analyst and analysand, the play of transference and countertransference, the mutual constituting of subjectivities, and so forth.

We find these criticisms compelling, but we do not think that it is necessary either to discard The Libido Theory or to show libido as a derivative of something else in order to meet the criticisms. To point an alternative way, we are going to chart the development of Freud's instinct theory through its major stages, concentrating on the historical moment when Adler and Jung brought their briefs against Freud's first draft.[1] We want to revisit Freud's responses to Adler and Jung, as these two critics moved him to begin modifying his original working hypotheses about the instinctual drives. Such a historical excursion is not necessary, of course, to approach the theoretical and technical indictment, but we think that this route not only shows up the problems of The Libido Theory clearly but offers a portrait of the psychological resistances that have stood in the way of the solution we propose. Very summarily, we believe that Freud eliminated from his own theory exactly the element he needed in order to meet his critics' criticisms: his notion of the ego instincts. He became unable as a consequence to provide psychoanalytic theory with a wider concept of object relations, with a third principle of mental functioning in addition to the Pleasure Principle and the Reality Principle—we'll call it the Growth Principle—or with a notion of instinctual drives in conflict and harmony over development.

LOVE AND HUNGER IN THE NEUROSES AND PSYCHOSES

In the first phase of his theorizing about the instincts, from the 1890s up to 1914, Freud was imagining a Darwinian struggle in the

---

1. Edward Bibring (1941) offered a good map of Freud's evolving theory by following Freud's own mini-histories; see particularly: "Instincts and Their Vicissitudes" (1915); "The Libido Theory and Narcissism" in *Introductory Lectures on Psychoanalysis* (1916–1917); "Beyond the Pleasure Principle" (1920a); "The Libido Theory" (1923a); "The Ego and the Id" (1923b); Chapter VI of "Civilization and Its Discontents" (1930); Chapter XXXII of "New Introductory Lectures" (1933), and Chapter II of "An Outline of Psychoanalysis" (1940).

mind. He spoke of the ego with its interest in self-preservation battling the sexual instincts and subduing them only at the price of suffering and restriction. Eventually he needed to give the ego's checking or guiding or repressing energy a designation, which was "instincts of self-preservation" and then, starting in 1910, "ego instincts."[2] Hysteria and Obsessional neurosis could be understood very efficiently as conditions in which sexual energy was tamed or dammed up by the counter-energy of the ego.[3]

Freud operated with the idea that ego had its own energy, its own drives, but neither before nor after he began to speak of "ego instincts" in 1910 did he ever really explore the assumed drives. Similarly, he did not question what "self-preservation" consisted of, and it seems that only once did Freud offer any indication of what the plural in self-preservative instincts might refer to. In that instance he noted (1913) that the sexual instincts are made up of component instincts and are also characterized by being initially "attached to the self-preservative functions of nutrition and excretion, and, in all probability, of muscular excitation and sensory activity" (p. 181). By contrast, Freud often discussed the sources, aim, and objects of the sexual instincts, offering several different variants on the basic idea that they are chemical in nature; arise internally, concentrating during different stages in various bodily zones; aim at pleasure, which consists crucially of tension discharge, and eventually at reproduction. The sexual instincts seek as their objects either the self (autoerotism) or others (alloerotism), at first in an undifferentiated or polymorphous way and later in more limited or directed search. But of the ego instincts he indicated only that their aim is self-preservation. Whence they arise, where they concentrate, and whether they have objects was not clear. In the period from 1910 to 1914, Freud did claim that the ego instincts have as their first ob-

---

2. The first use of this term is in "The Psychoanalytic View of Psychogenic Disturbance of Vision" (1910, p. 214).

3. In the "New Introductory Lectures," Freud (1933) wrote: "In the course of investigating the neuroses we came to know the ego as the restricting and repressing power and the sexual trends as the restricted and repressed one; we therefore believed we had clear evidence not only of the difference between the two groups of instincts but also of the conflict between them. The first object of our study was only the sexual instincts, whose energy we named 'libido'" (p. 96).

ject the maternal nourishing breast, but when he waxed retrospective, recapping his struggle to develop an instinct theory, he attributed no objects to the ego instincts at all, except perhaps the ego itself. Indeed, he said that initially he had opposed the ego instincts to the "object-instincts," his designation for the sexual instincts. "In what was at first my utter perplexity," he reminisced (1930), "I took as my starting point a saying by the poet-philosopher Schiller that 'hunger and love are what move the world'" (p. 117).

Although he cited Schiller, Freud was well aware that his first formulation was his Darwinian one. The idea that love and hunger are the prime movers of the animals was, of course, not original to Darwin, but Darwin was the first to provide a clear theory asserting that these two instincts or instinct groups—described as self-preservative and species-preservative or reproductive—and no others are at the basis of animal behavior (Sulloway 1979). Darwin's formulations, especially as they opened the territory of the sexual instincts for exploration, gained enormous currency, as Havelock Ellis (1939) acknowledged retrospectively: "The immense importance of sex is indeed implicit in the biological conception of life as it began to take shape in the middle of the last century and the ancient dictum that hunger and love are the pillars of life became developed in all the human sciences" (p. 316).

In this broad tradition of which Freud was a part, as in Freud's own theory, it is noteworthy that the self-preservative instincts were less explored than the species-preservative sexual instincts were. Darwin himself had made it clear that the idea of natural selection occurred to him as he read Thomas Malthus's *Essay on the Principle of Population* (1798). If the high geometrical rate of their increase dictates that all organic beings must struggle for their existences, Darwin (1859) thought, then any being that can "vary however slightly in any manner profitable to itself" (p. 37)—that is, preserve itself—under its life conditions will have a better chance of surviving, being naturally selected, and thus propagating "its new and modified form." So, of course, there arose for Darwin the key question: What constitutes fitness for survival?—for presumably the instinct for self-preservation would be an instinct aimed at this fitness.

Darwin's answer to this question was complex. He recognized that aggressive capacities for struggling and triumphing would be key, particularly under conditions of scarcity that aggravate competitiveness. And on the basis of this recognition grew up the theoretical tendency known as Social Darwinism, which emphasizes the "natural law" of ruthless competition among animals and humans. But Darwin also claimed, as he said in a famous passage of *The Descent of Man* (1871), that

> there can be no doubt that a tribe including many members who, from possessing in a high degree the spirit of patriotism, fidelity, obedience, courage and sympathy, were always ready to aid one another, and to sacrifice themselves for the common good, would be victorious over most other tribes; and this would be natural selection. [p. 166]

He was indicating that it is not strength or cunning but capacities for serving the common good that are, ultimately, preservative, increasing "the standard of morality and the number of well-endowed men" over time.[4]

Sigmund Freud was no Social Darwinist. When he took up the Darwinian vision, as he made very clear in his early essays, prior to

---

4. Among Darwin's many followers, the Russian Prince Peter Kropotkin, writing in 1902, became the most dedicated critic of Social Darwinism. He was a proponent of the notion his countryman, the naturalist Kessler, had called "the law of Mutual Aid," which, Kropotkin argued (1902), "for the success of the struggle for life, and especially for the progressive evolution of the species, is far more important than the law of mutual contest" (p. 407). Darwin himself had made it clear, Kropotkin stressed, that struggle is replaced by cooperation, which implies that the fittest animals are those that depend upon and support one another. "They have more chances to survive, and they attain, in their respective classes, the highest development of intelligence and bodily organization" (p. 411). In human societies, there is, then, an "unconscious recognition of the force that is borrowed by each man from the practice of mutual aid; of the close dependency of every one's happiness upon the happiness of all; and of the sense of justice, equity, which brings the individual to consider the rights of every other individual as equal to his own" (p. 408). Social Darwinists emphasized the war of all against all, the Hobbesian Darwin, but Kropotkin saw Darwin's barely adumbrated idea that animals have a drive that aims at development itself, which is a drive toward mutual dependency. The Prince's notion was that animals and men have instincts that attach them to objects that nourish them, protect them, grow them up, increase their physical abilities and intellectual capacities. Interestingly, Kropotkin's work is not mentioned in the most recent effort to reconsider Social Darwinism and create a vision of altruistic human behavior: Sober and Wilson's *Unto Others: The Evolution and Psychology of Altruism*, 1998.

"Three Essays on The Theory of Sexuality," he saw the great Malthusian problem epitomized in the challenge to curb the sexual instinct rationally. For him this meant, specifically, discovering contraception that would not interfere with or eliminate pleasure, and thus induce neurosis, which, in turn, would render sexual reproduction impossible. Freud's intrapsychic Darwinism, then, pitted a rational power, the ego, against the sexual drive, with the aim not of defeat but of pleasure preservation. But what has this power to control sexuality to do with Hunger? Why, when it came to exploring the ego's own source of power, look to Hunger? Why not to motives for aiding others, like Darwin's sympathy, or seeking aid from others? Or generally to what Darwin called "the social instincts." Or why not think of hunger as having its most elementary manifestation in a baby's suckling and a caregiver's aid to this dependent baby? To approach Freud's theory with these questions in mind, we are going to turn to the context in which, between 1910 and 1915, he finally put his attention to the self-preservative ego instincts—and to the baby at the maternal breast. These were the years of Freud's quarrels with, first, Adler, and then Jung, each with his challenge to The Libido Theory.

Alfred Adler first emerged as an independent and bold theorist with his claims, which Freud initially found very interesting and suggestive, that people generally suffer from biological weaknesses, unfitnesses for the struggle to live, which Adler called "organ inferiorities." Some people are able to compensate for these weaknesses by a conscious concentration of attention. Self-training can result in superior performance for an afflicted organ or another one: a blind person may become a superb musician, a deaf person a painter. Compensation, on the other hand, can initiate a neurosis if it involves the inferior organ in a neurotic sexualization process, particularly if the organ inferiority involves or entails weakness, specifically, of the sexual function.

Although Adler started out very interested in how sexualization of an inferior organ can induce neurosis, by 1908 he was explicitly countering Freud's emphasis on the sexual instincts. First he insisted that there is an aggressive drive: aggression is not the result of frustrated libido, but an inborn drive that has a role no less important than libido has in normal life and neurosis. Then in 1910 Adler emphasized the psychological hermaphroditism of all people, but especially neurotics, whom he thought of as also physically hermaphroditic (a condition of "organ inferiority"). Combining his developing lines of thought, Adler then claimed that all males protest against the femininity and passivity in themselves by asserting their masculine aggressivity. This is "masculine protest," a universal.

In the course of refining his ideas, and of responding to Freud's 1910 "ego instincts" formulation, Adler insisted that there are no ego instincts that are not part of the dominative nature of the ego itself—its striving for significance, for power, for control. The dependent hunger satisfaction of a baby was of no interest to Adler as he, the Social Darwinist of psychology, argued for an ego that always wants to be "above." And, further, for an ego always striving in culture, shaped by culture to such an extent that the ego instincts are, really, nothing more than the means by which culture's guidelines for dominion are laid down in people. Social pressures shape the expression of the ego's aggressive drives.[5]

When Freud decided that Adler had begun to create not a challenge to psychoanalysis but an alternative to it, he made it clear that Adler was at once too biological and too sociological. His strongest counter to Adler's notion that there is an innate aggressive drive for dominion or a predetermined protest against weakness was his idea that the child begins life not by being aggressively assertive of its wishes but by feeling that all its wishes will be satisfied, a feeling of omnipotence. Working collaboratively with Ferenczi, who wrote a seminal essay in 1913 on the ego's development of a sense of reality, and with Karl Abraham, Carl Jung, and Sabina Spielrein, who reinforced Freud's old Darwinian conviction that ontogeny is a repetition of phylogeny and the individual child's development, thus, a recapitulation of the species' development, Freud (1913) proclaimed: "The principle of avoiding unpleasure dominates human actions until it is replaced by the better one of adaptation to the external world" (p. 186). A child only gradually gives up its sense of omnipotence, its expectation that all its wishes will be fulfilled, to accept the teachings of reality; the Pleasure Principle gives way to the Reality Principle, as Freud put the matter

---

5. Adler's early work is discussed in Henri Ellenberger's *The Discovery of the Unconscious* (1970), as well as in Paul Stepansky's *In Freud's Shadow: Adler in Context* (1983).

(1911). The implication of this conception was that the ego instincts have as one of their main aims guiding the sexual instincts into realistic or reality-tempered channels, because they are more reality oriented than the sexual instincts. Summarizing this strand of Freud's thought, Ferenczi (1913) wrote:

> The stages in the development of the sense of reality have here been presented . . . only in terms of the egoistic, the so-called "ego instincts," which serve the function of self-preservation; reality has, as Freud has established, closer connections with the ego than with sexuality, on the one hand because the latter is less dependent on the outer world (it can for a long time satisfy itself autoerotically), and on the other hand because it is suppressed during the latency period and does not come at all into contact with reality. Sexuality thus remains throughout life more subjected to the pleasure-principle, whereas the ego has immediately to experience the bitterest disappointment after every disregarding of reality. . . . [p. 198]

After working with Carl Jung to establish the International Psychoanalytic Association at the 1910 Nuremberg Congress, Freud articulated his disagreements with Adler more forcefully and more politically—for the preservation of psychoanalysis as he understood it and as he had just successfully institutionalized it as a kind of mutual aid society, a Darwinian brotherhood. But even after Adler had departed the Vienna Society, Freud continued meeting his challenge by exploring the relation between the sexual instincts, which Adler had disavowed, and the ego instincts, which Adler had misconstrued.[6] He

---

6. In his "History of the Psychoanalytic Movement," Freud (1914a) noted that it was an important psychoanalytic task to show (as Ferenczi had begun to do in his essay) "the egoistic constituent in libidinal instinctual impulses," because psychoanalysis had been preoccupied with demonstrating that "every ego-trend contains libidinal components." But Adler had used his focus to deny the libidinal impulses: "He does what every patient does and what our conscious thought in general does, namely, makes use of a rationalization, as Jones [1908] has called it, in order to conceal the unconscious motive. Adler is so consistent in this that he positively considers that the strongest motive force in the sexual act is the man's intention of showing himself master of the woman— of being 'on top.' I do not know if he has expressed these monstrous notions in his writings" (p. 53). Adler had construed the ego instincts as aggressive instincts, ruthlessly competitive: "The view of life that is reflected in the Adlerian system is founded exclusively on the aggressive instinct; there is no room in it for love" (p. 58).

developed the idea that ego instincts—paradigmatically, Hunger—are object related from the beginning of life, from the moment when the baby takes the mother's nipple in its mouth to preserve itself by suckling and incorporating. Then he went further and made explicit his suggestion that ego instinctual object relations with the mother and other caregivers also guide the object relations of the sexual instincts. Self-preservative feeding at the breast prepares the way for erotic investment in the breast and then in the mother.

The key passage where these ideas come together is in Freud's 1912 essay "On the Universal Tendency to Debasement in the Sphere of Love." There Freud referred to the object-relatedness of the ego instincts as "the affectionate current," while to the developmentally later object-relatedness of the sexual instincts he gave the name "the sensual current."

> The affectionate current is [older than the sensual current]. It springs from the earliest years of childhood; it is formed on the basis of the interests of the self-preservative instinct and is directed to the members of the family and those who look after the child. From the very beginning it carries along with it contributions from the sexual instincts—components of erotic interest—which can already be seen more or less clearly even in childhood and in any event are uncovered in neurotics by psychoanalysis later on. It corresponds to the child's primary object choice. We learn in this way that the sexual instincts find their first objects by attaching themselves to the evaluations made by the ego-instincts, precisely in the way in which the first sexual satisfactions are experienced in attachment to bodily functions necessary for the preservation of life. The "affection" shown by the child's parents and those who look after him, which seldom fails to betray its erotic nature ("the child is an erotic plaything"), does a very great deal to raise the contributions made by erotism to the cathexes of his ego-instincts, and to increase them to an amount which is bound to play a part in his later development, especially when certain other circumstances lend their support. [p. 180]

In this passage, it seems clear that Freud's thought was moving in the direction of an image of the infant as initially a harmonious mix of ego instinctual and sexual instinctual drives. The harmony then gets disturbed as the sexual instinctual drives surge, in part stimulated by parental seductiveness. Aggression would, presumably, surge in such frustration. But in a passage written a year later, it seems that Freud also thought that something in the sexual instincts themselves disturbs the harmony. He calls it (1913) their independence, and he seems to have had in mind the initial lack of relation to reality or autoeroticism that Ferenczi had stressed:

> If we examine sexuality in the adult with the help of psychoanalysis, and consider the life of children in light of the knowledge thus gained, we perceive that sexuality is not merely a function serving the purposes of reproduction, on a par with digestion, respiration, etc. [that is, the self-preservative functions]. It is something far more independent, which stands in contrast to all the individual's other activities and is only forced into an alliance with the individual's economy after a complicated course of development involving the imposition of numerous restrictions. Cases, theoretically quite conceivable, in which the interests of these sexual impulses fail to coincide with the self-preservation of the individual seem actually to be presented by the group of neurotic illnesses. For the final formula which psychoanalysis has arrived at on the nature of the neuroses runs thus: The primal conflict which leads to neuroses is one between the sexual instincts and those which maintain the ego. The neuroses represent a more or less partial overpowering of the ego by sexuality after the ego's efforts at suppressing sexuality have failed. [p. 181]

Several things about these passages need noting. First, Freud was assuming that parental sensuality or seductiveness, always a part of parental affection and seldom failing to be obvious as such, will routinely stimulate the child's own sensual current. But, more fundamentally, he was assuming an interplay—a mutuality—of the child's affection and the parents' affection (admixed with sensuality). That is, Freud took a step in the direction of ego instinctual affectional mutuality between child and caregiver, a psychological grounding for the Darwinian preservative social virtue of sympathy. But he soon changed direction. By 1915 Freud would deny that there is any early affectionate current, any ego instinctual object relations guiding sexual object relations. In his 1915 additions to the "Three Essays" as in the essay "On Narcissism" (1914b), Freud redefined the affectionate current as a precipitant out of the sensual current, a desexualized leftover that appears when the Oedipus complex dissolves and sexual attachments to the parents are left behind. Why?

Freud's suggestions in 1912 and 1913 about how the ego instincts and the sexual instincts initially develop harmoniously and become disturbed in neurosis were prompted by Adler's theories, but they were also the product of his appreciative early exchanges with Jung.[7] In 1910, Freud had described the developmental sequence he was thinking about to Jung as a matter of early ego instinctual manifestations to which the sexual current "adds spice later on" (Freud and Jung 1974, p. 284).

Jung agreed with this sequencing, applying it both phylogenetically and ontogenetically, as Freud did. But as Jung developed his own ideas about it and reported them to Freud by sending the papers and lectures he was producing, Freud became alarmed. In response, Freud moved in the direction of exploring the instincts maintaining the ego, accepting Jung's challenge to look at the ego's energy. He took on Jung's suggestion that the nutritive instinct precedes the sexual instinct to the maternal breast. This is the "affectionate current" of Freud's 1912 paper, which echoes Jung's Fordham lectures, also of 1912, where an early pre-sexual (nutritional) stage with an emphasis on the mother is said to precede an oedipal (sexual) stage. But Freud considered this early stage a stage of dominance of the ego instincts, followed by one in which the sexual instincts gain power and influence—not as an emergence of the sexual from the nutritional in Jung's manner. At the same time, Freud reacted negatively as Jung shifted toward the idea that a single psychic energy underlies all psychic manifestations. In "Psychoanalysis and Neurosis," a text that summarized his thought of this period, Jung (1916) explained that this energy, which he sometimes (confusingly) called libido, "using the word in its original sense," is a "vital energy in general, [like] Bergson's *elan vital*." Further, the "first manifestation of this energy in infants is the nutritive instinct. From this stage the libido slowly develops through numerous variants of the act of sucking into the sexual function. Hence I do not consider the act of sucking a sexual act" (p. 557). The distinction between ego instincts and sexual instincts that Freud held so essential disappeared in formulations like this.

Further, in the theory of neurosis that Jung was sketching, which Freud recognized as much like Pierre Janet's, this postulated psychic energy becomes blocked in the course of adapting to reality, and then undergoes regression to an earlier and more primitive mode of adaptation. Jung (1916) cited hysteria as the most obvious case in which a disap-

---

7. In 1912, Ferenczi, too, wrote to Freud about "the ego instincts and sexuality, which despite their opposition, still exist side by side in more primitive stages and in neurosis" (Freud and Ferenczi 1993, p. 336).

pointment or thwarting in love precipitates a neurosis and all kinds of digestive disorders appear: "the regressive libido, turning back from the task of adaptation, gains power over the nutritive function and produces marked disturbances" (p. 557). Jung concluded: "Here the events of early infancy—*never before important* [italics added]—suddenly become so. They have been regressively reactivated. Remove the obstacle from the path of life and this whole system of infantile fantasies at once breaks down and becomes as inactive and ineffective as before" (p. 557). Jung was arguing that fantasies of the Oedipus complex, early incest fantasies, become reactivated and important in regression, in the face of a failure of adaptation in the present; they are not, as Freud held, always important and available as causal factors in neurosis. Freud forcefully and angrily rejected Jung's notion that dammed up and then regressed libido gives rise to or activates infantile sexual fantasies.

The difference between Freud's and Jung's views of the period that came to be called "the preoedipal" surfaced most forcefully in their discussions of psychosis, which had begun after Freud published his case study of Schreber. Freud argued that the psychotic withdraws his sexual instinctual drive from reality, and he suggested that the drive is then invested in the ego itself. Jung (1913) replied that withdrawal of sexual libido might produce an ascetic anchorite, but not a person suffering from dementia praecox, for such people do not "endeavour to exterminate every trace of sexual interest." He also remarked that he knew cases of dementia praecox "where all regard for self-preservation disappears, but not the very lively erotic interests." Freud's sexually oriented libido theory could not account, Jung said, for "functional disturbances which affect the indefinite sphere of the hunger drive just as much as that of sex" (p. 271). In other words, Jung was looking to withdrawal of the ego instincts or, more generally, what he called psychic energy, for the etiology of schizophrenia, which he viewed as fundamentally a condition of disunification or dissolution of the personality. There was a very valuable idea here, which many later Freudian theorists of "ego deficit" took up without knowing its source, but Freud could not see it while he was making two countermoves. First, he began to speak of the ego instincts in terms of their orientation or reorientation toward the ego itself—that is, of narcissism—and, second, he emphasized that the ego instincts are themselves *always* libidinal.

The more Jung created the general "psychic energy" out of a stress upon the ego instincts and a diminishment of the importance of the

58 / Cherishment Psychology

sexual instincts, the more Freud went in the other direction, sexualizing the ego instincts to the point where they virtually disappeared into the sexual instincts. The first consequence of this defensive rigidification, as noted, was that Freud missed the chance to learn from what was most valuable in Jung's theory of psychosis—how psychosis involves disturbance and withdrawal of the ego instincts in their object relationality and thus in ego dissolution. (But Freud did, as we will note in a moment, come back to this idea by another route in the 1920s as he focused his attention on anxiety.) The second consequence was that the notion of narcissism and narcissistic injury became more and more central for Freud in this period of his own intense narcissistic injury over Jung's disagreements and then his departure. In biographical terms, the theory of narcissism is Freud's reaction to his experience of losing Jung's love; it was his mourning. Eventually, Freud's understanding of psychosis came to focus exclusively on how sexual instinctual—not ego instinctual—cathexis is withdrawn from reality (and objects) into the ego.

NARCISSISM: MARGINALIZING THE EGO INSTINCTS

In the years just after his break with Jung, Freud became his own most strenuous critic. Specifically, he judged his first formulation of an instinct theory unsatisfactory because it could not explain the loss of self-regard or self-esteem that he now held to be crucial to the psychotic's break with reality. In the psychoses, Freud thought, the ego itself is the object of the sexual instincts, either because a person has not been able to grow out of a primary condition in which ego-libido rules ("primary narcissism") or because, wounded or frustrated in reality, the person has withdrawn libidinal investments onto the ego ("secondary narcissism"). The psychotic is someone who either has never been able to love or has become dependent on the object and then lost the object—and all object-libido with it—to abandonment, unrequited love, or death. A person of solid self-regard will not suffer loss of the object or of love in this way, but will, rather, withdraw his love investment in the object and turn it—return it—to himself for a period of mourning before turning it outward again, to new objects.

Underlying these ideas was a second instinct theory in which there are effectively no ego instincts, but only conditions of the sexual instincts: primary narcissism—autoerotism—alloerotism. To Jung's monistic energy theory, Freud replied with one of his own, as he recognized when he noted (1923a) that it was "as though the slow process of psychoanalytic research was following in the footsteps of Jung's speculations about a primal libido, especially because the transformation of object-libido into narcissism necessarily carried along a certain degree of desexualisation" (p. 257). Freud's supposition was that normal narcissism, healthy self-regard, would be self-preservative—as loss of normal narcissism would be ultimately self-destructive.

It was in his famous "On Narcissism" essay that Freud (1914b) turned his attention to the phenomenon of self-regard, which "has a specially intimate dependence on narcissistic libido" (p. 98). He had concluded that

> it is easy to observe that libidinal object cathexis does not raise self-regard. The effect of dependence upon the love object is to lower that feeling: a person in love is humble. A person who loves has, so to speak, forfeited a part of his narcissism, and it can only be replaced by his being loved.... [p. 98]

In this vision, being loved, which Freud understood as a replacement for self-love, came to be equated with receiving narcissistic supplies. But being loved can never bring security, much less restore one to the state of primary narcissistic bliss that Ferenczi had in 1913 equated with the "original omnipotence" of fetal and postnatal existence, for being loved always entails the vulnerability of dependence.

In another way, too, the influence of Freud's experience with Jung—his retreat from disappointment into narcissistic self-regard—seems to be reflected in his theorizing. He suggested that the primary narcissistic condition is maintained by being made over to the "ego ideal," which a person strives for as he or she once strove for the original narcissistic condition. The ego ideal is a futureward projection of that ideal past condition of narcissistic self-sufficiency. And it is very interesting to note that Freud (1914b) conceptualized this formation of the ego ideal as a way in which (for men) homosexual object choice is avoided: "In this way large amounts of an essentially homosexual kind of libido are drawn into the formation of the narcissistic ego ideal and find outlet and satisfaction in maintaining it" (p. 96).

In Freud's second instinct theory formulation, self-preservation is interpreted as self-love, ego-libido. There is no notion here that to preserve itself the ego must find an object—initially, the maternal breast—that nourishes, preserves. All mutuality is gone out of the concept of self-preservation and dependency is interpreted as a condition equivalent to lack of self-regard. Put another way: object relatedness, in this formulation, is derivative. It comes developmentally after what Freud called primary narcissism, primary investment of libido in the emergent ego itself. Further, it is no longer attributed to the emergent ego, but is entirely a libidinal matter.

In 1914, Freud was defending his sexual etiology theory to such an extent that he also recast his intuition that our first steps in the direction of object relations involve identifications. He came to assume (1920a) that we identify chiefly with objects in their specifically *sexual* characteristics, in terms of their female or male, masculine or feminine, anatomical parts or mental characteristics—that is, with the breast as female, the penis as male, with the mother, with the father, with femininity (often as passivity or penis-receiving) or masculinity (often as activity or vagina-penetrating). This constriction of view—one which later made Heinz Kohut's theorizing about mirroring seem novel—is obvious in Freud's two case studies of this period. During his famous primal scene, the one-and-a-half-year-old Wolf Man identified with his mother and her penis-receiving state, which is, in his mind, her castrated state. There is nothing here about his identifying in the same stage of his life with a caregiver's care (or lack thereof), with the breast as a nourisher, with the caregivers as a source of (or in their lack of) warmth, safety, caring, kindness, speech and songs, play, affection. In describing the eighteen-year-old female homosexual, Freud notes (1920b) that she went through a latency period of associating with young mothers and caring for their babies. This seems to him a stage of desire to bear her father's baby from which she then retreats; but it can also be understood as a period of expressing affection in identification with mothering figures who give it—and perhaps give it more than her own mother had given it to her after her little rival brother was born.

It is not an accident that these two key case studies of this period in Freud's work were both of homosexuality. The Wolf Man case, of course, focuses on male homosexual desire built upon a foundation of opposite sex identification with the mother and desire (passive) for the father. The eighteen-year-old's homosexuality was opposite-sex identification with the father (and brother) and desire for the mother. To note about these patients that their ego instinctual—taking this to mean chiefly their affectional—needs were not considered is to invoke the identifications and objects they may have had irrespective of sex or masculine or feminine characteristics (what is now called gender). Although affectional needs were typically met in patriarchal households more by female figures, mothers and nurses, they were *expected* to be met (as they are in all kinds of sociocultural conditions) by all caregivers. But, if Freud had gone in this direction, he would not have been able to accomplish his main polemical purpose in these two case studies, which was to continue his combat against the heresies of Adler and, especially, of Jung.

Freud's stress upon the sexual instinctual then began to have its profound—and, we think, distorting—influence on all the next generation Freudians now generally grouped as "object relations theorists." Those of his followers who wanted to set up object relations as primary thought they had either to reject primary narcissism (as Michael Balint and Melanie Klein did) or modify the libido theory, even reject it (as Fairbairn did) to consider primary object relations. Further, even among the object relations theorists like Balint and Klein, who retained the libido theory, primary object relatedness was not ego instinctual. They spoke of primary *sexual* object relatedness (or, in the case of Melanie Klein, primary sexual and aggressive object relatedness, to good and bad breast and penis representations, in the paranoid-schizoid position). The possibility invoked by Freud and by Ferenczi in 1912 and 1913 that the ego instincts are primarily object related and the sexual instincts primarily narcissistic was not developed—although, as we will note below, Winnicott came close to this formulation.

PHASE THREE: EGO INSTINCTS AND ANXIETY

When Freud moved away from the ego instincts/sexual instincts dualism, he no longer featured the ego instincts in his instinct theories, but he did not leave them completely behind. He was, in fact, able to give some attention to ego instincts other than Hunger. For example, he noted (1930) that one of the component sexual instincts stood out from the rest because its aim was very far from being loving. Sadism was, "moreover, attached to the ego instincts: it could not hide its close affinity with instincts of mastery which have no libidinal purpose" (p. 117). While Freud did not pursue his inquiry into "instincts of mastery," or question how mastery and aggression might be linked, some of his followers did—and those who did all came to the conclusion that the concept of the ego instincts needed to be revived in order to account for all that mastery entailed.[8] Freud himself, on the other hand, turned to the topic of anxiety, and eventually came back to mastery as mastery of trauma.

Most importantly, in the mid-1920s Freud was able to reconsider his early theory of anxiety, which had defined anxiety in terms of transformations of frustrated libido. He came to focus on anxiety as a reaction to danger and as an expectation of trauma based on previous experiences of danger and loss. Anxiety is a danger signal, instinctually based. As Freud had noted in the *Introductory Lectures* (1916–1917), two years after the "On Narcissism" essay: "realistic anxiety in the face of a danger seems to be a manifestation of the self-preservative instinct—which, after all, can scarcely be disputed" (p. 430).

As he worked out his new approach to anxiety, Freud's idea from 1912–1913 that the ego instincts are object related from the start of life slipped back into his theory. And, further, the new approach to anxiety brought Freud back to the Ferenczian task of tracing a developmental line for ego instinctual object relations.[9] Opened up was the

---

8. Freud's American contemporary, G. Stanley Hall, emphasized ego instinctual mastery, but the first to study it specifically was Ives Hendrick (1943). Robert White (1963) surveyed the history of psychoanalytic concern with the ego instincts and proposed to call mastery "effectance." Recently Eric Plaut (1979, 1984), has emphasized ego instinctual play and argued for thinking of three types of instincts (sexual, aggressive, and ego). Khantzian and Mack (1983) have revisited the concept of self-preservation.

9. Freud argued with Adler again in "Inhibitions, Symptoms and Anxiety" (1926), this time on the question of what distinguishes people who can control their anxiety from those who cannot, given that all people face the typical danger situations Freud had just pointed out, starting with separation from the mother and loss of love. Adler's answer had been: organic inferiority impedes those who cannot respond to danger. This answer "sets aside the whole wealth of material that has been discovered by psychoanalysis," Freud announced summarily (1926, p. 150).

possibility of thinking of the ego instincts as fundamentally expressed through the ego's concern with having and holding precisely those objects the loss of which constitute the key danger situations of life. The ego instincts, that is, are for safety, security, caretaking, affection. The paradigmatic anxiety situation in which they are first manifest is birth—separation from the mother. The next in line developmentally is loss of the mother's love as she becomes the frustrator, the absent or unavailable one, perhaps the abandoning one. And loss of love here means not loss of erotic satisfaction but loss of safety, care, concern for a helpless baby and an emergent ego—what might be called, generally, loss of growth promotion or loss of developmental help from reality. Castration anxiety is developmentally later—a manifestation of the phallic stage—and in many ways specific to males, while females generally tend to be more organized around loss of love, maternal and then paternal.

In "Inhibitions, Symptoms and Anxiety," Freud wrote explicitly of the "need to be loved," citing it as arising in reaction to the dangers entailed by being born into dependency and helplessness.[10] But he stopped short of saying that the need to be loved or the expectation of being loved is part of the endowment we bring into our uniquely long period of dependency and helplessness relative to the other animals. Instead he argued that helplessness is the cause of our need to be loved by caregivers; it gives rise, eventually, to the Oedipus complex. Danger spurs us to love, in other words. But, the entire weight of the argument Freud was actually making about anxiety falls in the other direction: our need to love makes us able to react with anxiety to danger, that is, to any threat to our need to love, any threat of loss of love.

---

10. See "Inhibitions, Symptoms, and Anxiety" (1926): "The biological factor is the long time during which the young of the human species is in a condition of helplessness and dependence. Its intra-uterine existence seems to be short in comparison with that of most animals, and it is sent into the world in a less finished state. As a result, the influence of the real external world upon it is intensified and an early differentiation of the ego and the id is promoted. Moreover, the dangers of the external world have a greater importance for it, so that the value of the object which can alone protect it against them and take the place of the former intra-uterine life is enormously enhanced. The biological factor, then, establishes the earliest situations of danger and *creates the need to be loved* [italics added], which will accompany the child the rest of its life" (p. 154).

64 / Cherishment Psychology

By the time Freud came to write "Inhibitions, Symptoms and Anxiety" in 1926, he was seldom using his ego instincts terminology, but he did clearly connect anxiety to the instinct of self-preservation and what he at one point in that text calls "the capacity for self-preservation." In this text, Freud was, in effect, propounding a new—or another, a complementary—definition of neurosis (and potentially of psychosis as well): neurosis is inability to control the anxiety that arises instinctually—ego instinctually—in a danger situation. This definition in effect says that the origin of a neurosis may lie in the territory of the instincts of self-preservation, not—or not only—the sexual instincts.

Put differently, we can say that Freud was moving in the direction of recognizing that reality tempers the sexual instincts in one way: by curtailing the infant's sense of omnipotence and its narcissistic libidinal wishes, by teaching that autoerotic satisfactions are limited, by showing that alloerotic satisfactions are initially beyond the child's physical means. But other dimensions of reality, those manifest in caregivers' care, temper the ego instinctual, self-preservative drive. Reality in this sense is growth-promoting or growth-arresting—the shaping principle of the ego instincts is a Growth Principle. The infant's expectation of love in this sense is satisfied or it is not. But this satisfaction is experienced not as tension discharge, like erotic satisfaction is, but as the absence of anxiety—calm. The well-cared-for, cherished child is not characterized by its sexual excitedness (although it can be, of course, sexually excited), but by its sense of security.[11]

THE DUAL INSTINCT THEORY

In a long footnote at the end of "Beyond the Pleasure Principle," as he was recapping the main developments in his instinct theory for the third time, in a kind of amazement, Freud remarked (1920a):

---

11. If we were hypothetically to translate this distinction into biological terms unavailable to Freud, we might suggest that the two broad categories of hormones are involved in the sexual instincts and the ego instincts: the so-called "sex hormones" and the regulatory hormones, especially the so-called "stress hormone" (ACTH, which we might call, in this context, the anxiety hormone). See E. Le Doux, *The Emotional Brain* (1996), Chapter 8.

It is not so easy, perhaps, to follow the transformations through which the concept of the "ego instincts" has passed. To begin with we applied that name to all the instinctual trends (of which we had no closer knowledge) which could be distinguished from the sexual instincts directed towards an object; and we opposed the ego instincts to the sexual instincts of which the libido is the manifestation. Subsequently we came closer to grips with the analysis of the ego and recognized that a portion of the ego instincts is also of a libidinal character and has taken the subject's own ego as its object. These narcissistic self-preservative instincts had thenceforward to be counted among the libidinal sexual instincts. The opposition between the ego instincts and the sexual instincts was transformed into one between the ego-instincts and the object-instincts, both of a libidinal nature. But in its place a fresh opposition appeared between the libidinal (ego- and object-) instincts and others, which must be presumed to be present in the ego and which may perhaps actually be observed in the destructive instincts. Our speculations have transformed this opposition into one between the life instincts (Eros) and the death instincts." [p. 61]

It is certainly not easy to follow this story, and particularly hard is the last transformation, in which the self-preservative function the ego instincts once had is turned over to the sexual instincts, so that Freud began to speak of "the self-preservative sexual instincts" (p. 55). And the ego instincts themselves become—invisibly, obscurely—associated with the death instincts and manifest only in the destructive instincts; that is, they once again virtually disappear from Freud's new picture. All that is clear from the text is that this conceptual upheaval came about as Freud focused his attention on the phenomenon he called "the compulsion to repeat" and drew the conclusion that the ego instincts are fundamentally conservative or regressive, that is, they are aimed at returning to an earlier state—ultimately, to the inorganic or preorganic state, death, or (in evolutionary terms) prelife. Only the sexual instincts are progressive, serving life, and thus they were termed life instincts.

In this last version of his theory, Freud (1920a) much more forcefully took care of both the Adlerian type of assault on the sexual instincts and the Jungian. He was able to posit an instinctual base for aggression, as Adler had, but without involving any repudiation of the sexual instincts or belittling of their importance. In his second key defensive direction, he was able, with his notion that the sexual (life) instincts are self-preservative, to assure that the sexual instincts could not be belittled or dismissed. Freud even thought for a moment that he had gone so far in this direction of "recognizing the sexual instinct as Eros, the preserver of all things" that he had landed again near his enemy, Jung, the monolithic theorist: "If the self-preservative instincts too are of a libidinal nature, are there perhaps no other instincts whatever but the libidinal ones?" No, Freud quickly assured his reader, he was not drawing close to "innovators like Jung who, making a hasty judgment, have used the word 'libido' to mean instinctual force in general" (p. 52). On the contrary, he was asserting a dualism, Eros and Thanatos, that was, finally, completely insusceptible to being reduced into a Jungian instinctual force in general, a "psychic energy." As he had with his theory of narcissism, Freud had protected his libido theory at the expense of the ego instincts disappearing: this time the ego instincts disappeared into the death instinct and their function, self-preservation, disappeared into the sexual instincts.[12]

This revision, unlike the earlier one, grew from Freud's attention to what he calls "the facts of the compulsion to repeat"—although it is not easy to understand why Freud would have put such stress on these "facts of the compulsion to repeat." He himself wondered whether he might not have "overestimated their significance" (p. 59). And he is also anxious to note that his new theory, which, he said, only shifts to a topographical rather than a qualitative dualism of the instincts, does not in any way change the old truth that "the transference neuroses, the essential subject of psychoanalysis, are the result of a conflict between the ego and the libidinal cathexis of objects" (p. 52). But, despite this important (and potentially undermining) declaimer, his

---

12. Some later Freudians actually attributed to Freud the view that the ego instincts and the death instinct are the same. See Nunberg (1955, p. 96), and Schilder (1951), who argues against this equation and against the existence of a death instinct with perhaps the strongest emphasis among the Freudians on ego instinctual mastery: "Thus I find myself in disagreement with Freud's theory of the death instinct and the repetition compulsion, and consider the ego instincts only the tendencies to seize, to hold, and to master, tendencies which are fully in accord with the general laws of instinct, namely, to strive after an object, and to turn to new objects with a renewed ardor" (p. 11). For Schilder, an unfortunately neglected figure in psychoanalytic history, an instinct theory is an object relations theory.

text prompts questions about how he estimated the facts of the compulsion to repeat, not whether he overestimated their significance.

Near the beginning of "Beyond the Pleasure Principle," as he was discussing how war neurotics' traumas reappear repeatedly in their dreams and how children use play to replay everything that has made a great impression on them in real life, Freud linked such repetitions to the instinct of mastery—as noted above, an ego instinct—which seems to have nothing to do with returning to an earlier state. Mastery is turning a passive enduring into an active surmounting and working through, which certainly seems like an ego instinctual preserving of life, promoting of survival. And this kind of mastery also certainly looks like an ego instinctual overcoming or controlling of anxiety. Indeed, it is Freud's own anxiety theory that contains a way to estimate the fact of the compulsion to repeat that is consonant with self-preservation, rather than pointing to a tending toward death: the ego (unconsciously) repeats its danger situation, its traumatic situation, in order to survive it, work it through, develop through it, and find security. Another definition of neurosis is implied: neurosis is a condition in which the compulsion to repeat cannot successfully work through a trauma, in which disturbed or arrested development is not put back on track. Similarly, a failed psychoanalysis is one in which such a neurosis persists, or one that becomes and remains a (transferential) danger situation. In a successful psychoanalysis, the patient is, as Freud said (1920a), "obliged to repeat the repressed material as a contemporary experience instead of, as the physician would prefer to see, remembering it as something belonging to the past" (p. 18). But the repetition does not clear the developmental path.

When Freud first discussed the unpleasure of repeating a trauma in a psychoanalytic treatment, he noted that it can be offset by the pleasure of releasing an instinctual impulse from repression. But then, in his next discussion of the analytic situation, he stated, to the contrary, that "the compulsion to repeat the events of his childhood in transference evidently disregards the pleasure principle *in every way*" (1920a, p. 36, italics added). Then he offered this sweeping generalization as the key reason to attribute to the instincts an urge to restore an earlier state of things. Immediately, however, having made this leap of argumentation, he cautioned that "this view of the instincts strikes us strange because we have become used to see in them a factor impelling towards change and development . . ." (p. 36). This familiar view of what we would call the ego instinctual Growth Principle would also have entailed a vision of the treatment situation as a situation for change and development, as well as transferentially a situation of danger. Nonetheless, Freud stayed with this new conception of the instincts as conservative—based on nothing more than the appearance of transference neurosis in treatments, and based on an interpretation of transference entirely in terms of transference of the sexual instinctual aims and objects into the treatment, onto the analyst. There are no ego instincts in the picture of transference, despite the fact that Freud claimed still to believe that a conflict between the ego and the libidinal cathexis of objects defined the transference neuroses. In the new picture of transference, it is quite impossible to imagine how any working through of the unpleasurably revisited past could ever come about. The dual instinct theory plunged Freud into the pessimism about treatment that is the hallmark of all of the reflections on technique in his late work. And it drew him away from what is now known as a "two-person" or interactive model of the analyst–analysand relationship.

ONCE MORE, THE EGO INSTINCTS

Defending his discovery of the enormous importance of the sexual instincts in human life against Adlerian charges that he was a monomaniac and Jungian charges that he was attributing to repression of the sexual instincts neuroses that were a matter of failed adaptation, Freud consistently pushed the ego instincts out of his evolving theoretical framework—and with them any notion of object relations other than sexual object relations. Consequently, in developing his structural theory in the 1920s, Freud did not think of the ego as having needs, goals, or purposes of its own, maintained by its instincts and what we have called its Growth Principle. Rather, he imagined the ego as the servant of three masters. As Freud said (1940) summarily in his last work, "An Outline of Psychoanalysis": "An action by the ego is as it should be if it satisfies simultaneously the demands of the id, of the superego, and of reality—that is to say, if it is able to reconcile their demands with one another" (p. 146).

By focusing on the ego's role as repressor of the id and, generally, all-around servant of the psyche, Freud also, as the group of his heirs called Ego Psychologists—chiefly Heinz Hartmann—insisted, underestimated the functions of the ego that these heirs called "autonomous ego functions." But even the Ego Psychologists worked without a conception of the ego instincts, or any conception that the ego got its energy from any other source than the id, the reservoir of the libido. It is important to note, however, that much clinical and empirical work within this tradition actually assumes that being related—seeking care and being cared for lovingly—is essential for self-preservation; without it, a child sinks into depression and can actually die, fail to thrive, as René Spitz's postwar research on "hospitalism" showed so clearly. Further, it was Spitz who gave to psychoanalytic infant research the concept of mother–infant "dialogue" to capture the cherishing mutuality that had, briefly, been in Freud's sight.[13]

Among the psychoanalytic successors to Freud it was not the Ego Psychologists but D. W. Winnicott—as he drew synthetically on the work of Klein, Balint, Bowlby's Attachment Theory, and Anna Freud—who came closest to the theoretical framework that we are describing as having been closed off by Freud's defense of The Libido Theory. Three innovations of Winnicott's brought this Freudian revenant to theoretical consciousness from its repression, and we will note them briefly, keying them to the four criticisms of The Libido Theory summarized at the beginning of this essay.[14] First, while retaining Freud's observations about instinctual tension discharge and his stages of libido development, Winnicott called attention to what he called "aliveness," which is not a Jungian *elan vital* but an instinct for development, for growth. Rejecting Freud's notion of the death instinct, he presupposed the developmental thrust of the ego and—without using the name "ego instincts"—the ego's energy, which he sometimes called "primary creativity." Second, Winnicott opened the concept of primary object relations by naming two types of them—that is, by realizing that in the Freudian tradition primary object love had always been only love of a sexual object. Winnicott (1971) spoke of the "good-enough mother" in two dimensions: she is the erotically invested object mother and the security providing environmental mother. The environmental mother is an object and a source of other objects who allows the child to re-

---

13. See the essays in Part 2 of *René Spitz: Dialogues from Infancy*, 1983.
14. Citations to *Maturational Processes*, 1965, and *Human Nature*, 1988.

late to reality generally: that is, she is and provides "transitional objects." Third, this concept of "transitional objects" opened into a concept of "cultural space," which, in a very preliminary way, allowed Winnicott to address the need for psychoanalytic social and cultural theory to be grounded in a reformed instinct theory. Fourth, Winnicott distinguished the "true self" from the "false self," which is the self built up like a shell from reactions to impingements—including frustrations—from the environment and from early sexual objects. The true self persists—survives—in its original and originary expectation of loving care, and is the font, in Winnicott's understanding, of the child's own developing "capacity for concern," its Darwinian social instinct of sympathy. The true self is the site of mutuality or interactivity, although it is closed off, to one extent or another, behind the accrued false self. Winnicott understood neuroses as variant forms of inaccessibility of the true self and blockages of its drive for mutuality, its expectation of being loved and loving, that are woven together with the traditional Freudian sexual fixations and regressions.[15] Thus his vision of the psychoanalytic treatment was of an analyst in dialogue with the patient's true self.

Out of these kinds of innovations, which allowed Winnicott to retain Freud's libido theory in a wider object relations frame, came a developmental picture that we could describe—using terms Winnicott did not use—as the ego instincts (the affectional current) and the sexual instincts (the sensual current) finding a *normal dynamic harmony*, one in which neither current preponderates to the detriment of the other or to the imbalance of the individual. Such a harmony could come about after a developmental progression in which it is typical and normal for now one and now the other instinctual drive to surge up and dominate. The ego instincts dominate and guide in the period of helplessness and dependency (the early preoedipal); then they are intensely intertwined with the sexual in the second year of life (in what Freud called the anal period, or Margaret Mahler the rapprochement sub-

---

15. The Japanese psychoanalyst Takeo Doi (1971) has identified "the expectation of being loved" with Freud's "ego instinct" and studied it in his Japanese patient population. He calls it *amae* and speaks of the child's drive to *amaeru*, to presume upon and seek sweet, indulgent love and care.

phase[16]), as conscious knowledge of sexual difference is attained. The ego instincts ascend again in latency as a child seeks affection out in the world and seeks mastery and skills, while the sexual instincts, which dominated in the oedipal period, do so again in puberty. Over the late adolescent and adult years, there are, in most people, fluctuations, for both physiological or hormonal reasons and emotional-relational reasons, sometimes because of external circumstances and traumata. Some people in adulthood seek chiefly sexual partners; some seek chiefly affectional partners; some seek both in one person, some seek both in a plurality or a series of persons; some oscillate, with a partner for sex or for affection and a friend or confidante or valet or guru or mistress— same sex or opposite sex—for the other current (more or less, a *menage à trois*); some are tricksters or role benders or crossers (perhaps both bisexual—having objects of both sexes—and bifurcated along affectional and sexual lines), and so forth. In late adolescence, many people would, in addition, settle into a style of being predominantly affection seekers or predominantly affection givers, but some would continue to fluctuate; similarly, many would settle into a style of being predominantly active or predominantly passive in the domain of sexuality, but some would continue to fluctuate. That is, along with bisexualisms of object choice and bifurcations along the lines of ego and sexual instinctual drives, there can be ambitendencies of seeking and giving, wanting concern and being concerned, activity and passivity.

Such a developmental picture, we think, stands behind much of contemporary psychoanalytic work that is in Winnicott's debt—and in which the hidden history of the ego instincts is having its most recent chapter.

---

16. In the terms that we are developing in this essay, Margaret Mahler's (Mahler, Pine, and Bergman 1975) rapprochement subphase is a time when the sexual instincts normally begin ascendancy over the ego instincts, which still dominate in the preceding "practicing" subphase. The rapprochement subphase is characterized by its "ambitendency," or the child's vacillation between wanting to be close to its mother and its desire to be independent. Being close means, for example, putting toys in her lap—staking out that libidinal territory, jealously guarding her as "my own" from siblings, fathers. The earlier period is not competitive and, affectively, it is characterized by exhilaration, elation, joy in exploring the world. Mahler reads this as libidinal investment in the world, but it can also be interpreted as the relatively unconflicted playing out of ego instinctual self-preservative drives for development and mastery, and for the child's caring as it has been cared for.

REFERENCES

Bibring, E. (1941). The development and problems of the theory of instincts. *International Journal of Psycho-Analysis* 22:102–131.

Darwin, C. (1859). *On the Origin of Species*. Excerpted in *Darwin: A Norton Critical Editon*, ed. P. Appleman. New York: Norton, 1979.

——— (1871). *The Descent of Man and Selection in Relation to Sex*. London: Murray.

Doi, T. (1971). *The Anatomy of Dependence*. New York: Kodansha, 1973.

Ellenberger, H. (1970). *The Discovery of the Unconscious*. New York: Basic Books.

Ellis, H. (1939). Freud's influence on the changed attitude toward sex. *American Journal of Sociology* 45:309–317.

Ferenczi, S. (1913). Stages in the development of the sense of reality. In *First Contributions to Psychoanalysis*. London: Karnac, 1980.

Freud, S. (1910). The psychoanalytic view of psychogenic disturbance of vision. *Standard Edition* 11:209–218.

——— (1911). Formulations on the two principles of mental functioning. *Standard Edition* 12:213–226.

——— (1912). On the universal tendency to debasement in the sphere of love. *Standard Edition* 11:177–190.

——— (1913). The claims of psychoanalysis to scientific interest. *Standard Edition* 13:163–190.

——— (1914a). On the history of the psychoanalytic movement. *Standard Edition* 14:1–66.

——— (1914b). On narcissism: an introduction. *Standard Edition* 14:67–104.

——— (1915). Instincts and their vicissitudes. *Standard Edition* 14:109–140.

——— (1916–1917) Introductory lectures on psychoanalysis. *Standard Edition* 15, 16:1–481.

——— (1918). From the history of an infantile neurosis. *Standard Edition* 17:1–124.

——— (1920a). Beyond the pleasure principle. *Standard Edition* 18:1–64.

——— (1920b). The psychogenesis of a case of homosexuality in a woman. *Standard Edition* 18:145–172.

——— (1923a). The libido theory. *Standard Edition* 18:255–262.

——— (1923b). The ego and the id. *Standard Edition* 19:1–59.
——— (1926). Inhibitions, symptoms and anxiety. *Standard Edition* 20:75–172.
——— (1930). Civilization and its discontents. *Standard Edition* 21:57–146.
——— (1933). New introductory lectures. *Standard Edition* 22:1–182.
——— (1940). An outline of psychoanalysis. *Standard Edition* 23:139–194.
Freud, S., and Ferenczi, S. (1993). *The Correspondence of Sigmund Freud and Sándor Ferenczi*, volume 1. Cambridge, MA: Harvard University Press.
Freud, S., and Jung, C. (1974). *The Freud/Jung Letters*. Princeton, NJ: Princeton University Press.
Hendrick, I. (1943). The discussion of the "instinct to master." *Psychoanalytic Quarterly* 12:561–565.
Jung, C. (1913). The theory of psychoanalysis. In *Collected Works of C. G. Jung*, trans. R. F. C. Hull, volume 4. Princeton, NJ: Princeton University Press.
——— (1916). Psychoanalysis and neurosis. In *Collected Works of C. G. Jung*, trans. R. F. C. Hull, volume 4. Princeton, NJ: Princeton University Press.
Khantzian, E. J., and Mack, J. (1983). Self-preservation and the care of the self. *Psychoanalytic Study of the Child* 38:209–232.
Kropotkin, P. (1902). Mutual aid. Excerpted in *Darwin: A Norton Critical Edition*, ed. P. Appleman. New York: Norton, 1979.
Le Doux, J. (1996). *The Emotional Brain*. New York: Simon & Schuster.
Mahler, M. S., Pine, F., and Bergman, A. (1975). *The Psychological Birth of the Human Infant*. New York: Basic Books.
Nunberg, H. (1955). *Principles of Psychoanalysis*. New York: International Universities Press.
Plaut, E. (1979). Play and adaptation. *Psychoanalytic Study of the Child* 34:217–232.
——— (1984). Ego instincts: a concept whose time has come. *Psychoanalytic Study of the Child* 39:235–258.
Schilder, P. (1951). *Introduction to a Psychoanalytic Psychiatry*. New York: International Universities Press.
Sober, E., and Wilson, D. S. (1998). *Unto Others: The Evolution and Psychology of Altruism*. Cambridge, MA: Harvard University Press.

Spitz, R. (1983). *René Spitz: Dialogues from Infancy: Selected Papers*, ed. R. Emde. New York: International Universities Press, 1983.

Stepansky, P. (1983). *In Freud's Shadow: Adler in Context*. Hillsdale, NJ: Analytic Press.

Sulloway, F. J. (1979). *Freud, Biologist of the Mind*. New York: Basic Books.

Waelder, R. (1960). *Basic Theory of Psychoanalysis*. New York: International Universities Press.

White, R. W. (1963). *Ego and Reality in Psychoanalytic Theory* (*Psychological Issues*, 7). New York: International Universities Press.

Winnicott, D. W. (1958). *Collected Papers: Through Paediatrics to Psycho-Analysis*. New York: Basic Books.

——— (1965). *The Maturational Processes and the Facilitating Environment*. New York: International Universities Press.

——— (1971). *Playing and Reality*. New York: Methuen.

——— (1988). *Human Nature*. New York: Schocken.

4

The Wise Baby as the Voice of the True Self

Sándor Ferenczi was fascinated by a typical dream that he called "the dream of the wise baby." In 1923, he wrote a short communication under that title. Eight years later, when he was in the midst of his controversial technical experiments, he referred to the dream again in "Child Analysis in the Analysis of Adults." Finally, he gave the dream a prominent place in "The Confusion of Tongues Between Adults and the Child," which he delivered at the Wiesbaden Congress in 1932, less than a year before his death. The dream of the wise baby, Ferenczi came to think, shows very clearly how people "autosymbolize" the narcissistic splitting in themselves that is their determinative way of responding to trauma. Now, after almost seventy-five years, Ferenczi's trauma theory is beginning to assume the important place it deserves in psychoanalytic theory, carried along by D. W. Winnicott's adoption of it into his theory of the split True/False Self. But the dream of the wise baby has not followed the split self theory into contemporary psychoanalytic writing. In order to appreciate how Ferenczi's and Winnicott's trauma theories can be used in dream interpretation, and how they can be elaborated by dream interpretation, we would like in this essay to present and discuss three examples of the dream of the wise baby.

FERENCZI'S WISE BABY: THE SPLIT-OFF SELF

Ferenczi's original short communication in German about the dream of the wise baby appeared in the *Zeitschrift fur Psychoanalyse*. A revised version of the whole note follows:

> Not infrequently patients tell their analysts dreams in which there are newborns, babies in their cradles, or young children, who are able to talk or write fluently, offer up profound sayings, carry on intelligent conversations, deliver harangues, give learned expositions, and so forth. I imagine that behind such dream contents something typical is hidden. The superficial layer of dream interpretation in many cases points to an ironical view of psychoanalysis, which, as is well known, attributes far more psychical value and permanent effect to the experiences of early childhood than people in general care to admit. The dreamer's ironic exaggeration of the intelligence of children, therefore, expresses doubt about psychoanalytic theorizing on this subject. But, because wise babies also appear in fairy tales, myths, and traditional religious history, as well as in paintings (see the Debate of the young Mary with the Scribes), I believe that they, furthermore, serve patients as a medium for deeper and graver memories of their childhoods. The wish to become learned and to excel over "the great" in wisdom and knowledge is a wish to reverse or overcome the situation of the child. Such a wish in dreams of this content that I have observed is also illustrated by the pithy exclamation of a ne'er do well: "If only I had understood how to make better use of the position of the baby." Lastly, we should not forget that the young child is in fact familiar with much knowledge that later becomes buried by the force of repression.

In 1926, when he included this short 1923 communication among his collected papers, Ferenczi continued on with his line of interpretation by adding a footnote to the effect that he had recently observed that wise baby dreams "illustrate the child's actual knowledge of sexuality." As an appreciator of the instinctual drive theory in "Three Essays on the Theory of Sexuality," Ferenczi was emphasizing what the wise baby knows about sexuality and what the dreamer remembers from babyhood about being helpless and at the mercy of those surrounding adults who know more. But by 1931 the wise baby dream had quite a different story to tell.

Ferenczi hoped to convey in "Child Analysis in the Analysis of Adults" how his innovative techniques had allowed patients to communicate their early traumatic experiences by sponsoring "deeper relaxation and more complete surrender to the impressions, tendencies and emotions" (p. 128) arising spontaneously in them during analytic sessions. He related that his patients would sometimes play childlike games of question and answer with him, if he spoke simply enough; that sometimes they actually played, drawing pictures or making up little poems and rhymes; and that sometimes they would sink out of such play into a "twilight state" in which they reenacted a childhood trauma, often while experiencing the analytic situation itself as a traumatizing abandonment.

When feeling hurt, disappointed or abandoned by their analyst, Ferenczi's patients developed a "split of personality," along the lines of their childhood splits in response to trauma:

> Part of the person adopts the role of father or mother in relation to the rest, thereby undoing, as it were, the fact of being left deserted. In this play, various parts of the body—hands, fingers, feet, genitals, head, nose, or eye—became representatives of the whole person, in relation to which all the vicissitudes of the subject's own tragedy are enacted and then worked out to a reconciliatory conclusion. . . . [1931, p. 135]

In their fantasies, too, the patients often presented or autosymbolized themselves as "a suffering, brutally destroyed part and a part which, as it were, knows everything and feels nothing" (p. 135). A knowing head part might be fantasized as connected by a thread, for example, to a suffering body part. Or, in dreams, the knowing part could be represented by the wise baby. What the wise baby of a dream knows is the child's trauma story.

Taking up the notion of splitting again in his general description of "the mechanism of the genesis of a trauma," Ferenczi noted that part of the patient's body, or even all of it, becomes the site of the patient's "deadness"—it becomes flaccid or inert, killed. He called the wise baby or the head the survivor, much as contemporary trauma theorists understand that the body has memories of trauma, which the head knows about and can sometimes recall—or dream. Ferenczi commented:

> It really seems as though, under stress of imminent danger, part of the self splits off and becomes a psychic instance self-observing and desiring to help the self, and that possibly this happens in early—even the very earliest—childhood. We know that children who have suffered much morally or physically take on the appearance and mien of age and sagacity. They are prone to "mother" others also: obviously they thus extend to others the knowledge painfully acquired in coping with their own suffering, and they become kind and helpful. It is, of course, not every such child who gets so far in mastering his own pain; many remain arrested in self-observation and hypochondria. [1931, p. 136]

In 1932, Ferenczi turned his attention from traumas of abandonment to traumas of abuse—traumas of "more love or love of a different kind" than children need—which may also be re-enacted in the analytic situation, especially if the analyst is hurtful in his "professional hypocrisy" or his "restrained coolness" or even his "dislike of the patient." Abused children often become paralyzed, Ferenczi noted, and unable to express their reactions of hatred, disgust, refusal. They cannot respond to sudden unpleasure with defense. In their anxiety, they are compelled "to subordinate themselves like automata to the will of the aggressor, to divine each one of his desires and gratify these" (1932, p. 162). The aggressor, with whom the child has identified, is installed intrapsychically, so the child loses any sense for the real person outside and is thus able to maintain tender feelings for the abuser. But, because the child has introjected at the same time the abuser's guilt feelings, the child is not able to consider the actions engaged in as entirely harmless and loving play—they become punishable offenses. The child then ends up feeling both innocent and culpable, "with the confidence in the testimony of his own senses broken."

When Ferenczi had described in more detail the mechanism of the genesis of a trauma of abuse, and suggested that splitting can go as far as the condition known now as multiple personality disorder, he noted the two main ways in which children struggle to overcome their hurt. They use denial: a split-off part regresses into the state of happiness that preceded the trauma. Or they may—and Ferenczi admitted he had only recently encountered clinically this mode of overcoming—activate "latent dispositions which, uncathected, waited in deepest quietude for their development" (p. 165). This traumatized child becomes a wise baby by activating latent wisdom and progressing developmentally:

> When subjected to a sexual attack, under pressure of such traumatic urgency, the child can develop instantaneously all the emotions of a mature adult and all the potential qualities dormant in him that normally belong to marriage, maternity, and fatherhood. One is justified—in contradistinction to the familiar regression—to speak of a traumatic progression, or a precocious maturity. It is natural to compare this with the precocious maturity of the fruit that is injured by a bird or insect. Not only emotionally, but also intellectually, the trauma can bring to maturity a part of the person. I wish to remind you of the typical "dream of the wise baby" described by me several years ago in which a newly born child or an infant begins to talk, in fact teaches wisdom to the entire family. The fear of the uninhibited, almost mad adult changes the child, so to speak, into a psychiatrist and, in order to become one and to defend himself against dangers coming from people without self-control, he must know how to identify himself completely with them. Indeed, it is unbelievable how much we can still learn from our wise children, the neurotics. [1932, p. 165]

WINNICOTT'S TRUE SELF SPEAKS

As he experimented technically, and as his theorizing developed, Ferenczi interpreted the wise baby as the knowing (particularly sexually knowing) part of the self, then as the self-observing and self-rescuing part, and then, finally, as the psychiatrist part that rescues everyone in the family. As these interpretations emerged, Ferenczi had shifted his attention from the intrapsychic effects of instinctual drive development to the intrapsychic effect—splitting—of abandonment traumas and, finally, of abuse traumas. But, because Ferenczi died soon after his "Confusion of Tongues" lecture, he unfortunately did not have the chance to report further what he was learning from his wise children, the neurotics.

His analysand and student, Melanie Klein, then became the major theorist of splitting. But her emphasis was always on *object* splitting as an inevitable effect of instinctual drive development; she did not follow Ferenczi in his concern for traumas—either of abandonment or

80 / *Cherishment Psychology*

of abuse—except insofar as she considered weaning an inevitable trauma of development. In Klein's theory, a "paranoid-schizoid" position in which both the infant's innate aggression and its weaning frustration are directed at an introjected mother, existing intrapsychically as "good" and "bad" part and whole objects, is normally followed by a "depressive" position in which the child tries to make reparations to the object-mother for its aggression. The child rescues the maternal object from its own anger.

More than any other analyst of the British group that heard the postwar Kleinians present this way of developing Ferenczi's theory, D. W. Winnicott (1965) understood both its importance and its limitation. He set out on his own path by assessing Klein's contribution (in a 1959 lecture):

> I would say that Melanie Klein represents the most vigorous attempt to study the earliest processes of the developing human infant *apart from the study of child-care*. She has always admitted that child-care is important but has not made a special study of it. On the other hand there have been those who developed an interest in the child-care and infant-care techniques. Those who did this ran the risk of being considered traitors to the cause of the internal process. The work of Miss Freud and Mrs. Burlingham in the Hampstead War Nursery (Burlingham and Freud 1944) led to a development of the study of external conditions and their effect. It is clear that this dichotomy between those who almost confine their researches to a study of the internal processes and those who are interested in infant-care is a temporary dichotomy in psychoanalytic discussion, one which will eventually disappear by natural processes. [p. 126]

In fact, of course, this dichotomy persisted for some thirty years more, because most of the Kleinians continued to confine their researches to study of the internal processes, relying upon Melanie Klein's insistence that object splitting processes result fundamentally from death instinctual aggression. Ferenczi's attention to external conditions as they are internalized or absorbed was not further developed in the Kleinian camp. Winnicott, by contrast, found the "death instinct" theory unnecessary as he studied *both* the Kleinian "introjection processes" and the "absorption into the individual child of the child-care elements." Concerned with how the child is initially dependent upon the mother for "ego support," Winnicott cataloged the types of faulty

The Wise Baby as the Voice of the True Self / 81

ego development that come about with traumatizing lack of maternal support and the child's reactions—including aggression—to being unsupported. In comparison to Ferenczi, he gave more attention to the preoedipal period and less attention to libidinal frustration in the oedipal period and to sexual traumatization. But even his comprehensive and balanced approach to faulty ego development or narcissistic illness contained a danger of misunderstanding. Winnicott (1965) held:

> It is as if in looking at narcissistic illness the clinician is liable to be caught up with the absorbed, or internalized, environment, and to mistake this (unless well prepared) for the real individual, who in fact is hidden and is secretly loved and cared for by the self within the self. It is the true individual that is hidden. [p. 127]

The self within the self, or as he came to call it, the "True Self," was Winnicott's wise baby. But, while Ferenczi had emphasized the wise baby as the survivor self split off from the dead or deadened hurt self, throughout his 1960s papers Winnicott more optimistically presented the hidden True Self as able to retain its original sense of aliveness and omnipotence and as being protected by the False Self, which, in order to protect, complies with the environment. Pathology, he held, comes about when this normal developmental kind of splitting proves impossible; so, in comparison to Ferenczi's, his theory was more about trauma prevention or adaptive splitting than about survivorship.

> The True Self comes from the aliveness of the body tissues and the working of body functions, including the heart's action and breathing . . . the True Self appears as soon as there is any mental organization of the individual at all, and it means little more than the summation of sensorymotor aliveness. . . . The infant then becomes able to react to a stimulus without trauma because the stimulus has a counterpart in the infant's inner, psychic reality. The infant then accounts for all stimuli as projections . . . [and] the infant is now able to retain the sense of omnipotence even when reacting to environmental factors that the observer can discern as truly external to the infant. . . . [Winnicott 1965, pp. 148–149]

It is the mother's adaption to her baby that permits the baby to retain its sense of omnipotence but also to adapt to the environment, to tolerate frustrations, to comply. Inevitably, a False Self is built up

82 / Cherishment Psychology

in this process. But the False Self can be either a healthy compromise with reality—manifest as a social manner—or, at the other extreme, an unhealthy, split-off, pathologically compliant False Self that is mistaken for the whole child or the whole adult (Winnicott 1965).

On the basis of his distinction, Winnicott developed his analytic technique, which always aimed at communication with the True Self.

> It is being recognized in the last few years that in order to communicate with the true self where a false self has been given pathological importance it is necessary for the analyst first of all to provide conditions which will allow the patient to hand over to the analyst the burden of the internalized environment, and so to become a highly dependent but a real, immature, infant; then, and then only, the analyst may analyze the true self. This could be a present-day statement of Freud's *anaclitic dependence* in which the instinctual drive leans on the self-preservative." [1965, p. 134, italics in original]

Very important to Winnicott's development of a technique for allowing the true self to be analyzed was the work of Mme. M. A. Sechehaye, which she had summarized in *Symbolic Realization* and *The Autobiography of a Schizophrenic Girl* (1951a,b). Mme. Sechehaye described how her schizophrenic patient Renée, who had made no progress with conventional psychoanalytic technique, responded when she was given objects—a doll, a toy monkey, some red apples—with which she could symbolically represent her hidden self. She could do unto her doll what she had wanted and needed done unto herself in her time of dependency; she could represent her desire to suck at her mother's and her analyst's breasts by eating the red apples her analyst gave her. Winnicott himself used a piece of string or a squiggle drawing for autosymbolizing: he invited his child patients to complete the squiggle drawings he started, and he interpreted to them the pictures of themselves they spontaneously made.

THE TRUE SELF'S EXPECTATION TO BE LOVED

What Winnicott added to Ferenczi's theory was a sense for the degrees of trauma, or a sense for how the hurts of everyday infant-care relate to the kinds of traumas of abandonment and abuse that Ferenczi studied. Winnicott also focused his attention on the preoedipal period and the formation of the ego, while Ferenczi had used Freud's notion of a trauma as a breaching of the stimulus barrier, an overwhelming of the formed ego, and focused on the oedipal level, emphasizing sexual instinctual disruption and frustration. Winnicott had assumed that some splitting is normal and facilitates trauma prevention; only splitting in which the False Self is mistaken for or experienced as the whole is potentially psychotic. As long as the True Self can still speak, it can be reached analytically. In Ferenczi's view, the analysis can foster a developmentally progressive leap forward by helping the patient draw on or cathect (in Ferenczi's words) "latent dispositions which, uncathected, waited in deepest quietude for their development" (1933, p. 165), and by fostering the integration of the child's wisdom into the whole of its developing self.

In Winnicott's view, such self-love comes about by means of dependency on the analyst, by "an anaclitic dependence that leans on the self preservative." That is, in Winnicott's view therapeutic action comes about by means of the instinctual drives that push for self-preservation, the ones Freud had in his early instinct theory called ego instincts and contrasted with sexual instincts. Winnicott implies, but does not say explicitly, that these are drives for nourishment and care, for maternal attention and attunement to the child's needs—drives for attachment, affection, and development.

We have just translated Winnicott's thought about self-preservative dependency into terms stemming from Freud's concept of the self-preservative ego instincts, which he, of course, abandoned in the 1920s when he posited the "death instinct," a step that Winnicott, as we noted, did not think necessary. Winnicott, in effect, worked with the older Freudian distinction between the sexual instincts and the ego instincts, and he found the ego instincts for preservation of the self by the caregiver to be the instincts primarily involved in healthy trauma prevention (as they are the ones primarily thwarted in preoedipally based splitting). In contemporary psychoanalysis, this thought of Winnicott's about dependency as the path to health—to the wise baby asserting itself—has been elaborated most clearly from within a culture that does not evaluate dependency negatively or say it is just for infants and pathological if appearing in adults (as Ferenczi's student Michael Balint argued, for example). The Japanese analyst, Takeo Doi, who was familiar with Ferenczi's and

Balint's work, went nonetheless right back to Freud's self-preservative ego instincts in order to elaborate in Freudian psychoanalytic terms what is called in everyday Japanese *amae*, "the expectation to be sweetly and indulgently loved." Doi (1971) argued that this type of dependency need or expectation addressed to first caregivers, which can also be expressed with an intransitive verb, *amaeru*, "to presume upon another's love," is thwarted in various ways and to various degrees in each type of pathology. Such traumatizing is the root of pathology, which may become entwined with sexual instinctual thwarting (including the traumas of abuse Ferenczi studied) as a baby grows into the oedipal stage. This, we think, is Winnicott's theory elaborated without cultural inhibition or inhibition induced by following the later Freudian instinct theory to the exclusion of attention to the ego instincts. Doi's position implies that the true self has a drive to be dependent and to be preserved in and by that dependency, to be developed and grown in it. The True Self, the wise baby, speaks to tell the adults—and the adult patient's analyst—what he or she needs; the baby speaks Truth to Power. And the Truth is: I expect you to lovingly care for me.

THE DREAM OF THE WISE BABY

This Japanese elaboration of the theoretical stream that flows from Ferenczi to Winnicott—this emphasis on expectation to be loved as an ego instinctual thrust for development—illuminates, we think, both the features of the dream of the wise baby that were observed by Ferenczi and the further features that we have observed and will present below. We have turned to Doi's *amae* concept to account for how wise babies represent in dreams the dreamer's wish for developmental rescue. We notice in wise baby dreams all of the caution about psychoanalysis and even mocking skepticism about it that Ferenczi's babies displayed, but also wisdom about how the analysis can work, about what help is needed.

In our experience, a dream of the wise baby first comes at a particular juncture between the opening and middle phase of an analysis. The patient is in a regressive period when dependency needs are prominent and frequently protested as the patient declares that the analysis is an indulgence. For the three patients we will present, who all play the family psychiatrist professionally as well as at home, this time of longing for tenderness, maternal care, and indulgence was especially frightening: dependence meant allowing the analyst (not themselves) to be the family psychiatrist. In this *amae* condition, the patient will typically produce a big dream (like a "big job," as the British call a big bowel movement) that she or he carefully remembers and brings in like a gift, with a sense of portentousness. The patient indicates that this dream is somehow the whole story; past and present—even future—are all in it. The dream may be long and involved, with a number of segments, or it may feel connected to other dreams or recurrent dreams, as though it were a piece of a larger panorama. Its themes feel so familiar. But interpreting the dream is unsettling. The dream feels like a map of recently traversed analytic territory, a summary, but also an indicator of something just off the edge of the map, something dark and frightening. The big dream is the wise baby's dream: it contains what the wise baby knows: the story of the dreamer's traumatization, the story of the deadening of part of the self (in Ferenczi's terms), or of genesis of the pathological False Self (in Winnicott's terms).

And then comes a dream *of* the wise baby, a dream in which the wise baby actually appears and speaks—and the patient immediately says "That is me." This dream may be a segment of the big dream—if so, it is usually one segment of three—or a dream dreamt during the next night or so. When the wise baby speaks, he or she issues an instruction to the dreamer and also to the analyst about the analysis. Generally, the wise baby tells the dreamer and the analyst to go slowly, not to work too quickly on the themes of the big dream. This is to keep the analysis from being retraumatizing as it comes close to the original traumas that the wise baby knows. Or the wise baby may indicate to the dreamer and the analyst that it is afraid that a step in the direction of freedom—freedom of speech—in the analysis will be followed by a setback, a repetition of the original trauma, so caution must be taken. In effect, the wise baby is the voice of the True Self saying to the analyst, "Do not explore the False Self too abruptly; I need it for now as much as I need you."

In a broader sense, the message that the wise baby delivers is about the dreamer's development. We think that patients are doing what we call "developmental dreaming." That is, they dream their development as it has been and as they wish it to be: their developmental dream is a disguised fulfillment of an ego instinctual—not primarily a sexual instinctual—childhood wish. The wise baby knows how the dreamer's development got arrested or troubled, and he or she can point the way forward, even though begging that progress not be faster than is tolerable. The healing direction is into relationship with a person who will help the dreamer achieve dependency, as Winnicott said. The baby communicates, "It is *this* kind of love that I need, to remedy specifically *this* kind of trauma." If the dreamer was neglected or abandoned, in the dream the wise baby gets the helper's intense, focused attention; if the dreamer was bewildered or intellectually stymied by being physically hurt or abused, the wise baby gets enlightenment or sympathy for its struggling intelligence (or for the dreamer's learning inhibitions). The period of expectant dependency in the analysis, entered into so cautiously and hesitantly, then allows the analyst to receive later the negative transferences, to allow exploration of the traumatizing figure and reconnection with that reality without the patient being retraumatized, so that the traumatizing can be worked through.

As noted, the wise baby frequently appears in the third segment of a dream (sometimes the big dream) or as one in a sequence of three dreams; it may also be in a dream that has three parts or three locales, three spaces. In one way or the other, the wise baby segment is *the third*, and it is related to the other two dreams (or segments or parts) as to "the mother" and "the father." The parents or parental figures appear as they were for the dreamer as a baby but also as the wise baby wishes they might have been for its best development. Signaling that they are coming into their baby relation with the parents, patients often represent themselves at some point in the dream sequence as naked, naked as a baby. In women, the wise baby may appear with the dreamer as an adult, a mother, and the dreamer is aware that she plays both parts in her dream, the mother and the baby—she is both of them.

When the wise baby appears, as Ferenczi had implied by alluding to the painting of "Mary Debating with the Scribes" and other artistic renderings of wise babies, he or she addresses a group. Frequently, the group is the family group—the group for which the wise baby, as Ferenczi indicated, may be acting as the psychiatrist. But we have noticed that wise baby dreams also typically contain groups that are multiples of the figure who was centrally traumatizing to the dreamer. If this figure was the mother, she appears as many women who are all alike in some way.

If the figure was a man—say, an abuser—the man appears as many men, all alike in their ominousness or their frightfulness. Sometimes both the family group and the traumatizing figure writ large and plural will appear. Both are represented in one of the dreams we will present below, where there is a group made up of the patient's disheveled, depressed, neglectful mother in multiple, and then, later, a group of "cold authority figures." In the second group, the whole adult family, including the dreamer herself, appears and is addressed by the wise baby.

THE LOBSTER DREAMER

Toward the end of the first year of her analysis, a middle-aged patient who has many hysterical traits brought a big dream, one that has three distinct parts set in different locales. She later made a transcription of the dream in her journal, placing it with two other dreams that she had in the same night, the third of which presents her wise baby. Although she worked with the big dream for only one session, she came back to it frequently over the whole course of the analysis; she concentrated on the first part, scanting the second, which centers on her remote father, who was preoccupied with his business and a mistress, and avoiding the final part, which features her depressed mother in multiple. This is the big dream (the three parts of which we will number):

> [1.] I was having a lobster dinner with [her child] and [her husband] on the wooded area at the side of our property. It was a Christmas Eve dinner. Strange to have lobster, I thought. Messy. I couldn't eat it all. "I'm not that hungry, I'll just have the claws," I said. One lobster hadn't yet been cooked for some reason, and at a point it started begging, claws snapping aggressively as it reached for food on the table, only to be pushed away like a dog. The scene had shifted here to my parents' kitchen dinner table with my husband and [child] seated in Mother's and Dad's places. I couldn't imagine that it would eat flesh of its own species, but at one point a piece of my lobster fell on the floor and the lobster hungrily scampered toward it. I thought to myself that we should have cooked the lobster because if it hadn't been fed for awhile it wouldn't make a very good meal—it's too starving. [2.] Then, for

some reason I left to go to my music lesson with F at his house. Christmas Eve. I got there and no one was home. I also forgot my recorder. I couldn't believe it. "Would I have to borrow his?" . . .Then there was a black girl waiting too, and I said, "Are you here for F, too?" I had seen her before, another student of his, but I was surprised he would schedule two people together. I said to her, "You won't believe it but I forgot my recorder." Then F and his family members came home. . . . I didn't have an exchange with him because he was preoccupied. [3.] Then I was in my car heading home. I realized that I was undressed and disheveled. I'd better get dressed before [my husband] saw me or he would be suspicious of me. I'm in my car naked, or almost naked, and I pull into an area that looks like I could change while driving—I'd done this maneuver before—looking for shirt, underwear—but as I'm in this area, all of a sudden [her modern dance teacher] and another person were there. I hid myself, crouched down, and they didn't see me naked or near-naked. Then there were all these other women around in bathrobes or so—as if there had been some sort of tailgate sale type thing—waiting in line to pay, or something. I was sort of trapped in this parking area but then I got out and was thinking how I'm sure no one at home cleaned up the dishes of the lobster dinner—typical—I'd have to do it . . .

Below are her transcriptions of the second and third dreams in the sequence:

The second dream: I went to Professor H's office and explained that I hadn't been in because I'd had so much work over the semester. She said she was glad I was there, that she really trusted/liked me and I could have come sooner. She wanted help with organizing books or something about helping her to import/export books or something from/to Germany and the USA. I knew it would be a lot of work and I was feeling lazy or inadequate, but I went along.

The third dream: A group of adults—cold authority figures—were trying to get this baby to do something—to cooperate in some way—they were surrounding him. I was one of the adults. The baby remained stubborn and difficult. Then I decided to take a different tactic so I picked the baby up very maternally and sweetly said, "What's wrong?" and kissed the baby (a boy). His face and lips were all scrunched and hard and he rejected the kiss but then he softened and very sincerely, articulately, and eloquently talked to me. He explained his behavior, but the only part I remember was that he said, "It's all going too fast, I can't do it that quickly, that's why I appear so uncooperative." The implication of what was going too fast was "to be myself," "to reveal myself."

This patient, whose trauma was cumulative, with all the types of elements Ferenczi studied—early childhood neglect by the depressed mother, abandonment by the preoccupied father, and abuse by a brother—knew immediately that she had autosymbolized herself as the starving lobster, begging for nourishment and attention. She has only herself to eat self-preservatively at the parental table, which she associated to the table of her present unhappy marriage. Then she represented herself as not having an instrument to attract or impress her male teacher, whom she associated to her preoccupied father. She could not draw him away from the other student, who is part of the father's other life. Finally, many months after the dream, associating back to it, she realized that she had represented herself in the third part, disheveled and nearly naked, as identified with her mother, who was often too depressed to get properly dressed in the mornings—and the mother is, then, multiple, which means very, very frightening.

This child-father-mother dream has no exit; she can only return to the home where the lobster dinner dishes await her. But the next dream in the series represents her as a favored student of a professor at her college who deals in German books, like the books about psychoanalysis the patient was reading at the time. Her developmental way is pointed: she must go into the world, find others who will love and respect her, finding her well-equipped, even if perhaps not entirely adequate, and who want her to help—that is, who appeal to her helpful self, her rescuing self. She associated the professor with her analyst. Then, in the third dream, the wise baby appears and is induced to speak by the dreamer's own sweet mothering kiss, a self-loving kiss, which softens the baby, dissolves his shell. He asks that the analysis not go too quickly—"to be myself" is hard.

THE AMPHITHEATER OF TERROR

A woman with many hysterical features, including an attention deficit, but more physically traumatized and narcissistically wounded than the Lobster Dreamer, reported a very powerful dream, which, like many of her dreams, was "architectural" and symbolized her body. During the session at the end of her first year of analysis when she was presenting the dream, she gnawed on her thumb as she often does, feeding on herself self-preservatively as the Lobster Dreamer does. She also sounded many of her recurrent themes: she is afraid she is not attractive, not intelligent; her analyst will surely find her disgusting and stupid. Introducing the dream, she mentioned that there was an amphitheater in it, up in the older part of a house that had both new and old sections. In her dream narrative, however, the amphitheater was only alluded to. We will present her and her dreams from process notes in order to convey her as she is and as she works in the analysis.

> I was going down steps which were getting older, more decrepit. There were cobwebs. [My husband] was maintaining this part of the house, but he had done nothing with it for a while, so it was funky. Then I was in this basement, stripped naked, getting ready to take a shower, and nothing was clean, so I felt very nervous. I found an old yellow mackintosh, which I was thinking about washing because it had not been used since I had the children. But then I thought I should get out of there, go up the rickety stairs—although that was very scary, too. But I thought maybe I should go back and turn out the lights. Then I debated whether to run away as I was so scared. I got into a linoleum area, neither new nor old, which I was thinking might make an office space for [the company she works for]. [A lesbian colleague from the company] was at the top of the steps, and I considered telling her about the amphitheater part of the house. That was it. This feels like a recurring theme, somehow.

In her associations, the three spaces in this house slowly revealed themselves to be her anus and urethra (the basement, with its dirt and its yellow coat), her vaginal opening (the linoleum area, "which is like a play area"), and her vagina and uterus (the amphitheater upstairs, in the interior of the house). Her urethra is the site of her first remembered physical trauma—an operation for urethral constriction when she was five. Her vaginal opening is the site of a second trauma—she was molested by an elderly neighbor when she was eight: he put his fingers in her vagina while holding her on his lap, and he scraped her, made her feel ragged, like the torn-up linoleum in an apartment she once lived in. In the dream, she was going to tell her lesbian colleague about the amphitheater, and (she said in associating to the dream) maybe take her there:

> Perhaps she's you [the analyst] . . . I don't know. This is somehow about the psyche. There were lights. Something epileptic, apocalyptic, seizure-like. I don't know why. It feels weird to talk about it—it's like not about me. It's like an object I'm describing, I don't connect to it. I have no idea what it's about, but I *should* know. But I don't . . . In many ways, it's beautiful. I guess seizures are being out of control. You're there and you're not; you shake—I shake a lot. For some weird reason I'm thinking about orgasms. Intense ones feel like there's a gap in time, seizure-like . . . What the hell is this?

When she came to the idea that the amphitheater represented her vagina and uterus, her further associations led to the speculation that she had had an orgasm when the neighbor molested her (perhaps also vaginal sensations during the earlier surgery), which she had found both exciting and repellent. If she had gone into this amphitheater, she said, it would have been riveting, compelling, she would never have gotten out, it would have been like she was under a spell. She came to understand, as she worked on the dream, that she had split off the vagina-uterus area—disconnected from it, made it the part of her body that is sometimes "dead" (she used terms like Ferenczi's), although sometimes it is lit up and beautiful, too, compelling, entrapping.

In the amphitheater, she said, remembering more of the dream, there was a group of men in long black frock coats with beards and mustaches, quite Victorian. Several weeks before, she had seen a photograph of the neighbor in his high old age. Hideous. He was, she was startled to notice, and then to remember, bearded, mustachioed. Quite Sigmund Freudian, she laughed nervously. Like Ferenczi's early patients,

92 / *Cherishment Psychology*

she was being ironical, in the dream and in associating to it, on the topic of psychoanalysis and its weird notions about dreams and about childhood sexuality. But this was just a surface layer of interpretation. The Victorian neighbor was so terrifying he became a group. Men. Then, later, she came to think that it is only one type of Men that terrorizes her: "men who have sexual power, who are sexually preoccupied, and have a weird effect on me—like they immobilize me . . . stick me . . . They are blood suckers."

As she became more and more amazed by what this architectural dream was telling her—"I said it was about my psyche, but it's about my body, isn't it? And my body was hurt, wasn't it, really hurt?"—she became frightened. Later she remarked, "It isn't exactly that I hate my body, it's that I don't know how to be in my skin." Enter the wise baby, in a dream she had after a weekend break in the analysis:

> [A female friend, a few years older, who mentors her] and I are walking through a kids' park. There is a heavy, plump, drab-looking mother, with dirty blond hair, wearing something in an ugly beige color. Her son, about three, is big, chubby. They are lower middle-class, below average intelligence types. The two of them were in a sandbox, and she was trying to pull him out while he struggled to step up and out himself. She said he went to a school for disabled children. She put his jacket on him, and I felt compelled to say—for him, you know, to speak for him—"He's doing the best that he can right now." I was surprised that [the mentoring friend] did nothing to help him, but sat off to the side, because she was going to do something more therapeutic later. She was observing him, and maybe was going to do something different than what I did. I was sticking up for the kid.

This patient has to disparage her wise baby—she explicitly says he is not smart, and he is awkward and chubby, as she herself was in her toddler years; so she has to come to his rescue herself, as she is also his drab mother. In this she is like the first patient, who had to kiss her wise baby to make him relaxed enough to talk wisely to her. But this patient has to go further and speak for her wise baby in order to get the wise baby's job done: the analyst is instructed about not going too fast. As she went on to associate to the dream, she said of herself that she felt stuck in all the issues her architectural dream had raised, but wanted to say, "This is the best I can do—I'm a little retarded, leave me alone." Her mentoring friend, who represents her analyst, will do something more therapeutic later, and is meanwhile being warned: Do it later, not now, and do not take me by surprise. "I guess I don't want you to think I'm smart, either, or you'll expect too much of me when I'm not ready to do adult stuff," she told her analyst, recognizing that she often plays the clown or the comedian in order to divert attention from the intellectual abilities she has but cannot trust.

Over the weekend, the patient had been feeling that everyone around her would find her stupid and incompetent. When friends came to visit, she had tripped on the stairs in front of them—"what a damn spectacle I made of myself!"—and spilled her drink all over herself. "I was like that child trying to step up out of the sandbox." Then she went on to tell about a woman resembling the lesbian colleague who had appeared in her architectural dream. Over the weekend, this woman had just confided in her that some years ago she had fantasized about having a sex change operation "because she had so many issues about being a woman, and she had had such a hard time when she was young because her mother pushed her all the time to be more feminine, giving her pocketbooks and things that would look right." The patient had told this woman that she herself had confusions about what it means to be female, and her mother, too, had been pushy and perfectionist. But even as she had said this she had thought, "I avoid those confusions," as in her dream she had avoided going into her interior feminine amphitheater room with the lesbian colleague.

The intense conversation about sexual identity, so exciting and disturbing to the patient, then provided material for a sequence of three dreams she had in one night, the third of which, once again, featured a wise child. In the first two dreams, she, who is not a homosexual, was making love to women—one with features in common with her mother, one associated with her brother, the mother's favored child:

> The first one looked like the prostitute in the film *Deconstructing Harry*, and I was going down on her and kissing her, but her genitals were inside this box kind of thing, like those . . . what do you call it? . . . stocks that the Pilgrims were punished in. In the second dream it was my brother's wife's sister, and it was

similar sex, and it felt very weird to me. In both dreams I was the aggressor, and I had an orgasm in one, and when I woke up I had my hand between my legs. I tried to call to mind how it had felt to have sex with [an emotionally abusive former lover] and what had been so compelling about it.

When asked, she told the third dream:

I was with one of my college roommates, S [whom she associated with her current mentoring friend of the playground/sandbox]. Back in college, in a dorm . . . There were guys across the hall that we were friends with, but the status of this was not clear—Were we just friends? Did these men like me? In the dream I said I had a lot of work to do [for her company] and would probably flunk the courses—I wasn't cutting it academically. S said, "You had an affair." What is the big deal? I thought. In another part of the dream I had nails—like thin hairs—in my lips, and I was going to have something done, surgically, to my lips. Like having braces. I worried people would know. And then the last scene was this big Fourth of July pageant, and I was a young child, elementary school age. We were skipping to some kind of patriotic song. "Yankee Doodle Dandy," she sang. It was a fun ending to the dream, I was talking and playing, and very successful in school.

In this third dream, the patient appears as a precocious child in a playground who has none of the academic difficulties of the college girl who is confused about her relationship with a group of men and defensive about a former lover. In these heterosexual relationships, her surgically "nailed" lips (an upward displacement for her urethra, genitals) might be discovered; she might be shown to be, like the prostitute, genitally boxed up, punished. Combining elements of regression to a pre-traumatic, happy, fun time and progression into precocious maturity, the performer child, the wise baby, parades beyond all this and entertains everybody; she is just dandy on the Independence Day that the analysis will bring. "Maybe this work we do is going to be the American Revolution, huh?" she joked with her analyst, nervously.

THE WISE BABY AT THE END OF ANALYSIS

After a year of analysis, a third patient, anxiety disordered and depressed, entered into a phase of great neediness, dependency, and expectation of the analyst's love. In sessions she often wrung her hands, as though these were (in Ferenczi's terms) the "dead" part of her. Dream after dream, the analyst appeared and was helpful, sweet, attentive. Then came a dream in which the wise baby entered in the guise of the patient's daughter, who, in waking life, is a late adolescent getting ready to leave home for college.

The dream of the wise baby opened with a scene in which the patient was traveling in a car with her analyst, her mother, and her daughter as a toddler. They were all returning to the patient's house, which she identified as both the house where she resides now and the house of her childhood, her parents' house. In the car, the toddler daughter was trying to speak, like an analysand in a session, as the patient explained:

> She was free associating for the first time, being articulate about feelings, and everyone was attentive. You [the analyst] were very attentive to the words forming. Something about a color. I said the color turquoise had meant something to me. She was expressing something about me—the mother—for the first time getting words out. Got to the top of the driveway, lots of cars in the drive, you [the analyst] were driving. Mother said, "You could drive on the grass." My husband would have had a fit! But first [the little girl] got out of the car; me too. An adorable toddler! Pants, shirt, a push toy—one of those with a canister full of colored balls that pop up and make sounds as you push it in front. She goes running with it down the drive, with me after her. Then, in the courtyard, something happened. She lost her toy, or something, and she was crying hard. When the baby started crying, and before I got to her, she was desperately but facilely climbing the vertical wall of the courtyard to get out. When I got to her, she clung so tightly it was frightening. Now she said slowly and clearly: "There will be nothing to love." And I thought this meant no bottle.

The rest of the dream was set inside the house and presented first her brother, who had just been visited by the analyst, acting the part of his dentist. The patient explained that she had once chipped her brother's front tooth during a roughhousing game and been harshly scolded by her parents. Then she encountered her sister, who was in her bedroom preparing to read the notebook in which the patient writes her dreams. She prevented this attempt "to invade my privacy." The brother and sister parts of the dream—like the father and mother parts of other patients' three-part dreams—show the siblings needing repair, instruction, correction, fixing, family psychiatry. In her childhood, the siblings had made the patient feel that she was inept, different, unlovable, and in these segments of the dream she was mastering these traumatized feelings.

What this wise baby conveyed to its dreamer and the analyst was: something happened, her toy was lost. Whatever it was, was terrifying—it made the baby climb the walls, cling to the dreamer-mother in fear, seeking help. The dreamer comforted her wise baby self, and was told by the wise baby: "There will be nothing to love." In the dream, the patient interpreted the statement: the baby will be hungry, unfed. The patient was frightened that more of the old trauma would follow upon the wise baby's moment of free speech and free association, in which she had revealed her feelings, shown her colors, including the color turquoise of her own eyes, which she typically associates with knowing and seeing that is dangerous. The moment in which the child runs off freely and gaily with the push toy is going to be brief. The analyst, after doing dentistry on the brother, has to go away, leave. She is abandoned.

As the analysis went on, the trauma story, which had all the Ferenczian elements—neglect, abandonment, abuse—became clear, and the large role her aggressive and invasive sister had played in it was established. The patient had been, literally and figuratively, time and again, pushed down, and this is what the patient associated to the "something happened" in the dream courtyard. Her joy and creativity and capacity to see, her wisdom—all symbolized by the colorful toy—had been taken away. When the patient was in the last week of her analysis, preparing to end, the wise baby appeared again, out of the timeless unconscious, in exactly the same form and developmental stage that she had assumed in the courtyard dream. In this termination week dream, the patient was not present as the mother; the baby was on her own. She had gained what Winnicott called "the capacity to be alone," which is the True Self's capacity to protect and preserve itself. Her toy was restored. The large cast of familial characters was absent; only a shadowy sister remained:

> I was a toddler—me as a toddler. With my sweeper toy—the colored balls and the popping sound. I was pushing it along. And there was the very vague presence of my sister, who felt very large, but not the size of an adult. She was hovering all around me, in and at me; she moved where I moved.

The patient said that the sister was like a guard on a basketball court, closely checking her every move, but not keeping her from moving, not pushing her down. To the patient, as she analyzed her own dream without the analyst's help, the sister seemed to be staying close out of envy, envy of the patient's current relationships, including with the analyst. The analysis had, she understood, released her from developmental immobility and brought her to the point where she had the wisdom to explain others' motivations. She was her own wise baby.

REFERENCES

Aron, L., and Harris, A. (1993). *The Legacy of Sándor Ferenczi*. Hillsdale, NJ: Analytic Press.
Doi, T. (1971). *The Anatomy of Dependence*. New York: Kodansha, 1973.
Ferenczi, S. (1926). The dream of the "clever baby." In *Further Contributions to the Theory and Technique of Psycho-Analysis*, ed. J. Rickman, trans. I. Suttie et al., pp. 349–350. New York: Brunner/Mazel, 1980.
——— (1931). Child analysis in the analysis of adults. In *Final Contributions to the Problems and Methods of Psycho-Analysis*, ed. M. Balint, trans. E. Mosbacher et al., pp. 126–142. New York: Brunner/Mazel, 1955, 1980.
——— (1932). The confusion of tongues between adults and the child. In *Final Contributions to the Problems and Methods of Psycho-Analysis*, ed. M. Balint, trans. E. Mosbacher et al., pp. 156–167. New York: Brunner/Mazel, 1955, 1980.

Gedo, J. E. (1976). The wise baby reconsidered. In *Freud: The Fusion of Science and Humanism*, ed. J. E. Gedo and G. Pollack, pp. 357–378. New York: International Universities Press.

Rudnytsky, P., Bókay, A., and Giampieri-Deutsch, P., eds. (1996). *Ferenczi's Turn in Psychoanalysis*. New York: New York University Press.

Sechehaye, M. (1951a). *Symbolic Realization*. New York: International Universities Press.

——— (1951b). *The Autobiography of a Schizophrenic Girl*. New York: Grune & Stratton.

Winnicott, D. W. (1958). *Collected Papers: Through Paediatrics to Psycho-Analysis*. New York: Basic Books.

——— (1965). *The Maturational Processes and the Facilitating Environment*. New York: International Universities Press.

5

A Developmental Matrix for the Ego Ideal

> The Master said, At fifteen I set my heart on learning; at thirty, I took my stand; at forty, I came to be free from doubts; at fifty, I understood the Decree of Heaven; at sixty, my ear was attuned; at seventy, I followed my heart's desire without overstepping the line.
>
> —*The Analects of Confucius*

In a series of children's illustrated biographies called The Value Books, there is a biography of Confucius called *The Value of Honesty*. In it, a latency-age child can read how little Confucius's mother told him that his father had wished on his deathbed for his son to grow up to be a wise man. "Why did he say that?" the child asks his mother, and she replies "Because he loved you." As she speaks, a little gray-bearded Chinese gentleman in a long white robe, his hands folded serenely over his chest, appears in a puff of magical smoke at the bottom of the page. For the rest of the biography, as the child Confucius grows into a youth, the youth into a man, this little sage is always at his side—his sidekick. As the book ends, Confucius, renowned for his wisdom and particularly his honesty, has come to look just like this little sage. They stand together on the last page, the little sage still child-sized, while the child who needed the ideal is fully grown and, resembling his ideal, is an ideal for others.

Beautifully translated into images for children, this is a psychoanalytic rendering of "the ego ideal." But the illustrated biography of Confucius—not to mention Confucius's own wisdom on the topic of ego ideals, as collected in the *Analects*—is actually much richer affectively than most of the psychoanalytic writings on the ego ideal. In the analytic literature, the concept is surprisingly undeveloped and flat, although there have been, of course, articles, passages in books, and one full book by the French analyst, Janine Chasseguet-Smirgel (1985), on the topic. In this essay, I want, first, to reflect on the theoretical history that has kept "the ego ideal" so circumscribed, and then to go forward by sketching a developmental matrix for the ego ideal based on a theoretical reappraisal and illustrated from clinical work.

FORMULATING THE "EGO IDEAL"— A PRELIMINARY HISTORICAL MAP

When Freud first introduced the term "ego ideal" in his 1914 essay "On Narcissism," he associated it with the transformations of "primary narcissism." "What man projects before him as his ideal is the substitute for the lost narcissism of his childhood in which he was his own ideal" (p. 94). Subsequently, this formulation about the "ego ideal" became controversial because the theory of narcissism and its transformations became so complex and full of difficulties. Debate also arose because Freud originally used the term "ego ideal" as a synonym for "superego." Both terms designated a single psychic agency responsible for the two functions of prohibition and idealization. But, by the time Freud wrote the "New Introductory Lectures on Psychoanalysis" in 1933, he was saying that the ego ideal's function was only one of the superego's three functions "of self-observation, of conscience, and of the ideal" (p. 66). The superego acts as "the vehicle of the ego ideal by which the ego measures itself, which it emulates, and whose demand for ever greater perfection it strives to fulfill" (p. 64). This description, however, left unexplored the role and the history of the ego ideal in, or in relation to, the more comprehensive superego structure.

Each contributor to the psychoanalytic literature on the ego ideal since Freud has felt obliged to begin by addressing these two conceptual problem areas: the ego ideal in relation to narcissism and the ego ideal in relation to the superego. Trying to settle the first area, Peter Blos (1974) very selectively reviewed the literature and stated that there is "universal agreement that the ego ideal's roots lie in the stage of primary narcissism" (p. 44). However, it is more accurate to say that all those who stress that there is such a thing as primary narcissism, as Freud did, locate the ego ideal in relation to it. Further, the more strictly the ego ideal is understood as a transformation of primary narcissism, and thus as involving fantasies of omnipotence, the more it is then understood as distinct in its origin and development from the superego. Among the exemplars of this rule is Chasseguet-Smirgel (1985), who views the ego ideal as a transformation of primary narcissism and also attributes to it an independent origin and development prior to the Oedipus complex, in which the superego is held to be formed.

But there is a second type of Freudian theorist, by contrast, who begins by distinguishing the ego ideal and the superego, sometimes even noting the ego ideal's preoedipal origins, but does not, then, embrace the idea that the ego ideal is primary narcissism transformed and distinct in its origin from the superego. Instead, this second type of Freudian stresses that both the ego ideal and the superego develop through identifications, the former positive and the latter negative.

Hermann Nunberg can stand as a representative of the second sort of Freudian concerned to distinguish ego ideal and superego developments without separating them by origins. In a much-cited section of his *Principles of Psychoanalysis* (1955), Nunberg suggested, for example, that the ego ideal consists of identifications with loved figures, while the superego derives from identifications with hated and feared figures. The ego, Nunberg went on, submits to the superego out of fear of punishment, while it submits to the ego ideal out of love. Then, making a third distinction, he concluded:

> The predominantly maternal ego ideal starts to develop as early as the pregenital stages, but the predominantly paternal superego is observed

first in the genital stage. The impetus for the formation of the superego [in the male] is the danger of castration, a danger which threatens the entire ego in consequence of its identification with the genitals. By taking his father into his ego, the boy not only escapes the danger of castration but also gains a protector in the image of the father absorbed by the ego. The superego is formed not only because of hatred but also because of love and fear for the endangered narcissistic ego. [p. 136]

Among the clinical writers who developed Nunberg's formulations, which were also reflected in the theoretical work of Heinz Hartmann, the most influential studies were offered by Edith Jacobson (1964) and Annie Reich (1975), pioneers in exploring the narcissistic disturbances. Both Jacobson and Reich thought of lack of self-esteem as expressing a discrepancy or disharmony between self-representation and the "wishful concept of the self," the ego ideal. Reich also described pathologies of self-esteem regulation resulting from persistence of a "primitive ego ideal" made up of "primitive identifications with idealized infantile objects." That is, she described the persistence of an ego ideal never tempered by encounters with reality and thus always retaining the omnipotence she assumed to be normal for an ego not yet differentiated from reality.

As his sense of reality grows, the child, recognizing his own weakness, endows his parents with the omnipotence he has had to forgo. From this time on, desires set in to become like the glorified parent. The deep longing to become like the parent creates constant inner demand upon the child's ego: an ego ideal is formed. In cases of insufficient acceptance of reality, the differentiation between ego and ego ideal may remain diffuse, and under certain conditions *magic identification* with the glorified parent—megalomanic feelings—may replace the *wish* to be like him. [Reich 1975, p. 188]

Expecting grand worldly achievements to come by magical means, or magically trying for a fit of self to primitive ego ideal, people with these pathologies are compelled to "compensatory narcissistic self-inflation" and then they suffer from the crashes of their hopes.

Nunberg, Jacobson, and Reich all assumed primary narcissism (and corresponding omnipotence fantasies), but they did not describe the ego ideal as a transformation of primary narcissism. As noted, they stressed the identifications making it up. By contrast, Chasseguet-Smirgel

A Developmental Matrix for the Ego Ideal / 103

(1985) is perhaps the most thoroughgoing emphasizer of primary narcissism, and she, accordingly, focuses on the ego ideal as an agency quite distinct from the superego, not as embedded in it. For her, the ego ideal is the "heir to primary narcissism," or, as Freud had it, the substitute for primary narcissistic perfection, while the superego is "heir to the Oedipus complex." The origin of the ego ideal is the moment when an infant is dislodged from its initial blissful symbiosis with its mother by its helplessness and frustration.

> The violent end to which the primary state of fusion is brought by this helplessness obliges the infant to recognize the "not-me." This seems to be the crucial moment when the narcissistic omnipotence which he is forced to give up is projected on to the object, the infant's first ego ideal, narcissistic omnipotence from which he is henceforth divided by a gulf that he will spend the rest of his life trying to bridge. This projection provides an impetus that then becomes the primum movens of his education and his activities in other spheres. [Chasseguet-Smirgel, 1985, p. 14]

Finding in the object a model and striving to emulate the model—as the boy does vis-à-vis his father in the oedipal period—are secondary, in Chasseguet-Smirgel's conception, to desiring restoration of the fused-with-mother state before part of the infant's narcissism was wrenched away. Behind all ideals lies the Ideal—an Ideal state. And throughout life, people are moved by their nostalgia, their desire to return to the fused state—to the womb—which the male can imagine as his destiny in intercourse, orgasm, as Ferenczi argued in his *Thalassa*.

The way in which these origins stories, development stories, and functional descriptions for the ego ideal fail to fit together seems to me to signal a theoretical or metapsychological impasse. If we step back from the particular technical psychoanalytic arguments, it seems very obvious that when people are striving for an ideal or for perfection, they are moved in part by nostalgia—hence the many myths worldwide of golden ages, paradises lost, utopias of the past. So there certainly is an element of nostalgia in the ego ideal, but the question is whether this is nostalgia for primary narcissism or for some other early condition. It also seems very obvious that in guiding themselves people operate with both prohibitions and encouragements, no and yes, stop and go, do not and do—hence the many ethical systems worldwide in which Thou Shalt Nots are combined with encouraging Thou Shalts (usually in

104 / *Cherishment Psychology*

some form that stresses relatedness and doing unto others as one would have done unto oneself). But the question here is whether the prohibiting and the encouraging agencies are the same or different, in origin and development.

SOURCES OF CONFUSION AND PROPOSALS FOR CLARIFICATION

In this essay, I want to approach these psychodynamic and cultural questions with a revision of psychoanalytic theory that can, I think, absorb and make orderly and fruitful the various strands of theory, clinical observation, and infant research that now seem so tangled.

As Chasseguet-Smirgel and others have pointed out, the confusions surrounding the concept of the ego ideal stem, historically and theoretically, from the fact that when Freud introduced the term he was in the middle of a huge theoretical transition. He was articulating the tripartite structural theory, and thus articulating "the superego" in which the ego ideal eventually got located. Secondly, he was also moving toward the theory of the life instincts and the death instinct—the dual instinct theory. And thirdly, he was launching a revised theory of anxiety, in which his notions about the sources of the ego's anxiety shifted. The ego ideal was a concept that suffered from neglect; it was never worked through all of these dimensions of transition. But I think it was, also, a concept that pointed to a theoretical loss that came about in these transitions, one that Freud did not want to acknowledge.

When Freud moved to the idea that there are two basic instincts, Eros and Thanatos, he certainly galvanized attention toward aggression, but he also left behind the insights that flowed from his earlier distinction between the self-preservative ego instincts and the species-reproductive sexual instincts—Hunger and Sex, for short. These earlier two instinct types were eventually gathered under the rubric of "the life instincts." But this move meant that Freud ceased exploring the ego instincts, and never questioned what his revised concept of the ego—the ego in the context of the structural theory—would mean for the aim of self-preservation. Self-preservation could have become a much wider notion, covering more than the functions necessary for physical preservation, as it did in fact become in later psychoanalytic infant

A Developmental Matrix for the Ego Ideal / 105

observational research. Most importantly, later research made it clear that self-preservation requires relatedness. René Spitz (1945), for example, did much to initiate this revision by describing "hospitalism" and demonstrating empirically that children in hospitals who lack warm, affectionate care lag in ego development and even fail to develop physically as they lapse into "anaclitic depression." D. W. Winnicott's famous remark that "there is no such thing as a baby"—that is, that only a baby with a mother, with a caregiver, can be a living baby—has been generally accepted as the foundation of relationality, but it is not usually considered for its implication: relatedness is the essence of self-preservation, the aim of the ego instincts.

Freud also removed from his theory a very rich vein of questioning about the ego instincts in relation to the sexual instincts, a vein signaled by passages like this from the *Introductory Lectures on Psychoanalysis*:

> It is not our belief that a person's libidinal interests are from the first in opposition to his self-preservative interests; on the contrary, the ego endeavors at every stage to remain in harmony with its sexual organization as it is at the time and to fit itself into it. The succession of the different phases of libidinal development probably follows a prescribed program. But the possibility cannot be rejected that this course of events can be influenced by the ego, and we may expect equally to find a certain parallelism, a certain correspondence, between the developmental phases of the ego and the libido; indeed, a disturbance of that correspondence might provide a pathogenic factor. [Freud 1916–1917, p. 351]

When he left this idea about ego instinctual and sexual instinctual interplay and harmony behind, Freud ended up with a fixed notion that the child's need to be loved arises out of its initial helplessness; the need to be loved is not original to the developing ego, or crucial to the ego's growth and self-preservation. For Freud the need to be loved—and from thence, the Oedipus complex—arises when the infant experiences frustration and danger, as he argued very forcefully in "Inhibitions, Symptoms and Anxiety":

> The biological factor is the long period of time during which the young of the human species is in a condition of helplessness and dependence. Its inter-uterine existence seems short in comparison with that of most

animals, and it is sent into the world in a less finished state. As a result, the influence of the real external world upon it is intensified and an early differentiation between the ego and the id is promoted. Moreover, the dangers of the external world have a greater importance for it, so the value of the object which can alone protect it from them and take the place of its former inter-uterine life is enormously enhanced. The biological factor, then, establishes the earliest situations of danger and creates the need to be loved which will accompany the child through the rest of its life. [Freud 1926, pp. 154–155]

If Freud had stayed with his own concept of the ego instincts, he could have formulated the need to be loved—not just physically preserved—as, like helplessness, a biological given; he could then have seen this need as, inevitably, to some degree frustrated, and the frustration thus giving rise to a nostalgia for the original state of expecting love. This view could have presumed that all the modes in which an infant is preserved in life—from being-gestated to being-nursed to being-protected to being-warmly-held to being-affectively-stirred—are experienced or represented by the infant as satisfactions of the expectation to be loved. Similarly, the ego ideal could then be understood not as projection of primary narcissism, but as projection of this lost or partially lost being-loved relational condition onto objects (and eventually onto the world in general).

I am suggesting that the ego ideal be understood as a transformation not of primary narcissism but of primary love. The ego ideal could, then, be defined as that agency that will restore or re-create new forms of what might be called "primary loving and being-loved," an ideal condition but not a condition of *omnipotence* prior to confrontation with reality.

This phrase "primary loving and being loved" is a way to evoke the Japanese word *amae*, which the Japanese psychoanalyst Takeo Doi has translated as "the expectation to be loved" in his many writings on how central this expectation is to Japanese child-rearing and culture. Alluding to Freud's first instinct theory, Doi (1971) understood *amae*, which I will translate in what follows with the old English word "cherishment," as an ego instinct propelling the ego to grow, and, further, making other ego instincts, like hunger, *relational*.

In the psychoanalytic writings on the ego ideal that stress its roots in primary narcissism, the ego ideal is understood as an ideal of "how I want to be," with that "I" understood as standing alone, autonomous, narcissistically restored and thus with healthy, regulated self-esteem. But the implication of the conceptualization I am suggesting is that the ideal is always an ideal of the ego in relatedness. To Winnicott's quip that "there is no such thing as a baby" could be added the elaboration that there is no such thing as an ego. When the ego ideal is formed, it, like the baby, is, so to speak, prepositional: the "I want to be" is *with* (someone who is holding), *for* (someone who is watching), *beside* (someone who is leading or following), *between* or *among* (group members, people, humankind), *within* (a living cosmos, a Being). When the ego ideal is suffused with grandiosity, it may be because the original condition of relatedness is longed for and recalled as totally secure and empowering, even after blows from reality have been sustained, or it may be because the ego ideal borrows heavily from the primary narcissism of the sexual instincts, or, most likely, both.

This formulation about primary being-loved or being-cherished does not imply that there is no such thing as primary narcissism—the conclusion leapt to both by most Object Relations theorists, who emphasize the primary relatedness of the infant, and by John Bowlby and his followers, who posit "attachment" as the quality of the sexual (not ego) instincts. It is certainly not theoretically difficult to say that the sexual instinct is primarily narcissistic (that is, libido is first ego-libido then object-libido) and the ego instincts primarily object-related in the sense just noted. And this is, in fact, the way Freud saw the matter in his first instinct theory. The ego or self-preservative instincts are, he had argued, "anaclitic" or attached to objects, while the sexual instincts are auto-erotic or narcissistic; and he also noted that this contrast implies that the sexual instincts, insofar as they lean upon the prior object relations of the ego instincts, have a kind of indirect object-relatedness from their start as well. Using other terms, Freud sometimes spoke before the 1920s of the ego instinctual "affectionate current" of love preceding and initially guiding the sexual instinctual "sensual current."[1]

Further, in this formulation the superego can be understood as the agency in and through which the sexual instincts are eventually chiefly

---

1. For a discussion of Freud's use of "affectionate current" and "sensual current," see Chapter 3 above, "The Hidden History of the Ego Instincts."

regulated, while the ego ideal is the agency in and through which the ego instincts are chiefly directed—although such a clear distinction exists only in the realm of concepts. To use slightly different terms: the superego is the agency that urges the ego to control the sexual instincts, which are under the sway of the pleasure principle; the ego ideal is the agency that urges the ego to develop its own instincts—to follow its growth or maturation principle—and to stay in harmony with the sexual instincts. Two developmental lines are implied, and, with the help of the concept of "anaclisis" (Strachey's erudite, Greekish neologism for translating Freud's ordinary language *Anlehnung*, leaning on), the two lines can be looked at in their links and contrasts.

As the descriptions below will show, two periods of "sexual efflorescence" or sexual instinctual dominance that Freud identified—the oedipal and the pubertal—are certainly observable (with much variation from individual to individual and culture to culture). But these sexual instinctual efflorescences punctuate periods of ego instinctual efflorescence and dominance. The first year of life, when physical (and especially brain) growth is so pronounced, is a period in which ego instinctual drives seem to preponderate, and so is latency, as can be gathered from the descriptions of psychoanalytic writers like Berta Bornstein (1951) and Anna Freud (in *The Ego and the Mechanisms of Defence*, 1936), who both stressed the growth of the ego in latency. Late adolescence is, ideally, the period when the ego instinctual and the sexual instinctual forces stop oscillating and come into harmony or co-dominance—so this is, as all psychoanalytic writers note, the period of character consolidation.

The general approach I am sketching also opens the concept of the ego ideal to a very rich vein of psychoanalytic work that has been left out of almost every contemporary account of the ego ideal: the literature, mostly from the 1950s and 1960s heyday of "Ego Psychology," on shame and guilt as the affects aroused in, respectively, failing the ego ideal and transgressing the superego's strictures. Further, without having to decide the question of whether to conceptualize aggression as "the death instinct" or as self-*preservative* and often related to frustration (the conceptualization I prefer), aggression can be considered as it gets woven into and flows from the agencies of the ego and the sexual instincts, as it gets suffused with shame and with guilt.

THE DEVELOPMENT OF THE EGO IDEAL

I want to begin tracking the development of the ego ideal and contrasting it to the superego by noting again that in Freud's structural theory, the superego, although it has preoedipal precursors like what Ferenczi called "sphincter morality," is formed within the Oedipus complex and under the threat of castration.[2] Freud developed the superego theory with regard only to males, indicating that a boy's hostility toward his father and jealous longing for his mother bring him into conflict. He loves his father, but now hates him as well. Resolution can come if he identifies with his father, and this means identifying with the father who proscribes the boy's sexual feelings for his mother and who threatens castration—the punitive father. The punitive father becomes, then, the central character in the boy's superego (while he may, as Nunberg indicated, be installed as a protective figure in the ego ideal). By contrast, a girl, who may have rivalrous feelings as well, toward either parent, does not have a penis to fear losing. She is not so inclined to identify with a parent felt as punitive. It was for this reason that Freud thought the female superego to be less firm, a thought at variance with the many observations by his contemporaries that girls often repress their pregenital sexuality rigorously. The less firm superego idea is also at variance with Freud's own observation that girls undergo a sexual "involution" (e.g., repression of masturbation) unknown to boys. In his late essays on female psychology, Freud went on to argue that a girl is also not so inclined to give up the earliest object-choice she and the boy share, the mother, toward whom (or toward whose breast), in the terms of the first instinct theory, her self-preservative instinct's "evaluations" have led her sexual instincts. How the girl later makes a turn toward her father becomes, then, a question for which Freud found only one controversial answer: penis envy. The girl wants a penis and finds one on the person of her father. Later, she symbolically equates the penis and the baby, so she can satisfy her penis-wish with a baby.

---

2. On the early development of the superego, see Holder (1982) and Spitz (1958).

In telling the boy's oedipal story and the story of the origin of his—*the*—superego, Freud mentioned but did not really develop his sense that there is also an earlier type of identification with the parents, one common to both boys and girls. This anaclitic identification, defined as expressive of the child's wish to be at one with (or, literally, to lean on) the parents, and, later, to emulate their nurturing, their loving, takes place with the first caregivers, with their care. If we think of such anaclitic identifications as the first ingredients of the ego ideal, then it becomes clear that omnipotence is not the defining characteristic of the primitive ego ideal (as Annie Reich held)—cherishing is. The early ego ideal holds the identifications that buffer a child against the frustrations of reality, that preserve its self-preservative expectation to be loved.

It also becomes clear that the object relations of the ego instincts need not be decisively shaped—as those of the sexual instincts are—by the gender of either the child or the objects. The "affectionate current" of a child's relatedness becomes intertwined with the libidinal current, the sexual current, under the superego's charge, so that the oedipal child's object relations are a combination of affection and sexuality. But the earliest cherishment layer of the ego ideal is not gendered as the later layers, the combinatory layers, very complexly are.

The original matrix for the ego ideal is the infant's sense of being boundaried, which we can think of concretely as having a skin, being defined by being touched and touching, coming to know an outside and an inside. As Freud said, the first ego is a body ego, and, by the same token, the first ego ideal is a body ego ideal. English is rich in having one word, "feelings," that captures both the affective and the tactile: "This is the way I want to be cherished and the way I want cherishing feelings on my body. These are the good feelings." The ideal is (to resort to words, again, for what is preverbal) "I want to be with Mommy like this." In Japanese, with its rich *amae* vocabulary, there is an intransitive verb for the infant's cuddling expectation of love—*amaeru*—and a corollary for the mother's sweet indulgence of this expecting—*amaiakasu*; both words imply the preverbal, tactile communication of cherishment.

This first body ego ideal can be thought of as a preconceptual (and thus pre-self-concept) vibratory skin, skin experienced as giving a shape, but also as being pleasurably receptive, feeling good, being welcoming to cherishment. In iconographies around the world, vibratory skin appears as a halo, a nimbus, an aura or an aureole—some form of powerful holding or enclosure, representing destiny. The halo connects a divinized child or childlike adult with the cosmos and its power, which is usually associated with solar warmth and light's growing power. In the divine child iconographies, the haloed child has a blissful, smiling expression, an expression of contentment or serenity. Similarly, in the earliest freestanding sculptures of the ancient world, East and West, the so-called "archaic smile" seems to represent the infant's ideal state of being-shaped as that ideal is carried into later life. These are images of a potency that is part of the primary expectation to be loved; and thus is quite different than primary narcissistic grandiosity or omnipotence, which stems from not having yet distributed libido outward, from maintaining what Freud called ego-libido (meaning ego-directed-libido, self-love).

Children play out of or play outward this first body ego ideal matrix with the first possessions they cherish—the things that D. W. Winnicott (1951) called "transitional objects." A piece of blanket, a pillow, a teddy, a mitten, maybe a place, perhaps a person or part of a person, becomes the medium through which children relate to the world, adventuring out of the two-in-one relation they need with their caregivers, their mother's breast or bottle. The transitional object is the prototype of all future forms of the ego ideal, the touchable version of an ideal based upon touch.[3] The practicing child (to use a term of Margaret Mahler's) can do unto the object as the child has had done unto it, and it can also say through the object, in effect, "This teddy is me, as I want to be, exploring, growing big, moving on my own into the world."

The products of a child's body, particularly its feces, are also versions of itself in this way, so children relish giving their feces as gifts, smearing or depositing them with special people. During the period that Margaret Mahler and her colleagues (1975) called the "rapprochement subphase," children separate from their caregivers, but keep rushing

---

[3]. Winnicott himself followed his original concept of the "transitional object" with work on its relation to the ego ideal's most public and plural form, the cultural ideal.

back, often to bring toys and objects as offerings, connectors—transitional objects in reverse, as it were—signs from themselves and from the world. They are by this developmental moment fully capable of object constancy and they cherish their constant objects with things, as they register their frustrations with tantrums. "This is me as I want to be: giving to you, cherishing you." "This is me as I want to be: in your reliable lap." Aggression, traditionally in theory so associated with the anal stage, is enormous under conditions in which cherishment is not available or bodily gifts like feces are despised, held to be dirty and disgusting, rejected. Among psychoanalytic educators, George Devereux (1956) was particularly clear about how important it is not to punish children for their bodily interests and exhibitions, but to discipline them: punishment, which generally serves the punisher's interests, not the interests of the child's developing ego, is assimilated into the child's superego, while discipline serves the ego ideal's growth and unfolding as a positive, encouraging matrix.[4]

It seems to me clarifying to think of shame as the affect that arises when early cherishment needs go unmet, when the child's expectation to be loved is thwarted, when good-feeling reciprocity—implying good-feeling separateness, without rejection—is not established. Shame is felt as falling short of the emergent cherishment ideal.[5] Guilt, in distinction, is the affect that arises when a child seeks to recover by means of sexual assertion from a shameful thwarting, and with its assertion crosses a boundary, transgresses, incurring superego punishment. Another way to put the interrelation of shame and guilt is to say that if a child's so-

---

4. In his *Therapeutic Education*, Devereux, an anthropologist as well as an analyst, the founder of the Devereux schools, distinguished superego and ego ideal in terms quite similar to those that I am arguing for in this essay. He sees the superego as made up of primitive introjections of parental charismatic power and punishment and the ego ideal made up of "functional identifications" that lead to positive injunctions, reasonable assessments of reality, and the possibilities for satisfying good conduct.

5. Because the psychoanalytic literature is so focused on the sexual instincts, and not on the ego instincts, as it is on the punitive superego and not the growth-promoting ego ideal, both shame and guilt at the anal phase are usually thought of only in relation to the sexual instincts and the superego. The shame involved in not living up to the ego ideal has been much less studied than guilt (except by Erikson, 1950, and Piers and Singer, 1953).

liciting of love by exhibition—trying to get touching and, derivatively, looking for attention—is thwarted (particularly if the child is punished, not disciplined, for its expectant behavior), the child turns to efforts to command love sexually, sadistically or masochistically, by beating or being beaten. The child sexualizes expectation of love. It was Freud who originally made the suggestion that shame is a defense against exhibitionism and scoptophilia, noting as he did the fact that in German the genital region is *die Scham*, and *Schamgefuhl*, the feeling of shame, is associated with it. Shame is sexual shame by common usage. But this usage obscures how shame, which can be thought of as initially not a defense but as the affect of frustration and disappointment over exhibition, becomes sexualized as a child seeks to overcome it and incurs guilt, often in the context of punishment.

As children become more visually oriented and conceptual, their ego ideals take on visual characteristics in addition to the earlier tactile ones; the process is cumulative. They move into the domain of body comparison as they move into the oedipal period, or, in libido theory terms, into the phallic phase. Their bodies are so small in comparison to their parents'; their genitals are male or female in comparison with the opposite sex. The ego ideal reflects the child's effort to reconcile his or her own sense of present size and future growth—so the little sage imagined by the boy Confucius in *The Value of Honesty* is both little and grown, like so many of the ideal images adored by children of this stage: dwarfs, elves, and gnomes who are their size but also grown-up, who can defend against an evil figure who proffers deceptive appearances, like the Witch's poisonous apples in *Sleeping Beauty*. In cultures where totemic animals are adopted by individuals and groups, the totemic animal can function for the child as an ego ideal representative, much as an assigned name does in other cultures.

The early oedipal child's visual ego ideals have a reparative or augmenting or aggrandizing quality: they counsel, "You will grow bigger, you will have the sexual characteristics of both sexes, you will win love." Suffering by comparison is the shame of this period. Those analytic writers, like Otto Fenichel (1945), who have focused their attention on the shame of this developmental stage (often mistaking it for the whole of shame) note it as "the specific force directed against urethral-erotic temptation. Ambition, so often described as an outcome of urethral-erotic conflicts, represents the fight against this shame"

(p. 69). Boys, particularly, are shamed by their inability to control their bladders, while girls are usually more concerned with the bowel (and as adults, are more commonly afflicted with constipation as a symptom).[6]

The first two versions of the ego ideal—the tactile and visual body ego ideal versions—provide the foundation for a third, which grows on top of them, sometimes obscuring them quite thoroughly, sometimes not. In the oedipal period, the child operates as an imitator of persons (sometimes called "role models" in non-psychoanalytic literatures, sometimes called "idols" in analytic literature). "I want to be like Mommy, like Daddy." Other figures—usually adults—meld into the ideal, as do their activities. "I want to be a fireman." When people more than bodily or affective states inform the ego ideal, it is sometimes called "the wished-for self image," a phrase originated by Edith Jacobson.[7] The wished-for self image is very bound up with the surge in the ego instinct of mastery, and with the child's fascination with activities and competencies, including the specific sexual activities of men and women, which are imitated in sexual games and games with sexual content. Curiosity grows strong. In this stage, the ego ideal has not only its earlier tactile and visual dimensions, but an internal *voice*: It says, like the Little Engine That Could, "I think I can! I think I can!" The superego, as it begins to take on its mature form in the oedipal period, is made up, as Freud said, of introjections of or identifications with not so much the parental figures as their superegos. It is in the domain of the auditory as well—it is the "voice of conscience." For sins of the domain of conscience, the sinner is struck dumb (and the child can feel compelled to mutism).

In latency, the ego ideal, like the ego generally, stabilizes and a normal latency could be described as one in which the ego ideal is neither too exacting and thus out of reach, nor too amorphous and thus without guidance; it neither says "you must!" (as opposed to the "you

---

6. Observing the child's wish not to be shamed, to be able to control, led analysts such as Hendrick (1942, 1943) to speak of an (ego) instinct of mastery manifest particularly in the phallic phase.

7. See the discussion of Jacobson's term "the wished-for self image" by Milrod (1982, 1990).

ought to!" of the superego) nor "don't bother!" Ego ideal stability in latency augurs well for a youngster's ability to weather preadolescence, when the cherishment ego ideal of early childhood, never abandoned, has a resurgence. In a growth spurt comparable to that of infancy in its intensity, the preadolescent needs again the protective surround, the protective skin, of the mother or caregiver. In terms of the sexual instincts, pregenitality in general has a resurgence with the onset of pubertal sexual instinctual drives, and is mightily defended against, so the youngster is also running away from the mother as a sexual and sexualized being. Thus ego instincts and sexual instincts push and pull in different directions; the ego instinctual nostalgia is indulged as a twelve-year-old nestles up to his or her parents, while the sexual nostalgia for the mother and for primary narcissism is felt as forbidden and rejected.

Like a latency child, the preadolescent idealizes states of undifferentiation or self-sufficiency or, in the nostalgic mode, states of ideal relatedness prior to sexual differentiation, but the ego ideal is also laced with the regressive fantasies typical of the period. While the body is changing so rapidly, these fantasies are very clearly expressed as concern with skin and with body image generally. The preadolescents' "Do not touch me!" is proportionate in vehemence to the complexity and contradictoriness of their desires to be cherishingly, affectionately touched and to be sexually touched. Both boys and girls imagine themselves lost in the undifferentiatedness of couples or groups. They imagine that it would be wonderful to run away from home and be everywhere and nowhere. Girls particularly worship androgynes—sometimes in the person of an older woman who is free, active, beautiful—and are often conscious of their desire to be both sexes. Meanwhile, boys are in awe or envy of female reproductive power, although they usually have this feeling under great repression and express it only indirectly in their creative projects.

As early adolescence is reached, parents are usually deidealized. A process of disillusionment is also usually spurred by particular episodes in which the parents are less than magnificent, and the adolescent's disappointment demands a new ego ideal to replace the one that grew with and in the Oedipus complex. Friends begin to fall heir to the parental idealizations or they fill the adolescent's need to reverse the parental idealizations, to *somehow* exit the resurgent Oedipus complex. Friends—or sometimes the friends' ego ideals—can become the main

116 / *Cherishment Psychology*

sources of a teenager's ego ideal ingredients or wished-for self-images. The ego ideal begins to function in the process of separating from the parents, individuating, consolidating "me" as an independent person. Parents are often distressed that their children choose companions who seem so unlikely, so different, weird, inappropriate, bad. But this is just the point: the companion is supposed to supply everything the child cannot find inside or in the parents. The companion—or later a group of companions, even a secret society—is the challenge, the "as I want to be" and the "who I want to be with." The friend is the adolescent's transitional object for adventuring into adulthood, for trying on identity possibilities, for doing "let's pretend we're. . . ." And if no friend quite fills the bill, a book or movie or concert hall hero or heroine is called upon. An early adolescent will often look to the present culture, or sometimes the romantic or idealized cultural past, for idols to replace the parental idealizations and supplement what friends can supply as well. Sometimes a teacher or coach can be half parent, half friend. Diaries can be the friend as well as being the place where a friend is idealized, eulogized.

From early adolescence and into adolescence proper, the friend or friendship circle comes to be chosen on a more and more explicitly narcissistic basis, as Freud (1914) noted succinctly: "Whoever possesses the qualities without which the ego cannot achieve its ideal, he is the one who will be loved" (p. 101). But Freud also assumed that the narcissistic characteristics of the ego ideal implied that it was also a homosexual construct because, Freud continued, the ego ideal has absorbed and is sustained by narcissistic and homosexual libido:

> The ego ideal has imposed severe conditions on the satisfaction of libido through objects; for it causes some of them to be rejected by means of its censor, as being incompatible. When no such ideal has been formed, the sexual trend in question makes its appearance unchanged in the personality in the form of a perversion. To be their own ideal once more, in regard to sexual no less than other trends, as they were in childhood—this is what people strive to attain as their happiness. [Freud, 1914, p. 100]

This passage of Freud's has been crucial to all who, like Peter Blos (1962), conclude that "the new distribution of the libido thus enhances the progression to heterosexual object finding, and serves to maintain stable relationships" (p. 77). That is, the ego ideal in adolescence prevents the normal homosexual ties of a boy to his father and then to male friends from becoming fixated; it brings about the resolution of the negative Oedipus complex that Blos takes as the most important adolescent task. So Blos (1962) can state categorically: "The origin of the ego ideal is to be found in the irreversible surrender of the negative (homosexual) oedipal position during early adolescence" (p. 184). And he can imply, thus, ridiculously, that male homosexuals do not have ego ideals!

This is the kind of problem that arises within Freudian theory when the ego ideal is simply understood as a libidinal construction and not (originally) an affectional one, when it is construed as a product of the sexual instincts (and narcissism transformed) not of the ego instincts. In Blos's work, the whole history of how the ego ideal develops out of the matrix of early caregiving is neglected, while the early adolescent form becomes "the origin," or, to say the same thing (quoting Blos [1962] again), "the ego ideal, at least in its typical and predominant form, has its roots in identification with the parent of the same sex" (p. 184).

In late adolescence, the ego ideal becomes a matter of values, maxims, philosophical propositions, worldviews, religious or spiritual beliefs, sometimes represented by a leader who is installed in the ego ideal as earlier identifications have been. The body ego ideal layers and person-centered imitative layers are not left behind, but they get woven into what might be called a character-ideal, an ideal way of being and an ideal of relating to others, eventually of relating to "the world," all others. Late adolescents can be idealists; that is, their ideals include ideas. They are artists of themselves with an idea before their minds, or promoters of their own evolution with a goal in mind, or they are cleansers of their own obstructions with an image of purity in mind. Characterologically grounded modalities of creativity take characteristic forms in late adolescence (see Young-Bruehl 1989).

AN EXAMPLE: THE SHAMEFUL GIRL

In adult analysis, the distinction between the ego ideal and the superego that I have been developing can be heard clearly in the very different languages of self-accusation or self-reproach relating to the two

118 / *Cherishment Psychology*

domains. The shameful person complains of being defective, permeable, empty or full of something nasty, disgusting, ugly or aesthetically marred. She always comes up short; he does not measure up. As it is often heard in younger or youngest children, the shame discourse can sound like sibling rivalry, part of an endless struggle to catch up, but it usually finds this form after starting out earlier as a sense of bodily inadequacy or inferiority. By contrast, the guilty person complains of being bad, morally, and of being a rule-breaker or deviant, a weed in the garden of life, a freak. A shameful person, as noted, can and usually does evolve into a guilty one, but some patients are more characterized by their shame and its different forms than by the guilt they incur for it. And these are people who have neurosis-determining ego ideal conflicts or deficits.

A patient of mine who is a vivid example of shameful self-accusation and ego ideal failure lamented one day that she had always felt the need to be like her perfect mother. Then she drifted back to the earliest layer of her ego-ideal formation: that is, she presented herself as a newborn, coming out of the relaxation of the womb—represented as a bathtub—all ruddy and fresh, her skin as she wishes it were, a good border, a cherished border.

> The headlines [of my relationships] always stay the same. I still have my shit. My problem is less depression than comfort in my own skin. I was never comfortable with myself. As a kid I was always looking to my mother for the way to be and saying, "I can't do it, I can't be like her." I had this image when I hit puberty that I was awkward, goofy looking, and I felt I could not leave the house and be seen. It lasted about six years. Maybe four, five years . . . I did everything I could not to interact, not to leave home, taking baths a lot. . . . Now I take hot showers, to relax. I come out with bright red skin. At night. But I used to lie in a bath for a long time. It was a whole body relaxation kind of thing. Like sex is, sometimes. I want to be enervated, a perfect release . . .

For this patient, who presents herself as "defective and unsatisfactory from the beginning, never the baby my parents wanted," the oedipal phase of ego ideal formation was made especially hard by a trauma: she was operated on for a constricted urethra when she was four—a very frightening and painful procedure, which left her with the sense that she was damaged and ugly "down there"—in her genitals, *die Scham*, this meant. She needed, then, to have her physical sense of her self, her body ego ideal, restored, and she later sought this restoration in her sexual life. She always hoped that making love would relax her, relieve her of her body anxiety, repair her, be her bathtub, her longed-for maternal cherishing, as well as her father's loving regard. When she is feeling damaged, she always describes herself as "cut off," and she makes a characteristic gesture, drawing her hand across her chest below her breasts, which was her unconscious signal that it was her "down there" from which she felt cut off, or that felt cut off, castrated, damaged.

Eventually, she tried to form the ego ideal with which she could outgrow her perfect mother ideal. She found a friend at age twelve who gave her an image of how she herself might be, an image to supersede the one that had governed her childhood—her main oedipal, parental image: her perfect mother. Time and again she had measured herself against the mother image and come up short, so she shifted, tried to break away, reconfigure—a necessary process, but deeply disruptive.

> I am so tired of reaching out to people and then fucking things up. I feel empty, lonely, and then go looking for someone to save me. I engage people on that desperate level, and then it becomes so frightening.... Yesterday I just worked like a maniac at the office, putting out fires all day long. And then in my need to fill the void, I reached out to X [a new woman friend], who is so-o-o-o needy herself. It's my seventh grade self speaking. You know, its a girlfriendy kind of thing, girl–girl....

Then she told me that at the end of her marathon day at the office she had had a drink with two of her female co-workers. Pretty quickly, their conversation had turned to men and sex, eventually to very explicit talk about orgasms.

> And I'm thinking to myself, why? Why am I doing this? Why am I once again in a situation where I feel uncomfortable, showing too much, and feeling I should have stopped somewhere well short of this. I don't cut off when I should [she makes her cutting-off gesture]. I was humiliated. But they were even more revealing, if you can believe it. The bottom line is I dread boredom, lack of some kind of excitement. Very little penetrates the surface. I don't interface enough with things, connect. I just do all these things, and walk away feeling disappointed. It's like when I was a kid and had the feeling "you're never going to be the one," so much so that when I was older and someone paid attention to me I would go

into shock. Now, attention is like a drug. I have a huge fear of being lost in the shuffle. And if I get noticed, I have this feeling like "I cannot let this go, it is too good to be true, it may never come again." I hold on for dear life.

A few weeks later, more about her girl–girl kind of friendship came forth:

I was thinking as I was driving over here about Yvonne, who was my friend when I was twelve. I was a good girl, absolutely afraid to do anything bad, getting all A's in school and never exploring anything. No dancing, no gymnastics, nothing physical. I took no risks, and I could not find any natural talents—what was I meant to do? That was my question—that is still my question. I did that twelve year old stuff when my parents came this weekend, like I was trying to find out from them if they thought I was somebody; did they know? But, anyway, when I was twelve Yvonne came into my life. She was the shortest girl in the school, and I was the tallest. She was very cute, but she had acne, and she was a little chunky and she had a big nose. She also had plenty of trouble academically. But she had learned to manipulate, to lie, so she got by. My mother thought she was malicious, conniving, and she certainly was. I was her doormat. This tall zombie who could be dictated to. She did get me to do normal teenage things—cigarettes and sneaking around with boys, alcohol, pot. She needed to be in complete control. When I was a senior and finally had a few other friends, I cut her off, I got apathetic about her.

Having other friends allowed my patient to release herself from the girl who had helped her detach a bit from the image of her perfect mother, but she knew that this reconfiguration was only part of her ego ideal story. The rest she described later in the same session:

It's like Yvonne and my mother were engaged in a power struggle. I was the medium through which their power struggle was played out. I removed myself from the scene. That's what I do. When there's conflict, I leave. Or I give up. Give in. When there is something painful, I go away before the pain gets to me. This all sounds so disturbed, it scares me. I either let people in too much, so they're going right through my fucking veins, or I cut them off. It's that way with my friends now. They're so important to me, but sometimes I don't care if I ever see them again. It's not really depression, it's like being cut off. It's like every time I assert myself I'm being mean. I don't know the difference between asserting myself and being mean, being a bitch and selfish. My mother never puts herself out for people; she does not go out of her way. But me, I go so far in the other direction! If I can do it, I will. But right now I feel just terrible saying bad things about my mother! She was, though, really kind of selfish. I could very seldom do or be what she wanted, so I got my needs met on a kind of provisions level. It was all about not being seen. I've been wandering all over the place today, can you follow it?

EGO IDEAL DISTORTIONS OR PATHOLOGIES

In this patient' s struggle, so full of shame, so full of not measuring up, there is a basic ego ideal distortion: In the oedipal period, already feeling not wanted as she emotionally and physically was, she took on a false ideal—comparable to what Winnicott called a "false self"—in the form of her mother's ideal for her, and then she could not get free of it. It galvanized her previous childhood effort to be comfortable in her skin, to be calmly boundaried. So she became a person of split ego ideal. Her own ego ideal had to grow, very weakly and uncertainly, in the shadow of the one she had imported from her mother.

Ego ideal splitting is one kind of ego ideal distortion, and its manifestation (from preoedipal roots) seems to be quite specific to the oedipal phase. But there are many other kinds of distortions, some also phase specific to a certain degree, and I will note some by reviewing the developmental line sketched above. I have proposed that there are three basic stages (or one might say matrices of factors) in the formation of the child's ego ideal and three basic stages of the adolescent's ego ideal. To use shorthand:

1. *The Radiant Child*: the tactile ideal of the preoedipal, oral/anal periods; distortion comes if the cherishment ideal is not met and the infant feels defective
2. *The Little Adult*: the comparative, visual ideal of the early oedipal, phallic period, marked by feelings of shame when failed
3. *The Mastering and Capable Boy/Girl*: the auditory ideal of the oedipal, the genital period, intersecting with superego prohibitions and guilt; distortions come if the child feels rebuked by those it imitates and tries to pursue erotically

4. *All (Again) and Nothing*: the ideal formed in latency and into preadolescence that echoes the infant's cherishment ideal and defends against resurgent pregenitality
5. *My Friend Is Me*: the ideal of early adolescence and adolescence, involving mirroring and complementarity
6. *The Philosopher's Way*: the ideal of late adolescence, a character ideal

Each stage in the development of the ego ideal addresses particular needs, but also assuages a core anxiety or fear. And, if the stage is not successful, if the anxiety or fear is not allayed, the ego ideal tends to become distorted. In the earliest stage, which is echoed in every succeeding one, the basic anxiety is about being out of touch, abandoned, and being an "untouchable"; about the condition of being-unanswered or unresponded-to, being-left-alone, being-lost. Uncherished. The ego ideal distortion that is typical is this: the child begins to love and cherish the negative state it falls into—it cherishes its unloved and unloving self, which is its only self. It cherishes lack of cherishment; it nurses its grudge, licks its wounds. And this condition then underlies all later distortions.

A DEVELOPMENTAL ILLUSTRATION OF EGO IDEAL PATHOLOGY: "MY PERFECT LIFE"

Because it is the ultimate function of the ego ideal to present the ego's wished-for relatedness, the way the ego wants to be in relation, its distortions can be seen most clearly in patients whose pathologies are in the realm of ego-reality relations, that is, in the narcissistic neuroses (a designation from the period of Freud's first instinct theory) or the borderline conditions (the current designation). I can illustrate a number of the distortions just discussed with a patient whose ego ideal pathology kept her in a condition of almost total unrelatedness. The development of the pathology through her childhood and adolescence was particularly clear in the reconstructive work of a nine-year analysis (usually four times a week) that focused on a fantasy-ideal.

The patient's earliest memories are of being shamefully "wrong" in physical terms and of being dressed in clothes that were filthy. She was a colicky baby and her overwhelmed mother, who had a third child only a year after her birth, either forced her to eat or wearily left her hungry and dirty; she was and remained painfully skinny. In her dreams, the patient represents herself as thin and hard. In one, for example, she was a metal ruler lying on a desk. She only feels comfortable with objects and furnishings that are square-edged, geometric, plain, and in her drawings of herself she appears as neat and pressed as a tin soldier. "Inhuman" is her word for herself.

When she was five, and her mother was expecting the next baby, the patient was diagnosed with nephritis consequent to a strep infection. The diagnosis was made late because the mother did not really register the child's symptoms, which included nearly death-like sleeps (the origin of her later chronic, fearful insomnia). A long hospital stay was traumatic, redeemed only by the presence of a good fatherly doctor who, for one miraculous evening, read a storybook to her. Her family mocked her for having fallen so in love with this doctor, so she made it a point during her six-month recuperation to keep her love secret. Her ego ideal eventually became centered on being good to children like the wonderful doctor, and her profession involves child care.

But this centerpiece of being good to children, her oedipal competence and mastering, is wrapped in a big distortion that set in at the time of the hospitalization. She became preoccupied with what she now calls "My Perfect Life." This fantasy was that her mother would wash her pajamas and then, when she put on the clean pajamas, suddenly everything would be right in her world—she would be clean, well taken care of, loved, happy. The nights when she wished for this transformation, she would be so wrought up in expectation that she could not sleep. Now she is convinced that her mother knew about this hope of hers and actively sabotaged it, not wanting her daughter to be happy or to be in any way better taken care of than the mother herself had been as a child. I take this theory to be a projection: the patient wants her mother to suffer and to have suffered just as she does, an eye for an eye—the law of talion rules. ("I want her to suffer as many years as I have been alive for what she has done to me!" is a common cry.)

In her latency, "My Perfect Life" was played out in a game involving a little plastic figure of Doc ("the least defective" of the Seven Dwarfs) who came sailing on a raft into a community of other little plastic figures ("The Creatures"). When Doc arrived, the Creatures could begin their perfect lives. In a key part of the game, Doc (who is a version of the good doctor in the hospital) turned one of the Creatures into a personal servant: "It's like a Frankenstein kind of thing, but he's not bad." There is something sexual, the patient says, about this transformation, and she had to play this part of the game in guilty solitude behind a rocking chair in the family's chaotic living room, while the initial transformation could be played out in front of her siblings. At about the same time, the patient invented another game: she would imagine that she had a little male figure, about six inches tall, naked but "without any marks of gender" (i.e., without a penis), which she could put in her pocket. As far as she remembers, she didn't do anything further with this imaginary figure, and didn't masturbate; it just made her feel temporarily good and perfect. It was part of her sexual assertion to overcome her shame. And the other part involved fantasies of being her father's wife, supplanting her mother, for which she punished herself with all kinds of imaginary tortures.

There are other indications that "My Perfect Life" is an ideal of bodily repair. When she was a young adolescent, she visited an aunt and uncle who seemed to her perfect people. In their perfect house, she came across an object that was imperfect: it was a ceramic figure of a horse, all irregular and dark brown, that a child had made at school. Wanting everything in this house to be regular and square-edged (like the blocks in Doc's village), she found this horse intolerable. But since she couldn't just throw it out, she had to leave the house and refuse ever to return. In associating to this feeling, and responding to my questions about whether the horse was like a diseased part, she said that she has always felt that the inside of her body was "all messed up" and had diseased parts—her brown, irregular kidneys—which would eventually kill her. This brown mess is also fecal, but the anal, urethral (kidney) and genital senses of mess and damage have all become related in her.

When she was twelve or so, the patient remembers, she tried playing the Doc and the Creatures game and found that it no longer consoled her. So she turned her attention to Barbie dolls, which she and her older sister dressed in all kinds of outfits, each new outfit representing a chance at the beginning of "My Perfect Life." There was a sexual variant of this game, too. Ken came and carried Barbie, who was naked, and somehow drugged (i.e., sleepy) to a bed; he was going to do something to her, and they were in a hospital surgery room. This part of the Barbie fantasy is vague, and it came up in a session in which she was associating to a dream reported a few days before: "My Dad and I both needed surgery and had it, and then we were all bloody—wet blood stains all over us. We woke up in the same bed, but I pretended that I was asleep. My Dad, or it could have been [a boyfriend] started to get up." Her associations also went to how ashamed she was of her menstrual period and how furious she was at her mother then for not helping her deal with her period or the excruciating cramps that came with it. She had wanted her mother to wash her underwear as she had once wanted her to wash her pajamas.

In her adolescence, "My Perfect Life" was played out in a number of obsessional forms. She took to saying only certain words, which were to have magical transformative power, while any other words would be dangerous. She regulated her eating to achieve transformation, and this habit has continued. At one point while she was seeing a male psychiatrist, she lost fifteen pounds in order to be thin like him, on the theory that this would also make her smart and psychoanalytic like him. Now she has trouble eating at all when she is angry and depressed, but she can sometimes help herself by imagining that I, her female analyst, have come to her kitchen and am eating with her or feeding her. In her adolescence, she also started list-making. She latched onto a particular model person (her aunt and uncle, a teacher at school, various Hollywood celebrities) and labored to make a list of all the wonderful and beautiful things that the model person must have, which she then set out to buy at a store or to order through catalogues. If the whole list could be acquired, which, of course, was impossible, "My Perfect Life" would begin in a perfect house with all the perfect things.

It is this adolescent version of the fantasy-ideal that dominated her adult life and that was manifest in every facet of her behavior until about five years into the analysis. For example: the pervasiveness of the "My Perfect Life" fantasy began to become clear in the analysis after the second summer vacation, and during a period when the patient started trying to buy a new (used) car. She could not make up her mind about a car, and she slowly admitted that this was because she was terrified that she would spend a huge amount of money on a car only to get it home and find that it was not perfect. Then she would hate it and want to get rid of it—"I would want to blow it up!"—but she would be unable to because she would not be able to afford to replace it. She then admitted that over the years she has bought many things and then had to return them or get rid of them because they were not perfect, so her apartment became almost bare.

Slowly, the conflicts that the distorted "My Perfect Life" ideal represents emerged. She fantasizes about living in the perfect house with the perfect husband and a family. In oedipal terms, she has to be "the best" woman for the best man. But she admits that she has never been able to let another person into her life in any but the most superficial of ways because she knows that she would be unable to tolerate anyone's things. She could not live with a man because she would have to furnish a house with him, and that would mean accepting to some extent his ideas and his possessions—and thus "My Perfect Life" would be unattainable. The fantasy has the function of preventing exactly what it is supposed to create; it does and undoes; it is, ultimately, masochistic (and in this sense it is a kind of a beating fantasy—she always gets beaten out in it, or it always fails).

Of course, as soon as the extent and depth of this fantasy, which isolates the patient so completely, was apparent, she was no longer able to conceal the ways in which it was woven into the analysis. She used me to model "My Perfect Life." Whenever she had to make a decision, she asked herself, "What would the doctor do?" She expected the perfect interpretation, which would suddenly make her well. The analyst should be perfect and live perfectly for her, which meant never misunderstanding her, never failing to think about her, never having any other patients, never taking a vacation. My Perfect Psychoanalyst. When she was trying desperately to go to sleep at night, she imagined me sitting by her bed saying just the right soothing thing. And, of course, when I failed any feature of the ideal, she railed, screaming that she was being used, abused, treated with incompetence, scammed—that is, she tried to eject me as she tried to eject the damage in herself, either conjuring up the next psychoanalyst, who would be perfect, or threatening to kill herself in despair. She became furious, as well, when the "My Perfect Life" ideal was exposed in the analysis, for she had no idea how she could possibly live without it, even though she knew that with it she could not *live*—that is, have a merely imperfect, but nonetheless real, life.

There are, of course, many ways to describe the therapeutic action of an analysis, as there are therapeutic actions along all the developmental lines and matrices. When a distortion of the ego ideal is as salient as it was in this patient, revealing and relieving the ego ideal distortion is key. The patient herself recently offered me a summary of where she is now in this process: "For my whole adult life, I tried to go to a store to buy something for myself, wishing that I could bring something home and keep it, enjoy it. I didn't know that you have to have a self to even have a home, and that if you do have a self, you might be more interested in a person to eat with than a full set of dishes."

REFERENCES

Bibring, G. (1964). Some considerations regarding the ego ideal in the psychoanalytic process. *Journal of the American Psychoanalytic Association* 12:517–521.
Blos, P. (1962). *On Adolescence.* New York: Free Press.
——— (1974). The geneology of the ego ideal. *Psychoanalytic Study of the Child* 29:43–88.
Bornstein, B. (1951). On latency. *Psychoanalytic Study of the Child* 6:279–285.
Chasseguet-Smirgel, J. (1985) *The Ego Ideal.* New York: International Universities Press.
Devereux, G. (1956). *Therapeutic Education.* New York: Harper.
Doi, T. (1971). *The Anatomy of Dependence.* New York: Kodansha, 1973.
Erikson, E. (1950). *Childhood and Society.* New York: Norton.
Fenichel, O. (1945). *The Psychoanalytic Theory of Neuroses.* New York: Norton.
Freud, A. (1936). *The Ego and the Mechanisms of Defence.* New York: International Universities Press, 1974.
Freud, S. (1914). On narcissism: an introduction. *Standard Edition* 14:67–104.
——— (1916–1917). Introductory lectures on psychoanalysis. *Standard Edition* 15, 16:1–481.
——— (1926). Inhibitions, symptoms and anxiety. *Standard Edition* 20:75–172.
——— (1933). New introductory lectures on psychoanalysis. *Standard Edition* 22:1–182.
Grinker, R. R. (1955). Growth, inertia, and shame. *International Journal of Psycho-Analysis* 36:42–53.
Hartmann, H., and Loewenstein, R. (1962). Notes on the superego. *Psychoanalytic Study of the Child* 17:42–81.

Hendrick, I. (1942). Instinct and ego during infancy. *Psychoanalytic Quarterly* 11:33–58.

——— (1943). Work and the pleasure principle. *Psychoanalytic Quarterly*, 12:245–272.

Holder, A. (1982). Preoedipal contributions to the formation of the superego. *Psychoanalytic Study of the Child* 37:245–272.

Jacobson, E. (1964). *The Self and the Object World*. New York: International Universities Press.

Khan, M. (1963). Ego-ideal, excitement, and the threat of annihilation. In *The Privacy of the Self*. New York: International Universities Press, 1974.

Lampl-de Groot, J. (1962). Ego ideal and super ego. *Psychoanalytic Study of the Child* 17:94–106.

Lewis, H. (1971). *Shame and Guilt in Neuroses*. New York: International Universities Press.

Mahler, M., Pine, F., and Bergman, A. (1975). *The Psychological Birth of the Human Infant*. New York: Basic Books.

Milrod, D. (1982). The wished-for self image. *Psychoanalytic Study of Child* 37:95–120.

——— (1990). The ego ideal. *Psychoanalytic Study of the Child* 45:43–60.

Novey, S. (1955). The role of superego and ego ideal in character formation. *International Journal of Psycho-Analysis* 36:254–259.

Nunberg, H. (1955). *Principles of Psychoanalysis*. New York: International Universities Press.

Piers, G., and Singer, M. (1953). *Shame and Guilt*. Springfield, IL: Charles C Thomas.

Reich, A. (1975). *Psychoanalytic Contributions*. New York: International Universities Press.

Sandler, J., Holder, A., and Meers, D. (1963). The ego ideal and the ideal self. *Psychoanalytic Study of the Child* 18:139–158.

Spitz, R. (1945). Hospitalism. *Psychoanalytic Study of the Child* 1:53–72.

——— (1958). On the genesis of superego components. *Psychoanalytic Study of the Child* 13:375–404.

Winnicott, D. W. (1951). Transitional objects and transitional phenomena. In *Collected Papers: Through Paediatrics to Psycho-Analysis*. New York: Basic Books, 1958.

Young-Bruehl, E. (1989). *Creative Characters*. New York: Routledge.

6

A Visit to the Budapest School

INTRODUCTION

In the early 1920s, in the aftermath of the First World War, there were three major centers of psychoanalytic study and practice, each dominated by one of the founding fathers: Sigmund Freud's Vienna, Karl Abraham's Berlin, and Sándor Ferenczi's Budapest. The history of Freud's Vienna is well known, and much has been written biographically not only about Freud but about the succeeding generation, particularly those who gathered around Anna Freud. Berlin in the 1920s has also been a magnet for historians. About Abraham himself, who died in 1925, when he was 48 years old, there is only a small biographical literature, but his analysands, especially Melanie Klein, have been subjects of biographies, just as their many disagreements have been the subject of theoretical and institutional histories. After the emigration of the 1930s, Berliners became the leaders in the American centers of psychoanalysis, while Berlin provided the model for many American training institutes, so this legacy had an ongoing historical interest, too. Relatively speaking, the unknown part of the early psychoanalytic map is Budapest, and the least appreciated seminal figure, until very recently, has been Sándor Ferenczi.

Within the past ten years, two American essay collections have led the way in evaluating and re-evaluating Ferenczi in this country: *Ferenczi's Turn in Psychoanalysis* (Rudnytsky et al. 1996) and *The Legacy of Sándor Ferenczi* (Aron and Harris 1993). Ferenczi's correspondence with Freud is being published volume by volume in English (Freud 1993, 1996), having appeared already in French; his correspondence with Groddeck is available in French (Ferenczi 1982); and his *Clinical Diary*, the work of his last year, is now available in English (Ferenczi 1988). But there is as yet no biography of him, and his followers—known since the 1920s as the Budapest School—are little known, with the exception of his literary executor and chief representative in the British Psychoanalytical Society, Michael Balint. Alice Balint's most important work, *The Early Years of Life*, published in 1931 in Hungarian, was not available in English until 1954; Imre Hermann's many books remain unavailable in English, although several articles have appeared, including his most influential one on the clinging instinct (in 1976, dating from 1936); Istvan Hollos's and J. Harnik's interesting works on psychosis were published in German but never in English, and so forth.

Nonetheless, it is certainly possible to look at the evolution of psychoanalytic technique since Freud's pre-First World War technical papers and say that the single strongest influence on technique has emanated from Ferenczi and the Budapest School. Although the Hungarian influence went with the émigrés to many places (as I will note in a moment), its most immediate effects were upon the British, during and after the war. In London, the Hungarians generally allied themselves with Anna Freud and the Hampstead Centre that she and Dorothy Burlingham developed. But their influence was greatest in the British Independent group, particularly upon John Bowlby and D. W. Winnicott. Winnicott became, as it were, the Ferenczi of the British Psychoanalytical Society, challenging it with his technical innovations and developing on the basis of those innovations a body of theoretical work that is to the preoedipal years of human life what Freud's work was to the years of the Oedipus complex.

But the influence of the Budapest School's technical orientation was slow accumulating because, as Michael Balint (1968) has pointed out, the controversy between Freud and Ferenczi over Ferenczi's technical experiments "acted as a trauma on the psychoanalytic world" (p. 152). Ferenczi's associates were marginalized, and their great interest in regression in the analytic situation was rejected until the 1960s. As Balint noted the tide began to turn when Anna Freud published a paper entitled "The Role of Regression in Mental Development" in 1963, after which it became possible to speak in "mainstream" Freudian circles of regression as something other than a terrible threat to psychic development and a destructive force in analytic situations.

In consequence of the change in attitude toward regression and of the slow assimilation of Winnicott's work into British and American psychoanalysis, the Budapest School has had its recent renaissance, and others in Britain who were influenced by the Hungarians—like Bowlby, Suttie, Fairbairn, and Guntrip—have come to be more widely known and appreciated. Similarly, the types of patients with whom the Hungarians made their most important discoveries—psychotics and those whom Ferenczi called "the most difficult cases," that is, those with character neuroses or antisocial tendencies, and those eventually known as "borderlines"—were the patients with whom the British Object Relations clinicians developed their techniques. The Hungarians and their British collaborators were thus the most important initiators of "the widening scope of analysis" that was heralded in the 1960s.

But even though the most visible and direct route of Hungarian influence was through London and into merger with the British Object Relations trend, it is important to note that individual psychoanalysts who were trained in Budapest, many by Ferenczi himself, also took the basic preoedipal orientation of the Budapest School, its technical innovations, and the commitment of its members to empirical research out to other centers. In postwar America, it was not to an émigré's advantage to have been trained by Ferenczi, as Ferenczi was thought to have been repudiated by Freud and by the Viennese and Berliner Freudians, so Hungarian training, although never denied, was not advertised. Sandor Rado, one of the original members of Ferenczi's circle, relocated to New York and presented himself as more of a Berliner than a Hungarian, although his work on the biological foundations of emotional life is obviously derived from Ferenczi. René Spitz, whose postwar work on "hospitalism," first published in *Psychoanalytic Study of the Child* (1945), had tremendous influence on child analysts everywhere, did not identify publicly with Ferenczi, and usually cited him only when using the concept of infantile omnipotence. Neither did Margaret Mahler, who immigrated via Vienna to New York, where she established the research program on which her separation and individuation framework was built up. Nor did Franz Alexander in Chicago, where he and Therese Benedek, who had a special interest in early mother–child bonds, did so much to bring psychosomatic factors into analytic work and into American medicine, as well as into the theoretical innovations of Heinz Kohut. By contrast, Clara Thompson, not an émigré but an American trained by Ferenczi, emphasized her Budapest School orientation to her circles in New York and Washington, establishing its influence upon the tradition called Interpersonalism and associated with Harry Stack Sullivan and William Alanson White, and giving an impetus to Harold Searles's 1960s studies of severely regressed patients at Chesnut Lodge. Finally, by a more circuitous route, John Bowlby's attachment theory, which was developed by Mary Ainsworth and Mary Main, discretely acknowledged the 1936 paper on clinging by Ferenczi's associate Imre Hermann. Then, forty years later, attachment theory received a more overt third-generational renewal and extension through the research programs of much younger Hungarians, like Peter Fonagy, who works out of the Anna Freud Centre. Fonagy and others of his age represent the continuing influence of the Budapest School in Budapest itself, where Imre Hermann taught continuously until his death in 1984, and which has, since the political events of 1989, opened again to the rest of the world.

In this paper, I want to describe briefly some of the key concerns of Ferenczi and his Budapest School. With all of the limitations of working on a small scale, not with the leisure of a book, I have organized my historical excursions to select out three broad areas of concern that are currently lively in psychoanalysis and that I think could particularly benefit from historical reflection. At the same time, I have constructed my expositions to caution against (but not argue against at any length) certain interpretations of Ferenczi's work that have been building up in the growing American commentary literature. Specifically, I try to show that Ferenczi was not a believer in occult phenomena, although both he and Freud believed in thought transference to a degree that has been underappreciated; that Ferenczi never abandoned the basic ingredients of Freud's libido theory, although he did become more interested in object relations as his work progressed (as did Freud); and, finally, that Ferenczi's late work on psychosis was not a new departure for him but a crucial change of emphasis.

UNCOVERING TRANSFERENCE AND COUNTERTRANSFERENCE: UNCONSCIOUS COMMUNICATION

It was chiefly with Sándor Ferenczi, whom he met in 1908, and Carl Jung that Freud explored the implications of transference as he had become aware of them in his retrospection on the case of Dora. To Jung he had announced in 1906, with an astonished tone, that in psychoanalysis "the cure is effected by love" (Freud 1974, p. 13), a phrase he repeated at the January 30, 1907, meeting of the Vienna Psychoanalytic Society (Nunberg and Federn 1962, p. 101): "Our cures are cures of love." This insight was the crystal around which Freud imagined writing what he described in a 1908 letter to Ferenczi (Freud 1993, p. 27) as "a general methodology of psychoanalysis"—a treatise that never got written, although he did write a series of six papers on technique between 1911 and 1915.

One can imagine the impact that envisioning a cure by love had on Sándor Ferenczi, who long before he met Freud had understood himself as a child deprived of maternal love, and even unwanted. He had been the eighth in a group of twelve siblings, his father's favorite but with an ambivalent mother whom he described as rigid and overworked even before her husband's death when Ferenczi was fifteen. Among Freud's early adherents, Ferenczi was the one most eager to view the analytic situation as the arena for re-creation of the child's love story and for the creation of a curative relationship. And he was the one most sensitive to how parents can traumatize children, spurring them to what he later described as "the colossal superperformance the child imposes on itself" (1988, p. 89) to win the love not given.

But it was Jung's and Ferenczi's present-tense love stories that provided the material for Freud's first elaboration of the countertransference dimension of his therapeutic action theory. As Jung was making his confession that he had started an affair with one of his patients, Sabina Spielrein, Freud coined the term *countertransference* to indicate the analyst's obstacle to understanding the patient's communications and the temptation to destroy the peculiar, unique love relation that is psychoanalysis (Freud 1974). Jung was Freud's model of how the "cures of love" can become traumatic, a model he held up two years later to Ferenczi when Ferenczi fell in love with one of his analysands, the daughter of his future wife, Gizella Palos, and begged Freud to help by taking the girl into analysis.

Both transference and what came to be called countertransference had often been in their thoughts through the months in 1909 as Freud, Jung, and Ferenczi had prepared to make their journey together to Clark University. The direction their conversations took can be inferred from an account of an excursion that Freud and Ferenczi made together to Berlin not long after their return from America. They went to visit a famous clairvoyant, Frau Seidler, in hopes of learning more about communication and blockages of communication "unconscious to unconscious." Their conviction was that the transference–countertransference relationship rests upon such "Ucs. to Ucs." (as their shorthand went) communications and their blockages and distortions in the analytic situation.

Through the fall of 1909, Freud and Ferenczi discussed the experiments with clairvoyants and mediums that Ferenczi was conducting in Budapest, working with Gizella. Freud was concerned that the discussions he and Ferenczi were having not be published prematurely, for he was sure that their interest in the occult would bring upon psychoanalysis another round of the hostility that had greeted his "sexual thesis" at the turn of the century. "I would like to request that you continue to research in secrecy for two full years . . . then certainly [publish] in the *Jahrbuch*, openly and aboveboard" he wrote to Ferenczi in 1910 (Freud 1993, p. 240). Freud also wanted Ferenczi to try to work together with Jung despite their personal tensions, and he appreciated Ferenczi's agreement about the importance of this collaboration: "I consider this matter consequential for the entire psychoanalytic cause—and in the event of failure or going astray, even fateful . . ." (Freud 1993, p. 277). It is clear that Freud and Ferenczi hoped that their investigation would bring insight as powerful, as monumental, as that Freud had found on the royal road to the unconscious, dream interpretation.[1]

In "Totem and Taboo" (1913) Freud himself made public the conviction to which he had come about the reality or actuality of thought transference. He also argued there that the assumption of a "collective mind" is necessary for there to be any social psychology, and for social psychology to have any understanding of how one generation of human beings can receive its "heritage of emotion" from its predecessors. This was Freud's psychological Lamarckism, for which he and Ferenczi continually sought the biological substratum. But, using different terminology, one could say that Freud was indicating here the psychological basis for what later researchers have investigated as "intergenerational transmission," which has been studied most in relation to transmission of trauma, although Freud clearly had a much more sweeping notion of what is transmitted. For example, he declared that "psychoanalysis has shown us that everyone possesses in his unconscious mental activity an apparatus which enables him to interpret other people's reactions, that is, to undo the distortions which other people have imposed on the expression of their feelings" (Freud 1913, p. 159).

For the rest of his life Freud vacillated over the reality of most types of occult phenomena (and Ernest Jones [1957] dutifully catalogued the vacillations in the "Occultism" chapter of his Freud biography). But Freud maintained his appreciation of thought transference between people and across generations, just as he kept using his image of a mental capacity humans have that enables them to read through the distortions—that is, defenses—"imposed on the expression of their feelings." As he put the image in a famous passage: "[The analyst] must turn his own unconscious like a receptive organ towards the transmitting unconscious of the pa-

---

1. As Freud's break with Jung was unfolding in 1913, Ferenczi wrote a critical review of a paper on libido that Jung had published, and in telling Freud about the review he offered a succinct catalog of the ideas about occultism that he and Freud rejected: "I have finally arrived at the most secret meaning of Jung's paper. It is none other than his hidden confession of occultism in the guise of science. Dreams tell the future; neurotics are mantically endowed people who foretell the future of the human race (progress, repression of sexuality). The unconscious knows the present, past, and future; the fate (i.e., the task) of humanity is revealed in symbols. . . . The little he has seen of the 'occult' was sufficient to bring down the obviously very shaky edifice of his psychoanalytic knowledge" (Freud 1993, p. 484).

tient. He must adjust himself to the patient as a telephone receiver is adjusted to the transmitting microphone" (1912, p. 115–116).

Ferenczi, also a firm believer in thought transference, shared Freud's skepticism about other occult phenomena, even portraying himself as a practitioner of what he called "de-occultization," although his self-analysis taught him that he was a deconstructor of reports on occult phenomena in order to defend against the very "magic-religious strivings" in himself that he and Freud had criticized in Jung.[2] But in relation to thought transference, he developed a different conceptualization than Freud's. His line of inquiry focused on the language of feelings; he hypothesized that humans have a language of feeling that develops prior to the languages adults speak—one might call it a prelanguage. This is a language of introjections (a word Ferenczi introduced into psychoanalysis) and elementary identifications, and a language in which affects, not cognitions or thoughts or even words, reign. (So Ferenczi really should have spoken about "affect transference" rather than "thought transference" when this language is transmitted and received.) This affect language is the substratum upon which those who transfer and receive "unconscious to unconscious" base their speech. They have special access to affective pre-language, as an adult has special access to it in the analytic situation, in regression.

Ferenczi always stressed that language arises in the relationship between a child and its caregivers; it is born in the original transference. There may be inborn, and possibly universal, templates for language (as later linguists, chiefly Chomsky, have argued), but the affective pre-language of body movement and sounds is built up among humans by mimesis, as it is among the higher animals. The child imitates the caregiving humans around it, but also all the things and creatures that come into its perceptual world, which are not, for the child,

---

2. On July 24, 1915, Ferenczi (Freud 1996) wrote to Freud about his "urge toward de-occultization, at the base of which there may be, in the final analysis, magic-religious strivings, which I am defending myself against by wanting to bring clarity to these matters. I am convinced of the actuality of thought transference. I believe, incidentally, that even an indication that prophecies are possible could or should not force one to abandon the scientific basis. Certainly I know of no proven case of foretelling the future" (p. 70). In his *Clinical Diary*, Ferenczi indicated (1988) that his patient RN (Elizabeth Severn) believed in telepathic healing, but not even in the privacy of his diary did he say that he himself was a believer.

disconnected from all the things in the world, from the world as a whole, by being packaged or boundaried into discrete objects.[3] The infant imitates and forms identifications in a stage prior to object relations, a stage in which, as Ferenczi emphasized in his late work (1988), the infant is unable to protect itself: "a state in which any act of self-protection or defense is excluded and all external influence remains an impression without any internal anti-cathexis" (p. 148).

As a mimetic microcosm, the child is, as Ferenczi put it "omniscient." This omniscience is then lost as the child develops, for developing requires adapting to a reality made up of discrete objects rather than introjecting and identifying with a world less differentiated or just becoming differentiated in the process of being introjected and identified with. A neurotic, in Ferenczi's terms, is a person who may not be very well able to adapt to reality, but who does keep extending his "circle of interests" by introjecting, while a psychotic (as I will show in more detail later) is someone who cannot adapt and also cannot contain introjections but must project all painful feelings back onto the world or into a split-off part of himself.

In *The Early Years of Life* (1931), Alice Balint, Michael Balint's first wife and frequent coauthor, wrote the most extensive Budapest School study of identification, emphasizing its relational quality:

> The ego, and more particularly the primitive "pleasure ego," plays the principal part in identificatory thinking, to a much greater degree than it does subsequently, after the development of what is called "objective" thinking. For the basis for the earliest identifications is not resemblance to the object (though naturally this plays its part) but *the manner in which the object in question enters into relation with the child's instincts* [and is imitated as such]. Indeed, this is self-evident: since whatever does not belong to our ego is alien to us, and thus the starting point for identifications must necessarily be our own body and our own instincts. [p. 93, italics added]

---

3. As early as 1909, in a paper called "Introjection and Transference," Ferenczi had supported the mimetic origin of language, citing the work of Kleinpaul (*Das Stromgwebeit der Sprache*, 1893), which Karl Abraham had written about in *Traum und Mythos* (1909): "man succeeds in representing the whole audible and inaudible environment by means of the ego, no form of introjection or projection remaining untried thereby."

138 / *Cherishment Psychology*

She went on to describe the way in which identifications serve (from birth onward) to attach a child to the external world in "a kind of incorporation or assimilation, or, inversely, as an extension of the ego":

> This can be demonstrated very clearly from a child's relation to its toys. It is a remarkable fact, for instance, that the essence of a small child's play consists in the child itself becoming a dog or a motor car or a railroad train though the corresponding toys are close at hand. Until this mental incorporation has been achieved, the toy remains something alien and frightening. The preference felt by children for a piece of paper or wood, for an empty box or a bit of string, is easily explained by the fact that these things can assume a greater diversity of shape and consequently afford wider possibilities for identification. [p. 96]

The child makes its world familiar and unfrightening by identifications. At the same time, its inner world fills with identifications, with the actions, words, and unconscious affective transmissions of the people around, so it will be either love-filled, if they are loving, or hate-filled, if they are hating, or—as is usual—a confusing mixture, to which the child then adds its own mixture of fantasy.

As I noted, Ferenczi held that in analysis the earliest affective transferences can be reached through regression. So in the Budapest School, regression became the key technical topic (while resistance and defense dominated the agenda in Vienna, particularly under Wilhelm Reich's influence). Ferenczi's experiments with "active therapy" (in which he instructed patients to act or refrain from action) and "relaxation" (in which he tried to help patients relax and be passive) were understood as experiments in inducing or permitting regression. Then Michael Balint, who clearly rejected the extremes of both of Ferenczi's methods, viewing them as ways of reinforcing just the inequality between patient and analyst that Ferenczi had criticized in Freud's technique, developed the emphasis on regression, adding explicitly that in regression the patient moves beyond—or before— oedipal level language to a silence (not a resistant silence, but a preverbal silence). The analyst must refrain from interrupting this silence with interpretations or efforts to organize it; the analyst must instead be "a provider of time and of milieu" (Balint 1968, p. 179) that will allow the patient to communicate from this silence. For the patient this means:

to find himself, to accept himself, to get on with himself, knowing all the time that there is a scar in himself, his "basic fault," which cannot be analyzed out of existence; moreover, *he must be allowed to discover his way to the world of objects* [italics added]—and not be shown the "right" way by some profound or correct interpretation. If this can be done, the patient will not feel that the objects impinge upon or oppress him. It is only to this extent that the analyst should provide a better, more "understanding" environment, but in no other way, in particular not in the form of more care, more love, more attention, gratification, or protection. [p. 180]

Balint used the word *empathy* for the analyst's listening to the patient's regression and silence, but his description makes it clear that for him (unlike many users of the word) empathy meant introjection and identification; that is, the analyst works out of his or her own "language of feeling" level. This is what the capacity for countertransference was in this Budapest School conceptualization: the capacity to access the thought transference or the affective pre-language in the patient and in her- or himself.[4] Ferenczi had once called this "tact," stressing that when the analyst has received the patient's affective trans-

---

4. The first published vignettes about thought transference between adults and children gained from clinical work were written not by a Hungarian but by Dorothy Burlingham, who was very much interested in psychoanalytic investigations of the occult. The original 1935 version of her paper "Child Analysis and the Mother" was written in German (in Anna Freud's style); then it appeared in English (also in 1935) and finally it was collected by George Devereux (a Hungarian émigré to America, trained in anthropology) for his very interesting and neglected 1953 volume *Psychoanalysis and the Occult*. The vignette seems likely to be about Dorothy Burlingham herself, as a mother who was in analysis with Freud at the same time that her children were in analysis with Anna Freud:

> The most striking example that I know of a child being influenced by his mother's thoughts is the following. The mother was in analysis and in her hour she had a fantasy of throwing a jug of boiling water over someone when in a rage. She had witnessed a similar scene in her childhood. An hour later she was sitting at the table with her children. The younger child quarreled with his older sister. He suddenly left the table and returned a few seconds later carrying a glass of steaming water. He advanced on his sister crying: "You will see what I will do to you," and he threatened her with the water. The action was entirely unusual and unexpected from him. Where would such an occurrence fit in the child's analysis? Had it really anything to do with the child? If not, what is this strange form of communication?

ference, he or she must draw back and decide on the appropriate response—whether to speak in turn or not, and what to say.[5]

THE MOTHER–CHILD DYAD, DEPENDENCY, AND TRAUMA

Freud's first interest in Ferenczi's work was concentrated on unconscious communication and its implications for human relationships in general and for the analytic relationship specifically. He was slower to appreciate the context in which Ferenczi's interest in telepathy arose. It was not until 1926, as Freud was formulating his revised theory of anxiety and publishing "Inhibitions, Symptoms and Anxiety," that he really registered in his own theorizing the key conviction of the Budapest School analysts, who were, by that time, a much larger and stronger group than the little band Ferenczi had assembled in 1913, the founding year of the Budapest Society.[6]

The conviction that united all the Hungarians was that human beings are born with an instinct for relatedness to their caregivers, chiefly (at first) their mothers, and that all humans are centrally influenced by the manner in which they undergo eventual separation from the caregiver to whom they are related, on whom they are completely dependent. "Primary object love," to use the phrase Ferenczi originated and Michael and Alice Balint developed, is each child's natal condition, and we are all fundamentally—"in sickness and in health"—the history of, the fate of, our primary object love. To put this orientation in allegorical terms, we are all living, traumatized to some degree, moved by our memories, in Paradise Lost.

Ferenczi was the originator of this shared conviction, and he made it quite clear in his address to the first international psychoanalytic

---

5. In "The Elasticity of Psychoanalytic Technique" (1928) Ferenczi, describing tact, concludes: "Before the physician decides to tell the patient something, he must temporarily withdraw his libido from the latter, and weigh the situation coolly; he must in no circumstances allow himself to be guided by his feelings alone . . ." (p. 89).

6. The founding group was Ferenczi, Istvan Hollos, Lajos Levy (a physician, married to Kata Levy, later an associate of Anna Freud's), Sandor Rado, and Hugo Ignotus (a publisher and Freud's translator).

meeting (1910), arguing with great optimism and enthusiasm for educating parents about the powerful influence they have over their children's development. He was imagining psychoanalysis as a kind of trauma preventative medicine. And he continually emphasized the ways in which parents can harm or disrupt the natural maturational course of their children's separation—that is, the ways in which parents traumatize their children. From his first address to his last, called "Confusion of Tongues between Adults and the Child" (1933), Ferenczi inquired into the motives of adults for traumatizing their children and destroying the original relationship of primary object love, in which the child loves a mother who is entirely given over to her child's communications, having no wishes of her own. Others in his school focused less on parents and more on how, in the course of maturation, every child undergoes separation, with some degree of traumatization being inevitable. Similarly, Ferenczi's technical experiments all had as their goal finding ways for the analyst not to be a traumatizing parent in the analytic situation, while his followers tended to put the emphasis on finding ways for the analyst to facilitate the inevitable separation process and the inevitable regressions it involves.

One consequence of the difference in emphasis between Ferenczi and his associates is that he, concerned specifically with parental traumatization and eventually more and more with sexual traumatization, focused much of his attention on the child's reactive eroticization of its genitals. His associates, who shared Imre Hermann's great interest in primatology, ethology, and evolutionary psychology, emphasized an innate clinging instinct and the way in which it is manifest in a child's use of its hands to cling to its mother, and the eventual eroticization of the hands and the whole clinging body. Ferenczi imagined the child's genitals—particularly the male's genitals—as the primary organ of longing return to the mother, of Paradise Regained, while his associates looked to the clinging hands. Importantly, neither Ferenczi nor his associates focused their attention on the child's mouth or on the "orality" or "oral greed" that was so much a feature of Freud's own theories and of Karl Abraham's (and from thence, of Melanie Klein's).[7] They

---

7. Phyllis Greenacre commented (1966): "It is my impression that in early psychoanalytic theory, anchored too strongly on the libido theory, there was too exclu-

142 / *Cherishment Psychology*

did not emphasize the child's relation to "part-objects" or claim that "whole objects" are only slowly attained. For them, the child related from the beginning to the whole, embraceable real mother or caregiver.[8]

At a 1937 Four Nation Conference meeting in Budapest, as Michael Balint set out to distinguish the Budapest School from Freud's group in Vienna and Klein's in London, he described the chief characteristic of the School as rejection of "primary narcissism." It is impossible, he argued, to speak of the infant, living in a biological unit with its mother for the first months of life, as having a self; and when this unit begins to differentiate, as it begins to do from the first days of extrauterine life, the infant directs its libido not at some emergent self but at its mother. There is an active clinging—to use Imre Hermann's term—directed not at the mother's breasts (as part objects) but at the mother's whole body. Describing the analytic situation, the Budapest School analysts saw the analysand repeating this primary object love bond, as they saw the analyst engaged in the bond, like the mother, not sitting outside of it as a mirror or a blank screen or an interpreter.

Interestingly, it was Ferenczi, the originator of this shared view, who was the least committed among the Hungarians to its elaboration, and this is because he was the most Freudian of them, the most committed to Freud's various instinct theories and to emphasis on the sexual instinct.[9] Ferenczi developed a detailed and highly speculative "sexual

---

sive an emphasis on orality in the first phase of life, and that the importance of clinging (Hermann, 1936), touch, smell, vision, and kinesthetic stimulation was insufficiently appreciated" (p. 744).

8. When Michael Balint (1952) prepared a birthday essay for Melanie Klein, he did speak of part-objects, but this seems to have been a diplomatic exception in a paper actually dedicated to a very strong critique of the primacy Melanie Klein attributed to the paranoid position (with its emphasis on part-objects) over the depressive position. In Balint's view, as in that of the whole Budapest School, loss of love (of the archaic primary love) is the first step of development out of the original "harmonious mix up" of baby and mother—and it entails depression (or what might be called a primary depressive position).

9. Ferenczi did not reject the notion of primary narcissism, which was so important a part of Freud's second instinct theory. His followers came to this position on their own, as is apparent in a footnote that Michael Balint added in 1954 to Alice Balint's book *The Early Years of Life*, which dates from 1931. She had made the claim (following Freud and Ferenczi) that an infant in the first stage of development "has no need of anybody in particular to love in order to gratify the wishes arising from its

theory," worked out in his book *Thalassa: A Theory of Genitality* (1924), which was his main contribution to the Freudian libido theory, the centerpiece of his biological concerns. In a very literal way, Ferenczi imagined libido coursing through the developing human body and coming to concentrate, finally and maturely, in the genitals. But this part of his work, which he called into question only in the last pages of his *Clinical Diary* (1988), did not receive elaboration from his followers, although they never repudiated it More recent appropriators of Ferenczi's work have tended to erase his sexual theory from his legacy, however, finding it incompatible with their view of him as the seminal object relations theorist. But in his own mind his sexual theory, the implications of which for the cure of impotence constantly compelled Ferenczi, was central. His interest through the 1920s was guided by his understanding of male homosexuality, while his followers turned more and more to what were known then as "the ego instincts."

However, although they did not follow Ferenczi into his sexual theory, the Hungarians certainly never would have accepted any dichotomizing of instinct theory and object relations theory. On the contrary, they introduced a very important modification of Freud's first instinct theory while they developed a very important critique of his second instinct theory. Ferenczi had been enthusiastic about the Death Instinct notion because he read it right into his recurrent concerns. In his 1929 essay "The Unwelcome Child and His Death Instinct" he wrote poignantly—fifteen years before René Spitz's classic paper on hospitalism—that "children who are received in a harsh and unloving way die easily and willingly" (p. 105). His argument was that human infants, unlike animal ones, need love to overcome the pull of the death

---

primitive sexuality." Michael Balint commented: "This was the generally accepted theory in the early thirties. Since then, important developments have taken place, among them that outlined in A. Balint's "Love for the Mother and Mother-love" [in German in 1939]. For present purposes it is only necessary to note that in that paper the author calls attention to the 'archaic love' between infant and mother, 'the fundamental condition of which is the complete harmony of interests'" (M. Balint, quoted in A. Balint 1931, p. 63). Michael Balint is crediting his wife with the recognition of "archaic love," and this makes her paper the "new beginning" of the Budapest School after Ferenczi's death. Unfortunately, she herself died in the year of its publication, 1939.

instinct and that if love is absent in the unconscious communications their mothers make, they cannot keep from dying.

Ferenczi's followers, putting their emphasis on clinging and its manifestations, connected their work with Freud's first instinct theory, which distinguished sexual instincts from ego instincts.[10] Clinging is a key ego instinct, serving self-preservation, and it appears in conjunction with an urge to go-in-search, which Imre Hermann described as a precursor or preliminary form of the sexual instinct, serving reproduction. Separation is a reactive tendency, a pulling away from the loved object, but even in separation there is always a regressive pull toward clinging to the mother, toward primary love, and toward the fetal condition that Michael Balint called "the harmonious mix-up" of mother and baby. Hermann and Balint denied that there is a Death instinctual pull toward stasis or inactivity, arguing that the two phenomena that Freud wanted to explain with the Death Instinct concept—the compulsion to repeat painful experiences and masochism, taking pleasure in pain—could be explained in relation to the ego instinctual clinging. Hermann (1936), for example, defined masochism as a reaction formation to the urge to cling and sadism as a frustration of the desire

---

10. In a 1933 paper called "Two Notes on the Erotic Component of the Ego Instincts," Michael Balint imagined an instinctual drive continuum with ego instincts and their functions at one side, sexual instincts and their functions at the other. Moving across the continuum, one would find the sexual instinct more and more intermingled with the ego instincts.

> Such a line could be constructed as follows: heartbeat ... breathing ... muscular activity ... intake of fluids ... of solids ... the diverse excretory functions ... the considerably erotised "herd instincts," such as ambition, domination, submissiveness, etc. ... and lastly one could include the various character traits which in an adult certainly appear to be of a libidinal nature, but which doubtless contain also a strong ego-component, such as: obstinacy, steadiness, envy, but also magnanimity, generosity, cold-bloodedness, imperturbability, etc. Such a series could be continued further in both directions, and many more items could be inserted. [p. 42]

Muscular activity includes the function of clinging; the next step in line is being fed (orality), and the next excretory functions (anality). That is, Balint is stressing the underlying ego instinctual and relational aspects of the Freudian libidinal stages, and noting that clinging precedes the stages in which libido begins to be commingled with ego interests.

to cling, and he saw both as developing in the context of intensification of the dynamics of clinging and separating.

Balint (1968), building on and revising Hermann's work, eventually distinguished two fundamental character types, which he called "ocnophilic" and "philobatic" (two Greek neologisms that mean, literally, loving-to-cling and loving-spaces). In response to the traumas of separation that every child must experience, as well as in response to more specific traumas of neglect or abuse, children develop either a love of clinging to supporting objects or a denial of need for objects and a focus on empty spaces. An analyst should be able to empathize with each patient's particular experience (by identifying with it) and respond accordingly, giving the ocnophile the desired dependable object—being the good parent—or giving the philobat the respect for silence and quiet that the philobat desires. Failing to identify with or read the patient correctly will lead to retraumatizing.

It is interesting to observe that in the elaboration of Bowlby's work that came from his followers, chiefly Mary Ainsworth and Mary Main, there are two fundamental styles of insecure attachment, called ambivalent/resistant and avoidant, which are the potentially pathological forms of ocnophilism and philobatism. Basically, the ambivalent/resistant child is one who clamors for attention, who clings and seeks soothing—not usually with success—from its inconsistent, often rejecting parental figure. The avoidant child, reacting to a parental figure who is dismissive, tries to live without objects, to close down all the demands of the attachment system, and to assume an affectless emotional posture. (That these two types are very like the hysteric and obsessional characters described by Freud neither Balint nor Bowlby and his followers seemed to notice.)

THE WIDENING SCOPE OF PSYCHOANALYSIS: PSYCHOSIS

Even though he questioned it in his "Fetishism" (1927) paper, the distinction Freud had made repeatedly in the 1920s between a neurotic, whose ego "in the service of reality, suppresses a piece of the id" and then suffers from that conflict, and a psychotic, whose ego "lets itself

146 / *Cherishment Psychology*

be induced by the id to detach itself from a piece of reality,"[11] and thus is cut off, withdrawn, became a commonplace. But not in Budapest.[12]

When he had begun to develop his view, Freud had assumed that the psychotic patient who is cut off from reality is regressed to the stage of primitive narcissism (1916–1917). Not accepting the idea that there is a stage of primitive or primary narcissism, the Budapest School analysts emphasized the psychotic's (ego instinctual) tie to reality. In Michael Balint's words about the so-called withdrawal of the schizophrenic: "In fact, it would be more correct to say that the schizophrenic has a much closer tie with, and is much more dependent on, his environment than the so-called 'normal' or 'neurotic.' True, a superficial observation of his behavior will not reveal this close tie and this desperate dependence; on the contrary, it creates the impression of withdrawal and lack of any contact" (1968, p. 54). "Desperate dependence" is also characteristic to a lesser degree of a narcissist. In order even to survive, the narcissist, who is far from being a paragon of independence, must attach him- or herself to a figure who is capable of object love and who is truly capable of independence and realism. As Balint said in illustration, every Don Quixote must have a Sancho Panza.

In the Budapest School, psychoses are pathologies of dependency. They are dependencies that became desperate as "primary love" was either lost in childhood—often traumatically—or continued on into adulthood without any modification by reality. In either case the adult remains a helpless baby or, as Ferenczi put it, a "wise baby." Ferenczi himself was

---

11. Freud's first summary statements about psychosis are to be found in the Schreber case (1911); then as he developed his structural theory, he summarized the view that followed from it three times: in "Neurosis and Psychosis" (1924a), in "The Loss of Reality in Neurosis and Psychosis" (1924b), and in "Fetishism" (1927), where he points in the direction of the notion of splitting of the ego that Ferenczi was developing at the same time.

12. Ferenczi had started thinking about psychosis in the terms Freud used, but he had always emphasized introjection and projection. He wrote in 1909: "The dement completely detaches his interest from the outer world and becomes autoerotic (Jung, Abraham). The paranoiac, as Freud has pointed out, would like to do the same, but cannot and so projects onto the outer world the interest that has become a burden to him. Whereas the paranoiac expels from his ego the impulses that have become unpleasant, the neurotic helps himself by taking into the ego as large as possible a part of the outside world, making it the object of unconscious fantasies" (p. 47).

the main contributor to the study of the destroyed-love kind of psychosis, while Michael and Alice Balint contributed most to the unmodified dependency kind of psychosis. Alice Balint's "Love for the Mother and Mother-Love" (1939) shows how a child's unmodified demand for absolute unselfishness from its mother can keep the child in a kind of slavery to the mother and propel the grown-up child to demand excessive care or attention from loved ones, being incapable of reciprocity and without "reality sense in regard to the interests of the love object" (p. 114).

The Hungarians also disagreed with Freud's judgment that patients suffering from "narcissistic neuroses" or psychoses cannot be analyzed because they cannot form transferences—that is, because they cannot overcome their primary narcissism to form object relations or be connected to reality. Ferenczi went so far as to assume that if a patient could not be analyzed it was because the analyst was not able to analyze him or her. This perspective, then, had a profound effect upon those who later treated the kind of difficult character neurosis and psychosis cases that Ferenczi specialized in. For example, Winnicott, reflecting on the history of psychoanalytic technique, said, "Gradually and in the course of time the study of psychosis began to make more sense. Ferenczi . . . contributed significantly by looking at a failed analysis of a patient with character disorder not simply as a failure of selection but as a deficiency of psychoanalytic technique" (1959–1964, p. 125).

The technique that Ferenczi had searched for was, as I indicated above, one that would allow the patient's regression, or even promote it. But, viewed as a matter of his own quest for self-understanding, it was a technique that would allow him to complete the intermittent analysis he had begun with Freud. Ferenczi felt that he had simply been left with unresolved anger at Freud for not analyzing him completely and for discouraging him from his love for his wife's daughter. To compensate himself, he launched upon his most controversial—and disastrous—technical experiment, a "mutual analysis" with a psychotic patient, Elizabeth Severn. When she became his analyst, Severn took him well beyond where he had gone analytically with Freud. Ferenczi claimed (1988) that this analysis had revealed to him his own early history of traumatization and that he was—as he said in his *Clinical Diary*—schizophrenic.

Ferenczi's *Clinical Diary* is as much about himself—overtly and covertly, in the first person and in the third—as it is about his patients, particularly Elizabeth Severn. On the basis of his understanding of himself as a schizophrenic—a diagnosis that reflects the experience of mutual analysis, which was that the two analyzing each other come to share their conditions—Ferenczi developed a theory of psychosis with three key elements: traumatization, ego splitting, and absorption of the traumatization and splitting into the body.

In 1929, at the Oxford international conference, Ferenczi began to speak of the psychotic not just as projecting upon the world but as splitting internally in response to traumatizing events or, one might say this in another way, as projecting unwanted feelings onto a part of the ego. Ferenczi (1988) attributed (pp. 121–122) this formulation to Elizabeth Severn, but he took it much further. He developed the idea that the psychotic patient creates internally a whole dramatic scene, a cast of characters—in fact, an oedipal cast of characters or (to use later terminology) internal objects.

For example, in his "Confusion of Tongues" paper (1933), using the introjection and identification concepts that he had worked out for describing the normal development in a child of a language of feelings, Ferenczi wrote:

> The misused child changes into a mechanical, obedient automaton. His sexual life remains undeveloped or assumes perverted forms . . . [The] weak and undeveloped personality reacts to sudden unpleasure not by defense, but by anxiety-ridden identification and introjection of the menacing person or aggressor . . . One part of [the patient's] personality, possibly the nucleus, got stuck in its development at a level where it was unable to use the alloplastic way of reaction but could only react in an autoplastic way by a kind of mimicry. [1933, p. 163]

Ferenczi came to define schizophrenia as a "mimicry reaction" to trauma, which takes place in children "before they possessed a personality"—that is, before they could assert themselves or protect themselves.

With his theory of psychosis, Ferenczi was struggling to formulate a basic philosophical belief in the innate goodness of newborns and the primacy of kindness—the belief that most fundamentally distinguished him and those who followed him from Freud. This conviction, tacit in Ferenczi's work from the start, but formulated as such only in his *Clinical Diary*, was that all human wickedness or vileness develops in consequence of a traumatic disturbance of the child's primary state: "man becomes passionate and ruthless purely as a consequence of suffering." Trauma jolts a child into self-assertion, interrupting its ability to "share its pleasure with the environment and to take pleasure, without a feeling of envy, in the development and well-being of the environment" (1988, p. 151). Psychoanalysis, in this last conceptualization of Ferenczi's, was a method for guiding those injured most drastically and early—the schizophrenics—and those less injured—the neurotics— "back to trusting kindness," a journey to selflessness that exceptional sagacious people, religious people, can make by means of spiritual disciplines. Psychoanalysis should "promote a child's nature . . . particularly its conciliatory and balancing aspects that delight in progress." Like a Taoist or a Buddhist, Ferenczi imagined the child's original nature as goodness and as openness to the world, a feeling for the whole (the universe). This was his final formulation of the child's omniscience, and he stated very clearly that adults know nothing of this omniscience because, unlike children, they use their sense organs to "exclude a large part of the external world" (p. 154).

As he explored his basic sense of psychosis as involving introjection of and identification with an aggressor, and then splitting off of the aggressor within, Ferenczi often returned to his earlier questions about the human capacity for thought transference and telepathy. He summarized his speculation in the *Clinical Diary* as he described a patient who was hypersensitive to the important people in her world, a result of her childhood of "anxious listening for any wish impulses of a cruel person." Ferenczi hypothesized that "all mediums are such overanxious people, who are attuned to the slightest vibrations, those accompanying cognitive and affective processes, too, even from a distance. Here link with the telegraphic, electro-radio-telegraphic and telephonic hallucinations of the [psychotic]. Perhaps there are no hallucinations, but only an illusory working through of real events" (p. 140).

CONCLUDING REMARKS

In the 1960s, psychoanalysts began to be more conscious of the history of psychoanalysis, and it seems to me that the main reason for this was the publication of Jones's biography of Freud in conjunction with the celebration of Freud's centenary, which helped make Freud into a historical figure. It became more common for analysts to try to understand and take into account in their own theorizing the pendulum swings in psychoanalytic attention. For example, in 1963, D. W. Winnicott positioned himself between Anna Freud, on the one hand, and Melanie Klein, on the other, which meant for him between a clinician attuned to all kinds of external factors in a child's development and one who was entirely focused on internal objects. In that position, he took note of an observation made by Elizabeth Zetzel. "As Zetzel said in a seminar recently: first Freud thought all neurotic persons had had sexual traumata in childhood, and then he found that they had had wishes. And then for several decades it was assumed in analytic writings that there was not such a thing as a real sexual trauma. Now we have to allow for this too" (1963, p. 251). Then Winnicott used this observation to argue that in thinking about an analysis we also have to allow for the real factor of the analyst, who may be, like a not good enough mother, not good enough.

Winnicott was very well aware that in the early history of analysis it was the Budapest School in which the tendency to ignore external factors in a child's life—especially its earliest years—or in a patient's analysis was never dominant. But even Winnicott, the great appreciator of the Budapest School, was unaware that Ferenczi's attention to the child's experience of its caregivers was tied to a vision of the child as innately good and only corrupted by being traumatized: a vision of the child as innately capable of a loving receptivity to the world that mediums retain and sages—including psychoanalytic ones—in their emotional attentiveness try to emulate.

REFERENCES

Aron, L., and Harris, A., eds. (1993). *The Legacy of Sándor Ferenczi*. Hillsdale, NJ: Analytic Press.
Balint, A. (1931). *The Early Years of Life*. New York: Basic Books, 1954.
——— (1939). Love for the mother and mother-love. In *Primary Love and Psychoanalytic Technique*, by M. Balint, pp. 109–127. New York: Liveright, 1954.
Balint, M. (1933). Two notes on the erotic components of the ego in-

stincts. In *Primary Love and Psychoanalytic Technique*, pp. 42–48. New York: Liveright, 1954.

——— (1952). New beginnings and the paranoid and depressive syndromes. In *Primary Love and Psychoanalytic Technique* (pp. 244–265). New York: Liveright, 1953.

——— (1968). *The Basic Fault: Therapeutic Aspects of Regression*. London: Tavistock.

Deri, S. (1990). The great representatives of Hungarian psychiatry: Balint, Ferenczi, Hermann, and Szondi. *Psychoanalytic Review* 77:491–502.

Devereux, G., ed. (1953). *Psychoanalysis and the Occult*. New York: International Universities Press.

Federn, P. (1933). Sándor Ferenczi (1873–1933). *International Journal of Psycho-Analysis* 14:467–485.

Ferenczi, S. (1909). Introjection and transference. In *First Contributions to Psychoanalysis*, ed. M. Balint, trans. E. Mosbacher, pp. 35–93. London: Karnac, 1980.

——— (1910). Psychanalyse und Pedagogik. *Zentralblatt für Psychanalyse* I:129.

——— (1924). *Thalassa: A Theory of Genitality*. London: Karnac, 1989.

——— (1928). The elasticity of psychoanalytic technique. In *Final Contributions to the Problems and Methods of Psychoanalysis*, ed. M. Balint, trans. E. Mosbacher, pp. 87–101. London: Karnac, 1980.

——— (1929). The unwelcome child and his death instinct. In *Final Contributions to the Problems and Methods of Psychoanalysis*, ed. M. Balint, trans. E. Mosbacher, pp. 102–107. London: Karnac, 1980.

——— (1933). Confusion of tongues between adults and the child. In *Final Contributions to the Problems and Methods of Psychoanalysis*, ed. M. Balint, trans. E. Mosbacher, pp. 155–167. London: Karnac, 1980.

——— (1982). *Correspondance Ferenczi-Groddeck*. Paris: Payot.

——— (1988). *The Clinical Diary of Sándor Ferenczi*, ed. J. Dupont, trans. M. Balint and N. Z. Jackson. Cambridge, MA: Harvard University Press.

Freud, A. (1963). The role of regression in mental development. In *The Writings of Anna Freud*, vol. 5, pp. 407–418. New York: International Universities Press, 1969.

Freud, S. (1911). Psychoanalytic notes on an autobiographical account of a case of paranoia. *Standard Edition* 12:3–84.
——— (1912). Recommendations to physicians practicing psychoanalysis. *Standard Edition* 12:109–120.
——— (1913). Totem and taboo. *Standard Edition* 13:1–162.
——— (1916–1917). The libido theory and narcissism. *Standard Edition* 16:412–430.
——— (1924a). Neurosis and psychosis. *Standard Edition* 19:149–156.
——— (1924b). The loss of reality in neurosis and psychosis. *Standard Edition* 19:183–190.
——— (1926). Inhibitions, symptoms and anxiety. *Standard Edition* 20:75–172.
——— (1927). Fetishism. *Standard Edition* 21:149–158.
——— (1974). *The Freud/Jung Letters*, ed. W. McGuire, trans. R. Manheim and R. F. C. Hull. Princeton, NJ: Princeton University Press, Bollingen Series.
——— (1993). *The Correspondence of Sigmund Freud and Sándor Ferenczi, Vol. I, 1908–1914*, ed. E. Falzeder, E. Brabant, and P. Giampieri-Deutsch, trans. P. Hoffer. Cambridge, MA: Harvard University Press.
——— (1996). *The Correspondence of Sigmund Freud and Sándor Ferenczi, Vol. II, 1914–1919*, ed. E. Falzeder and E. Brabant, trans. P. Hoffer. Cambridge, MA: Harvard University Press.
Greenacre, P. (1966). Problems of overidealization of the analyst and analysis. In *Emotional Growth*, vol. 2, pp. 743–761. New York: International Universities Press, 1971.
Hermann, I. (1936). Clinging—Going-in-Search: a contrasting pair of instincts and their relation to sadism and masochism. *Psychoanalytic Quarterly* 45:5–36, 1976.
Jones, E. (1957). *The Life and Work of Sigmund Freud*, vol. 3. New York: Basic Books.
Nemes, L. (1980). Biographical notes on Professor Imre Hermann. *International Review of Psycho-Analysis*, 7:1–2.
Nunberg, H., and Federn, P., eds. (1962). *Minutes of the Vienna Psychoanalytic Society*, vol. 1, trans. M. Nunberg. New York: International Universities Press.
Rudnytsky, P., Bókay, A., and Giampieri-Deutsch, P., eds. (1996).

Ferenczi's Turn in Psychoanalysis. New York: New York University Press.

Spitz, R. (1945). Hospitalism. *Psychoanalytic Study of the Child*, 1:53–72. New York: International Universities Press.

Winnicott, D. W. (1959–1964). Classification: Is there a psychoanalytic contribution to psychiatric classification? In *The Maturational Processes and the Facilitating Environment*, pp. 124–139. New York: International Universities Press, 1965.

——— (1963). Dependence in infant-care, in child-care, and in the psycho-analytic setting. In *The Maturational Processes and the Facilitating Environment*, pp. 249–260. New York: International Universities Press, 1965.

PART II

SEXUAL AND GENDER IDENTITY

7

Reflections on Women and Psychoanalysis

INTRODUCTION

For this fine occasion to meet that Post-Graduate Mental Health has provided us, I wanted to prepare a historical and clinical talk that would bring us to the present tense of "Women and Psychoanalysis." Let us reflect on how we in the field of psychoanalysis have come a long way on this topic, baby, and where we might be going. So I thought about writing a brief history—a multibiography—of women psychoanalysts, our foremothers, and comparing their situations with ours. Then I thought about writing a brief history of women in psychoanalysis—of women as patients—focusing on how women patients now are understood and treated. With these possibilities, I wanted to avoid writing a history of changing views in psychoanalysis of female psychology, as that has been done many times, for many purposes. Not one of you is in need of such a talk, for you have all taken whole courses on this "changing views" theme at your training institutes, and many of you

158 / *Sexual and Gender Identity*

teach such courses. In fact, one of the key features of the present moment of "Women and Psychoanalysis" is that we are all well aware of the history of changing views in psychoanalysis of female psychology; we are thoroughly historicized.

Reflecting on our historical consciousness, I decided to walk a path in relation to it that is—to use a fancy term—metahistorical. We are in a moment in the history of the conjunction "women and psychoanalysis" when it is important to share with each other not just the history of theories but our questions about how and why the history of theories has been constructed as it has been. And to work metatheoretically, asking psychoanalytic questions about what kinds of theoretical strategies have shaped the history—doing what I once, on another occasion, called "psychotheoretical critique" (Young-Bruehl 1998). Our collective self-consciousness about the history of women and psychoanalysis should by now be helping us not to be condemned to repeat that history, in our theorizing or in our consulting rooms.

Getting myself oriented, I made a list of characteristics of the present moment of "women and psychoanalysis." At the top of it I wrote, a little facetiously: "The most famous question that the conjunction 'women and psychoanalysis' brings to mind is Freud's 'What do women want?' This question is no longer being asked; it could no longer, for example, be the focus of a seminar as it was so famously for Jacques Lacan in 1972–1973." Why not? First, because it presumes that there is a Woman doing the wanting who is or represents all women, as it presumes that there is one reference for the what that She wants. But ours is—thank goodness—an era of suspicion as far as such general concepts go, or as far as any essentialist definition of Woman goes. Correlatively, in research terms, ours is an era in which much psychoanalytic interest is focused on phenomena that call the categories Woman and Man, Masculinity and Femininity, directly into question *as categories* of sex and gender—for examples, the phenomena of intersexuality, transsexualism, and gender identity disorders.

From other angles, too, the categories Man and Woman have come into question. Historians working in the relatively new subdiscipline history of sexuality have shown the many ways in which even physiological and anatomical differences between the sexes, once thought to be matters of objective knowledge, are always interpreted. A single great dichotomy of types of interpretations has appeared. Sometimes the biological "facts" have been interpreted as indicating that males and females are sexually very different and at other times as indicating that they are very much the same. Biology is no more without prejudices or prejudgments than psychology or psychoanalysis.

One of the most remarkable of the new histories of sexuality, Thomas Lacquer's *Making Sex* (1990), for example, begins by showing how the basic picture of human sexuality that arose in Europe with the ancient Greek Hippocratic physicians featured the idea that men and women have similar desires and similar sexual organs, in the sense that their genitals—penis and testicles—are structurally just the same. For centuries, physicians accepted as fact the idea that these genitals, apparent on the exterior of a man's body, are to be found on the inside of a woman's. By the mid-nineteenth century, however, this sexist conviction, this product of narcissistic inability to tolerate difference, which now seems so bizarre, had given way and its opposite prevailed: scientists believed that there are fundamental differences between the male and female sexes, and, further, that the sexes are different in every conceivable aspect of body and soul, in every moral and physical aspect. A theory of radical dimorphism replaced the "one sex" everyone-has-a-phallus model, and, in terms of relations between the sexes, a theory of radical incommensurability reigned. This nineteenth-century emphasis on difference was a very important development for opening the way toward exploring female sexuality and also female psychology as not phallic and not a subset of male psychology. In this crucible, psychoanalysis was born.

But the way has proven a very hard one to go, and it has—as I will note later—its own distortions and difficulties. Breaking away from thinking of women in male terms allowed Freud's question, "What do women want?" to be posed, but, as generations of feminists have pointed out, the question has remained all set to be sexist in its own way. It can so easily presume that what men want is already known and normative, which means that whatever women want is going to be something peculiar or deviant or lesser. The answer will turn out to be that women want something men already *have*—like a penis—or men already *are*—like in power. And the desires and needs—two sorts of wants—common to men and women in their conditioned existences will go unexplored.

So "What do women want?" is out of favor now among the heirs of Freud. And those for whom it is out of favor—I include myself and most of you, I will assume—are struggling to avoid all the pitfalls that come with thinking of Woman categorically, definitionally. What we do, rather, is think of all the fundamental psychoanalytically discovered ingredients of identity generally (and the subsets of sexual and gender identity particularly) IN THE PLURAL. We exist in the moment of the pluralization of psychoanalytic concepts. The concept "developmental line," for example, has become: plural and overlapping and interactive lines of development leading to maturity as a quilt of traits, not a static condition. Or, to take another example, we think not of identification and introjection, but of plural identifications and introjections. A girl child—or a boy child—identifies with female figures and male figures, and with the femininity of masculine figures and the masculinity of feminine figures, and, over the course of her development, we expect that there will be shifting and changing in her identificatory mélange. We think—to take another example—of "object choice" not so much in end-result type categories—say, heterosexual, homosexual, bisexual—but in processes. We do not think of there being bedrock in identities, much less a single bedrock. And, in the clinical situation, we think of a diagnosis as a working description of a great variety of interacting psychic tendencies and mechanisms, more like a simulation of a journey than like a map. Our psychodynamic formulations are more dynamic than formulaic. We do not think of "the transference" as an entity but as an interactive field of forces and figures, kaleidoscopic; not the analyst's authority, but the mutuality of analyst and analysand and the analysand's experience of dependency are crucial to cure.

Nonetheless, accurate as this characterization of what we do may be, it is still, in many respects, ahead of our metapsychology or of our ability to understand what we are doing, as it is ahead of contemporary inquiry into human sexuality from biology or psychology. And I think you can see this by noting that in our literature as well as in the literatures of biology and empirical psychology the question, "How do men and women differ?"—the question that really lies behind "What do women want?"—is still being asked without benefit of historical reflection. So is "How are men and women similar?"—although this variant is less common. These questions ought to be suspicious, too, for the same postmodern reasons that knocked off "What do women want?" in the ways that I have been sketching. But, interestingly, they linger. I will take the persistence of "How do men and women differ?" as my lead-in to the further reflections on the present tense of "women and psychoanalysis" that I want to offer.

THE QUESTION "HOW DO MEN AND WOMEN DIFFER?"

If you look back over the one hundred years of psychoanalysis, I think you can observe a pattern that is very instructive. Every time psychoanalysis has asserted differences between the sexes very strongly, while asserting at the same time that men are superior in their difference, there has been a reaction, led, not surprisingly, by women, who have not appreciated being judged inferior, regardless of the scientific pretense of the judgment. There have been, basically, two kinds of reaction.

First, it has been asserted against patriarchal, sexist psychoanalysis that, yes, there are differences between men and women, but those do not indicate any inferiority of women; in fact, the differences point to a superiority, which men envy. Most frequently, the difference focused upon is that women are capable of motherhood, and the assertion is made that this is their destiny: anatomy is destiny. Arguments of this sort I will call "reversals" after the defense mechanism that Anna Freud was the first to describe in detail. Generally in the history of psychoanalysis, reversal arguments have been polemical and polarizing, becoming beacons for camps and schools of analysts and thus living long lives because complexly institutionalized.

The second way that the sexist psychoanalytic emphasis on differences and male superiority has been combated is by means of theories about an underlying similarity between the sexes that is of much greater significance than any differences or alleged differences. This underlying similarity may be said to be hidden by the historical circumstances of patriarchal culture, which create differences and set hierarchies in place. In the future, when circumstances change, the similarity will become manifest. Or, in a variant on this argument, the similarity may be specifically named as "undifferentiation," and a claim be made that there is a period of undifferentiation in human development when boy and girl infants are the same in every significant psychological way. This psychological sameness is, then, held to be more significant than either inborn

162 / *Sexual and Gender Identity*

biological differences or the kinds of psychological differentiations that come about after the period of undifferentiation.

While the first strategy I noted resembles "reversal," this one can resemble to one degree or another "disavowal," for it can involve setting aside or denying differences that are experienced as traumatic. As perceiving the absence of the penis in women or the presence of the penis in men can be traumatic, so can conceiving sexual difference in theory—and for some people the theoretical plane may actually echo an earlier traumatic experience of perceiving. But it is also apparent, looking over the history of psychoanalysis, that sameness arguments, when they involve little disavowal, when they acknowledge differences but try to keep them in sameness perspective, are less polemical and distorting than reversals. (Similarly, one might note that a disavowal taken to a great degree prepares the way for a mere perversion, but a reversal taken to a great degree opens on psychosis.)

Sigmund Freud, the most powerful articulator in all of psychoanalysis of differences between the sexes, both anatomical and psychological, also supplied the paradigms for the two forms of sameness argument. Both men and women, he said, are bisexual, both physiologically and anatomically and in terms of their object choices. They only become monosexual in object choice, if they ever do, over the course of their development, as they repress some choices and follow others or an other. If the historical circumstances promoting the cessation of bisexuality of object choice and "polymorphous perversity" of modes of sexual pleasure-seeking were not in place, men and women might remain more similar than different. "Civilized morality" promotes constriction. And, under conditions of constriction, Freud argued, women remain more bisexual in object choice than men because nothing prompts them to resolve their Oedipus complexes as definitively. (This assertion of eventual difference with which Freud concluded his argument about bisexual sameness has, of course, been greeted with reversals: yes, such arguments go, women are more bisexual than men and that is truly wonderful and indicative of their superiority in being able to relate to both sexes intimately.)

Freud also supplied the paradigmatic sameness as a developmental stage argument. He made the claim, after 1914, that all human beings begin their development in a state he called "primary narcissism," and only slowly leave it. Men leave it much more clearly than women do, so they become capable of object love while women remain predominantly narcissistic lovers, being pulled toward object love and beyond their narcissism—most manifest in their attention to their own bodies—only by their children, especially their sons. (Of course, this assertion of eventual difference between men and women has been greeted with many reversals in which the narcissism of men is asserted and the object-related nature of female desire and the caringness of women is extolled as superior.)

As I will indicate in a moment, I think it was really a very unfortunate turn of theoretical events for psychoanalysis that the way Freud explored the possibility that there is a period of pre-differentiation in human development was exclusively through the notion of primary narcissism. This turn effectively kept out of consideration for two generations any other kind of period of pre-differentiation. It is one of the key features of our current moment that the notion of primary narcissism, so long problematic, no longer blocks the view psychoanalytic infant researchers take toward object relations or attachments in the first year of life.

But let me return to my overview of the theoretical territory. Because the responses to Freud's sexist emphasis on difference were so few and so stereotyped, they did not really have much reform effect. It has been the experience of many persecuted groups that neither responding to the prejudices directed against them with reversals—by asserting that the differences between groups have been misevaluated and the oppressed are really the superior group—nor responding with humanistic pleas for the realization that all human beings are really more similar than different—has much effect on the prejudiced group or on the various internalizations of their prejudices that some in the victim groups have suffered. Neither "reverse racism" nor appeals to the common humanity of blacks and whites have had much effect on the everyday, ordinary white racism, for example. These responses meet with the same fate that interpretations meet with in the clinical situation when work on the resistances has not preceded them, when the way has not been properly prepared for their reception. Prejudices are resistances, or, as I have elsewhere argued, they are social mechanisms of defense, and they only yield to defense analysis—that is, analysis directed by the question, "Why do you need this prejudice?—What does it do for you? What does it defend against?"

164 / *Sexual and Gender Identity*

But this matter of reversals and disavowals in psychoanalytic theory has another dimension, too. Over the history of psychoanalysis, as critics of Freud have offered various kinds of reversals and disavowals, it has become more and more obvious that the way in which Freud's own assertions of difference and sameness were structured had great implications for the way his critics structured their counterarguments and found themselves unable, eventually, to break through the prejudice or shift away from its terms. I'd like to linger over two key movements in Freud's thought (and thus in the thought of his critics) when alternative ways of thinking almost surfaced. My plan is to show how these might-have-been possibilities have finally appeared, or reappeared, in the present moment; this will give us a way to judge whether an exit from the impasse I am describing is really at hand.

NOSOLOGICAL SIMILARITY BECOMES THE NOSOLOGICAL DIFFERENCE

The first moment I want to consider is the one that I take to be paradigmatic for psychoanalytic psychopathology. It is a story of how preoccupation with sexual difference pushed diagnostic-theoretical thinking into channels that were much more narrow than they needed to be.

When Freud set out on the road that led, eventually, to psychoanalysis, he was, as you know, studying hysteria. The road had begun in Paris, in Jean-Martin Charcot's Saltpêtrière clinic, where the great French neurologist was defying conventional neurological wisdom by working clinically and by taking an interest in hysteria, a disease most researchers then thought incurable, inevitably degenerative. Freud followed Charcot in claiming that the conventional wisdom on hysteria as a hereditary degenerative disease was wrong, and he also agreed that it was to be found in men, not only in women. The disease named after the female womb, *hysteros*, is not a mark of sexual difference. Men and women are similar as hysterics.

Freud was making a very important and clinically accurate sameness argument against an existing prejudicial difference argument. Then, as he developed his own approach to hysteria, and distinguished it from Charcot's, he took the sameness approach further, placing more and more emphasis on the etiological factor, which he identified as early sexual experience. He also broadened his study to compass the role of early sexual experience in obsessional neurosis as well, which he had the distinction of identifying as a distinct psychoneurosis. "I was obliged to begin my work with a nosological innovation," Freud explained. "I found reason to set alongside hysteria the obsessional neurosis as a self-sufficient and independent disorder, although the majority of the authorities place obsessions among the syndromes constituting mental degeneracy or confuse them with neurasthenia" (1896, p. 146).

The isolation of obsessional neurosis was exhilarating in and of itself to Freud, but also because it gave such support to his theory of the traumatic origins of hysteria, the so-called "seduction theory" postulating that a childhood sexual experience was causal in all hysterias. He noted:

> The obsessional neurosis arises from a specific cause very analogous to that of hysteria. Here too we find a precocious sexual event, occurring before puberty, the memory of which becomes active during or after that period . . . There is only one difference which seems capital. At the basis of the aetiology of hysteria we found an event of passive sexuality, an experience submitted to with indifference or with a small degree of annoyance or fright. In obsessional neurosis, it is a question on the other hand of an event which has given pleasure, of an act of aggression inspired by desire (in the case of a boy) or of a participation in sexual relations accompanied by enjoyment (in the case of a little girl). The obsessional ideas . . . are nothing other than reproaches addressed by the subject to himself on account of his anticipated sexual enjoyment, but reproaches distorted by an unconscious psychical work of transformation and substitution. [1896, p. 155]

Although Freud was quite clear that both males and females can be hysterics and obsessional neurotics, when he read his monocausal understanding of the two psychoneuroses through a supposed biological differentiation—activity and passivity—he moved in the direction of a differentiating generalization about men and women. "The importance of the active element in sexual life as a cause of obsessions, and of sexual passivity for the pathogenesis of hysteria, even seems to unveil the reason for the more intimate connection of hysteria with the female sex and the preference of men for obsessional neurosis" (1896, p. 156). Once he had stepped in this direction, bringing into the foreground the biological difference he unquestioningly assumed between passivity and activity, Freud began to lose the complex view he had of how both sexes become both hysterical and obsessional. Similarly, he lost sight of how hysteria and obsessionality as forms of psychoneurosis intertwine, overlap—as both sexes are bisexual, including in terms of the activity he associated with males only and the passivity he associated with females only. Although Freud alluded to his early insights as late as his case study of the Wolf Man, he did not explore further his idea that there is a hysterical core to every obsessional neurosis and that obsessional symptoms are part of every hysteria, while both conditions share the common ground—common, also, to both sexes—of phobias. Psychoanalysis began to move in the direction of discrete diagnostic syndromes, each of which was to have one cause. Later, when that one cause was no longer early sexual experience but fixation at or regression to one libidinal stage, hysteria was said to have passive "oral" origins, and obsessional neurosis active "anal" origins. Psychoanalysis was headed toward a very rigid diagnostic thinking—not as symptom oriented as the *DSM* eventually became, but nonetheless, very boxy.

I offer this diagnostic story as an example of what has happened time and again in psychoanalytic theory when an unexamined biological assumption about sex difference has been brought forward in such a way as to undermine a clinically perceived similarity. In psychopathology, hysteria and obsessional neurosis came to be seen only in their differences. And that is one of the main reasons, I think, why, by the late 1930s, when analysts were noting that they saw very few hysterics (that is, hysterics of the fin de siècle symptomatology) in their clinics, a pathology called "borderline" was outlined, covering the clinical phenomenon of severe hysteria with aggressive obsessional features. "Borderline" was—like the fin de siècle hysteria—thought to be much more common in women than in men (the *DSM* claims twice as common). Then, again, in the late 1970s, another form of severe hysteria with obsessional features appeared in epidemic proportions and was thought to be "for women only": anorexia nervosa. It took many years for the realization to spread through the clinical community that males suffer from anorexia, and, further, that both women and men can conduct their anorexia in the medium of obsessions, like obsessional exercising or body culture, and, further, that cultural conditions influence the way an illness develops.

One-cause thinking in combination with sex stereotyping led psychoanalysis away from the realization that the psychoneuroses are culturally shaped—hysteria more than obsessional neurosis, but both to some degree—but even more generally it led psychoanalysis away from developing any broad-based, multidimensional, flexible, descriptive character typology. This meant that there never appeared any Freudian characterology drawing on the whole range of Freud's developmental lines rather than just on the libidinal stage theory and the unexamined biological notions about activity and passivity. It became unusual for Freudian psychoanalysts to appreciate that similarities and differences in character among people are a broad arena—an arena of PLURALS—of which similarities and differences in sex and gender are a part, an appreciation that is fundamental to contemporary Jungian multi-type analysis, as it had been to the whole characterological tradition in Europe from the Hippocratic physicians forward.

A SECOND KEY EXAMPLE OF DIFFERENCE THEORY DOMINATING

I have been sketching how psychoanalysis was tilted toward diagnostic particularism as Freud focused on sexual difference and how it contributed to closing off clinical exploration of the psychoneuroses in their intermixtures, exploration of the psychoneuroses in cultural context, and study of character. The present moment is a moment for the return of all these represseds. But I want to turn my attention now to a second moment in the history of psychoanalysis and a second type of theory construction.

As I indicated before, and as is well known, Freud eventually abandoned his so-called "seduction hypothesis," having become convinced that it could not completely explain the origin of the psychoneuroses—that is, neither of hysteria nor of obsessional neurosis, and neither in women nor in men; and seduction especially could not, being less than universal, explain the universal presence of psychoneurotic traits. Recently, this abandonment of the seduction hypothesis has been the focus of much controversy fostered by polemicists or reversalists concerned only with seduction of women and only with hysteria. The critics have claimed that Freud disavowed the ubiquity of seduction of women in his patients' milieus. But Freud was looking for a single, truly universal cause of both the two psychoneuroses, in men and in women, and of all the psychoneurotic symptoms common to everyone. So he turned his attention to the language of dreams, which all of us do have in common. *The Interpretation of Dreams* (1900) was the book in which he hoped to show the universality of a sexual experience of another sort than seduction, that is, of the experience of the incest taboo, the experience of desiring familial figures and having to renounce that desire. Later, "Totem and Taboo" was the text in which Freud read his claim about the universality of the Oedipus complex across the history of the species—his ultimate sameness argument, as big as Darwinism.

In *The Interpretation of Dreams*, as in "Three Essays" (1905), Freud stressed the similarity of males and females in their oedipal object relations—both love the opposite sex parent and develop a rivalry with the same sex one. His drive to find a single sexual etiology and to universalize it made him maintain that girls take as their *first* love object their fathers while boys take their mothers—the Oedipus complexes of the two sexes, that is, are structured similarly. And the similarity was kept clearer, too, by another disavowal. Freud noted but minimized parental desire for the child, parental seductiveness; that is, he did not conceptualize the Oedipus complex as an interactive formation. Among the early Freudians, emphasis on the interactive Oedipus complex came from Sándor Ferenczi and his Budapest colleagues. (Among social psychologists and anthropologists, it was the Hungarian-trained George Devereux (1953) who pioneered in studying the interactive Oedipus complex.)

Later, having given more attention to the period that came to be called preoedipal (or, in libido theory terms, the oral stage), and under pressure to rethink his views on female psychology, Freud, of course, changed his mind and said that both girls and boys take their mother as their first love object. Initially, that is, there is a period of undifferentiation or pre-differentiation. This position, which is by now accepted in one form or another by analysts of the most diverse views, had as its consequence, Freud thought, that he had to show how differences arose—which really meant showing how women ever moved toward heterosexuality, leaving their mother bond. (Or, as he put the matter in later terms, how they moved from their negative [same sex] to their positive [opposite sex] oedipal bond.) Freud felt he had to identify a determinative mark or point of differentiation, and for that he turned to a staple in his clinical observation—penis envy—to which he gave greater determinative weight than he had ever given it before. The girl turns toward her father, having discovered that she lacks the penis, unconsciously wanting his, and wanting a baby who unconsciously is a penis.

As has often been noted, this makes female heterosexuality, which Freud often identified as the "normal" type of outcome from the initial bisexuality, into an achievement that comes about only from frustration and a sense of lack. Reversalists protested and put together all kinds of arguments about how heterosexuality is the inborn, biologically determined direction of female sexuality, as is motherhood. In the 1920s and early 1930s Karen Horney was the leading reversal theorist, but others—Ernest Jones, Melanie Klein—came forth, each with his or her own version of the reversal. The crux of the debate was really whether an event turns the woman's sexual instinctual drive to men and to motherhood or whether this happens naturally unless an event interrupts, deflects.

Interestingly, before these debates of the 1920s, Freud had pointed to another experience of frustration, not sexual instinctual, as the truly universal experience of frustration for children, and also as the *earliest* experience of frustration. Very clearly in his "Three Essays on the Theory of Sexuality" (1905) Freud had cited children's experiences of not being cared for—including nursed—as much or as well or as securely or constantly as they need and wish as crucial for them. He was indicating not experiences of unpleasure, in erotic or libidinal terms, but what he usually called helplessness (sometimes he spoke of dependency) in the relationship he called anaclitic. Much more than animal babies, a human baby is completely dependent on its caregiver's care, and feels any lapse of that care, no matter the intention, as loss of love. Anxiety over loss of love in this sense, Freud would note in his 1926 "Symptoms, Inhibitions and Anxiety," is the elemental anxiety—and it is common to males and females.

Why did these experiences, and a child's reactions to them, not come to be thought of as determinative for a child's developing object

170 / *Sexual and Gender Identity*

relations? Because in his work of the 1920s, when he was operating with an instinct theory organized around Eros and Thanatos, Freud had only one instinct to interpret in object relational terms—the sexual instinct. To be able to credit as determinative for future object relations the infant's or the child's experiences of deprivation of care, he would have needed to think in terms of an instinctual object other than the sexual instinctual object. (Similarly, Melanie Klein, the great theorist of the importance of weaning in a child's psychic life, was only able to view weaning as loss of an erotic object.) Freud, in fact, once had such an object in his theoretical scheme Between 1910 and 1914, he had spoken of the sexual instincts and the ego instincts or self-preservative instincts—those of Hunger as contrasted with Sex—as the two fundamental instincts. The ego instincts, he had said then, are the ones that draw an infant to its mother's nurturing breast, preparing the way for a later sexual instinctual investment in her breast and in her. Males and females are similarly drawn, by implication.

I am dwelling on this undeveloped avenue in Freud's work because I want to note in a moment how it has opened within recent psychoanalysis and is coming to transform it deeply. The avenue was, in fact, developed in the 1920s by the group that surrounded Sándor Ferenczi in Budapest, while Freud himself was going where the dual instinct theory and his strong emphasis on sexual difference led him. But the Hungarian work, although it was, of course, known in the psychoanalytic community, was marginalized as Ferenczi himself was marginalized in the years before his death in 1932 and thereafter. What Ferenczi called "primary object love" was the ego instinctual love Freud had started to explore in the period between 1910 and 1914, as I will show later. But for the moment, let me put the question: "Why did Freud move away from his consideration of a love that is equally determinative for both sexes and toward his emphasis on sexual differentiation?"

HOW SEXUAL DIFFERENCE CAME TO DOMINATE OVER SIMILARITY IN FREUD'S LATE THOUGHT

In the history of psychoanalysis, the first woman to play a major role was Lou Andreas-Salomé, who arrived in Vienna in 1908, as her wonderful journal (1964) relates, just as Freud was quarreling with

Alfred Adler. He was charmed that she chose him rather than Adler as her teacher, but she was not ever a "passive" student.

During the period from 1910 to 1914, while Freud was writing about the sexual instincts and the ego instincts, stressing that the ego instincts are from the start oriented toward objects—toward the mother's breast—and that they set down pathways in which the sexual instincts *later* flow, Lou Andreas-Salomé was with him. But as Freud began to think of the primal state of undifferentiation as a narcissistic state, dominated by sexual instinctual drive directed at the ego, not by an ego instinctual drive directed toward the mother's breast or toward the first caregiver, Lou objected. She thought Freud was pathologizing the primal sexually undifferentiated state, making it the origin of the "narcissistic neuroses," while in her estimation it had a positive influence on all later development. It symbolizes Woman, she held, and the bond of mother and child. Wanting to regress to it, she held, is a sign of health—and, she stressed, drawing on her interest in artistic creativity, and anticipating later descriptions of "regression in the service of the ego," regression can be a sign of creative power. Such a regression could signal, to use a term later employed by Ferenczi's student Michael Balint, a "new beginning." For the present moment in psychoanalysis, the main theorist of creative regression and new beginnings has been D. W. Winnicott.

Frau Lou also disagreed with the way Freud, in his anthropological speculations of the time, in "Totem and Taboo" (1913), associated the undifferentiated beginning with a primal patriarchy, while she thought in terms of a primary matriarchy, a reign of mothers, which, she reminded Freud, had been written about by contemporary anthropologists. In their correspondence, neither Freud nor Frau Lou pursued further Freud's reasoning for the position he took in his famous 1914 essay "On Narcissism." The correspondence in which Freud's shift is chronicled, however, is the one with Carl Jung, for it seems very clear that it was Jung's move in the direction of a concept of undifferentiated beginnings, with more and more stress on the earliest mother–child bond, that provoked Freud's thoughts on narcissism. Objecting to what he viewed as Jung's abandonment of the libido theory and his substitution of a nonsexualized primary energy for libido, Freud insisted on having the primary state defined as sexual, libidinous. To do this, he pushed his own concept of the ego instincts to the side—eventually so far to the side that he subsumed the ego instincts completely in his later theory of Eros. Then, as Freud put more and more emphasis on his libido theory, he brought the differences in libidinal development between the sexes to the fore.

In the "On Narcissism" essay, which should be read, I think, as Freud's great good riddance to Jung, Freud was on the path that later led him to emphasize female difference as centrally a matter of wounded narcissism. As I noted earlier, he stressed that girls envy the male penis, and after 1914 he described their sense of lack in terms of wounded narcissism. The one of his followers who did most to buttress the emphasis on female wounded narcissism was Karl Abraham, whose 1920 essay Freud never ceased to praise. In the strongest possible terms, Abraham presented penis envy as (to use Freud's later term) "bedrock" in the psychology of women. And Abraham also drew overtly the conclusion that Freud and many other of the early Freudians accepted: penis envy is of a piece with the feminist desire for sexual and every other form of equality. Feminism and "the masculinity complex" became two descriptions of the same phenomenon. This development was of great consequence, for it meant that thereafter any clinical or political protest against Freud's and Abraham's difference theory, whether in the mode of reversal or in the mode of disavowal, could be dismissed as a form of penis envy or wounded narcissism. With this strategy, psychoanalysis, once a politically progressive mode of thought, began to metamorphose into a reactionary mode of thought.

A SLOW CHANGE OPENS INTO THE PRESENT

It is no exaggeration to say that from the 1920s to the mid-1930s all of the protests against the view that Freud ended up advocating (which excluded any sense that all humans originally seek loving care, with their erotic or sexual lives following in the paths of this earliest seeking and its fulfillment or lack of fulfillment) were reversal protests. Lou Andreas-Salomé's critique was lost. And, as I said, the work of the Budapest School was marginalized. It is also the case that even after the 1930s, whenever Freud's journey toward his final view was repeated, as it was very self-consciously by Jacques Lacan in the early 1970s, for example, the resulting protests took very similar reversal forms. Among the Lacanian trainees who questioned their master's views, many varieties of reversal were articulated, but they all had and have in common the idea of motherhood as the natural destiny of women and of women as essentially different than men, different in their sexuality as in their *écriture feminine*.

After the 1930s the alternative path of critique emerged, one that I described as asserting that an underlying sameness is gong to be revealed in the future as the situation of women is reformed. Karen Horney, who had been the great reversalist of the 1920s, shifted to this view and in the mid-1930s warned women that it was a trap for them to concern themselves with what is feminine and what is masculine, with sex differences. A true understanding of the sex differences that are apparent in any given time and place, she said, will only come when women have developed their potentialities as human beings, as she made very clear in *New Ways of Psychoanalysis* (1939). Horney had become convinced, helped along by the interpersonal psychology of Harry Stack Sullivan and the anthropological work of Margaret Mead, that most personality traits, behaviors, and types of pathology attributed to sex differences with roots in biology are, in fact, products of culture, and, specifically, products of parental transmission of cultural values. Femininity, is, as we now say, a social construct.

Horney's culturalist view had little impact within psychoanalysis itself before World War II, but by the late 1960s American feminists who put achievement of equality in all domains at the center of their political work converged upon all kinds of psychoanalytically buttressed emphases on sexual difference. Difference became the enemy. And it became especially important for radical feminists to try to separate— as Freud once had in his own way—biology and social identity or social role, sex, and gender. A full-scale attack was mounted upon prescriptivism about "natural" female roles and domesticity, even to the point of Shulamith Firestone's famous suggestion—taking Simone de Beauvoir's position in *The Second Sex* to the max—that in a brave new technological future women should be freed from biological motherhood, which had always been the anchor of patriarchy. Radical feminists in one way or another argued that anatomy is not destiny and that the humanity men and women have in common, not their differences, should be the focus of all political vision.

In terms of human sexuality, the debates of the day focused on the female genitals and the question of whether the clitoris or the vagina should be designated the defining sexual site. The emphasis that in the 1920s Karen Horney and other psychoanalysts who had stressed motherhood as the essentially female destiny had put upon the vagina and upon the Freudian claim that a mature woman is one whose sexual pleasure has been transferred successfully from her clitoris to her vagina in puberty was challenged by sex researchers like Masters and Johnson as well as by the psychoanalyst Mary Jane Sherfy, who was famous for arguing that women are capable of multiple orgasms. The "clitoridal woman," the woman whose masculinity complex doomed her to unsuccess as a woman or to lesbianism or to feminism, began to disappear from the psychoanalytic nosologies where she had resided since the 1920s.

Both within psychoanalysis itself and from feminism, the intense attention trained on female sexuality, and specifically on the nature of female orgasm, in the late 1960s and early 1970s was eventually criticized. From within feminism came a form of reversal. Those of the so-called "cultural feminist" schools insisted upon the differences between men and women, emphasizing the value of virtues alleged to be specifically female, particularly those involved in establishing caring and concerned relationships and specifically female cultural achievements. Investigation of differences between the sexes was, once again, given impetus, and female superiority was argued in many ways. But, at the same time, among psychoanalysts, there was pressure to reassess not just female sexuality but the whole range of questions that contests over female psychology had raised. Robert Stoller was particularly forceful in speaking the obvious, that orgasmic response as it was debated by Sherfy and others is no measure of a total personality, while psychoanalytically oriented feminists, led by Juliet Mitchell, began to reassess the history of psychoanalytic theory about female sexuality. Much of this 1970s struggle was just polemical, but it did, by stirring things up, make possible the admission into psychoanalytic theory of a strand of work that had been building in child analysis, distinguishing itself both from the camps of those adhering to Freud's late views and those in dissent. As has always been the case in psychoanalysis, it was from the margins that a challenge arose both to orthodox Freudianism and the critical stances that have arisen to try to reverse or disavow that orthodoxy.

A NEW BEGINNING

The story of the rise in modern psychoanalysis of the tradition called Object Relations has been told in quite a number of recent studies. What I want to emphasize about this story, in the context of considering the psychoanalytic concern with differences and similarities between males and females, men and women, is that there came about, from its origins in the Budapest School and through the work of D. W. Winnicott, a renewal of concern, now at the very center of psychoanalytic infant research, with development prior to differentiation along sexual lines and with objects other than sexual objects. Slowly, into consideration came Imre Hermann's remarkable work on clinging, which was mediated through John Bowlby's work on attachment; Michael Balint's work on "primary object love," which took off from Ferenczi; Alice Balint's work on the first year of life and the development of it by René Spitz; Margaret Mahler's work on separation and individuation; and Ferenczi's own controversial explorations of psychoanalytic techniques that might reveal or even re-create the mother–child dyad.

These revenants deserve a paper to themselves, but here I am just going to say that when the majority of the Hungarian group moved to London, they had great influence on the British Middle Group. In Winnicott's work, the fundamental developmental line is not the libidinal line marked oral-anal-phallic-genital (although he certainly acknowledged this line), but one that goes: absolute dependence or helplessness, relative dependence, toward independence. His notion of the infant's mother is twofold: she is "object mother," the object of excited sexual desire, but she is earlier—from before her child's birth—"environment-mother," source of care, provisions, safety, place of holding, rest, and eventually ego integration She is the mother without whom the self cannot be preserved. Winnicott is the great theorist in psychoanalysis of dependence and of the way in which we all come into our humanity in a process of being supported in our helplessness—our helplessness that never entirely ceases, that is carried over into our maturity, and that is always there to be regressed into, as Lou Andreas-Salomé had said.

Into current theory and treatment has come Winnicott's basic idea that out of our reactions to and memories of our dependence and the support we got (or did not get) in it, we become able (or not) to support ourselves and eventually show concern for others. But we are still assimilating the significance of this basic idea for the construction "female psychology"—about which Winnicott did not write specifically because his concern was with sameness far more than difference—as we are still assimilating it to our understanding of sexism, in psychology and more generally. With his focus on dependency and development, Winnicott was the first to compass a crucial ingredient of sexism, one just as important as the ingredient that stems from narcissism or inability to tolerate signs of sexual difference, the ingredient that is so apparent in the images of genital sameness that Lacquer studied in *Making Sex*. As Winnicott expressed his insight in a 1950 talk called "Some Thoughts on the Meaning of the Word 'Democracy'":

> In psychoanalytical and allied work it is found that all individuals (men and women) have in reserve a certain fear of WOMAN. . . . The root of the fear of WOMAN is known. It is related to the fact that in the early history of every individual who develops well, and who is sane, and who has been able to find himself, there is a debt to a woman—the woman who was devoted to that individual as an infant, and whose devotion was absolutely essential for that individual's healthy development. The original dependence is not remembered, and therefore the debt is not acknowledged, except in so far as the fear of WOMAN represents the first stage of this acknowledgement. [1965, p. 262]

Winnicott implied that the main reason it has taken psychoanalysis so long to come to an appreciation of dependency and of the determinative role of dependency experiences in human psychic life is that fear of dependency—fear of WOMAN—makes it impossible for us to remember our dependency, to re-feel those feelings. Lifting the amnesia that surrounds WOMAN, along with the amnesia about original and paradigmatic sexual desires that Freud pointed to, is not just crucial to psychoanalytic therapy but crucial for psychoanalytic theory of development, including theory of sexual and gender identity.

This conclusion could be put in other words by saying that the key similarity between men and women is that the figure of dependency, called WOMAN (although in some people's stories, the figure may be male), is the original and paradigmatic object of both love and fear for both women and men. In the light of this conclusion, the question of difference becomes: In what ways (the plural is crucial) do women and men of all sorts—all developmental courses, all characters, all pathologies—grow from the original (and historically influenced) condition of dependency, and what roles do sexual differences (also historically influenced and interpreted) play in those ways of development and become influenced, in turn, by those ways of development?

I have put this conclusion in these terms in order to highlight how the topic of today's conference, "women and psychoanalysis," has shifted on its axis since the turn of the last century. The conjunction "women and psychoanalysis" now points beyond all the ways in which psychoanalysis has tried to understand women, the history of theories of female development. That long history of theories, in which "women" stood out as either the unknown or the misknown province, the key challenge to psychoanalysis, the main location of its errors and prejudices, can be seen as covering over the deeper territory that is now being explored in the dynamic and pluralizing clinical settings I described earlier and in infant research that is focused on the nature of primary and subsequent dependencies or attachments. It is our challenge now to come to know that deeper territory of WOMAN in everyone's love and fear, in everyone's primary relatedness. And we as women, and women of many different sorts, have many distinctive experiences that we are bringing to bear on that challenge.

REFERENCES

Abraham, K. (1920). Manifestations of the female castration complex. In *Selected Papers of Karl Abraham*. New York: Brunner/Mazel, 1979.

Andreas-Salomé, Lou. (1964). *The Freud Journal.* New York: Basic Books.

Devereux, G. (1953). Why Oedipus killed Laius. *International Journal of Psycho-Analysis* 34:132–141.

Freud, S. (1896). Heredity and the aetiology of the neuroses. *Standard Edition* 3:141–156.

——— (1900). The interpretation of dreams. *Standard Edition* 4/5.

——— (1905). Three essays on the theory of sexuality. *Standard Edition* 7:123–243.

——— (1913). Totem and taboo. *Standard Edition* 13:1–161.

178 / *Sexual and Gender Identity*

────── (1914). On narcissism. *Standard Edition* 14:67–102.
────── (1926). Inhibitions, symptoms and anxiety. *Standard Edition* 20:75–172.
Freud, S., and Jung, C. G. (1974). *The Freud/Jung Letters*, ed. W. McGuire. Princeton, NJ: Princeton University Press.
Horney, K. (1939). *New Ways of Psychoanalysis*. New York: Norton.
────── (1967). *Feminine Psychology*. New York: Norton.
Lacquer, T. (1990). *Making Sex: Body and Gender from the Greeks to Freud*. Cambridge, MA: Harvard University Press.
Winnicott, D. W. (1965). *The Family and Individual Development*. London: Tavistock.
Young-Bruehl, E. (1998). What theories women want. In *Subject to Biography*. Cambridge, MA: Harvard University Press.

8

Are Human Beings "By Nature" Bisexual?

PART I: POSING THE QUESTION

Even to pose the question in my title, I had to put "by nature" in postmodern quotation marks, signaling thereby that we all understand how very modernist, how very essentialist—thus outmoded and un-hip—it is to speak of human nature. But the main problem with my question is that the word "bisexual" is in the process of changing meaning, as it has done many times since its invention at the turn of the last century.

I could skirt these problems by defining bisexuality pragmatically, say, as the condition that allows you to double your chances for a date on Saturday night (as Woody Allen once quipped). But even this delightful claim, with the windfall of pleasure it conjures up, is contestable because recently "biphobia," fear of people who are bisexual, has been added to the list of prejudices; so, pragmatically, bisexuality is a condition that might get you a rock thrown your way on Saturday night. Prejudice like this is a uniquely intrahuman phenomenon. Members of

180 / *Sexual and Gender Identity*

the fish species who are able to mate acting as males and releasing sperm one day and then the next day acting as females releasing ova, are not punished for their versatility. No one even bothers to call these creatures pathological.

With just this much brief acknowledgment that my title question is complicated, I am going to work along with it slowly, exploring its complexity, and also using it to travel into a very large arena. I hope to show that we human beings are at a fascinating historical juncture in which we are struggling to appreciate the complexity and variability of our human sexuality; and to overcome another kind of prejudice, with us for more than a millennium: "erotophobia," fear of the erotic, fear of sexuality. From every disciplinary direction and in all kinds of cultural venues, people are realizing how often in the last century the complexity and variability of human sexuality were scientifically grasped and then promptly denied. Now the categories in which human sexuality has been scientifically circumscribed are breaking up. We are in a category shift. And I want to suggest that "bisexuality" has been the category shifter, the category that never quite fit with any of the general categorical schemes for thinking about sexuality. Further, "bisexual" itself is being transformed in the transformation. I think it is turning into something like "multisexual," a term I suggest because it can evoke another neologism, "multicultural," a possibility, a virtue we hope for in the global millennium. Already there are among us many celebrators of multisexualism or multisexual diversity.

To begin picturing this new appreciation of the complexity and variability of human sexuality, and to prepare the way for turning at the end of this paper to some clinical studies showing the front on which I think this new appreciation currently needs particular fostering, I am going to start off with four flashbacks into the history of scientific thought about bisexuality in the last one hundred years. I'll put the question "Are human beings by nature bisexual?" to four different vintages and kinds of experts.

The Fin de Siècle Sexologists

Let's pretend it is 1900 and we have before us a distinguished panel of sexologists—a new type of scientists, some with backgrounds in biology and medicine, some from psychiatry. All have taken seriously

Charles Darwin's theory of evolution, and all have studied the pioneering work within their own emergent specialty, Richard von Krafft-Ebing's *Psychopathia Sexualis*, published in 1886. Not all the men (there are no women in this new field) on our panel would agree with Krafft-Ebing's key causal idea that hereditary degeneration rather than environmental influences like childhood seduction cause sexual pathologies. But, whether congenitalists or environmentalists[1]—as the advocates of nature and nurture were then called—the sexologists would reply to our question in chorus: "Yes, all human beings are by nature bisexual as you can see by the evidence that the invertebrates and many lower vertebrates are bisexual (and sometimes reproductively hermaphroditic like some flatworms and fishes) and by the universally accepted knowledge that human embryos differentiate sexually only after the twelfth week of their gestation."

All our informants would then go on to describe various forms of anatomical hermaphroditism in human beings as reversions to the ancestral bisexual type.[2] Krafft-Ebing himself had contributed the idea to sexology that same-sex sexual desire or homosexuality is "psychical hermaphroditism," a disturbance in the psychical sphere completely analogous to reversion in the anatomical sphere.[3] Like the whole first generation of sexologists, and like his younger colleague at the University of Vienna, Sigmund Freud, Krafft-Ebing considered the universal condition of bisexuality to stand revealed in all people who are not what they called monosexual, a term for which slightly later theorists would use the neologism "heterosexual." Among the turn-of-the-century sexologists, homosexuality meant bisexuality, and heterosexuality was monosexuality. And all fully developed or evolved people were heterosexual/monosexual.

The shared conviction of the Darwinian sexologists was that human beings start out like the lower vertebrates and the other mammals in their bisexuality and then they refine themselves through their development; they become, as it were, specialized heterosexuals to best

---

1. The nature vs. nurture debate has a long history and has been known by many names. In the eighteenth century, there were preformationists and epigeneticists.
2. See Sulloway (1979) pp. 292–294.
3. Late in his life, Krafft-Ebing conceded to the growing influence of environmentalists and gave up his conviction that it is only hereditary degeneration that brings about reversions to the bisexual past, and is, thus, at the root of homosexuality.

serve the reproduction of their species. Krafft-Ebing, who believed for most of his career that homosexuality was a degenerative disease, felt that this meant that homosexuals should not be prosecuted by legal agencies or churches for an inherited condition. Biological determinism could be, in this sense, a progressive political position, as it had been for the pioneer homosexual theoretician and advocate for legal reform Karl Heinrich Ulrichs (1864), who had famously described and invented names for "a feminine soul in a male body" (a Uranian) and a "masculine soul in a female body" (a Urning). Biological bisexuality explained the feminine man and the masculine woman—those two turn-of-the-century prototypes of "the homosexual."[4]

Among Krafft-Ebing's sexological heirs, however, those favoring homosexual rights soon realized that they would have to depart completely from Krafft-Ebing's disease model if they wanted to win equality before the law for homosexuals. They would have to argue that homosexuality is a variant form of sexuality, not a pathology. The reformist hero of this sexological generation was Havelock Ellis, author of *Studies in the Psychology of Sex* (1905). It was also Ellis who first acknowledged that if choice of objects, not degenerative reversion to the biological past, is placed in the definitional foreground of human sexuality then one should also conclude that there is: "a broad and simple grouping of all sexually functioning persons into three comprehensive divisions: the heterosexual, the bisexual and the homosexual."[5] With emphasis on choice of objects, bisexuality began to emerge as a possibility distinct from homosexuality. But this trend was short lived—except among Freudians.

Freud and Freudians in the 1920s

Let me go forward in time to 1920 and consult Sigmund Freud and his followers. I have chosen this date because we need to take into account that Freud's view of bisexuality evolved after 1900, as he developed psychoanalysis and as he distanced himself from early associates

---

4. A good, brief summary of Ulrich's classifications can be found in Haeberle and Gindorf (1998), p. 17–20.
5. See Firestein (1996), p. 5.

like Wilhelm Stekel, who specialized in the theory that homosexuality is a pathology. The record of Freud's evolving view can be found in the additions and footnotes he made to all the editions of his 1905 text "Three Essays on the Theory of Sexuality." The record there shows that Freud was usually a great appreciator of the complexity and variability of human sexuality, but he could also lapse into being a monosexualist in the Krafft-Ebing tradition, thereby demonstrating that human beings' theories about sexuality are just as complex and variable as sexuality itself.

Freud (and his then friend Wilhelm Fliess) had started out with the Krafft-Ebing idea that homosexuality is a reversion to the original bisexuality, but by the 1920s his attention had shifted more and more to the psychological domain. His clinical observations had taught him that all people, regardless of their particular physical or sexual constitutions, make bisexual object choices. As he said summarily:

> It is well known that at all times there have been, as there still are, human beings who can take as their sexual objects persons of either sex without the one trend interfering with the other. We call these people bisexual and accept the fact of their existence without wondering much at it. . . . But we have come to know that all human beings are bisexual in this sense and that their libido is distributed between objects of both sexes, either in a manifest or a latent form. [Freud 1937, p. 243]

The implications of this thought were enormous. Freud rejected the idea that homosexuals are feminine souls trapped in male bodies or masculine souls trapped in female bodies, insisting, instead, that all souls choose both same-sex and opposite-sex objects. Over time, however, and through a process of repression, most people choose one sex or the other predominantly and manifestly, that is, consciously, all the while retaining in their unconscious minds the road not taken. Not all desires and choices are evident in behavior, but more are evident in the bisexuals, who are in less conflict, who do not repress so relentlessly as do heterosexuals or homosexuals.

All human beings are by nature bisexual, in Freud's view, both biologically and psychologically. But Freud went even further and realized that the psychological domain is not just a domain of object choice. It is a domain of what we would now call gender identity: of how a person feels and imagines himself or herself to be in terms of maleness and femaleness, masculinity and femininity, and how a person is in relation to prevailing conventions about what is masculine and feminine. In this domain, too, we are all bisexual in the sense that we are all a mixture of masculine and feminine traits and characteristics, some of which—like activity and passivity, perhaps—are closer to the biological domain and some more social or conventional. Very clearly, in his case study of a female homosexual, Freud (1920) distinguished three domains that make up an individual's sexuality: physical or biological characteristics (maleness and femaleness), mental sexual characteristics (masculinity and femininity), and the kind of object choice (p. 170). These are three domains or types of bisexuality. And it seems that the three domains vary independently to one degree or another in every individual.

In effect, Freud was acknowledging that one predominantly male person who takes males as his predominant sexual objects may have predominantly masculine mental characteristics, while another who does the same may have predominantly feminine mental characteristics. These are two different sorts of males behaving homosexually, the products of two different developmental routes and object-choice histories. Freud and his colleagues, like Ferenczi, studied developmental differences, using concepts like identification and noting that some men identify more with men and masculinity, some more with women and femininity. At this period in his work, the process of identification—a process of ego shaping—was more salient in Freud's thoughts than the process of ego control over or repression of libidinal drives, which had been central to his thought in 1900. When their egos are emergent, children attach themselves bisexually, and then as their egos mature and become shaped, they become delimited in their identities and their object choices. All human beings are in mourning for roads not taken.

Freud was not the only theorist of the 1920s who was trying to speak of variant types, to appreciate the complexity and variability of human biological bisexuality, gender mixture, and bisexuality of object choice. The leading German advocate of homosexual rights, the sexologist Magnus Hirschfeld, who appreciated Freud and was appreciated by him, issued a summary of his own research in 1926.[6] Although Hirschfeld (unlike Freud) thought of homosexuality as a biological

---

6. On Hirschfeld, see Haeberle and Gindorf (1998), pp. 20–28.

phenomenon, he nonetheless insisted that males and females can be described and differentiated in terms of (1) their sex organs, (2) their other physical characteristics, (3) their sex drive, and (4) their other psychological characteristics. If these four domains of variability are taken into account, Hirschfeld argued, then four broad types of what he called "intersexual variants" can be catalogued:

1. hermaphroditism as an intersexual formation of the sex organs
2. androgyny as an intersexual mix of the other physical characteristics
3. metatropism, that is, bisexuality and homosexuality, as intersexual formations of the sex drive
4. transvestism as an intersexual expression of the other psychological characteristics

But Hirschfeld's classification, like Freud's, was not recognized as a departure because they both kept considering their ranges of variants in relationship to heterosexuality, which stood outside the range as the norm. Both kept ending up saying conventionally that there are two fundamental types of human sexuality: normative heterosexuality and all else—intersexuality, homosexuality, bisexuality, and so forth. The radical tendency of the 1920s was to acknowledge variability, but it was very difficult for theorists not to slip back into the basic dichotomy articulated by the turn-of-the-century sexologists: the normal (heterosexual) and the pathological. In Freud and among the Freudians, too, the sexological repressed kept returning.

Kinsey and the Sex Researchers

One of the key consequences of Freud's radical view that all human beings are bisexual all their lives, even though most will limit themselves by repression to monosexuality of fantasy and behavior, was his opposition to separating homosexuals (or bisexuals) off for study as a separate group. "Psychoanalytical research is most decidedly opposed to any attempt at separating homosexuals off from the rest of mankind as a group of special character" (Freud 1905, p. 145, n. 1). Until quite recently, no one in the later Freudian tradition took this statement of Freud's as seriously as he did, however, because the Freudian heirs were

186 / *Sexual and Gender Identity*

more impressed by the idea that homosexuality is not heterosexuality, which they saw as the normal outcome of development.

The post-Freudian for whom Freud's radical lesson rang truest was not a psychoanalyst. Alfred Kinsey was a zoologist, and his tendency to think as a student of animal behavior is obvious in the metaphor that frames the most famous passage in his very famous book, *Sexual Behavior in the Human Male* (1948), which created a sensation when it was published:

> Males do not represent two discrete populations, heterosexual and homosexual. The world is not to be divided into sheep and goats. Not all things are black nor all things white. It is a fundamental law of taxonomy that nature rarely deals with discrete categories. . . . The living world is a continuum in each and every one of its aspects. [p. 639]

Dr. Kinsey's method of study was to interview hundreds of men—and later women—asking them not about their biology or their mental sexual characteristics, but about their sexual responses to other human beings and about their sexual behavior. The result was astonishing, even to Dr. Kinsey.

In the various male interview samples Kinsey studied, he found that between 25 and 50 percent were in some way and to some degree behaviorally bisexual; that is, they admitted to engaging in both heterosexual and homosexual sex to the point of orgasm. Kinsey ranged these respondents on a scale, called later The Kinsey Scale, between a group who had had only heterosexual experiences and a much smaller group that had had only homosexual experiences.

So, Dr. Kinsey's answer to the question "Are all human beings by nature bisexual?" would have been, consequently, a complex "yes and no." He recognized that human beings as a species may possess the capacity to react to same-sex as well as opposite-sex stimuli, and that this is their mammalian heritage. Behavior involves delimitation of possibilities, as Freud had said. But a certain number of the species do react only to same-sex or only to opposite-sex stimuli, for whatever reasons, biological or cultural. Like Freud, he recognized that it is a fallacy, however, to think that people *are* their behaviors, that behaviors and identity (to use a later term compassing desires and choices) are the same. Thus Kinsey recommended that instead of using the words *heterosexual* and *homosexual* as substantives that stand for persons, or even as adjectives to describe persons, they be used to describe the nature of the overt sexual relations, or of the stimuli to which an individual erotically responds. This clarification also explains why Kinsey did not say that 25 to 50 percent of his samples were bisexuals—this would be just another misleading substantive or adjective.

In a preliminary statement of his findings about males, Kinsey (1941) made his non-pathologizing, non-essentializing perspective and his conclusions crystal clear, aiming his words right at the old sexological emphasis on finding biological causal explanations:

> Any hormonal or other explanation of the homosexual must allow for the fact that somewhere between a quarter and a half of all males have demonstrated their capacity to respond to homosexual stimuli; that the picture is one of endless intergradation between every combination of homosexuality and heterosexuality; that it is impossible to distinguish so-called acquired, latent and congenital types; and that there is every gradation between so-called actives and passives in a homosexual relation.
>
> Any hormonal or other explanation of the homosexual must allow for the fact that both homosexual and heterosexual activities may occur coincidentally in a single period in the life of a single individual; and that exclusive activities of any one type may be exchanged, in a brief span of a few days or a few weeks, for an exclusive pattern of another type, or into a combination pattern which embraces the two types [that is, bisexuality].
>
> Any explanation of the homosexual must recognize that a large portion of the younger adolescents demonstrates the capacity to react to both homosexual and heterosexual stimuli; that there is a fair number of adults who show this same capacity; and that there is only a gradual development of the exclusively homosexual or exclusively heterosexual patterns which predominate among older adults. [p. 428]

Contemporary Sexperts and Sexual Politics

After the initial shock they caused, Kinsey's results and his tolerant attitude had little effect upon the intolerance and ignorance that were characteristic of Americans in the 1950s and 1960s, before the Women's Liberation Movement. The majority of the population continued to do as Kinsey's respondents had done: that is, to be much more

188 / *Sexual and Gender Identity*

complex and variable in their acting than in their thinking. They continued to deny the discrepancy between the complexity and variability of their sexuality and the rigidity of the legal codes and religiously framed prohibitions they lived under. Nonetheless, until the 1970s, Kinseyan research did dominate the little field of sexology, becoming more and more refined and complicated as more nuanced questionnaires were designed to elicit more kinds of information than Kinsey had sought. His successors particularly focused on the second of Freud's domains, what we would now call—thanks to the feminist theorists who began to inspire the Kinseyans—gender identity. At the same time, Kinsey's stricture on the use of the terms *heterosexual* and *homosexual* as substantives was reinforced by a generation of historians of sexuality—most importantly, Michel Foucault—who pointed out that these terms had only come into existence in the late 1860s and that they were very much the product of the turn-of-the-century social and cultural conditions that had supported the Krafft-Ebing, sexological or disease model for explaining homosexuality.

While Kinsey's stricture on the terms heterosexual and homosexual—and, implicitly, bisexual—was being appreciated by sex researchers and historians, it posed a problem for political activists. In the late 1960s, activists in the emergent Gay Liberation Movement recognized that Kinsey's liberal spirit animated those researchers who furthered the empirical task of demonstrating that homosexuality is not a pathology (not a disease and not a reversion to a more primitive bisexual state of the species). The activists used Kinseyan research to press the American Psychiatric Association to drop homosexuality as a diagnostic category.[7] However, the courageous people who worked for this change were also seeking affirmation of their lives and lifestyles. And this meant that they did not try to destroy the substantive "homosexual" but, instead, identified themselves as a distinct group seeking equality. The homosexuals saw themselves as a group with a history and a culture distinct from that of their oppressors (now called "homophobes" or "heterosexists"). Homosexuality became an identity, with "Gay is

---

7. In a chapter entitled "The Fall and Rise of Homosexuality," the political history in America of the diagnosis "homosexuality" has been told most recently by Kutchins and Kirk (1997).

good" as its slogan (on the model of "Black is beautiful"). "Bisexuality," however, was not part of the definition. So, once again, now for political reasons, there were but two kinds of sexuality: homosexuality and heterosexuality, gay and straight.

In the context of the remarkably effective Gay Liberation Movement, the field of sex research itself began to organize along a continuum. At one extreme, there was a group exclusively dedicated to the biological investigation Kinsey had criticized; their search was for the biological substratum that causes heterosexuality and homosexuality, the two kinds of sexuality. Some in this group felt that finding the biological substratum for homosexuality would lead—as Krafft-Ebing had hoped—to greater tolerance for people who could not help being as their biology dictated. Others hoped that with modern scientific therapies, biologically based homosexuality could be cured or eliminated.

At the opposite end of the continuum, among those whom the lesbian comic writer, Susie Bright, calls "sexperts," homosexuality is questioned as a category while it is being studied as "socially constructed" or "socially scripted." "Script theory" is the more sociological theory, which emphasizes that in any given historical moment people have available from their families, schools, churches, media, and so forth all kinds of sexual modalities out of which they cut and paste a personal script, just as the students of sexuality in any given culture have their scripts, which define what does and does not constitute normal and deviant sexual behavior.[8] "Social construction" usually points to a more psychological process of not just learning but growing in and through relationships.

Psychological processes are, of course, more complex to study and understand than people's appearances and overt behaviors, which certainly have changed dramatically among "the homosexuals" over the last two decades of the Gay Liberation Movement and the community it worked to call into being. In public arenas and in terms of visual presentation, the most commonly followed social script for being a male homosexual—biologically male, predominantly feminine in gender characteristics and predominantly attracted to males—gave way to bio-

---

8. The touchstone work of script theory is Gagnon and Simon's *Sexual Conduct* (1973).

logically male, predominantly masculine in gender characteristics, and attracted to males. The virile homosexual, fresh from the gym, not the effeminate one, headed for the drag show, became the most visible male type. Meanwhile current Kinseyan interview research shows that many gay men identify neither as predominantly masculine nor predominantly feminine; in terms of their objects and sexual activities, they enjoy variability, role playing, diversity, and, not infrequently, bisexuality. Changes are also apparent in the lesbian population, where diversity of self-description is also increasing, and where the number of parents grows, with "Heather's two mommies" frequently either taking turns being "daddy" or working to rid the role "parent" of gender binaries. One could say, then, that there is much more bisexuality (in gender identification and sometimes object choice, too) among the self-identified homosexuals.

At the same time, into the ranks of the Gay Liberation Movement have come people who want the designation "bisexual." They are committed, on the one hand, to a struggle with the many gay and lesbian people who think bisexuality is only a transitional phase, a way station on the journey toward coming out as gay or lesbian, and, on the other hand, a struggle with prejudiced people of many sorts who imagine that bisexuals are a major conduit for the AIDS virus. The bisexuals' struggle for recognition is being helped by the fact that sexperts are now studying them and their place in the more inclusively named LesBiGay Movement. The typical stages for their coming out processes are being formulated, and, in a growing autobiographical literature, the bisexuals are also studying themselves as gays and lesbians have done so brilliantly over the last two decades.

PART II: CHALLENGES TO THE CATEGORIES

This brief historical tour of sexologists, psychoanalysts, sex researchers, and contemporary sexperts, in which I have not even tried to be psychobiographical, shows that study of biological bisexuality gave way to study of heterosexuals and homosexuals as types of people defined by their object choice, and that this focus slowly yielded to emphasis on object choices and behaviors, which are known now to be very diverse and changeable. However, wrapped in identity politics, this last moment features both a great deal of identity claiming and a great deal of protest against restrictive or dichotomizing identity categories. These cross-currents exist with a great surge of reactive homophobia and biphobia among people who are frightened by the deconstructing and bending and blurring of sexual identities now in course. At present, in each of the three domains distinguished by Freud, the ways of thinking generated during this century of shifts and changes are all being challenged.

The Biological Domain

Contemporary biologists do not usually speak of biological bisexuality, but they do use terms like *sexual bipotentiality*, *sexual neutrality*, or *sexual dimorphism*. "None of these modern terms," the psychoanalyst Robert Stoller (1973) has claimed, "denies that aspects of both sexes are present in all animals, including man" (p. 361). So, there is general agreement that the biological answer to my question "Are all human beings by nature bisexual?" would still be yes. But, really, biological sex as the turn-of-the-century sexologists studied it has disappeared.

The more biologically oriented sex researchers—most of them essentialists—looked for the anatomy that is destiny, the more they found that "biological sex" is not a matter of anatomy; it is made up of a multitude of different, heterogeneous elements. Now, to be at all accurate in speaking of sexuality, people should always use an adjective, as they should use a qualifier when speaking of a person's maleness or femaleness. Specifically, they should distinguish (1) chromosomal sex, (2) hormonal sex, (3) gonadal sex, and (4) anatomical sex (with a distinction between internal accessory reproductive structures and external sex organs). Then, all of these subdomains except chromosomal sex should be looked at in temporal frames: there are embryological sex, natal sex, childhood sex, adolescent sex, adult sex, and late adult or postmenopausal sex.

While debating the Freudian distinctions among sex, gender, and kind of object choice, and considering the proposition that there is no simple relation among these domains, researchers are now realizing that there is no simple relation among the subdomains or the periods of sex either. Certain very specific, and not yet well understood, biological syndromes have conveyed this lesson and suggested that each human being's biological sex is a unique conjunction, changing over the course of a lifetime, of the various sexual elements.[9]

When hormones were discovered in the 1930s, the Darwinian and Freudian view that all human beings are biologically bisexual seemed confirmed, for both men and women were found to have the hormones most responsible for male development (androgens) and the ones most responsible for female development (estrogen), in varying proportions and produced in different sites. However, since the 1940s, it has been understood that all embryos, whether chromosomally male or female, begin with female tissues and mature as females unless testicular tissue is added; that is, unless there are available at a critical juncture the hormone testosterone (as produced in the male gonad, the testis) and another known as "Mullerian-inhibiting hormone" (MIH), which halts the development of the Mullerian ducts into female organs. By the late 1940s, it was clear to researchers that the gene on the Y chromosome known as the "testis determining factor" (TDF) sets off the androgenization process. So, the Darwinian-Freudian proposition that we all begin bisexual should be modified to say that by the time we are born we are chromosomally monosexual (usually) and hormonally bisexual in terms of the gonadal hormones.

But this usual story also needs a qualification. When the biology of chromosomes was first worked out, it seemed that there were clearly two combinations, XX for females and XY for males. The Y chromosome was designated the "male" one simply because a gene on it controls the testosterone level in a developing embryo, and this was held to determine the embryo's development into a male. But then came the discovery that not all human beings are either XX or XY. Men with Kleinfelter's syndrome are XXY, for example, which means that they have an extra copy of the chromosome labeled "female," and in this sense, they are not chromosomally monosexual, but rather bisexual. Their Y chromosome fulfills its function of sustaining testosterone levels through gestation and on into childhood. But, nonetheless, at puberty some Kleinfelter males—but not all—experience a dip in testosterone level and a degeneration of their testes; many have a decreased inter-

---

9. A good popular summary of the biological topics I am going to review briefly can be found in Mondimore (1996), Part II.

est in sex in comparison to XY males. But researchers have not been able to establish any direct correlation between these effects of the syndrome and manifest adult sexual object choice.

Study of variants that can come about in the embryological developmental process has refined the realization that even visible sex cannot be accurately discussed as simply male or female. There are different types of intersexuality—sex ambiguity or duality.[10] For example, chromosomally male fetuses with "androgen insensitivity syndrome" have defective receptor sites for testosterone, so they are born with female genitalia and are usually medically assigned as females, to be raised by their parents as girls. But when they fail to menstruate at puberty, or later when they are discovered to be infertile, their male chromosomal sex is discovered. The majority of women with "androgen insensitivity syndrome" are manifestly heterosexual on the Kinsey Scale, so, from a chromosomal point of view, they are males attracted to males, while from an anatomical point of view they are females attracted to males. In another syndrome, chromosomal females with a defect called "congenital adrenal hyperplasia" (CAH) have levels of testosterone from the adrenal glands that are too high, so they develop masculinized genitalia. From a chromosomal point of view, they are females, while anatomically, they are intersexual or, one might say, bisexual (but not hermaphroditic in the sense of having the genitals of both sexes). In a third syndrome, chromosomal males with normal testosterone levels but lacking an enzyme necessary for the normal development of external genitalia, are born with what appear to be female genitalia and are raised as girls. With the normal upsurge of testosterone at puberty, such girls develop a penis-sized genital and male secondary sexual characteristics. Many males with this syndrome assume a male sexual identity at puberty, and the majority of these locate themselves on the heterosexual end of the Kinsey Scale, being attracted primarily to women. Some of these men also report that they have felt themselves to be male all their lives, while they were being raised as girls. But others with this syndrome prefer to continue as females, helped by hormone treatments to stop their masculinization. Here, chromosomal sex and preadolescent ana-

---

10. Fausto-Sterling (1993) has summarized her review of intersexuality types under the title "The Five Sexes. Why Male and Female Are Not Enough."

tomical sex differ, as do, in many cases, medically assigned sex and self-identified sex (or gender identity).

In the 1960s biological research on sex identity tended to focus on hormonal sex and its eventual relation—if any could be found—to object choice. More recently, the focus has been on genetics and the "sex" of the brain. There has been a much-publicized search for "the homosexual gene," a phrase that makes no sense whatsoever if the multiplicity and complexity of the subdomains making up sexuality are taken into account. What would such a gene control? None of this genetic research has yielded anything that resembles a causal explanation for homosexuality or heterosexuality, and the most that can be said for it is that it shows that biological factors of diverse sorts seem to have an influence upon gender identity and object choice, but that this influence cannot be specified. The influence seems to differ from person to person, or, to use Kinsey's language, to range along a continuum from very influential to not very influential. At the extreme where biological factors seem least influential are to be found those known to Ulrichs as "feminine souls in masculine bodies" and "masculine souls in feminine bodies," except that such people are not now called homosexuals, they are called transsexuals.

The Psychological Domain

As sex variation has been more intricately mapped, it has become evident that the subdomains making up biological sex do not, individually or together, determine gender identity and object choice. The biological sex subdomains have influence, of course, to different degrees in different people and in different syndromes, but usually—if not always—biological factors are overridden by gender development, including sex assignment, and a person's history of object choices and experiences. This conclusion can be reinforced by turning for a moment to modern evolutionary thinking.

We can observe that human beings, of all the mammals, are the ones whose sexual drive is least tied to biological functions, specifically of reproduction. For example, most—not all—of the other mammals engage in mating behavior only when the female's estrus signals her readiness. Human (and a few primate) females, on the other hand, are distinctive for being always ready for sexual encounter and, further, for having a sexual organ, the clitoris, which serves no direct reproductive purpose but can provide intense pleasure as it plays its role in orgasm, a phenomenon that also serves no direct reproductive purpose and can be part of heterosexual, homosexual, bisexual, or autoerotic behavior.[11] Further, we can state that toward the human end of the evolutionary line, as biology has less and less sway, psychology and social organization have greater and greater consequence, including upon the biological domain. We human beings can imagine and choose sexual possibilities for ourselves that are not known to the other mammals. We can organize the sexuality of other animals and ourselves as breeders, trainers, educators, legislators; we can manipulate the sex of our young very complexly, by proscribing or promoting some of their sexual expressions and not others, or by doing something like taking them to a clinic for sex assignment and treatment if their biological sex is ambiguous. This capacity goes to the point, now, of intervening in the biological domain with hormone treatments, sex change operations, technologically aided reproduction, manufacture of genetic components, cloning, and so forth. Apparently it is "human nature" to act upon human nature, challenging it, pushing it, or, as the psychoanalytic sexpert Robert Stoller (1985) once put the general conclusion: "the more advanced the evolutionary development, the less absolute is the effect of somatic factors and the more we are dealing with a psychology into which the concept of choice enters" (p. 13).

Showing that sexual destiny arises from what people choose to make of their biology has been the common project of modern Freudians like Stoller, heirs of Kinsey, and contemporary sexperts of the social constructionist sort, although it has not prompted much investigation of how people's ways of organizing themselves psychically and socially specifically affect their biology. Even in these days, when scientists are rediscovering ancient wisdoms of the East and West about how regimen can change neurophysiology, reinvestigating the insights

---

11. One could note that the human male contributes to the organization of pleasure his mammalian uniqueness, too: his penis is always exposed and its state of unarousal is as visible as its state of arousal; it does not retreat into his body or into the safety of a sheath (although clothiers have tried to make men safe like the other mammals with various kinds of codpieces). But these are ways in which anatomy determines pleasure, not destiny—or identity.

196 / *Sexual and Gender Identity*

of psychosomatic medicine, considering how psychotherapy can affect physiology, and exploring how environmental forces shape sexual functioning, causal explorers still travel more strongly in the opposite direction, from body to mind, in the fin de siècle manner.

But to steer clear of "anatomy is destiny" or "biology is destiny" causal arguments, theorists have needed an approach that would establish the priority of the psychological domain and the importance in people's identities of gender, the ingredient of identity that is more psychological than sex. Since the late 1960s, feminist gender theorists, working from within and from without Freudian psychoanalysis to reform it and contest the idea that women are destined to be less than men because they lack the phallus, the emblem of male sexuality, have led the way to a general conclusion that resembles the one I noted earlier about biological sex: as biological sex is not a single thing—certainly not just anatomy—so gender is now known to be complex. No single line of gender identity development ends up at the single destination "masculinity" or the single destination "femininity." It is also too simple and biased toward heterosexual normativity to say as Freud did that there are three lines of gender development for women with three outcomes: normal (heterosexual) femininity, the masculinity complex, and asceticism (Freud 1931). Not only does biology alone not determine gender identity, but neither does any other single cause or type of construction: not infant- and child-rearing methods, not identifications within a family configuration, not the Oedipus complex, not object choices or experiences of being an object chosen (including traumatic ones), not adolescent rites of passage and societal and cultural institutions of gender-creation. But all of these forces converge in any given person's gender identity in any given time.

So adjectives are needed here, too, to mark the subdomains of gender and the developmental periods of gender. That is, gender identity is not a fixed and stable entity, definitively set at a given point (say, the preoedipal period) and definitively manifest in behaviors at a given point (say, late adolescence). People often—and in some circumstances typically—do want their own and other people's gender identities to be fixed and stable, so they self-identify, subscribing to ready-made substantives or scripts like "I am a heterosexual." But they do have to work at that achievement of stability. Again, as Freud had said about object choice, there is a process of delimitation, there are roads not taken, and there is mourning for disavowed gender (femininity, masculinity, and mixtures). And, further, efforts to achieve a stable and fixed gender identity can become ingredients of prejudices like sexism, homophobia, and biphobia, which are prejudices against gender identities perceived as "deviant" or unstable and prejudices against appreciation of the complexity and variability of human sexuality.

Of the many hypotheses comprising gender theory, one has been of particular importance for enforcing this emphasis on gender identity as multidetermined, complex, and variable. This is the hypothesis that women are more "bisexual" than (heterosexual) men. Freud was the originator of this hypothesis as he observed in his late essays on female sexuality that women, like men, retain their intense tie with their mothers in all their later relationships.[12] (Indeed, Freud went so far as to argue that it must be penis envy that turns women toward men—otherwise, what would move them to leave their mothers?) For heterosexual women, this means that their opposite-sex relationships are, in effect, bisexual, while heterosexual men who are transferring their mother love into their later loves of women are more likely to be caught in a conflict between two or more women. Many later Freudians have acknowledged that the Oedipus complex in heterosexual women is frequently a "bisexual relational triangle" (Chodorow 1992). And they acknowledge a second implication, too: that women may be more inclined to transfer their mother-love into love of a woman rather than turning toward a man; that is, the woman's mother-love may incline her toward "homosexuality."

Such contemporary psychoanalytic work on bisexuality of gender and of object choice has detached study of gender identity and role development from biology, but it has seldom focused in on the topic of how gender is and is not related to object choice. Consequently, many of the fin de siècle sexological notions linking gender role reversal—femininity in men and masculinity in women—with same-sex sexual preference have lingered on. This inertia was most influentially evident in the work of Stoller, who had so importantly argued that what

---

12. Freud (1908) had actually always emphasized the bisexuality of women, and particularly of hysterics, when he emphasized the idea that regression to bisexuality underlies pathology.

198 / *Sexual and Gender Identity*

he called "core of gender identity" is not a biological product but an assertion, a self-representation, "I am a male" or "I am a female." As much as he appreciated that biological sex is not indicative of gender identity, Stoller did not appreciate the corollary: that gender identity is not indicative of sexual object choice. And this became obvious when he turned his attention to transsexualism.

Biological males who desired to be women and biological females who desired to be men were known to Krafft-Ebing, who had read about them in the pamphlets written in the 1860s by Ulrichs, the man who spoke of "feminine souls in male bodies" and "masculine souls in female bodies." To both Ulrichs and Krafft-Ebing the so-called Uranian males were homosexuals; the term *transsexual* dates from 1949, and only came into common nosological usage in the late 1960s.[13] That is, Krafft-Ebing, like most sexologists until very recently, had assumed that a man who wants to be a woman wants, also, to be the object of male desire—that is, he wants to be the passive partner in a male-male homosexual relationship. A woman who wants to be a man wants, similarly, to be the active partner in a female-female relationship. The model or ideal within which the Uranians were understood was heterosexuality; that is, they were judged to be failed heterosexuals.

The legacy of the Krafft-Ebing sexological understanding of transsexuals, which was, of course, developed long before "sex change" procedures became available in 1953, has been strong, even among the Freudians who distinguished biological sex, gender, and kind of object choice.[14] So Stoller thought that any "male primary transsexual" who sought sex change would be attracted postoperatively to heterosexual men and not to homosexual men or people of the opposite natal sex, that is, women. However, recent Kinsey-like research among transsexuals and a growing transsexual autobiographical literature have begun to show clearly that they are very diverse in terms of object choice, preoperatively and postoperatively. The supposition that transsexuals are only attracted to people of their natal sex has been disproven. Many transsexuals behave bisexually and are attracted to members of the gen-

---

13. See John Money's helpful lexicon in Haeberle and Gindorf (1998), p. 126.
14. Males who live as females and females who live as males without wanting to undergo genital change are now known as transgenderists.

der they join (Firestein 1996). Further, transsexuals themselves consistently indicate that their condition consists of unhappiness over their genital sex, not over their gender identity or their object choice, and this is why many transsexuals reject the current psychiatric designation "gender dysphoria."

Stoller's understanding of the object choice of those males he called "primary transsexuals" followed from his description of them as males who, without any biological intersexuality, were characterized by having developed a feminine "core gender identity," a basic sense "I am female." Such a male does not deny his male anatomy and sex assignment, but he is nonetheless decisively shaped from birth by his mother's promotion of his feminine characteristics. His mother revels in his beauty and grace, and tries to keep him close—so close that his typically very passive and distant father is not available as an object of identification and never becomes a rival for the mother's love. The mother's love envelops such a male child; their symbiosis never ends—his gender identification is all with his mother. Even puberty does not influence such a male's marked femininity.[15] So Stoller concluded that as an adult the primary transsexual would only be attracted to a heterosexual man, and would not think of himself as homosexual or respond to the advances of homosexual men, whom he would consider to be interested in his male genitals.[16]

As far as women desiring sex change were concerned, Stoller, like most psychiatrists and psychoanalysts, assumed that a female-to-male (FTM) transsexual was a butch homosexual, that is, that she had become male in order to be the active one in partnership with a woman (usually feminine, whether heterosexual or homosexual); in effect, she wanted to be in a heterosexual-like partnership. However, the most

---

15. Stoller distinguished "male primary transsexuals" from "secondary transsexuals." One sort of the latter has experienced periods of masculine identity and activity growing up, but comes to think of himself as a feminine homosexual seeking a masculine homosexual partner. A sex change can seem to this type a way to be more successfully feminine. Similarly, a male transvestite can want a sex change as a way to enjoy being a woman. Neither of these sorts is propelled to escape a male body.

16. Stoller (1985) also indicates that he does not think there are subtypes of female transsexuals but considers all to be homosexuals drawn typically to feminine and heterosexual women. This view, too, is oversimple.

extensive study to date of transsexual men (FTM) showed that although all but one of the forty-five transsexual men in the study had been attracted to women before their sex changes, more than half of them had also been attracted to men at some point in their lives—that is, they were in the middle of the Kinsey continuum. Postoperatively, they were often attracted to men, including gay men, and the greater the number of years they had lived as men, the more likely they were to be attracted to gay men.[17]

These studies show that bisexuality of object choice exists in Kinseyan proportions among transsexual people, as does attraction to people of the transsexual's new gender. But, further, they show that assumptions made by researchers about how gender identity and object choice or sexual preference are related have been too simple (and too heterosexist). Sexual preference, too, is less monolithic than has been thought.

Bisexual Object Choice and Choice of a Bisexual Object

As contemporary researchers have considered bisexual object choice in the wake of Kinsey's research and in the light cast upon gender by feminist-influenced sexperts, it has become clear that bisexual object choice comes in many varieties. So here, too, adjectives are needed. In *The Bisexual Option*, Fred Klein (1978), for example, has suggested that there are four main bisexualities, distinguished by time frames. First, the name "transitional bisexuality" signals a time-limited transition from heterosexuality toward homosexuality or (more rarely) vice versa. Second, "historical bisexuality" names the past behavior of people currently engaging exclusively in heterosexual or homosexual relationships. In their pasts, they can have various kinds and combinations of same- and opposite-sex relationships, either sequentially or during the same period of past time. So, "sequential bisexuality" is a third type, and "concurrent bisexuality" a fourth. Within these types, bisexuality can be more or less open or acknowledged, more or less understood, more or less approved by the individual or by the familial or social context.

---

17. On Devor's 1993 study, see Firestein (1996), p. 94.

Other sexperts have noted that some bisexual behavior is more socially scripted than others. In societies where marriage is prescribed and there are no sanctioned alternative forms for sexuality, homosexual behavior takes place extramaritally and clandestinely. This is so-called married bisexuality. For unmarried people in such societies, without sanctioned heterosexual outlets, bisexuality may be adopted temporarily (secondary bisexuality). In many cultures, by contrast, it is expected that married men will have homosexual lovers outside their homes, and this behavior is sanctioned as long as the married man assumes an active role in sexual acts (particularly anal intercourse). "Greek love" was of this type, and currently it is known as "Latin bisexuality," with the difference that in the modern form the married men usually identify themselves as heterosexual while the ancient Greeks did not operate with the heterosexual/homosexual dichotomy. Some cultures—the best known among them being certain Native American tribes like the Lakota and the Navajo—have a particular bisexual role that enjoys great status. Individuals who are revered for being "two-spirited," feminine and masculine, adopt the gender role of the opposite sex, sometimes marrying a person of their own sex. Their versatility is celebrated and they are consulted on tribal matters as repositories of wisdom and healing power.[18]

In conditions where homosexuality is strongly proscribed, conversely, bisexuality can be adopted as a disguise, a cover, or a form of transitional experimentation before committing to the proscribed mode. There are other circumstances conducive to experimental bisexuality as well: bisexuality is, in many cultures, typical of adolescence and of adolescents' institutions, like boarding schools, clubs, military cadet units, reformatories. In some societies, adolescent bisexual behavior takes very specifically scripted forms. In Melanesia, for example, most youths engage in bisexual sex as part of their rites of passage, with their homosexual acts being of only one sort—for example, oral fellation of

---

18. Among anthropologists, this arrangement is known by its French name, *berdache*, although Native Americans generally reject this term as an imposition. Descriptively, it is called "gender-reversed homosexuality" (see G. Herdt in Haeberle and Gindorf, 1998, p. 162). Different tribes have different names for the two-spirited individuals; the Navajo *nadle* is not the same as the Lakota *wintke*. More tribes have male *berdaches* than have female ones.

202 / *Sexual and Gender Identity*

an older man, which is thought of as incorporation of the older man's manliness.[19] Some societies seclude their young women in all-female institutions where homosexual sex (often including breaking of the hymen) is preparatory for later heterosexual marriage, as was the case on Lesbos in the time of the great poetess Sappho. The bisexuality of adolescent or adult prostitutes and sex workers is sometimes referred to as "technical bisexuality." Finally, if the sex—or genitalia—of an object does not enter into a person's object choice, that person practices what is known as "equal bisexuality." A celibate person, for example, may have bisexual fantasies that do not focus on the objects' genitals but emphasize their spiritual qualities (which may be neither masculine nor feminine).

These typologies of bisexualities are, of course, made largely from the outside; they do not speak to object choice as a matter of inner life. Further, they concern an object only as a female or a male, that is, as identified by sex (or, more specifically, anatomical sex, genitals) and role in sexual activities, not by gender, and not by the object's own inner life or type of object choice. Until the 1990s empirical sex researchers did not even inquire simultaneously into the sexual behavior and the sexual identities of their respondents (Firestein 1996). To go into the territory of sexual identity further than questionnaires and even extensive interviews can take you requires something like a psychoanalytic setting, or at least a psychodynamically oriented inquiry.

In my view, understanding of the bisexualities would be deepened considerably by recognizing that the most underestimated and thus understudied of the three Freudian bisexuality domains—sex, gender, and kind of object choice—is the last, where the emphasis has always fallen on the choice, not the object. This is for (at least) four reasons. First, as long as classifications followed the fin de siècle sexology guidelines and had people choosing their sexual objects by and for their anatomies, no other characteristics of the sexual object were much

---

19. As Herdt (in Haeberle and Gindorf, 1998, p. 162) notes, "age-structured homosexuality" is a ritualized form of sexual practice, like the *berdache*, but the two forms are mutually exclusive and do not occur in the same geographical regions. The *berdache* feminizes males while age-structured practices masculinize young men; the *berdache* masculinizes women while the age-structured (lesbian) practice feminizes them.

noticed. Second, there was no precedent in psychoanalysis for speaking about the effects objects had on those who chose them; object choice was not viewed interactively or relationally, as a two-way street. In an interactive view, the sex, gender, and type of object choice of the chosen object (in reality and in the chooser's mind) must be accounted for. Third, objects and object-choice were not often viewed contextually or socioculturally. There was no way to account for the obvious fact that in different times and places, different types of objects have been deemed the most desirable (or the least), different combinations of sex and gender characteristics in objects have been valued (or devalued). In the late 1960s in America and Europe, for example, the favored object for many women who would have registered on the heterosexual end of the Kinsey Scale was a male who was virile but feminine—a Hirschfeld androgyne. There was much lamentation that all the men of this sort were homosexual. Culture critics, meanwhile, lamented loudly the feminization of American youth, while the same feminization was being celebrated by Aquarian visionaries who wanted to make love and not war. In the current cultural moment, there is a phenomenon that goes by the name "bisexual chic," which the 1960s androgyne presaged. Some people, like the rock star, Mick Jagger, have survived public life long enough to have been exciting as androgynes and then to have been rediscovered as bisexually chic.

A fourth reason study of object choice has not progressed far is that Freud's original insights about universal bisexuality of object choice have awaited, to this day, a systematic description and utilization in sexology and in clinical work. His basic orientation was toward the ways in which people choose their later objects on the basis of their earlier experience, that is, toward the phenomena of transference. Object choice was determined historically, by transference from primary object choices. What this meant was that Freud assumed bisexuality of object choice in everyone, not just because of (in some unspecifiable way) biological bisexuality, but because everyone carries over into later objects the early representations of a beloved mother and a beloved father (a female and a male) as well as representations of other beloved familial figures, like siblings and grandparents and nannies, who are both female and male. This much of Freud's framework is commonly assumed, but it seems to me that different processes of transferential object choice have nonethless not been explored.

In my reading of Freud's work, I see four elementary processes of transferential object choice, which I will indicate with very brief descriptions and examples. First, there is infant choice of a part-object, often a body part, like the breast, but also traits, like warmth and coldness, affectionateness and lack of affectionateness. When a child is capable of whole-object choice, the part object can stand for the whole and define how the whole is experienced. If the part-object is sexed or gendered, so too—in some way—will the whole object be. This mode of object choice operates in everyone, but some people are dominated by it, particularly those who incline toward perversions.

Second, there are split or doubled objects onto which a person will place separated desires and needs and sometimes separated sides of an ambivalence, a hate and a love, once felt toward a single object. A woman can, for example, love a man—perhaps a successor to her father—consciously, and a woman unconsciously, as Freud's patient Dora did. Or a person can, for another example, love a woman who is the successor to his or her mother and concurrently a man who is the successor to his or her father, or engage these objects sequentially. In one of Freud's most well-known examples, a man can love concurrently a woman who is chaste and a woman who is sensual, but it is not unusual for a man to love a woman who is chaste and a man who is sensual, as is often the case in the so-called married bisexuality or Latin bisexuality. When people divorce and remarry, to cite another example, they are often moving from an object of one kind (and gender) to an object of another kind (and gender). Recently, in areas where divorce is common, one can observe a trend for women to marry, raise a family, and then turn for a second "marriage" to a woman. Freud once remarked that women will not infrequently first marry a man with whom they have continued their relationship with their mother (a mother-man) and then in a second marriage continue their relationship with their fathers (possibly with a female), repeating the developmental order of their object relations.

The split object has been such a staple of psychoanalytic study that it has obscured the ways in which an object, singular, can be bisexual, that is, can be a composite (or composed) object, which blends parts, traits, and characteristics from at least two, and almost always more, sources. A woman, for example, loves a woman who is her mother plus her brother, as did the female homosexual about whom Freud wrote in his 1920 case study. Here it is the object's bisexuality that is of great importance to the chooser. It may be the object's biological characteristics, mental or gender characteristics, choice patterns, or all of the above, that matter.

Fourth, there is another type of composite object, which might be called a layered object or a manifest-and-latent object. As noted, people frequently relate to one object consciously and another unconsciously—a splitting situation. But they can also relate to the same object on both conscious and unconscious channels; this is a layering situation. For example, a woman might love a man consciously for his masculine qualities while she simultaneously loves this man unconsciously for his feminine qualities. This layering phenomenon is, I think, particularly crucial in the ways in which transvestites and transsexuals love and are loved.

You can hear woven through these brief descriptions the two fundamental types of contrast that Freud saw playing out in all the transferential processes of object choosing. First, people are attracted to and aroused by an object's sexuality, which includes an object's sex and gender—maleness and masculinity, femaleness and femininity—and an object's own kind of object choice or way of being an object chosen. People are attracted to these domains as they experience them or represent them to themselves. Second, people are attracted by an object's felt capacity to satisfy narcissistic needs and anaclitic dependency needs, or (to use Freud's earlier terminology) sensual needs and affectional needs. In patriarchal societies, where women do the primary child-rearing, dependency and affectional needs have tended to be associated originally with maternal objects. So the primary anaclitic or dependency object is usually someone chosen on the model of the woman who has fed us, and a later version is chosen on the model of the man who has protected us, as Freud (1914) noted. Narcissistic needs and choices are complexly sex-specific. We love people who are like ourselves in the present tense or like we have been or like we would like to be in the future, or we choose someone who was once part of ourselves. We can observe, for example, that the intergenerational ritualized bisexualities of Melanesia or Lesbos satisfy future-oriented narcissistic needs: the same-sex sex functions as a conduit through which boys are given manly virtues by men and girls are given feminine virtues by women.

These fundamental male/female and narcisstic/anaclitic contrasts show up in the four processes of transferential object choice in the most varied combinations and are socially supported in very complex ways. For example, a man might love a boy who is male and growing into his masculinity and who resembles himself when he was the growing boy his mother (or his father) loved. "Greek love" institutionalizes a version of this possibility. A woman might love a person—male or female—who has her father's masculine qualities and looks and her mother's feminine qualities as well as her mother's typical kind of object choice, say, of a woman like herself. A man might split his love object into a woman who is chaste and supplies his affectional needs and a man who is sexual and supplies his narcissistic need to be loved by someone who is as he wishes himself to be (thus making him feel like a powerful man). So-called married bisexuality institutionalizes versions of this possibility, which is related to societal institutions promoting arrangements in which a man has a chaste wife at home and a mistress in the servant's quarters or at the bordello or down in the dark ghetto. Or, consider the man who takes pleasure in observing two women, one more masculine, one more feminine (perhaps one a stranger and one a familiar like his wife), having sex with each other, and then he has sex with both of them, sequentially, one in a more passive way, in which he experiences himself as the woman he would like to be, one in a more active way, which satisfies his narcissistic need to feel himself the man he wishes to be. Generally, group sex (including sex in Carnival situations, group sex in disguises) satisfies more than one or two desires and needs at once, as does the fixed bisexual fantasy enjoyed by many people of lying in a bed between a male figure and a female figure, simultaneously being penetrated and penetrating.

PART III: THE BISEXUAL OBJECT IN THE ANALYTIC SITUATION

In my clinical practice, I assume that one of the key stories that will be reconstructed and experienced by my patients and me in the analytic transference is the story of how the patient's objects got to be bisexual. I do not, by contrast, focus on the patient's bisexuality or homosexuality or heterosexuality—what Kinsey called "the substantives"—because I think it is a mistake to assume that the patient will be one of these, defined by the sex of his or her object (or objects). To put the matter another way: I assume that a patient's desired object will always be bisexual but not that the patient will always be bisexual or homosexual or heterosexual. The identity side evolves and fluctuates, but the prevailing type of object desired becomes clear at least in adolescence and stays constant, even if appearances are to the contrary, that is, even if a person chooses (for example) now a male object, now a female one. (I am using the phrase "object desired" to indicate that an individual may actually choose a particular person who does not meet desire criteria.)

To show how the bisexuality of the object can be revealed in an analysis, I am going to present briefly three patients in whose analyses the bisexual object emerged with particular clarity and intensity. This clarity and intensity reflected the fact, I think, that all three patients came from families in which they were one of three siblings, so their bisexual objects were composites containing traits associated with a masculine and a feminine sibling as well as with the two parental figures. That is, the objects were very thickly bisexual, and the transference was, correspondingly, very crowded, layered, composite.

The first two patients, a man and a woman, have much in common psychically. These precociously bright, highly verbal people are both characterologically quite obsessional, meticulously micromanaging their daily lives and operating as what we know in slang as "control freaks," always vying with their love objects and with rivals for control. Both have highly ambivalent attitudes toward their conservatively religious parents and toward their younger siblings.

The female patient let me know right from the beginning of her analysis the lineaments of her ideal object, the woman she was questing after. She brought along to the second session a piece of paper on which she had listed this ideal's characteristics, in the order of their importance, and it was clear that I was going to be measured by the standards in this document as all her previous lovers had been and as her previous therapist had been. Through high school and college, her lovers had been male, thereafter, female, and she identifies now as a lesbian, having felt compelled "to end my bisexual period," as she put it. However, she is also aware that her lesbianism is largely political and her fantasy life is still quite bisexual.

Physically, her ideal object is a "soft butch" with blue eyes. She imagines this person as quite masculine in bed, perhaps wearing a dildo; although she also thinks of herself as highly sexual and usually more interested in sex and more aggressive about getting it than her partners, male or female. Sexual aggressivity is what she associates with her father, a very strange man, whom the patient, consulting psychiatry textbooks, diagnoses in retrospect with Asperger's Syndrome, emphasizing his total lack of social skills or empathy. But she understands her own sexuality chiefly as, like her mother's, "needy and greedy."

The patient has a sister whom she describes as wild and promiscuous in her youth, hysterical, and a Daddy's Girl, despite the fact that the Daddy beat her and railed against her for her sinful ways, her whorishness. The brother, passive, excruciatingly sweet and nice as a child, chronically depressed in his adolescent years, was the mother's favorite. The patient had to go outside the nuclear family to be the favorite of her grandmother, and this strategy has been followed up in her later life by going to professionals of various sorts—doctors, therapists—who can be paid to be reliably there for her; if they are not, she fires them. The love supplies in this family were so short that the patient became very attacking toward her siblings, competing with them for every emotional scrap. But these competitors—a father-sister and a mother-brother—are also built into her bisexual object. Once she had a dream in which her two pets, a boy and a girl, were in two cages and a third pet, who resembled the boy pet but was younger, came along and felt excluded from the cages. A storm came up and all three pets ended up huddled together under a protective washbasin, burrowed in the ground, partially buried. There she was, in the only safety available—outside the house—with her boy pet and her girl pet.

The male patient told me at the beginning of his analysis that his unhappy love history is a history of falling for his mother. The women he is drawn toward are marked by their melancholy—they have sad, sorrowful eyes. Further, they have been damaged in bad relationships with their fathers, who were neglectful, hypercritical, unappreciative, or hurtful. He sets out to rescue the women, giving them the sensitive appreciation they never knew. Initially, the women find him wonderful, but eventually they retreat from his controlling behavior—the manifestation of his insecurity—and become attached to other men, his rivals; he suffers terribly from jealousy.

From behind the oedipal story as the patient told it to me, another eventually emerged in bits and pieces. He mentioned that as a boy he had had the fantasy of being a girl; that in high school he and some buddies had once dressed up as cheerleaders, balloons for bosoms, and had a blast; that he had recently wanted to buy a dress in order to play the part of a little girl in a community center skit. As the little girl in the skit, he said, he imagined himself sitting on his father's lap, snuggling, so happy. It became apparent that when he falls in love with the girls needing rescue from their abusive fathers, he is also falling in love with himself, the little girl with an abusive father. While they are his mother, the women he loves are bisexual objects—man and little girl.

After about a year of analysis, the patient developed an intense crush on a woman of the requisite melancholy. But for some reason, when the relationship began to heat up, he felt compelled to telephone an ex-girlfriend. This was a woman who had shocked him by flinging herself at him aggressively; she was what he called a "manhandler." Why did he do this—jeopardizing his new relationship? His associations turned toward his sister, and then toward the second sister. He made it clear that the older sister was very like his mother in her victimhood: she was very feminine, but also angry and hurt. The younger one had identified herself with his father: she was tough, critical. He discovered that he could not be with a woman who was like the mother-sister without calling in one who was like the father-sister. Looking back, he realized that a woman he had once loved had been both sisters in one—and she had had lovers of both sexes. When she showed herself to be too much like the father-sister, too much of a manhandler, too frighteningly castrating, he had had to flee her.

The male patient's object contains his mother, his father, his mother-sister and his father-sister. He loves as a boy and as a young girl. The female patient's object contains her ideal mother, her ideal father, her sister-father and her brother-mother, and her grandmother. She desires a girl who is an ideal parent and (less strongly) a boy.

The third patient I want to sketch is a woman who was attracted to men and women in her youth, turned to men and married, then turned to women and had several long relationships. She thinks of herself as bisexual while she lives as a lesbian. Her lovers, both male and female, she told me, have had in common that they are tall, beautiful and elegant, artistic and cultivated, somehow European (by birth or association); all were androgynous, but the men had traits the patient thought of as feminine, the women had traits she thought masculine. The women's masculine traits—particularly physical energy and athleticism—were connected to the patient's father; the men's feminine traits—particularly a kind of exhibitionism tempered with reaction formation, somewhat depressive—were maternal. The patient felt herself to be a composite of her father's and her mother's traits and was aware that she chose her bisexual objects on a narcissistic basis, but the love objects were, importantly, not ideal—they had to be brought into ideal condition by the patient's love. She is a mentor or promoter rather than a rescuer, thrilled when her loved ones flourish artistically. But what she has always wanted is also to be the mentored one, to have a lover who could do unto her what she does unto others.

It puzzled this patient that every now and again she would find herself drawn to a woman who was not of her dominant desired object type: the variant type was a hysteric, very unstable, very feminine and petite. The patient, who would quickly find these women frightening and exhausting and run away from them, determined in the analysis that they were reminiscent of her sister, who, as a frail youngest child, was in the mother's care and formed with the mother a symbiotic bond. The patient was attracted to a woman who was loved by the mother in a way that she herself never could be loved because she would not allow herself to be frail; that is, in the object she was attracted to a role she could not play. The patient's brother did not figure explicitly in the gallery of her objects, but the patient did involve herself as a kind of surrogate mother to his children.

The first two patients were always getting involved in struggles for power and control with their complexly constructed objects, and the transference was similarly a struggle for control. Would the analyst give love on demand? This seems to me the characteristic obsessional's question, and it is put to the analyst as the analyst is experienced as a bisexual object. The third patient struggled to allow the analyst to analyze and not to do everything herself. This was also a struggle not to be disappointed that the analyst was not everything and everybody, not the total and bisexual object, as multifaceted as the patient herself.

CONCLUSION

I hope I have convinced you of the claim I made at the outset of this paper: that the complexity and variability of human sexuality is coming to be appreciated now that the one hundred year reign of the substantives heterosexuality and homosexuality is breaking up. This breakup has come about as people have tried to understand bisexuality: (1) biological bisexuality, (2) psychological or gender bisexuality (or, one might say, bigenderality), (3) bisexuality of object choice, and (4) the newest frontier, bisexuality of the object desired/chosen. But all of these substantive uses of "bisexuality," even carefully qualified with adjectives, give way, too, as soon as they are looked into at any depth. I suggested that we are becoming accustomed to thinking of human sexuality as multisexuality. But this word, too, is just a warning not to judge the book by its cover, the human being by his or her or his/her behavior, as our experiences are richer for not being understood in categories that do not do any of us justice.

REFERENCES

Chodorow, N. (1992). Heterosexuality as a compromise formation: reflections on the psychoanalytic theory of sexual development. *Psychoanalytic Contemporary Thought* 15:267–304.

Ellis, H. (1905). *Studies in the Psychology of Sex*. New York: Random House, 1942.

Fausto-Sterling, A. (1993, March/April). The five sexes. why male and female are not enough. *The Sciences*, pp. 20–24.

Firestein, B., ed. (1996). *Bisexuality: The Psychology and Politics of an Invisible Minority*. Thousand Oaks, CA: Sage.

Freud, S. (1905). Three essays on the theory of sexuality. *Standard Edition* 7:123–245.

——— (1908). Hysterical phantasies and their relation to bisexuality. *Standard Edition* 9:155–166.

——— (1914). On narcissism: an introduction. *Standard Edition* 14:67–104.

——— (1920). The psychogenesis of a case of homosexuality in a woman. *Standard Edition* 28:145–174.

——— (1931). Female sexuality. *Standard Edition* 21:223–246.
——— (1937). Analysis terminable and interminable. *Standard Edition* 23:209–254.
Gagnon, J., and Simon, W. (1973). *Sexual Conduct: The Social Sources of Human Sexuality.* Chicago: Aldine.
Haeberle, E., and Gindorf, R., eds. (1998). *Bisexualities: The Ideology and Practice of Sexual Contact with Both Men and Women.* New York: Continuum.
Hirschfeld, M. (1926). *Gechlechtskunde.* Stuttgart: Jullius Puttmann.
Kinsey, A. (1941). Homosexuality: criteria for a hormonal explanation of the homosexual. *Journal of Clinical Endrocrinology* 1(5):424–428.
——— (1948). *Sexual Behavior in the Human Male.* Philadelphia: Saunders.
Klein, F. (1978). *The Bisexual Option.* New York: Arbor House.
Krafft-Ebing, R. von. (1886). *Psychopathia Sexualis.* New York: Bantam, 1965.
Kutchins, H., and Kirk, S. (1997). *Making Us Crazy: DSM: The Psychiatric Bible and the Creation of Mental Disorders.* New York: Free Press.
Mondimore, F. M. (1996). *The Natural History of Homosexuality.* Baltimore: Johns Hopkins University Press.
Stoller, R. (1973). Facts and fantasies: an examination of Freud's concept of bisexuality. In *Women and Analysis,* ed. J. Strouse, pp. 343–364. Boston: G. K. Hall, 1985.
——— (1985). *Presentations of Gender.* New Haven, CT: Yale University Press.
Sulloway, F. (1979). *Freud: Biologist of the Mind.* New York: Basic Books.
Ulrichs, K. M. (1864). *Forschungen uber das Rathsel der mann-mannlichen Liebe.* Leipzig: Selbsverlag der Verfassers.

9

Beyond "The Female Homosexual"

It is not news that over the decades of psychoanalysis's history, psychoanalytic investigation of female homosexuality has been relatively neglected. But, at the same time that female homosexuality was being judged relatively unimportant, a creature known as "the female homosexual" was quite remarkably pathologized; the specter of a very disturbed, father-identified, mother-fixated, narcissistic Child Amazon came to haunt the feverish case studies of analysts who were hard pressed even to imagine what their subjects did in bed.

Currently, there is a welcome surge of effort within psychoanalysis to get beyond the spectral female homosexual and to reconsider female homosexuality—or, better, homosexualities—without intent to diagnosis or cure it. This essay is intended both as a marker of the reconsideration and a contribution to it. I will make a thumbnail historical map of how "the female homosexual" came into existence, then characterize some of the efforts made over the last several decades to confront both the general topic of homosexuality and HER in particular. The revision that I want to propose and illustrate with a case vignette is designed to help open the ghetto gate for "the female homosexual"—to dissolve the walls around HER rather than to continue describing HER or even to continue critiquing descriptions of HER.

THE ORIGIN AND DEVELOPMENT OF A STEREOTYPE

"The female homosexual" was the precipitate of a history of theorizing that had two basic assumptions. First, it was assumed that the female homosexual is just that, *the* female homosexual, one and only one type, who is masculine.[1] "The female homosexual" loves women like a heterosexual man does. And, second, this single mannish type was defined essentially when she made her deviant or same-sex *sexual* object choice; this choice summed up her instinctual drive and object relations story, which was a causal or etiological story of developmental divergence.

These assumptions held through a history made up of three main moments, which are fairly distinct, although nothing once laid down about the female homosexual was ever completely eclipsed in later developments. As the picture accrued layers, however, she did became more and more pathologized, her sexual object choice more and more deviant. Correlatively, as she became more ill, the ideal of curing her—converting her to heterosexuality—became more entrenched.

In the first moment, Freud's, the female homosexual was characterized by her masculinity complex.[2] However, it is important to note that in Freud's one extended case study, the eighteen-year-old homosexual patient's masculinity complex was more a matter of identifica-

---

1. No single male homosexual type appeared. Freud and his contemporaries—notably Ferenczi—explored different types of male homosexuals, and the plurality was later taken seriously, even if a strong and early mother-bond was posited as a common element. When de Saussure (1929) made a first review of the literature on homosexuality, he noted the plural male types and then wrote about the female homosexual.

2. See Freud (1920), "The Psychogenesis of a Case of Homosexuality in a Woman." It is interesting to note that Freud himself acknowledged in his case study of the eighteen-year-old homosexual that there are "various forms of homosexuality, which, to be sure, are manifold" (p. 170), but he did not, then, go on to explore them. Recently, a collection of critical essays on this case has appeared: Lesser and Schoenberg, editors, *That Obscure Subject of Desire* (1999).

tion with her father, into which she regressed after being disappointed in her father-love, than it was of the penis envy or shocked discovery of sexual difference that Freud usually presented as the centerpiece or the bedrock of the masculinity complex. That is, her story was more an object relational story than a libidinal developmental story.

This female homosexual loved a bisexual society woman, successor to the young woman's mother, in what Freud described as a masculine manner: overestimating and idealizing, being the active lover and not the passive beloved. In Freud's later terms, it would be said that the female homosexual's Oedipus complex was negative; she did not develop securely beyond her mother-love to father-love but, rather, slipped back. However, Freud also gestured in other explanatory directions by, for example, noting that his patient's bisexual object represented her brother as well as her mother. For another example, Freud implied that female homosexuals can choose love objects on a narcissistic basis, as he had earlier argued that one type of male homosexual does when loving a boy who is like the boy his mother loved—that is, like himself as a boy.[3] But Freud did not linger over these suggestions that the female homosexual loves a composite male–female figure or that she loves as she was loved or might wish to have been loved. Nor, in his eagerness to describe the single female homosexual type, did he consider the other woman, the society lady. Since the Freud era, homosexual or bisexual women who are predominantly identified with women, who are either very little or very indistinctly masculinely identified, have been overlooked—that is, assumed not to exist.

The second moment of the female homosexual's creation, launched by the work of Ernest Jones and Melanie Klein, centered upon a defense interpretation: the female homosexual takes a flight away from her oedipal love of her father when she turns to a woman. Some theoreticians stopped at this description of flight from heterosexuality, but, as psychoanalysis shifted more toward focus on the preoedipal, the female homosexual was seen as oral-sadistic and defending first against a frightening—poisoning, devouring—preoedipal mother imago, whose fearfulness was then transferred to the second object of defense, the

---

3. Homosexual love on a narcissistic basis was first described by Freud (1908) in "Leonardo da Vinci and a Memory of His Childhood." See also the footnote added in 1905 to "Three Essays on the Theory of Sexuality" (p. 144, n 1).

216 / *Sexual and Gender Identity*

father, from whom she took flight.[4] In this version of the female homosexual, "primary femininity" or a normal maturational program aimed at heterosexuality and motherhood, was assumed, whereas Freud had assumed primary bisexuality. So this female homosexual was categorized as pathological, whereas Freud had explicitly said that his eighteen-year-old was "in no way ill," that is, she was not a psychoneurotic repressing her desires—she was acting upon them.

The third moment, which incorporated much of the developing imagery of the first two moments, was given particular spur by Helene Deutsch's *The Psychology of Women* (1944). The female homosexual became pathologically tied—even fused or merged, in her fantasy—to her preoedipal mother and did not, thus, enter into her Oedipus complex, much less fail at exiting it or become defined by defending against it. In this model, homosexuality is a psychoneurosis or even a borderline condition, not, as Freud had it, an inversion, the negative of a psychoneurosis. Primary femininity became an even more strongly held assumption, often more biologically interpreted (and this bias was used to explain how "the female homosexual" might appear at menopause, in an "involution," too).

The third phase of theorizing also produced a curious paradox: although subtypes of "the female homosexual" had been identified ever since Jones's first typology in 1927, the many subtypes now identified had no impact whatsoever on the singularity of "the female homosexual." To cite a particularly pathologizing example: in his *Homosexuality* (1978), Charles Socarides identified ten subtypes of female homosexuals, including one who is conventionally feminine in appearance and behavior, but he still spoke psychodynamically of a single female homosexual whom the psychoanalyst should set out to cure:

> The homosexual woman is in flight from men. The source of this flight is her childhood feelings of rage, hate and guilt toward her mother and a fear of merging with her. Accompanying this primary conflict are deep anxieties and aggression secondary to disappointments and rejections, both real and imagined, at the hands of the male (father). Any sexual wishes poses

---

4. See Ernest Jones (1927) and Melanie Klein (1932), where she confirms Jones's observations about female homosexuals and their oral sadism in chapters 3 and 11.

[sic] further masochistic danger. On the other hand, her conscious and unconscious conviction that her father would refuse her love, acceptance and comfort produces a state of constant impending narcissistic injury and mortification. The result of this conflict is to turn [sic] to the earliest love object, the mother, with increasing ardor. [As Deutsch had argued,] what prevents her complete regression to this primitive unity is her unconscious fear of merging with and being engulfed by the mother. [p. 134]

To a certain extent, each of these three claimants to the title "the female homosexual" can describe some homosexual women. There are female homosexuals who are arrested in or regress into a negative oedipal relationship, those who take some kind of defensive flight from heterosexuality, and those who are merged with their mothers at a preoedipal level. One limit of the models can be noted, however, by observing that there are women who have made male sexual object choices who can also be thus described—to a certain extent. Each of the models has a prefabricated, abstract quality to it; none seem to have arisen from sustained or comparative clinical observation; none were shaken by an exception or by a challenge, homosexual or heterosexual, or even by the noted existence of subtypes. All three models involve adaptations to females of thoughts about masculinity or masculine modes of loving or male homosexuality, or they presuppose conclusions arrived at simply by saying "the female homosexual differs from the female heterosexual by virtue of the sex of her object . . ." The female homosexual is either a not-a-man man (father-identified but "maimed" in Jones's formulation; "castrated" in Socarides's terms) or a not-a-woman woman.

If the present moment of going beyond "the female homosexual" is to break free of HER, if psychoanalysis is to become less reductionistic over the topic of female homosexuality, circumscribing the use of these models will be required. But more than critique of past theoretical models is needed.

STUDIES IN PREJUDICE AND PROTESTS

In the last two decades, a different kind of reconsideration of female homosexuality has been pioneered by feminist culture critics and psychoanalysts, some of them identifying as lesbians. As they have looked at "the female homosexual," they have emphasized the prejudiced social and cultural contexts in which she has appeared or been constructed, and they have included in their view the contribution of psychoanalytic theorizing to those contexts. Because the history of sexism and homophobia so enwraps the territory these critics have wanted to explore and liberate, and because psychoanalysis is so implicated theoretically and institutionally in the modern history of sexism and homophobia, the focus of this critique has been on ideology, on how ideas about homosexuality have served power—societal power generally and power within institutionalized psychoanalysis particularly. This critique points out that psychoanalysis, despite its radicality in many respects, was and remained culturally syntonic in the matter of separating out a group, the homosexuals, as though their same-sex object choices were definitive of them as persons, species characteristic.

Because Freud himself was as much concerned with instincts and their aims (and deviations of aim) as with objects (and deviations of object), and because he assumed the universality of bisexuality and saw *all* sexual object choice as a process of delimitation, he usually did not think of homosexuals as essentially different from heterosexuals. He specifically said (1905) that "Psychoanalytic research is most decidedly opposed to any attempt at separating off homosexuals from the rest of mankind as a group of special character" (p. 145, n 1).[5] But most of the succeeding theoreticians who generated "the female homosexual" did assume—or subscribe to the ideology—that a person's sexual object choice defined the person, so that after the turn of the last century it was widely presumed that with the noun "homosexual" all that needed to be said about a person engaging in same-sex sex could be said. "A homosexual" was a person whose real or true object choice was—no matter what evidence of variability might be to hand or what repressions might obscure the multiplicity of desire—same-sex and exclusively so. In a similar way, given the ideology of racism, a person with a drop of "Negro blood" was a Negro.

Drawing on the work of Michel Foucault, whose *History of Sexuality* (1980) has been the key work in propelling study of the designa-

---

5. Similarly, Freud (1905) commented: "The pathological approach to the study of inversion has been displaced by the anthropological. The merit for bringing about this change is due to Bloch (1902–3), who has laid stress on the occurrence of inversion among the civilizations of antiquity" (p. 139, n 2).

tion "a homosexual," and, correlatively, study of the modern "invention of heterosexuality,"[6] the cultural ideology critique very generally calls into question the way in which Freudian psychoanalysis has enshrined heterosexuality, genital primacy, phallocentrism, and the biologically grounded oral, anal, and phallic-genital developmental stages of Freud's libido theory, all within the category "normal." Sometimes, this postmodernist or deconstructionist critique rejects the notion of identity altogether as "essentialist," but the main thrust of the critique has been to claim—or reclaim—the multiplicitousness of sexual and gender identities and the fluidity of desire. Along with that claim go calls, taking different forms, for liberation from the socially constructed norms that theoretical normativity both articulates and buttresses.

This kind of cultural critical reconsideration grew up without direct connection to the empirical research within psychology that supported the early 1970s political program of the Gay Liberation Movement. Kinsey's work in the early 1950s set a powerful precedent for the idea that homosexuality is neither rare nor synonymous with pathology. Then in the late 1950s psychologists like Evelyn Hooker (1965) showed carefully and conclusively that psychopathology was no more prevalent among self-identified male homosexuals than it was among male heterosexuals. Such empirical work was turned into weaponry by the political activists who successfully questioned the linkage of homosexuality and pathology assumed by most psychoanalysts. Protests aimed at the inclusion of homosexuality as a pathology in the *Diagnostic and Statistical Manual of the American Psychiatric Association* were successful by the 1974 edition.[7] Eventually, in the 1980s and early 1990s, comparable empirical work was being done with lesbian and female heterosexual populations. One psychoanalyst, Martha Kirkpatrick (Kirkpatrick and Morgan 1980), for example, produced a number of

---

6. This phrase is the title of a rich history of classifications by Jonathan Katz (1995), whose bibliography is a good guide to works on the history of homosexuality and heterosexuality as classifications. Katz is very clear that it was lesbian writers like Adrienne Rich and Monique Wittig, rather than Foucault, who pioneered in questioning heterosexism.

7. This story has been told by Ronald Bayer in *Homosexuality and American Psychiatry* (1981) and more recently by Herb Kutchins and Stuart Kirk in *Making Us Crazy: DSM, The Psychiatric Bible and the Creation of Mental Disorders* (1997).

different kinds of studies showing that lesbian mothers are no different in terms of psychological health and parenting capacities than heterosexual mothers (as the children of lesbian couples are not different in terms of their gender identity development, sexual orientation, or psychological well-being than children of heterosexual couples).

It is important to note that there was quite an imbalance in the attention given to male homosexuality in comparison to female homosexuality both in the research and in the political activism of this period. For the most part, this discrepancy was a matter of sexism, both because then as now what is male commands more investigative attention generally. Also, male homosexuality—conceived as men being like women—was and is more threatening to the patriarchal social order than women being like men, and it had to be criticized first, to open the way for a more general review of homosexuality that would include women. So George Weinberg's pioneering *Society and the Healthy Homosexual* (1972), in which the word "homophobia" was first introduced, was all about men. (Similarly, the female homosexual, conceived as masculine and a competitor to males, was and is more threatening to patriarchal order than the woman she might compete for, so she had to be confronted as a stereotype before any more nuanced view of female homosexuality could emerge.)

But it was also the case that reconsideration of female homosexuality was slow to come because of internalized sexism and homophobia within the Women's Movement. In the 1970s, lesbianism was widely viewed within the Women's Movement as a threat to feminism—it was politically pathologized—and as a threat to non-lesbian feminists, many of whom feared that reconsidering female homosexuality would win them the label *homosexual*. Revisionist study of female homosexuality was carried out by lesbians, in the context of their struggle to identify the homophobia woven through the feminist battle against sexism. As the rapprochement between feminism and psychoanalysis was slowly forged over reforming the Freudian psychology of female development, it became available for supporting new approaches to female homosexuality.[8]

---

8. I cannot survey here the many contributors to this rapprochement, of which full histories are now being written: for example, Mari Jo Buhle, *Feminism and Its Discontents: A Century of Struggle with Psychoanalysis* (1998).

But female homosexuality was not a salient topic in the key feminist works of the 1970s, which launched that rapprochement between feminism and psychoanalysis, overcoming the stridently critical attitude toward psychoanalysis so powerfully argued in, for example, Kate Millett's *Sexual Politics*. Female homosexuality and Freud's case study were mentioned only a few times in Juliet Mitchell's path-breaking *Psychoanalysis and Feminism* (1975), for example, and each time in connection with how torturously complex was Freud's journey to the domain of the earliest mother–child attachment. Mitchell did not question the assumption that a female homosexual is libidinally locked in her preoedipal mother-attachment; rather, her purpose was to point out clearly that, for Freud, this was a psychological matter and not—as for the later stage two and three pathologizing Freudians—a matter of failure to achieve the biological program of "primary femininity." Jones had announced in 1935 that "the ultimate question is whether a woman is born or made," and Mitchell (1975) was concerned to show that Freud, unlike Jones, had answered "made ": "To Freud society demands of the psychological bisexuality of both sexes that one sex attain a preponderance of femininity, the other of masculinity; man and woman are *made* in culture" (p. 131, italics in original).

Common in the feminist reform of psychoanalysis in the late 1970s and 1980s is this "made in culture." There was, for example, an appreciation that focus on genital sexuality, which is of such consequence for male castration anxiety and sexual identity and for the way masculinity is constructed in our culture, obscures the multiplicitous modes of female sexual engagement. From many directions have come descriptions of differences between men and women couched in terms of differences in relational needs. Women, so this trend goes, have greater needs for emotional intimacy, connection, relatedness, than men do. They often satisfy their need in relations with other women, so there is often a "relational asymmetry" in a heterosexual couple. Some theorists, usually building on Nancy Chodorow's *The Reproduction of Mothering* (1978), which did so much to promote feminist appreciation for object relations theory, emphasized the role that mothering plays in producing the relational asymmetry, noting that men give up their relationality as they disidentify with their mothers and with mothering; thus, they are rejecting of their own needs for relatedness.

Other theorists, not connected to feminism but influenced by it, like Otto Kernberg (1977), stressed the way in which girls, making a transition from mother-love to father-love, must trust in relationality—trust the more distant father to be loving—and thus learn early to develop their capacities for emotional commitment. Boys, so this argument goes, who keep their first object, the mother, are more prone than girls to anxiety about being engulfed in this mother-relationship, drawn regressively into it, and their anxiety then extends to other relationships and to relatedness. Again, the male's move away from mother—his disidentification—is a move away from relatedness. Psychoanalytic theories of this sort, stressing differences between men and women, and also connecting up with sociological assessments that point up the differences in various spheres of social life, set the stage for reconsiderations of female homosexuality, but did not produce them because they remained primarily concerned with heterosexuality.

However, in the course of these shifts in understandings of gender and of the complexity of heterosexuality, starting in about the mid-1980s, the inadequacies of "the female homosexual" began to be announced. For example, Robert Stoller (1985) wrote: "Homosexuality, like heterosexuality, is a mix of desires, not a symptom, not a diagnosis . . . [No] single clinical picture with common underlying dynamics and etiology holds for all homosexual women . . ." (pp. 184, 185). Words like these propelled the revisioning of female homosexuality that is presently in course within psychoanalysis, which draws upon all of the currents I have noted—the new history of sexuality, empirical research supporting depathologization, and the feminist reform of Freudian views on female sexuality. But the new revisioning also has a social context that needs acknowledging: it comes during a period when the Gay and Lesbian Liberation Movement has succeeded in establishing conditions that permit lesbian lives that are not only lived openly but frequently lived with children, in family units, so that lesbians are not distinguished as "nonreproductive" so quickly in popular or psychoanalytic consciousness. "The female homosexual" was not a parent, and lesbian parenting is a challenge to many of the psychodynamic explanations of why she would never desire to be a parent. The range of motivations and meanings involved in lesbian parenting is no less extensive than that involved in heterosexual parenting, so this socially and politically sponsored change suggests to those who theorize about female homosexuals that they should not be separated off (in Freud's words, noted earlier) "as a group of special character."

The theoretical revisioning now in course also needed the presence within psychoanalysis of openly lesbian and gay analysts who insisted on making homosexuality a topic inseparable from examination of homophobia in psychoanalytic theory and also in practice and training. This growing presence of the objects of study—this presence of actual female homosexuals—among the studiers, as practioners and theorists, does not, of course, eliminate prejudice any more than the presence of women in the first six decades of the psychoanalytic movement, including the two feminist-influenced decades, eliminated sexism. But it is certainly the case—minimally—that among lesbian clinicians "the female homosexual" is known to be a stereotype, and the ideal of converting homosexuals to heterosexuality does not reign. There are now individual female homosexuals in analysis, not HER. And different clinical material comes forth from female homosexuals in analyses where relative lack of homophobia is expected or where the topic of prejudice can be explored, as it does in analyses where shared experience is assumed. This development is not, of course, a simple correlation, as I was reminded the other day when a lesbian analysand told me, with great hesitation, that she often fantasizes about men when she makes love with her girlfriend and that, assuming—not knowing—that I am lesbian, she expects me to reject her for this "politically incorrect" admission!

Official depathologization of patients came twenty-five years before changes in training curricula and criteria for admission of candidates to psychoanalytic training. Similarly, discussions at conferences and in journals of how to revise models of homosexuality—growing out of revisions of Freud's views on female sexuality—came twenty-five years before discussions of how sexism and homophobia have shaped the models needing revision. A recent anthology, *Disorienting Sexuality* (Domenici and Lesser 1995), contains papers given at a 1993 "Perspectives on Homosexuality" conference where, for the first time, the panelists included lesbian psychoanalysts who could speak from both sides of the couch, both sides of the closet door, and before and after being defined by "the female homosexual." Then in 1997 Maggie Magee and Diana Miller, both analysts, brought out their encyclopedic *Lesbian Lives: Psychoanalytic Narratives, Old and New*, which, although it surveys the whole field, focuses on the position of lesbians in psychoanalysis and in the production of psychoanalytic theory. Their plural—lesbian lives—signals that the last chapter of the singular "the female homosexual" is open.

A STORY OF INSTINCT THEORIES

For the remainder of this essay, I will work on the field of critical forces that I have been sketching: accepting the basic argument that ideas of developmental normativity understood as natural, objective, and without cultural context, serve power; benefiting from the political and institutional reform that has delinked homosexuality and psychopathology; using the feminist psychoanalytic reconsiderations of female sexuality and development generally; and comparing my own clinical work with lesbian patients to the work recently reported by colleagues. But, while learning from all these critical literatures, political practices, and clinical experiences, I will raise a particular question and add a particular developmental topic to the evolving theoretical and clinical reconsideration. I want to look again at the part of Freudian theory that has been contested most in these recent trends: the notion that there are human instinctual drives and normal—in the sense of typical—developmental stages.

Like all the critics I have been reviewing, I see it as a prejudice to define homosexuality as a deviant object choice, placing the main burden of "normal" on heterosexual object choice and then emphasizing the differences between heterosexuals and homosexuals rather than the multiplicity and variability of human sexual modes and the oscillations of object choices within individuals that Freud had recognized and that object relations theory highlights. Unlike many (but certainly not all) of the critics, I do not find it necessary, however, to give up or downplay attention to instinctual drives in order to emphasize object relations non-normatively conceived. But then the question "Which instinctual drives and how manifest?" has to come first. I want to suggest that among the many theoretical, technical, and cultural reasons why homosexuality and heterosexuality have been so difficult for psychoanalysts to consider flexibly and non-prejudicially was the lack in Freud's science, in its original forms and in its many revisions, of the instinctual drive theory that Freud almost articulated but then rejected.

Between about 1910 and 1914, Freud made a formulation of his instinct theory that featured two classes of instincts: the self-preservative ego instincts and the species reproductive sexual instincts, which he presented in shorthand as Hunger and Love. Later, in the 1920s, after several reworkings of his instinct theory, Freud attributed the function of self-preservation to the sexual instincts, calling them the life instincts, and opposing them to the death instinct, which is manifest in aggression. The life instincts he called Eros, a name which signals Freud's claim that he had discovered that the ego instincts are also of a libidinal nature in the sense that they are sexual instincts that have taken as their object the ego itself (thus he spoke of narcissistic "ego-libido") rather than investing in external objects ("object-libido").[9] The ego instincts disappeared from Freud's theory as Eros and Thanatos were installed, and ever since sex and aggression have been routinely spoken of as the fundamental human energies by psychoanalysts of quite diverse sorts—even those who question the instinctual drive theory altogether and those who do not subscribe to the notion of a death instinct as the foundation of aggression.[10]

---

9. In his short article "The Libido Theory" (1923), Freud summarized:

> It was found that the pathogenic process in dementia praecox is the withdrawal of the libido from objects and its introduction into the ego, while the clamorous symptoms of the disease arise from the vain struggle of the libido to find a pathway back to objects. It thus turned out to be possible for object-libido to change into cathexis of the ego and vice versa. Further reflection showed that this process must be presumed to occur on the largest scale and that the ego is to be regarded as a great reservoir of libido from which libido is sent out to objects and which is always ready to absorb libido flowing back from objects. Thus the instincts of self-preservation were also of a libidinal nature: they were sexual instincts which, instead of external objects, had taken the subject's own ego for an object. Clinical experience has made us familiar with people who behaved in a striking fashion as though they were in love with themselves and this perversion has been given the name narcissism. The libido of the self-preservative instincts was now described as narcissistic libido and it was recognized that a high degree of this self-love constituted the normal and primary state of things. [p. 257]

For a historical discussion of Freud's evolving theory, see Chapter 3, "The Hidden History of the Ego Instincts."

10. The possibility, which I cannot take up in this context, that there are aggressions of various sorts with their roots in frustrations of both the ego instincts and the sexual instincts, was not considered by Freud before he posited the death instinct. That frustrations of libido alone are insufficient to account for the range of clinical

In the period between 1910 and 1914, before he formulated his ideas about narcissism or ego-libido and before the Eros and Thanatos duality, Freud had the idea that the ego instincts are object related from the start. This meant from the moment when the emergent ego begins to develop the interests that both support its growth and are, eventually, under its guidance; from the moment, primordially and paradigmatically, when the baby takes interest in the mother's breast that satisfies hunger.[11] Subsequently, Freud said, the ego instincts offer the child's sexual instincts their interested evaluations of objects and the sexual instincts follow, trenching upon the original ego instinctual object relatedness. The breast, first an object of ego instinctual interest, then gives oral pleasure, meaning discharge of sexual tension. By contrast, Freud's later dual instinct scheme features a developmental line for the composite life instincts that runs from narcissism ("ego-libido") to object relations ("object-libido"), from auto-erotism to allo-erotism. In terms of pathology, this meant that arrest in (or, later, splitting in the phase of) narcissism or regression to narcissism became the mechanisms of the earliest-rooted, gravest disturbances—the psychoses. Insofar as homosexuality was construed as an object choice on a narcissistic basis, it became assimilated to this concept of pathology; that is, it became quite pathologized. As Freud himself placed more and more emphasis on the

---

and social phenomena Freud examined when he posited the death instinct seems to me quite right, but Freud left frustrations of the ego instincts out of his account. Melanie Klein highlighted envy as the primary manifestation of the death instinct, but it seems to me that raging envy is the self-preservative instinct—Hunger, at the most elementary level—frustrated.

11. See "Three Essays on the Theory of Sexuality" (1905, p. 182) and "On the Universal Tendency to Debasement in the Sphere of Love" (1912) where Freud summarizes:

> [The affectionate current] springs from the earliest years of childhood; it is formed on the basis of the interests of the self-preservative instinct and is directed to the members of the family and those who look after the child. From the beginning it carries along with it contributions from the sexual instincts—components of erotic interest—which can already be seen more or less clearly even in childhood and in any event are uncovered in neurotics by psychoanalysis later on. It corresponds to the child's primary object choice. We learn in this way that the sexual instincts find their first objects by attaching themselves to the evaluations made by the ego instincts, precisely in the way in which the first sexual satisfactions are experienced in attachment to bodily functions necessary for the preservation of life. [p. 180]

sexual instincts, both while he was formulating his ideas about ego-libido or narcissism and during his articulation in the 1920s of the Eros and Thanatos theory, he effectively closed off any inquiry into the ego instincts. The possibility that it is the sexual instincts that are originally narcissistic and the ego instincts that are originally object related was never explored, even though it flickered in theoretical half-light. Freud's notion of "self-preservation" was left very narrowly framed on the model of hunger satisfaction. He did not ask, for example, if the ego instincts have a developmental history that is not libidinal. How does the sphere of self-preservation grow beyond the hunger-and-breast stage? Doesn't the theory of signal anxiety worked out in "Inhibitions, Symptoms and Anxiety" (1926) imply that ego instinctual life grows progressively more concerned with dangers in the environment and threats to the ego's own growth and development? Isn't being-related itself—for example, as expecting and seeking care and being cared for lovingly—essential for self-preservation, as René Spitz's studies of "hospitalism" (1945) showed empirically? Freud did speak of the "need to be loved" arising in reaction to the dangers entailed by being born into dependency and helplessness.[12] But his original thoughts about self-preservation had implied that the need to be loved or the expectation of being loved is part of the instinctual endowment we bring into our uniquely long period of dependency and helplessness relative to the other animals, not a consequence of that period's experiences.

Among Freud's followers, of course, much attention has been given to "primary love" (the phrase is Sándor Ferenczi's), especially by those of the object relations tradition who agree with W. R. D. Fairbairn

---

12. See "Inhibitions, Symptoms, and Anxiety" (1926):

> The biological factor is the long time during which the young of the human species is in a condition of helplessness and dependence. Its intra-uterine existence seems to be short in comparison with that of most animals, and it is sent into the world in a less finished state. As a result, the influence of the real external world upon it is intensified and an early differentiation of the ego and the id is promoted. Moreover, the dangers of the external world have a greater importance for it, so that the value of the object which can alone protect it against them and take the place of the former intra-uterine life is enormously enhanced. The biological factor, then, establishes the earliest situations of danger and *creates the need to be loved* [italics added], which will accompany the child the rest of its life. [p. 153]

(1994) that an infant's first object relations guide its libidinal development, rather than any inborn libidinal developmental program guiding object relations. (What moves the infant to those first object relations is not clear in this conception.) "Primary love" has also been considered by those of various intersubjectivist traditions—followers of Sullivan or of Horney—who emphasize the mother–child relationship as the crucible of all development. Further, many complex means for rejecting or adjusting Freud's "primary narcissism" have appeared among those who in these different ways emphasize primary love. But the only psychoanalyst I know who has suggested recovering the distinction between sexual instincts and ego instincts by positing an ego instinctual "expectation of being loved"—indeed, an "expectation of being sweetly and indulgently loved"—is the Japanese Takeo Doi, who has described this universal expectation among the Japanese, where he thinks it shows up most clearly because it is most valued.

Doi (1971) uses the everyday Japanese word for this expectation, *amae*, and a related intransitive verb, *amaeru*, which denotes the child's drive to presume upon and seek sweet, indulgent love and care. Languages that do not have a word for the ego instinctual expectation to be loved, Doi has argued, are typical of cultures where this expectation—this dependency—is not valued, and where children are urged to achieve independence as quickly as possible. And Doi has noted in criticism of Freud that such an ego instinct would also be unlikely to find a secure place in an instinct theory that stressed active pursuit of pleasure, especially sexual pleasure, and that defined all object relations as libidinal object relations. From this critical stance, however, Doi himself tended to neglect the sexual instincts, and he has so emphasized *amae* that his psychopathology consists entirely of different types of frustrations of *amae*.

In the period between 1910 and 1914—let me recapitulate the argument I have been making so far—Freud's theory briefly opened in the direction of the possibility that Doi grasped. The context of the theory's closure seems to be the tumult of Freud's quarrel with Carl Jung who had, Freud thought, backed away from the libido theory into a vague desexualized theory about "psychic energy." Freud responded by increasing his own emphasis on libidinal development, that is, by adding "ego-libido" or narcissism and using it to explain the pathologies in which Jung specialized, the psychoses. This meant that Freud abandoned the idea that normal development in the sphere of love depends upon a harmonious intertwining of the ego instinctual "affectionate current" and "the sensual current." Or, as Freud (1916–1917) once put it: "the ego endeavors at every stage to remain in harmony with its sexual organization as it is at the time and to fit itself to it . . . [so] we may expect . . . to find a certain parallelism, a certain correspondence, between the developmental phases of the ego and the libido; indeed, a disturbance of that correspondence might provide a pathogenic factor" (p. 351).[13]

In those people without such harmony, or with a pathogenic disharmony, Freud had argued (1910), there is a splitting of the object choice into an affectional ego instinctual object and a sexual instinctual object—often, into a saintly object and a promiscuous one, an elevated one and a debased one. This is a condition that Freud, importantly, did not study in women, despite the observation he made in his case study of the eighteen-year-old homosexual woman that her love was adoring and affectionate, chaste, not sexual. (Asceticism could also be described as involving various types of splits and the condition that neither the affectional object nor the sexual one be physically engaged.)

While he outlined this splitting, Freud stated explicitly that "the affectionate current," the current of the object-related ego instincts, is the older of the two currents. But as his theory shifted during the quarrel with Jung he gave up this formulation and began to speak of the affectionate current as precipitating out of the Oedipus complex. When the Oedipus complex dissolves, so this post-Jungian formulation goes, the affectionate current consists of the relatively desexualized remains (not the precursors) of the child's sexual love of its caregiver figures.[14] In the sexual upsurge of puberty, the derivative affectionate current should be folded into the sensual current as the adolescent seeks love objects outside of the family with whom to be actually, maturely, genitally, reproductively sexual—meaning heterosexual. In this formulation affection, then, had no instinctual base; no ego instincts underlay it.

---

13. This quote, from the "Introductory Lectures," post-dates Freud's essay on narcissism, but it is typical of Freud that he continued to work with his basic contrast of sexual instincts and ego instincts long after he officially modified it.

14. See a 1920 addition to the "Three Essays" (1905): "the affectionate current comprises what remains over of the infantile efflorescence of sexuality. . ." (p. 207).

230 / *Sexual and Gender Identity*

Freud nonetheless continued to make very astute observations about the intertwining of the affectional and the sexual currents, like this one about a common pattern in heterosexual relationships (1921): "It is also very usual for directly sexual impulses, short-lived in themselves, to be transformed into a lasting and purely affectionate tie; and the consolidation of a passionate love marriage rests to a large extent upon this process" (p. 139). But without his earlier notion of ego instincts, he had no way to ground the affectionate tie—he had to see it as a transformation of sexuality, a desexualization. The consequence of this theoretical situation for the evolution of "the female homosexual" became clear when later Freudians made the observation that female homosexual relationships often follow this same pattern of consolidation, and then went on to explain it Freudianly as a desexualization, which meant as a flight from heterosexuality or as a merger with the mother.

DEVELOPMENTAL LINES: BEYOND THE STEREOTYPE

When Freud shifted toward the late Eros and Thanatos instinctual drive theory, he narrowed his concept of development. He emphasized the sexual instincts, Eros, finding the *proper object*—meaning a person of the opposite sex with whom to reproduce—rather than considering the *normal harmony* the ego instincts (the affectionate current) and the sexual instincts (the sensual current) can achieve—meaning a condition in which neither current preponderates to the detriment of the other, producing intra-instinctual conflict. Such a harmony would come about after a developmental progression in which it is typical and normal for now one and now the other instinctual drive to surge up and dominate.

Such a developmental line—let me leave Freud at this point and create this line out of the possibilities he abandoned and the possibilities suggested by recent research in child development—would show the ego instincts dominating and leading in the period of helplessness and dependency (the early preoedipal). It would then show the two instincts intensely intertwined in the second year of life (in what Freud called the anal period, or Margaret Mahler the rapprochement subphase[15]) as conscious knowledge of sexual difference is attained. The line would show the sexual instincts dominating in the oedipal period, and then the ego instincts ascending again in latency as children establish affectionate relationships outside of their immediate families, with friends, neighbors, teachers, and various kinds of ideal figures. The sexual instincts surge again in puberty, and adolescence can be viewed as the time in which harmony appears only in and through much fluctuation. Over the late adolescent and adult years, there are, in most people, continued fluctuations, for both physiological or hormonal reasons and emotional-relational reasons, as well as in reaction to external circumstances and traumata.

In adulthood, we can go on, some people seek chiefly sexual partners; some seek chiefly affectional partners; some seek both in one person, some seek both in a plurality or a series of persons; some oscillate, with a partner for one current (sex or affection) and a friend or confidante or valet or guru or mistress—same sex or opposite sex—for the other current (more or less, a *ménage à trois*). In their adulthoods, other people are tricksters or role benders or crossers (perhaps both bisexual—having *objects* of both sexes—and bifurcated along affectionate and sexual *currents*), and so forth. In late adolescence, many people, in addition, settle into a style of being predominantly affection seekers or predominantly affection givers, but some continue to fluctuate between these possibilities. Similarly, many settle into a style of being predominantly active or predominantly passive in the domain of sexuality, but some continue to fluctuate. That is, along with the bisexualisms of

---

15. In the terms that I am developing in this essay, Margaret Mahler's rapprochement subphase is a time when the sexual instincts normally begin ascendency over the ego instincts, which still dominate in the preceding "practicing" subphase. Mahler noted that the rapprochement subphase is characterized by its "ambitendency," or the child's vacillation between wanting to be close to its mother and its desire to be independent. Being close means, for example, putting toys in her lap—staking out that libidinal territory, jealously guarding her as "my own" from siblings, fathers. The earlier period is not competitive and, affectively, it is characterized by exhilaration, elation, joy in exploring the world. Mahler reads this as *libidinal* investment in the world, but it can also be interpreted as the relatively unconflicted playing out of ego instinctual self-preservative drives for development and mastery, and for the child's caring as it has been cared for.

object choice emphasized in object relations narratives, there are bifurcations along the lines of ego and sexual instinctual drives, and ambitendencies of seeking and giving, activity and passivity.

Thinking this way, too, one would also want to note that before he abandoned the ego instincts, Freud (1921) had come to the clear insight that our first step in the direction of object relations is identification, "the earliest expression of an emotional tie with another person" (p. 105). But he eventually came to assume that identifications are made with objects in their specifically *sexual* characteristics, in terms of their female or male, masculine or feminine, anatomical parts or mental characteristics—that is, with the breast as female, the penis as male, with the mother, with the father, with femininity (often as passivity or penis-receiving) or masculinity (often as activity or vagina-penetrating). This focusing of the concept of identification on physical and mental *sexual* characteristics, which leaves out of account what might be called affectional characterisitcs, is obvious in the two case studies of the post-1910–1914 period in Freud's work. The one-and-a-half year old Wolf Man (1918), during his famous primal scene, identifies with his mother and her penis-receiving state, which is, in his mind, her castrated state. There is nothing here about his identifying in the same stage of his life with a caregiver's care (or lack thereof), with the breast as a nourisher, with the caregivers as a source of (or in their lack of) warmth, safety, caring, kindness, speech and songs, play—in short, affection. In describing the eighteen-year-old female homosexual, Freud notes that she went through a latency period of associating with young mothers and caring for their babies. This seems to Freud a stage of desire to bear her father's baby from which she then regresses into love of mother substitutes, but it can be understood in addition as a period of expressing affection in identification with mothering figures who give affection—and perhaps give it more than her own mother had given it to her, especially in the period after her little rival brother was born.

In my estimation, thinking in this way elaborates the vision of a multi-line developmental scheme for female sexuality and psychology that is implied by work within the critical traditions I sketched before: a vision assuming that there are many routes to female homosexuality, or many types of female homosexuality, as there are many types of heterosexuality, some of them virtually indistinguishable from homosexuality except for the sexual partner's actual (not fantasized) anatomy.[16] Such a multi-line developmental scheme would show everybody's instinctual life and object relations involving intertwinings of the ego instincts and their interests and the sexual instincts and their cathexes, intertwinings that have normal (in the sense of typical) shifts and dominances through different developmental stages. People oscillate in their instinctual modes, not just in their object choices. To sketch again these oscillations stressing their developmental features: sexual instinctual demands tend to dominate in the oedipal period and again at the upsurge of puberty; ego instinctual interests dominate in the preoedipal and during latency, when a child is usually hungrily looking for affection, tender care, warm relatedness more than for sexual tension reduction. When the ego instinctual drives dominate, maternal—or more generally, caregiving—figures are the chief objects sought by both sexes. In latency, for example, when a child goes out into the world beyond its family, the relations she or he seeks—including the "chum" (in Sullivan's term) relations, the buddies—are figures for giving and taking affectionately, while its sexual instincts are usually muted and very autoerotically focused, masturbatory. When puberty sets in and the sexual instincts begin to dominate, there is a transitional period of powerful mixture: many boys initially take flight from their mothers and all girls and then approach again, while many girls lurch toward boys but stay, at the same time, deeply embedded in their largely affectional girl groups.

In both boys and girls, the affectionate current—to use Freud's original term—is the oldest object relationally; it remains strong in all, although it may be quite repressed, particularly in those who have been thwarted in their searches for affection or those (typically males) for whom cultural norms forbid displays of affection-need. In boys, as Freud observed, the affectionate current is not infrequently split off in puberty from the sensual current—and the boy's objects are split accordingly, one being chastely maternal, the other purely sensual. Like one of the women described below, many women are similarly

---

16. The literature now available that in some way shares this vision is vast, and, for the purpose of considering female homosexuality, it is well represented in the bibliography to Magee and Miller's *Lesbian Lives* (1997).

organized, and they have one sensual object—male or female—and one chastely maternal object—not always but often female (say, a best girlfriend and confidante, but maybe a lover, or maybe a homosexual male who can, of course, play the "girlfriend" role, too). The often remarked "bisexualism" of women is frequently, it seems to me, not (or not just) a bisexualism of sexual object choice; it is a bifurcation or split between affectional and sexual instinctual needs and expressions, or an oscillation between their respective dominances—perhaps an oscillation through different life stages, which may, then, be manifest in a bisexualism of object choice.

Many (not all) female homosexuals, I want to suggest, prefer (often consciously) to satisfy both their affectional and their sexual needs in one person—another woman—whom they imagine as having features that can satisfy both needs. They have an object relational ideal who is caregiving and sexual, which may mean maternal-and-paternal in some way, although the ways differ very much from one female homosexual to the next, and there is no "the female homosexual" in these terms any more than in the terms of previous theories. Freud's eighteen-year-old, for example, loved a woman who was both a mother-successor and reminiscent of her brother, an androgyne. This ideal of the beloved being, as one of my patients put it, "all things and everyone," is often configured with an emphasis on the affectional. But more distinguishing for certain female homosexuals is the way in which the ideal reflects an ego ideal (and the narcissistic basis of the object choice is thus an ego ideal basis): the beloved is to be affectional-and-sexual in the way that the lover herself is or wishes to be.

But a woman who has both her affectional and sexual needs focused on one object can be experienced as overwhelming or engulfing by that object (as in the case below). This is especially so if the woman who is expected or idealized to be "all things and everyone" is herself someone who splits her needs or who has suppressed one—the affectional or the sexual—dimension of herself to some degree. A woman who focuses both her affectional and her sexual needs on a man can similarly be experienced by the man as overwhelming, and a man psychically prone to splitting his object choice may be reinforced in doing so by his feeling that his partner demands "all things and everyone" of him. "The other woman" is an escape, and frequently a culturally sanctioned one, while a woman's affair, whether she is heterosexual or homosexual, is not usually thus sanctioned.

The implication for clinical work of this sketching I have been doing is that the balance of ego instinctual and sexual instinctual drives and objects in patients is foundational for understanding them—and the sex and gender of their typical objects—and should be taken into account along with the history of their identifications and relations, their rivalries, their narcissism, their character traits and formations, and so forth. To show what this therapeutic stance implies, I want to turn to a patient who could be presented as an older version of Freud's eighteen-year-old. Like Freud's patient, mine is "in no way ill"—she is not psychoneurotic, although she has neurotic traits in her character. Also, since puberty, her important loves have all been female, and she is what Freud would have called masculine, loving in the idealizing mode he called masculine. I will present her briefly, stressing what I take to be the complexity of her instinctual drive oscillations while I note the identifications, object relations, and character traits that Freud emphasized in his study. As I go, I will give some indication of her partner's make-up as well, but this, of course, is a portrait extrapolated from my patient's reports and from her transference to me and not derived from direct therapeutic work with the partner.

The social situation in which my patient lives is the one in which, as I noted, "the female homosexual" is ceasing to exist: the lesbian parenting situation. She and her lover are separated after years of a marriage-like partnership in which they had a child together and lived both in the predominantly heterosexual world and in a world—not a ghetto or even a distinct subculture, but more like an ethnic enclave—of lesbians, all professional women, quite successful in career terms, many with children. Both partners were adolescents in homophobic family milieus and then moved into situations where they could be "out" in parts of their lives but not in others. The homophobia characteristic of my patient's parents and (to a much smaller degree) her siblings was woven into her ideal of monogamous family life, and this ideal is still firmly lodged in my patient: she was ashamed not to be living up to this ideal before her marriage and she is ashamed now in her divorce. Unlike Freud's patient, mine did not challenge or taunt her parents with her homosexuality; instead, she has sought accepting, affectionate parents in other figures—including her therapist.

SCENES FROM A MARRIAGE

Alexa came to psychotherapy in extreme distress because her lover, Barbara, who is the biological mother of their preschool child, conceived by artificial insemination, seemed to be gravitating toward another woman. Eventually, over the course of the next three months, Barbara moved out of the couple's house and in with the other woman, while Alexa tried to salvage her parental relationship with the child through a joint custody agreement, which she could only hope would have something like the legal status of a joint custody agreement made by a divorcing heterosexual couple. Alexa also tried to leave a path open for Barbara to return, should Barbara come to her senses. All of the couple's family members and friends, furious with Barbara and frightened for the child, agreed that Barbara was crazy and destructive to leave Alexa, who is a generous, sensitive, honest, hard-working, attractive woman—an excellent parent and spouse. The couple's whole circle also agreed that I had the wrong one of the two in therapy, but my patient was savvy enough to tell them she thought that in some way she was repeating the unhappy history of her love choices.

And she is. On the simplest level, she explains that she is a "blue" and all her lovers have been "pinks"—this is the suburban version of "butch" and "femme"—and all have been younger than she is. Her pinks have been beautiful, but also troubled. Barbara, who is artistically talented, charming, smart, the first to be openly lesbian, has a history of turning to intelligent, powerful older women and of then being "incapable of commitment." "She never got past the passion stage," Alexa told me. Barbara's sense of herself as very alluring, her confidence in her allure, seems to amaze Alexa, who thinks of herself as, before Barbara, unattractive and incapable. As she talked about Barbara and the women Barbara has found exciting, Alexa confessed that she fears she is not really very intelligent. She wondered anxiously whether Barbara had discovered that she is really childish and lacking in the intellectual power Barbara seeks. Alexa was the first in her large family to go to college, and no one around her in childhood knew how to appreciate her abilities.

The most gifted person in Alexa's family was her father, and Alexa told me that she wants to be like him. Just before her child was conceived, while Barbara was taking fertility drugs, Alexa's father died, and she still feels a sharp grief. She hopes she made it clear to him before he died how much she adored him and emulated him. She wanted to parent as he fathered when he was at his best, and she wanted to be "the provider" in her partnership. His death seems to have increased the intensity of her identification, which came about originally in the context of her disappointed oedipal love of him. She has powerful memories of herself as an elementary school girl waiting for him to come home from work and play with her, his youngest child, "the baby."

The father was an Irish-American working-class man who had struggled to support Alexa, her older siblings, and his wife, who, for all of Alexa's life, was in and out of hospitals with a condition that progressively crippled her—although she outlived her husband and, despite her physical frailty, was "tough and in possession of every one of her marbles" until she died, two years into the psychotherapy. The father worked long hours, but when he came home he was affectionate with his children and fascinating to them because he was an accomplished amateur artist who, without any formal training, could produce remarkably complex compositions. My patient felt stupid in comparison to him. But Alexa's father was also the family disciplinarian, and he could chastise his children ferociously, beating them with his belt, blowing up over details. As a child, Alexa was afraid of him, and also afraid that he didn't like her because she had no artistic talents and was distinguished by her earnestness more than any imagination. So she thought, and so she thinks again now in relation to Barbara. Generally, in this large family, however, the message was: Do not be outstanding, do not shine, be reliable and inconspicuous. The father, who had little opportunity to show his talents, never celebrated his children, and neither did the mother. She, in fact, constantly compared her children unfavorably to their cousins. Interestingly, all of the siblings, reacting against the parental policy, are avid celebrators of their own children, proud promoters.

In her own career, Alexa, a lawyer, has been able to be successful as second in command to a gifted male lawyer who is often emotionally abusive to his workers, has little heart, little warmth—she supplies his lack. This lawyer is like Alexa's father: he blows up and chastises people, so that Alexa has to intervene and "get around the bad to bring out the best in him." But the boss is also a male version of Alexa's mother, whom she describes as "a matriarch" with tremendous influence over her family. In Alexa's mind's eye, when her mother entered a room, the family became, as if by magic, organized and efficient, like troops before their general. Both of Alexa's parents were mixtures: generous caregivers sometimes and harsh lawgivers at other times. But her emotional barometer registered her mother as cold and her father warm. In a rare moment of confidence, the mother once confessed to Alexa that her husband was "kind beyond belief," "much too good for me," and that she had never been able to show her husband the affection or gratitude he deserved. Alexa got the message that behind her mother's lack of demonstrativenes there was real appreciation, and maybe it could be elicited.

In her parental home, Alexa functioned as her father's substitute or second in command in the role of kind caregiver to the mother. The father worshiped his wife, and my patient admires his attitude completely. But she was concerned to make it clear to me that as a girl she had been "all organized around Mother," who seemed to her always about to leave home and go to the hospital, maybe to die. In her anxiety about her mother, Alexa saw her father as not able to make the mother better, so she was inhibited in her appreciation of his fine qualities, and she regrets this. Her mother was, she felt, formidable in her capacity to run the household, even while ill, but she was also without what Alexa calls "passion": she never returned the father's ardor when he kissed her goodbye each morning on his way to work. As her relationship with Barbara deteriorated, Alexa identified more and more with her father as an unrequited lover, a thwarted romantic, not just a man whose kindness was not acknowledged.

Alexa found her parents' morning goodbye scene pathetic. All through her childhood, while she had a bedroom next to the parental one, she listened in regularly on their intimacy, but she never heard them making love. She was not a witness to a primal scene, but she was certainly deeply influenced by its absence, by the sexual blank in the parents' lives. She thought that she, like her mother, was passionless; after all, as a girl she had felt nothing for boys and later had had only brief, perfunctory affairs with men. Even when she did discover the pleasures of loving women she would enjoy bursts of passion and then grow sexually remote. She said " I always liked the cuddling part of it, the showing affection," without being able to mention her need for receiving affection or to consider her sexual needs. The women she got involved with were needy and, for nearly ten years, she lived with and supported one who was clinically depressed and "emotionally abusive," exploitative. Alexa had let herself be used, and had needed a psychotherapist then to help her protect herself against that lover's threat to expose their closeted relationship. But when she got together with Barbara, who had flatteringly courted her, taking the sexual initiative and putting Alexa in the conventionally feminine role, Alexa had come to feel that she was passionate and would remain so—that she was not only normal, healed, but powerful—and she then worshiped Barbara, indulged her. She had flourished as she came out to her siblings and in her workplace and as she took on the public complexities of lesbian parenting.

In this role of inspirer of passion, Barbara was not like Alexa's mother; she was, on the contrary, romantic, fascinating, smart, artistic—like the father. But, in a more basic way, Barbara *was* like the mother: she was a woman who was able to get her way, issuing commands, being imperious—even narcissistically privileged—and she could be cold and emotionally unavailable, especially when she was not obeyed. Barbara had clearly intimidated her own family, making her siblings feel that if they crossed her she would ice them out. One of Barbara's sisters had told Alexa, however, that she had sometimes been surprised to encounter "another Barbara" inside the imperious one, and this kinder, sweeter one was the woman Alexa longed for—consciously. This was the father-Barbara, the predominantly affectional object, which became sexualized—in a sense, heterosexualized. Unconsciously, she was also drawn to the harsher ruler-of-the-household. Barbara herself had once confessed to Alexa that she was "double," that she had "demons inside" and sometimes hated everybody; she even gave her demonic self a proper name.

True to her most familiar pattern, Alexa had been the caregiver for Barbara while Barbara struggled through trying to get pregnant and then through periods of bed rest and illnesses during and after her pregnancy. Usually, Alexa is a giver of affection, not a receiver; but she is not a sexual initiator, she responded when Barbara courted her, and she made no effort to try to woo Barbara back sexually—she felt crushed and defeated, cast back into her sense of herself as unattractive. Like her father, she hovers around, afraid of doing the wrong thing, afraid, when Barbara began to show interest in the other woman, "that the other shoe is going to drop," and terrified that she would do something to produce that result, to alienate Barbara. This pattern continued even after Barbara left, as Alexa was for months and months afraid she would precipitate by some mistake the definitive break—the death of the relationship being analogous to her mother's death. After her mother did die, Alexa began to be able to realize that Barbara was not coming back.

There is a great deal of fluctuating of identifications and desires in Alexa's story, but her operation in the mode of blind devotion and idealization is a constant. Her expectation to be loved by her mother was quite thwarted, but she does not allow herself to admit this very often or very far; she has adopted her father's view of the mother—"she could do no wrong"—and her father's mode of being affectionate, as she had adopted her father as the supplier of the affection she could not get from her mother. Beneath the worshiping level, she expected rejection from her mother and she feared rejection—until later in her life—from her father. It was a great relief to my patient when she could finally present herself to her mother as a family person, a producer of grandchildren like—as nearly as possible—all the rest of her siblings, a capable provider like her father. Producing a family was the medium in which my patient felt that she had at last secured her family's affection. But, importantly, she was never able to talk about her lesbianism with her mother, who was in all ways Catholic-puritanical and contemptuous of those she called "queers." "Why should I hurt her? There's no need for her to know." She took her child to visit her mother, but did not speak about her home life; they had a pact of silence and shame. Alexa feels that she "got mothering supplies" from an aunt, older by fifteen years, whom she describes as the one who took over all tasks like talking about sex, and this woman is Alexa's family confidante in the matter of her lesbianism. The successor to her father is her favorite older brother, to whom Barbara bears a certain physical resemblance. She enjoys telling me funny anecdotes about both of these accepting parental figures, drawing me into their circle in her mind.

I hear in Alexa's story as she tells it a long struggle to find affection—from the father when it was unavailable from the mother, from the father's gentle mode when it was unavailable in his angry, punishing mode, from the substitute mother, from the kind brother, from me. Like so many affection-starved people, she cast herself as the affection-giver: her hope was to get through giving, without ever appearing grasping—eventually, without even being able to identify her own need for affection. She delayed her own sexual life, deferred it, as though having accepted the idea that sexuality would disturb the peace; that only affection binds; that positioning yourself for not competing, not having rivals, not being a winner or outstanding, is the only way to keep everyone alive and stable. My patient fears she is "a doormat," and she laments that when her lover drew away she had no power—no sexual power—to win her back. She says, correctly, of Barbara that Barbara needs both a reliable, sensitive person and someone for novelty, for not-settling down—and that is the other woman. Barbara loves in the way Freud thought typical of men: she has a good, caregiving "man" and one for whom she can be more of a sexual object. She told Alexa, quite cruelly, that the other woman gives her expensive presents "for being good in bed." "When something goes wrong," Alexa sighs, "Barbara will come to me for help." Barbara, that is, sensed that Alexa is a "saint" and that she needs this saint to be there while she goes off with the unsaintly other (although it would not be surprising if the other woman is converted over time into a caregiver figure and Barbara looks elsewhere for sex and novelty).

Slowly, as we worked along, with me offering a good deal of support to Alexa in her parenting as Barbara became more and more overwhelmed by her child's demands, Alexa came to the realization that her lover was very ambivalent about being a mother. Barbara wanted to be able to love her child but "was not bonded" (as my patient put it). She had suspected this when the child was born and Barbara had been so unaffectionate. But Alexa's realization crystalized when I pointed out that Barbara had proposed a clause for their joint custody agreement that stipulated that the child could, upon reaching a certain age, make a decision about which of the parents to live with. This was exactly how old Barbara had been when she had quit her parental home to live with relatives, leaving behind an alcoholic and abusive father and a mother who had so collapsed under her husband's regime that she required her daughter's parenting rather than being able to do any parenting herself. Barbara, too, was a child of thwarted expectation to be loved, and the woman for whom she left my patient is notorious in their circle for being unrelated, self-absorbed, driven, narcissistic, and not interested in children. Barbara told Alexa that she had felt "trapped" in her marriage-like relation with Alexa—Alexa was too good for her, and expected too much of her. She really does not want so much to have a child as to be a child, but she keeps going to women who cannot really love her, as her father in his self-absorption could not and her mother in her collapse could not. Alexa was an affectional supplier—a good, loving father-mother—while the other woman is for the sexual repetition compulsion.

Alexa is a woman driven most strongly by her "affectionate current," which has become manifest, through identifications, as a current interested in rescuing—in the paternal manner. Her expectation to receive affection has been muted in the reversal, in the commitment to giving affection. She had hoped for affection from and then tried to give it—as she had before—to a woman who was struggling to be able to give or receive affection, a woman whose affection needs were also very great but whose sexual choice pattern dominated. In many respects, Alexa's relationship repeated the basic pattern of her parents' marriage: she made herself the adoring servant of a matriarch, a capable but self-enclosed woman. Recently, when Alexa gathered up her courage to accept an invitation from a new woman, one of her oldest friends very insightfully cautioned, "Be sure this time you find a kind one." Barbara, on the other hand, asked Alexa if the new woman was "a bitch like me" and speculated that Alexa really needed someone bitchy. Each commentator could see part of Alexa's pattern: the beloved must be both an affectionate father and a bitchy mother who—it can be hoped—has hidden dimensions of warmth.

Alexa could not begin to detach herself from Barbara until she let her anger and disappointment surface in the psychotherapy. It was particularly difficult for her to express her jealousy of the other woman, for she deemed jealousy a petty emotion and was chagrined to be feeling it. Her dream life let her know: she dreamed repeatedly of Barbara and the other woman doing things together or entering her house together, acting presumptuously. In one dream, she was with her favorite older brother, borrowing his strength, but also experiencing him as paternal in the sense that he, like the father and like she herself, cannot assert himself with women. Together, she and her brother used a truck to try to pull her child out of a swamp while, off in the distance, Barbara was driving away with the other woman in a sports car. The dreams always show Alexa helpless to do anything—stuck—but they also show her full of the rage she would not admit to in waking life. As she considered her dream images of Barbara, Alexa was finally able to say, "She wants everything, to have her cake and eat it, to have me as a babysitter while she plays around." She admitted that Barbara would never come back when she was able to say that she did not want her to because "she would come in my house and try to make me a slave."

It was very difficult for Alexa to show me herself in a rage, herself critical of Barbara, herself jealous, herself with angry feelings about her mother. She wanted me to have a good impression of her in her loyalty and constancy, and whenever she "lost it" and wept she was terrifically embarrassed. She feared she was slow to figure things out and she thought I must think, as all her friends did, that she was "slow to get real" about Barbara. She did not want to disturb me, to let the other shoe drop in front of me, for her deepest fear was that her mother would die if she did not show constant kindness and keep the good-girl house rules perfectly. Over time, she has shifted, and, as she has gotten accustomed to my acceptance of her in her less than perfect control and in her lesbianism, she expresses more directly her neediness; the transference is predominantly on the affectional channel—it is, so to speak, homoaffectional. What this feels like is that she is allowing herself to expect from me the affection she had hoped for from her mother, admired in her father, sometimes found in her lost lover, and erotized in both her lover and her father. She can joke with me now, laughing at herself as "coming out," this time "as foolish, like any other human being." She says of the woman who wants to date her—a woman with a child near the age of Alexa's child: "Now, if she wants me to be my father for her or for her child, I'll have to say 'been there, done that.' I'll see if I can explain to her that I'm paying you to help me work on letting her pay the check at the restaurant!"

This work, which is about being able to receive nurture, is not the work that "the female homosexual" did with her psychoanalysts at any time in her history. But it is an example of the kind of work that can happen when SHE does not overshadow a female homosexual in psychoanalysis.

REFERENCES

Bayer, R. (1981). *Homosexuality and American Psychiatry*. New York: Basic Books.
Buhle, M. J. (1998). *Feminism and Its Discontents. A Century of Struggle with Psychoanalysis*. Cambridge, MA: Harvard University Press.
Chodorow, N. (1978). *The Reproduction of Mothering*. Berkeley: University of California Press.
——— (1992). Heterosexuality as a compromise formation. *Psychoanalysis and Contemporary Thought* 15(3):267–304.
De Saussure, R. (1929). Homosexual fixations in neurotic women, trans. H. F. Bernays, In *Homosexuality*, ed. C. Socarides, pp. 547–601. New York: Aronson, 1978.
Deutsch, H. (1944). *The Psychology of Women*, 2 vols. New York: Grune & Stratton.
Doi, T. (1971). *The Anatomy of Dependence*. New York: Kodansha, 1973.
Domenici, T., and Lesser, R. (1995). *Disorienting Sexuality: Psychoanalytic Reappraisals of Sexual Identities*. New York: Routledge.
Fairbairn, W. R. D. (1994), *From Instinct to Self: Selected Papers of W. R. D. Fairbairn*, 2 vols., ed. D. Scharff and E. Birtles. Northvale, NJ: Aronson.
Foucault, M. (1980). *The History of Sexuality*. New York: Vintage.
Freud, S. (1905). Three essays on the theory of sexuality. *Standard Edition* 7:125–243.
——— (1910). A special type of object choice made by men. *Standard Edition* 11: 163–176.
——— (1912). On the universal tendency to debasement in the sphere of love. *Standard Edition* 11:177–190.
——— (1916–1917). Introductory lectures on psychoanalysis. *Standard Edition* 15/16.
——— (1918). From the history of an infantile neurosis. *Standard Edition* 17:3–125.
——— (1920). The psychogenesis of a case of homosexuality in a woman. *Standard Edition* 18:145–172.
——— (1921). Group psychology and the analysis of the ego. *Standard Edition* 18:67–143.
——— (1923). Two encyclopedia articles: the libido theory. *Standard Edition* 18:255–259.

——— (1926). Inhibitions, symptoms, and anxiety. *Standard Edition* 20:77–175.
Hooker, E. (1965). Male homosexuals and their "worlds." In *Sexual Inversion*, ed. J. Marmour, pp. 83–107. New York: Basic Books.
Jones, E. (1927). The early development of female sexuality. In *Papers on Psychoanalysis*, 5th ed. Baltimore: Williams & Wilkins.
——— (1935). Early female sexuality. In *Papers on Psychoanalysis*, 5th ed., n.p. Baltimore: Williams & Wilkins.
Katz, J. N. (1995). *The Invention of Heterosexuality*. New York: Dutton.
Kernberg, O. (1977). Boundaries and structure in love relations. *Journal of the American Psychoanalytic Association* 25(1):81–114.
Kinsey, A., Pomeroy, W. B., and Martin, C. E. (1948). *Sexual Behavior in the Human Male*. Philadelphia: Saunders.
Kirkpatrick, M., and Morgan, C. (1980). Psychodynamic psychotherapy of female homosexuality. In *Homosexual Behavior*, ed. J. Marmor. New York: Basic Books.
Klein, M. (1932). *The Psychoanalysis of Children*. New York: Delta, 1975.
Kutchins, H., and Kirk, S. (1997). *Making Us Crazy: DSM, the Psychiatric Bible and the Creation of Mental Disorders*. New York: Free Press.
Lesser, R., and Schoenberg, E. (1999). *That Obscure Subject of Desire: Freud's Female Homosexual Revisited*. New York: Routledge.
Magee, M., and Miller, D. (1997). *Lesbian Lives: Psychoanalytic Narratives, Old and New*. Hillsdale, NJ: Analytic Press.
Mahler, M., Pine, F., and Bergman, A. (1975). *The Psychological Birth of the Human Infant*. New York: Basic Books.
Millett, K. (1970). *Sexual Politics*. New York: Doubleday.
Mitchell, J. (1975). *Psychoanalysis and Feminism*. New York: Vintage.
Socarides, C. (1978). *Homosexuality*. New York: Aronson.
Sptiz, R. (1945). Hospitalism. In *René Spitz: Dialogues from Infancy: Selected Papers*, ed. R. Emde. New York: International Universities Press, 1983.
Stoller, R. (1985). *Observing the Erotic Imagination*. New Haven, CT: Yale University Press.
Weinberg, G. (1972). *Society and the Healthy Homosexual*. New York: St. Martin's.

PART III

CHARACTER THEORY AND ITS APPLICATIONS

10

The Characters of Violence

VIOLENCE NOW

As the turn of the millennium approached, Americans were asking all the questions about violence that had been urgent since the 1960s, when our streets flowed over with race war and antiwar protests, when the daily coverage from Vietnam was punctuated with assassination footage. Social scientific literatures on violence had exploded right along with the violence back then, and the frame of reference was so shared that Hannah Arendt had published a book in 1970 called *On Violence* and no subtitle was needed to explain what violence she was addressing. For the next two decades, questions about why we are such a violent people were repeated, while our attention focused not so much on war and revolution—political violence—as on our homicide rate (so much higher than that of any European nation), the frightening statistics on the spousal battering and child abuse among us, our film industry's anything goes attitudes, our incivility. A new question became pressing as well, to which experts and pundits and op-editorialists flocked starting in the early 1990s: Why are children going to school with knives, guns, even bombs to assault their classmates, their teachers? Why do we have so many juvenile criminals? Columbine High School galvanized us. Even the usually unpolitical American Psychoanalytic Association made a "position statement" on violence in May 2000 that referred to the "crisis of violence in our country." And, as is characteristic of our reactive social science industry, government funding for violence research was on the rise. We needed solutions, interventions, quickly!

Since September 11, 2001, it has hardly been possible in America to speak of any violence except the terrorist violence perpetrated against us in New York and in Washington, DC on that horrifying day. But I think it is important, nonetheless, not to lose the thread of attention to our own violence that the "Attack on America" so overshadowed, not least because there are many clues in it to the way in which the American government has responded to the terrorist attack and to the way in which the vast majority of the American people has supported the government in its "war on terror."

In the millennial year, when George W. Bush was running for President, both he and his Democratic Party opponents made a major theme out of juvenile violence in America. At that moment, juvenile homicide and most other juvenile crimes had actually decreased nationally, and deaths in schools were less than half what they were in 1993. Young people were, overall, "at less risk of participating in violence than any time in a generation," as *The Nation* noted editorially in 2000. But, nonetheless, the election campaign whipped up fear about "the culture of carnage surrounding our children" that is "turning some of them into killers," as Joseph Lieberman, the Democratic Party vice-presidential candidate said, evoking a common image of a pollution of violence that is seeping into people, like environmental pollution. This image was meant to justify putting constraints on the pollution that comes from the entertainment industry, in order to protect our children—and to protect us from our children.

In this pre-September 11th anti-violence rhetoric, which, as I will note again in a moment, had a very obsessional quality to it, were present all of the many ways in which Americans have typically misposed their questions about violence and reached for simple answers to them. We have long felt compelled to talk about a single thing: violence. The American Psychoanalytic Association statement, for example, contained the sentence "Violence is a major public health issue." And we have felt compelled to find a single reason, a single cause for this single thing, violence, a cause that will be either located in our nature or supplied by our nurture—an either/or of amazing persistence. The single cause is always referred to as "the root of violence," because, of course, if there is a root that can be named and located it can also be torn out, extirpated. The hope is clearest in the recurrent search for a genetic root to violence, a quest which, like the quest for a "homosexuality gene," ignores all that is known about how complex human behavior is. The metaphor means we must find a tangible root for which a procedure of uprooting can be designed.

Along with the "violence gene" research, there were, I think, three other major types of "root of violence" research being funded and widely reported before September 11th, when attention shifted to violence inflicted upon us.[1] As Robin Karr-Morse and Meredith Wiley (1997) have shown in *Ghosts from the Nursery: Tracing the Roots of Violence*, there is neuroscientific research concentrating on all kinds of childhood traumas that have effects on children's brains, which, in turn, make affect regulation nearly impossible for them: head injuries, including from child abuse, environmental toxins, and so forth. Secondly, various sociological projects concentrate on all the ways in which violence breeds violence, or in which violence is intergenerationally transmitted. "Risk factors" are weighed. One criminologist, for example, has very intricately mapped a process he calls "violentization," a developmental line along which a child becomes violently molded and shaped for violent behavior.[2] And, finally, evolutionary psychologists are suggesting that violence is our legacy from the great apes, and specifically from the "demonic males" among them who gathered in "small, self-perpetuating,

---

[1]. See the recent summary of current research in *Science* (2000).

[2]. See Richard Rhodes (1999), who tells the story of the work of criminologist Lonnie Athens, but insists that Athens is a maverick among social scientists, whereas his work is, it seems to me, not at all incompatible with psychoanalytic insights about the intergenerational transmission of trauma and violence, with which both Athens and Rhodes are apparently quite unfamiliar.

self-aggrandizing bands" for the paradigmatic acts of intra-group violence (Wrangham and Peterson 1996, p. 248).

These four types of research have much to teach us, but they definitely perpetuate simplifications. They ignore the many forms of violence, serving many functions, as they ignore the complex interplay of nature and nurture in any given form.[3] Similarly, the research focuses simply on a group, those who have committed violent crimes (especially very violent crimes, especially homicide and rape), and then makes inferences about violence in general or in any specific form from this construction, "the violent ones." Further, within this focus, given that images of children and adolescents wielding lethal weapons were so salient in our current national consciousness of violence, it was not surprising that research on violent children and delinquent adolescents was growing as fast or faster than any other kind, as research on people involved in political violence—student rebels, terrorists, revolutionaries—did in the 1960s. And it was even thought, as an FBI report showed, that "the violent ones" among adolescents could be identified—some would use the word "profiled"—before they

---

3. First, there is the extra-species violence that all animals engage in to feed themselves, and the inter-species violence that they all engage in as part of mating. Then there is the inter-species violence that only humans and a very few primates engage in, which has been taken for granted through much of human history and has only been considered abnormal or pathological recently. (Child abuse, for example, has only recently been considered abuse and not the right of parents and other adult disciplinarians.) There are many degrees of violence and types of violent acts, running from a punch right on up to genocide and the specter of species destruction from weapons of violence capable of eliminating even the perpetrators, an extreme which was novel to the twentieth century. There are many locations of violence: in the private sphere—domestic violence; in unregulated or extralegal public spheres; in regulated public spaces, under the rule of governments, which have their own agencies of violence like police and militaries. There are many types of criminal violence and some types for which legal exceptions are made, like violence in self-defense or violence by reason of insanity. There is violence in fantasy or in art and violence in action; impulsive violence and premeditated or meditated violence. Different kinds of violence are possible at different stages of a life-course, from childhood through adulthood. Different kinds of people—say, in characterological terms—and different kinds of social or cultural groups engage in different kinds of violence. Finally, there are many motives and functions for the violences of these many kinds and appearances.

make it into the criminal justice system. The corollary now in public attention is the literature that purports to describe "the terrorist," a young male who resembles in many respects the delinquent American adolescents who were "the violent ones" before September 11th. And terrorism is something we have to define in such a way that we can extirpate it, root and branch.

CLINICAL VIGNETTES: OBJECT CHOICE FOR VIOLENCE

Bearing in mind these approaches that focus on "the violent ones" and work backward reconstructively toward roots of their behaviors, and also bearing in mind the contexts in which the approaches have been advanced (or revisited)—the contexts in which "the violent ones" begin as children and grow up into the full form—let me consider now what psychoanalytic clinical work and theory can offer. To begin negatively, I will suggest that psychoanalytic inquiry ought to avoid conceptualizing violence or violent deeds as the endpoint of a process, like the leaves of a plant that has grown up from "the roots of violence," for this conceptualization blocks questions about whether the violence or violences serve some function other than expression of the designated roots, completion of the process.

Let me continue by going to my research lab—my consulting room—and considering three patients. None of these three is violent in deeds, but all three have persistent and repetitive violent fantasies, as all three frequently report very violent dreams. They have in common that they tell me often how they would like to kill this or that person. So, they are not "the violent ones," but I assume that their dreams and fantasies are not very different in content from those who are less able or willing to keep themselves from acting on their images. However, I think it is noteworthy that my patients have not to any great degree *consciously* connected up their images with images existing in their sociocultural surrounds and received, thereby, social sanctioning of their prejudices and violence; on the contrary, they are consciously pacifistic, anti-prejudice people, firmly defended (often by reaction formation) against associating with violent people or violence. In their conscious minds, they abhor the very prejudices that their images and associated violences resemble, so they consciously inhibit themselves.[4] Their violence is, as it were, private, mental, although their images of their victims resemble those available in common social prejudices.

First a woman, extremely bright, a professional who spends her days assessing and helping children, told me at the beginning of our work that revealing her sexual fantasies would be the hardest part of what she knew she had to do in order to figure out why she gets so depressed, with suicidal thoughts, and why she has to engage in so many obsessional actions, especially ones involving scheduling her time, doing her laundry, and managing her money. Like her dreams, her fantasies, she told me, are violent, full of mutilated bodies, shooting scenes, people getting torn apart by wild animals. Very ashamed, she confessed that all through her adolescence she had attacked her two younger siblings in what she now describes as "a sexual manner." Her current partner has complained that she is sometimes too rough in bed. She bites, and she has said bitingly mean things. Why does she want to do this? she begs me to explain. The only thing harder for her to talk about, she said later, is religion and that's because, even though she has extricated herself from the fundamentalist milieu in which she grew up, she fears that she still has that harsh, punitive mentality in her, and that it will come out in her relationships, that she will punish with a terrible swift sword someone she loves. Certainly, violence was normal in her house—her father beat her on her bare buttocks with a belt or a yardstick for any infraction, her mother threatened her with God's wrath. Now she is "a pacifist." But, then, she tells me, she gets frightened and imagines that everyone is "trying to get a piece" of her—everyone wants her time, her care, her money So she has to guard herself constantly against being intruded upon and "sucked dry." The image that guides her violent thoughts is "everyone is a bloodsucker." Ultimately, she finally tells me, she wants anybody who tries to take advantage of her time or her money "to disappear." She wants them cleaned out.

Second, there is a woman, characterologically hysterical, with a great deal of anxiety, who, despite her anxiety, is enormously capable

---

4. The phenomenon of inhibition of violence is of great importance, but I cannot take it up in this essay.

and productive, charming and sensitive. But sometimes too sensitive, she notes, for her own good, and too given to making dramas all the time, getting herself and others into uproars, anxieties. She tells me one day that, once again, she has had one of her torture dreams. A wounded man was brought in on a stretcher by a group of medics. They were going to try to save his life, but then they turned on him, and they were going to torture him with their scapels, kill him. She wanted to go down and help the man, but she didn't, because it was too dangerous, the medics were so menacing, and also—this was the part of the dream that filled her with horror—because she really wanted the man to be hurt. She would like to have cut him up herself. Why does she keep having these dreams in which she wants to torture? Can she be so angry with her wonderful, larger-than-life father, a war hero, who was, as she always says, "the love of my life"? She had been so angry that he was an alcoholic; that he kept having heart attacks and deteriorating, becoming a terrible burden for her; that he died and left her alone with her anxious, clinging mother and with his other children, a group of crazy half-siblings who were old enough to be her parents. Slowly, over many months, with much resistance, she told me the two types of fantasies she built up as a child to compensate herself for her sense of powerlessness to help her beloved father. Both fantasies involve complex identifications with racial "others" who overcome white people. In one type, she is a great (male) Indian warrior who triumphs over all his enemies, winning tremendous adulation for skill with knives and spears in hand-to-hand combat. In the second type, she is an Arabic princess who gets to be loved by a king, and who is more able than any other woman to win men, to get power over any man who tries to get power over her. In both versions, her enemies are the bad ones, and this projection of her own badness and her father's badness onto them is key to what her violence against them does for her. They are strong white people who will be cut down and humiliated, while she gets her father—in an idealized form.

Third is a man who, although he has many obsessional features, is a narcissistic character. Some days, he knows himself to be better than all the people around him—smarter, more talented; other days, he feels terrible about himself, thinking he has been ruined by his harsh, perfectionistic parents. During a recent session, he told me about spending the evening before with a new love interest, a woman who excites him tremendously but also baffles him and hurts him with her remoteness, her coldness. She can be so enchanting, he sighed, but she has "this unavailable quality." Maybe, he speculated, her harshness comes from her relationship with her father, who abused her verbally and physically, who was brutalizing. Our thoughts went to his pattern of choosing women who have been hurt by their critical fathers, as he has been by his mercilessly critical father. Narcissistically, he loves himself in them. After a long pause, he said that he needed to tell me something awful about the evening. Shameful. They were in the kitchen cutting up vegetables for a ratatouille when she turned away from him and suddenly an image flashed before his eyes of himself plunging the knife he was using into her back, deep, between her shoulder blades, blood gushing from the wound. The really awful thing, he said, crying, is that this very image has jumped into his mind with other women, in other kitchens. In fact, with all the women he has dated. "I feel like a murderer just telling you this. I know it's about being with my mother in our kitchen, and how angry I am at her for rejecting me. Or for loving me sometimes and rejecting me. Or whatever it was that she did that made me feel so goddamn weak." His image of the woman he stabs is "women—they all betray and abandon." This is the sexism of a man who supports feminism conscientiously and well.

The obsessional woman wants to eliminate from her life all the people who creep in and threaten to steal her time, her money, suck her dry. The hysterical woman wants to humiliate all rivals for her father's love and be able to idealize him, assigning his disappointing qualities to others. The narcissistic man wants to wield phallic control over his girlfriends, whom he experiences as phallic women who have control over him, so he fantasizes cutting the women down, cutting them off.

When I consider these patients—and others—and consider at the same time the psychoanalytic literature on violence, one feature common to all kinds and degrees of violence emerges. This is not a common root or ultimate cause; it is a feature, a mechanism. No matter whether just fantasized or enacted, violence against people (or against people indirectly, representatively, in the medium of violence against institutions or things or nonhuman creatures) seems to me to be always aimed at a target who is felt by the perpetrator to be a member of a group previously constructed in the perpetrator's mind. Or, to put the matter another way, the violence expresses a prejudice in the most literal sense of the word, a prejudgment. Even with violence that looks like it could be described with words like impulsive or reactive or unpremeditated, the perpetrator is always carrying prefabricated images in his or her mind of hated enemies, dangerous people, hurtful people, destructive people, disappointing people, people who are different, and the one or ones against whom the perpetrator acts or fantasizes acting is *one of them*, part of that group. Unlike objects of love and of sexual desire, which are, I think developmentally earlier, objects of violence are not individual, they are "them." We have little motivation to generalize or make group formations out of our experiences of sex and love satisfaction, out of our happiness; our prejudices are formed mostly on the basis of experiences of frustration or rejection; they are negative images, composites, generalizations that anticipate future frustrations that will be like past frustrations.

Now this claim brings me immediately onto the territory of theory of violence and aggression, not to mention theory of object relations and object choice. I am assuming that as their instinctual drives for connection (affectional or sexual) are frustrated, people—initially, as children, but over their lifetimes—build up images of the source of their frustration in a generalizing manner, arriving at an image of the frustrating group. Over time, for example, my narcissistic patient's neglectful mother became "women, who will not care for me." As expectation of care turns into expectation of hurt and rejection, these generalizations also attach to or are displaced onto generalizations shared with others, pre-existing social and cultural prejudices. In this process, the painful experiences of particular loved ones who were frustrating are covered over, removed from consciousness, while the group image dominates. New group images come into being in evolving social circumstances, as the image of "the violent ones" is doing now, appealing to people who can use such a group image of domestic or foreign terrorists to focus their frustrations.

This conceptualization, which I have sketched so briefly, depends upon an assumption about instinctual drives, which I want to make explicit. In Freud's second instinct theory, there are two broad types of drives: the life instincts and the death instinct, from which aggression, the energy source of violence, is ultimately derived. For reasons that I am not going to argue here, I do not accept this formulation, but find it much less abstract and speculative to think of aggression as a frustration reaction to thwarting of one or both of the two types of instinctual drive Freud compassed in his first, more Darwinian instinct theory, namely, the species reproductive sexual instincts and the self-preservative ego instincts, or, Sex and Hunger as Freud named them for short. People's objects of violence, I think, tend to fall into two broad categories, or represent two broad groups: (1) rivals for sexual satisfaction, and (2) disappointers of ego instinctual or nurturing and caregiving object relations. People attack people whom they construct as getting the sexual satisfaction they want and people whom they construct as withholding the nurture and affection they need.

The categories or images simultaneously operate as the legitimators and rationalizers of the violence, permitting the perpetrator to say in one way or another that the violence was justified or necessary because this *kind of person* deserves it, asks for it, provokes it, can only be controlled by it, and so forth. The feeling that the victim is a member of a group means that the victim does not have to be viewed or experienced in his or her personhood, as a specific person, or in his or her association with a frustrating person who was or remains close, loved. The literature on prejudice long ago informed us that people are more able to be violent when they do not experience their victims as individuals. This is as true for a child attacking a familial rival as it is for a soldier attacking enemies who have been dehumanized for him by a propaganda campaign or located out of his sight by virtue of his long-range, technologically sophisticated weapons.

Each individual's central and derived group images are unique to him or her and critically shaped by the object relational experiences of early childhood, the oedipal period, and early adolescence. But, as I noted, each individual's images will fit in with, meld with, be reinforced by, be displaced onto, existing images available in the social surround, that is, existing prejudices shared by groups. A man who attacks a woman is attacking her but also her as a member of a category, like "women, who cut men down" or "women, who abandon." Violence expresses the way a person has learned to classify people and to interpret relationships among them, how the person's mechanisms of defense have over time been generalized and structured into social mechanisms of defense or prejudices. For example, if a person operates characteristically with the defense mechanism Anna Freud and others called "identification with the aggressor," that person will also, over time, construct (consciously or unconsciously) a category of aggressive people and operate by identifying with them and attacking their victims.

When people's images of groups are shared and become normative for a social unit—a family, a society, a nation—they legitimate all kinds of actions toward the groups imaged, including violent ones. When violent actions become linked to some ideologically justified image of a group or some cultural system of meaning that pervades the social unit, they are no longer perceived as violent and certainly not as pathological. They become normal. So child abuse was normal—it was called discipline—in many European and American social milieus until the eighteenth century because there was a pervasively held image of children as born bad, born sinful, and in need of chastisement so that they did not hurt those who disciplined them. This idea has hardly disappeared, and there are certainly many who still hold to it among those now who would like to imprison violent children.

CHARACTERS AND PREJUDICES

When you think of violence (or violences) in the way I have briefly sketched, it is logical to explore the types of violence through the types of images or prejudices that people construct. And, I want to suggest further, it is logical to consider the types of images or prejudices through the lens of people's character types. As people's modes of loving are central to their character types, so are their modes of aggressing.

In Freudian theory, different types of characters are dominated by different types of defense mechanisms against the instincts (or the id), against the superego, and against reality (as experienced by the ego).[5] There are three basic character types that Freud proposed, which he called hysterical, obsessional, and narcissistic. Each has a typical direction of defense and defense structure. Repression, Freud always emphasized, is key to hysteria and to the hysterical type of character in which

---

5. Some of the descriptive material in what follows has been previously published in Young-Bruehl (1997).

threats from the powers of the instincts, the reservoir of the id, are most salient. Dissociation, too, is common, particularly among hysterical people who have been abused. By contrast, obsessionals are those who are most strongly dominated by or threatened by their own aggressive superegos, their internal commands of conscience, their agency of refusing pleasures. Among obsessionals, the more "intellectual" defenses are typical: rationalization, externalization (or blaming of others), isolation (particularly of intellect from affect), doing, and undoing. Narcissistic characters are those most determined by their relationships with external reality. Freud did not study the defenses of narcissistic characters specifically, but from considering the subsequent literature and my own experience, I think that narcissistic characters operate chiefly with forms of denial or disavowal of reality: they deny other people's desires and thoughts and characteristics, even going so far as to deny their existences as separate beings. Certain of the mechanisms of defense—like identification with the aggressor—are common to all character types, but take different forms in each. For example, the narcissist will usually identify with the aggressor's power, inflating his own power thereby. The obsessional will identify with the aggressor's ability to control and set up protections; the hysteric with the aggressor's capacity to get sex or love.

I would argue (and have argued at length in a book called *The Anatomy of Prejudices* [1996]) that each person also has typical social mechanisms of defense, by which I mean characteristic ways in which his or her ego uses social categories or social designations—social prejudices—to defend against felt threats from reality or from the dimensions of the psyche that Freud called id and superego. Images of "the other" are used to keep forbidden wishes out of consciousness, to appease the demands of conscience, to shape and mold reality, and so forth. And, as I have suggested, along with the characteristic prejudices go characteristic types of violence, which are a way of expressing the prejudices. Violence, imagined or enacted, helps fulfill the purpose of a prejudice. Prejudice is the idea for which violence is a mode of action. Prejudice says what violence does.

To make this case for the relation of character types to types of prejudice and, correlatively, types of violence, let me begin by sketching in greater detail the three character types (following the order followed in my case illlustrations), indicating their prejudices, and then turning to their violences. I will try to indicate briefly, too, the kinds of social relations in which each of the character types is fostered or promoted. Societies do not have characters—as though they were large individuals, macrocosms of an individual microcosm—but they definitely are influenced by the predominance (in terms of power and/or numbers) in them of people of one character type or another, and their arrangements reflect those predominances.

I'll begin by considering characterologically obsessional people like the first patient I described, who often have paranoid features and are marked by their rigidity, moralistic conventionality (reflecting either a very severe or a very faulty superego), and tight-fisted focus on money; by conformity, being unable to keep from splitting affects off from intellectual operations; and by a kind of cold rationality or hyper-rationality. Obsessional people tend to sweep all kinds of out-groups or others into their prejudices because all groups seem connected in a vast conspiratorial system, a plot, usually one controlled by what they believe is a scheming, wily leadership group, like "the Jews." This character type flourishes in families and institutions (especially the military) that promote money discipline, order for order's sake, the Protestant Ethic or "Prussian" values, sexual suppression, enviousness, and affectless intellectualism.[6]

A second type is characterologically hysterical and most recognizable by the way in which he or she splits up or dissociates into opposing "selves": a good, chaste self and a bad, lascivious self; a real self and an impostor self; a conventional self and a renegade. In her fantasy life, the second patient I described was a much more powerful and violent

---

6. This obsessional type appeared in quite a range of postwar psychoanalytic research projects and descriptive works: in the Frankfurt School research on "the authoritarian personality," in the sociologist William Whyte's *The Organization Man* (1956), and in the work of cultural psychoanalysts like Eric Fromm, who wrote about the rigidly conformist "marketing character" and Karen Horney, who described "the neurotic character of our time." Many young adults who ended up as research subjects for Frankfurt School-influenced projects had grown up in the 1930s in milieus marked by the fears and austerities of the Depression and then reached adulthood during the War or in the early 1950s, in a period in which the prevailing social style was obsessional.

self than she is in her day-to-day self. Such a person's split can allow him or her to be an upstanding citizen by day and live another life by night; hypocrisy is so much his way of life that he will disavow or dissociate from his "other" half's activities, as do people who belong to secret societies, clubs that engage in rebellious or outlaw activities, histrionic gangs, and so forth. Contemporary hysterics often have the bodily symptoms (conversion symptoms) that are typical of the "classic" hysterics known to Freud, especially the disordered eating and preoccupations with food, body image, and health (often involving some form of hypochondria). But many hysterical people (particularly males whose upbringings shape them for projecting their conflicts outward) have their bodily symptoms on the bodies of others—they make others ill, keep them down in sickening conditions, beat them, and focus all kinds of violence (real or symbolic) upon their genitals, from castration to rape.

This hysterical type flourishes in milieus where the family life is double or two tier, where a family of slaves or domestic servants or colonials is woven into the primary family, so there are two mothers, two fathers, two sibling groups, and the hysterical character can assign one part of himself to each family. In contemporary America, the two-tier family is often a merged or blended family, one in which adults bring children from previous relationships into a new unit, and this was the case in the family of my hysterical patient. The hysterical person's lower and darker self goes for love to the low (in class terms) and/or dark people (in race terms) or new (in merged family terms), while his lighter and higher self idealizes the light and high people or the original parent or sibling group. Incestuous desires and rivalries can be fantasized or acted out with a parent or sibling who is not the biological parent or sibling. So the prejudices (and violent actions) of such characters are endlessly sexualized. Their victims are imagined as archaic, primitive "natives" of grotesque sexual appetite—the id personified—whose intellectual abilities are inferior.

A third type is characterologically narcissistic and its male members are identifiable by their grandiosity, their complex phallocentrism. They worship both their own phalluses and the phalluses they magically attribute to their female victims; they have little empathy or ability to see things from another's perspective, and they radiate the expectation that they should be privileged, lucky, indulged.[7] At the same time, however, they may—like the third patient I described—have a very low opinion of themselves, a damaged sense of self, and oscillate between the two poles with what the psychoanalyst Annie Reich named "faulty self-esteem regulation."

I think it is helpful to distinguish body narcissists, who emphasize that everyone has or should have a body like their own, from more developmentally complex mental narcissists, who, having recognized that not all bodies are alike, having registered the fact of sexual difference, insist that the "other," the not-us, is mentally inferior, culturally deficient.[8] But most mental narcissists retain their earlier bodily narcissism, so that their images of the "other" are layered, contradictory. Their "other" is both the same and different, as she is both saintly and whorish, pure and impure, spiritually adept and mindless, beautiful and dangerous, desirable and terrifying, and so forth. The victims of the prejudice called sexism are compelled to battle their own confusion when they are elevated and despised in the same act, the same sentence, the same institutions.

---

7. I am going to discuss male sexism here, but female sexism certainly exists in the muted forms that patriarchal social conditions permit. Women do not generally have the expectation that all beings are phallic; rather, they usually imagine all beings are like themselves and their omnipotent mothers. Their disillusionment may lead to penis envy—as Freud assumed, falsely universalizing—but it can have many other outcomes, among them denigration of the phallus and alliance with other women, extended mother-bonding. But the great variability of female developmental lines away from omnipotence seems to me to contrast sharply with the relative invariability of the male story.

8. In terms of their visions of human sexuality, male bodily narcissists imagine that all people have the male genital. Females have an interior or inverted phallus—that is what their genitals consist of. Mental narcissists recognize that there are two different sexes, with different genitalia, but they believe that there is only one kind of mind, the masculine; women are mindless. There are, accordingly, two types of in-group sexism: that which attributes all sexuality and reproduction to male organs—the male sperm is, for example, a little man who is harbored for nine months in the female's inverted phallus—and that which acknowledges female reproductivity and ova but wants that reproductivity under male domination. On these sexual theories, cf. Thomas Lacquer (1992).

264 / *Character Theory and Its Applications*

Among psychoanalytically influenced feminists, the sexism of males has usually been attributed to their need to disidentify with their mothers and be taken up into male peer groups. Men disparage the femininity that they must reject in themselves, and this necessity also explains, then, their homophobia in the sense that they reject all forms of femininity in males. But I think that this prevailing feminist psychoanalytic understanding of sexism is partial because it does not rest on an interpretation of narcissism, and thus it has not been linked to social investigations of what kind of institutions and societies promote narcissism. The rule here is, I think, that the smaller and more insulated and intra-generationally eroticized families are, the more they are focused on reproduction and prolonging of childhood; the more nuclear they are, the more they support elaborate narcissistic entitlements and the more complexly, layeredly, contradictorily sexist they are. The central feature of the complex sexism of nuclear families is male control over every controllable facet of reproduction, which means that men reproduce themselves in every way but the actual bearing and birthing of children. More extended families or clans in more agricultural settings do, of course, repress women, often very violently and in bodily forms like genital mutilation, but the primary reason for this repression is to secure claims of paternity and ownership of the children who are future laborers. The aim is not to become, as much as possible, the reproducers. Awe over female reproductivity gives way in complex industrializing cultures to envy and the characteristic of the envious—that they attack what they cannot be or have.

TYPES OF VIOLENCE

I have been sketching three types of characters and their characteristic prejudices, and I'd like now to track back over the terrain of these distinctions by sketching the characteristic victim groups and forms of violence of these types. Each type both finds its appropriate victim group, paying attention to real qualities in the people, and constructs or imagines the group, fictionalizes it. The types of violence used against the victims reflect the imaged relationship between victimizer and victim, that is, what the victimizer wants (consciously or unconsciously) to accomplish with his or her prejudice.

Obsessional characters react with particular intensity and violence to groups that they perceive as penetrating the fortresses of defenses they have erected to keep their acquisitive (especially their anal, hoarding) desires in control. Their enemies come in from the outside, as immigrants or refugees, and penetrate—the metaphors are usually of anal rape—right into the commercial bowels that the obsessional considers crucial to the workings of the society. The penetration is usually imagined to be slow and invidious; but when the obsessional is reacting to actual violence (and one can hardly imagine violence more horrible and symbolically laden than the penetration and explosion of a locus of capitalism like the World Trade Center) the obsessional's fantasies concentrate on threats of ever greater violence. The strangers are or become what sociologists call "middleman minorities." By the obsessional's definitions, they become spies, secret agents, infiltrators, propagandists, for the vast network residing in their place of origin and in the new homes of their relatives and co-conspirators. Animosity against such people simmers among obsessionals, but it turns deadly on a large scale, in social and political terms, under specific conditions: an economic depression or an ongoing economic deterioration wipes out the savings and the security, the sense of future, of classes that have pulled up with huge effort or spent great amounts of prestige on staying in power, while war conditions have destroyed many of the rules and regulations that have checked aggression. Someone must be blamed and eliminated to restore law and order. The blameworthy group is accused of taking over the government, so that obsessional prejudice becomes anti-state, ultimately supranationalist. The world becomes supranationally Manichean: East vs. West, Muslim vs. Christian. Genocide is the logical punishment; it is the purgative "final solution" to a threat that threatens with its survivability, its remnant.

The anti-state, antipolitical rhetoric of the obsessional prejudices—so obvious currently in America in the pronouncements of the Christian Coalition and its leader, the Rev. Pat Robertson, against Jews and against homosexuals—is one of the key features distinguishing the obsessional prejudices from the hysterical. Hysterical characters need victims that they can humiliate, so they do not try to eliminate them from an expansionary supranational movement; they are not "ethnic cleansers." Rather, they appropriate existing political means to split up the victim group so that the victims cannot breed normally or gather their resources for rebellion. They rape and impregnate the victim group women, they beat and castrate the victim group men; they treat both women and men as rivals who need to be bested in every domain, especially any domain that involves intelligence, which the victims are said to lack as they are people of the body, the appetites. Discrimination and violence against these victims grow worse whenever they threaten to move up in the world, out of their place in the hierarchy that hystericals think is natural. Moving up is most critically represented by marrying up, so miscegenation is the cardinal sin in the sexualized world of the hysterically prejudiced. The apparatus of the state is coveted by the hysterically prejudiced for institutionalizing their prejudices; they are not anti-state but states rights in political orientation—they like their politics very local, very familial, very like La Familigia.

In America, racism has been fostered by a long tradition of two-tier families, in the contexts of slavery and then domestic servitude, in the South and in the North, to the point where an entrenched image of the African Americans as a servant group is pervasive, across classes. Much of the anti-immigrant fervor that is so widespread in America now is hysterical and modeled on the traditional racism: the point of its legislative forms is to humiliate the victims and break up their families (even to attack the health and safety of their children as the recent California initiatives against illegal immigrants do). Miscegenation that in any way admits the lower into the higher group is, as always, the central racist focus (Hockenos 1993). Men of color are usually beaten up, in more or less symbolic acts of castration, as we have seen in recent highly publicized episodes, from the police beating of Rodney King in Los Angeles to the dragging of James Byrd through the streets of Jasper, Texas.

In Europe, where anti-immigrant activity, supported by right wing political parties, is also very common, there are many episodes of racist violence, but also many episodes of anti-immigrant violence that are more obsessional—that is, aimed ultimately at eliminating rather than humiliating. In Germany, for example, fire-bombings of buildings in which Turkish families live fulfill the obsessional purpose of eliminating a group that in terms of their clan organizations and business success is very "Jewish," a middleman minority group. Currently, the attacks upon and detention of men who are associated with "the terrorists" is more obsessional than hysterical: "the terrorists" are wily, intelligent, ruthless agents connected to a network of their Muslim clansmen at home, who are capable of living among "us" undetected, plotting.

The violence that is associated with narcissistic prejudices is often domestic violence or violence in places that are understood as arenas of sexual display. It is aimed at people who are threatening to narcissists because of their sex and gender, their key marks of difference. Narcissistic violence is violence against the marks of difference, either to eliminate them or to appropriate them. Typical is the violence of the anti-abortion movement, which is male violence against the control women have over their difference, their reproductive difference.

Racism and sexism are obviously very closely linked, in the sense that racism is gendered—it falls differently on its male and female victims as it takes different forms in its male and female perpetrators. Racism, as Frantz Fanon wrote in *Black Skin, White Masks* (1952), exists "on the genital level." But it seems to me that the sexism that is directed by the men of one group at the women of another, construed as lower, should be called sexist-racism (or sexist-classism) to distinguish it from that sexism which is directed at women of a sexist's own group. Narcissistic characters, I think, focus first on women of their own group, women whom they model on their own mothers. But "other" women, darker, lower, can become carriers of the images first constructed for in-group women, particularly the bodily narcissistic images of phallic women. Among whites, dark-skinned women are phallicized; even when they are construed as "mammy" figures, hypermothers, they are said to be matriarchal, male-dominating, often castrating, dangerous. Rape is a way to keep them in their place, but also to assign their halfbreed children to a lower status. The obsessionally prejudiced, by contrast, forbid all sexual relations with the polluting people they hate.[9]

---

9. One measure of the complexity of the situation that evolved during the 1990s in the former Yugoslavia is that the Muslims, who are "Jews" to their Serbian oppressors (that is, they are construed as an interloper mercantile and culturally conspiratorial group with clan connection across the Middle East), were displaced and sent to concentration camps on the Nazi model, but their women were also subject to programmatic rape, something that is usually a feature of hysterical but not of obsessional prejudices. What may be reflected here is a difference in psychic and sociocultural formation between the rural Serb army soldiers—the rapists—and the more urban, more educated ideologues who envisioned and engineered the "ethnic cleansing" campaign against the Muslims, focusing their attention on the cosmopolitan Muslim culture of Sarajevo.

There are, of course, many people in whom the traits of the various character types mingle, as there are social circumstances that promote more than one kind of prejudice and associated violence. But it does seem to me that most people have a main prejudice, as they have a prevailing trait or characterological pattern. On the other side, many groups will be primarily suited to be targets of one type of prejudice, but there are some groups that can serve a plurality of prejudices. Adolescents, homosexuals, and immigrants or foreigners, for example, are three kinds of groups that include a number of subgroups anyway, and can be construed as cunning infiltrators like Jews, as primitively sexual like blacks, or as lacking the phallus as (or like) women. They can be blamed and envied, put in their places, or controlled in their reproductive sexuality. The group of "the violent ones" (particularly juveniles) is currently being constructed in this multipurpose way. The main reason why study of homophobia is still so preliminary, so riven with clichés, and so overburdened with the whole history of social scientific bias about prejudice is that homophobia is usually construed as a single prejudice—when we ought to be, at the least, speaking of "the homophobias," and not just because prejudices against male and female homosexuals take different forms. Homophobic violence can be directed toward homosexuals construed as infiltrators or underminers of family life (in the Christian Coalition manner); against homosexuals construed as a "lower" type living too close for comfort among the "straights" and representing, thus, a constant temptation or the possibility of another life; or against homosexuals construed as threats to the stability of the gender order, challenges to narcissistically grounded identity, so that they must be violently reduced to being "like us." I think that conversion therapy for homosexuals is a kind of psychic violence reflecting the narcissism of the therapists who practice it and who insist on making homosexuals "like us."

CONCLUSION (WRITTEN IN JANUARY 2002)

An essay like this one, which surveys wide territories and proposes a multifaceted speculatively theoretical approach, is bound to raise many questions. I am well aware that I have made assertions at every turn that are arguable, while there is no space for argument, much less nuance. But the recent months, during which we have witnessed such a stunning act of violence against America—a criminal, terrorist act, not an act of war—and a "war on terrorism" in response (on the territory of Afghanistan and at the cost of many Afghanistan civilian lives and ruined cities), leave me more than ever convinced that it is urgent that we try to shift our discussion of violence away from pursuit of "the root of violence" toward more phenomenologically complex descriptions and interpretations. From the perspective that I have outlined here, the enormous danger of our present circumstance is that the attack made against us by an internationally networked terrorist organization is an obsessional nightmare come true, come real, and it thus seems to call for and justify all the classic, characteristic obsessional responses. Overriding constitutional rights for the sake of security, sweeping innocent people of many nations into a vision of conspiracy (all who "harbor" terrorists), and assuming a fortress mentality that rigidly defines what is and is not patriotic—these tendencies have attracted widespread support. Under attack of this sort, the obsessional in everyone is mobilized, and especially the obsessional in obsessionals, who are very numerous in military and governmental bureaucracies. But slowly, voices of caution about how we conduct the "war on terrorism" and voices of concern about how we uphold our constitution and protect the human rights of all are being heard; these critics need a diversity of voices of psychological (especially psychoanalytic) and sociopolitical analysis to draw upon.

REFERENCES

Arendt, H. (1970). *On Violence*. New York: Harcourt, Brace & World.
Fanon, F. (1952). *Black Skin, White Masks*. New York: Grove Press.
Hockenos, P. (1993). *Free to Hate: The Rise of the Right in Post-Communist Eastern Europe*. New York: Routledge.
Karr-Morse, R., and Wiley, M. S. (1997). *Ghosts from the Nursery: Tracing the Roots of Violence*. New York: Atlantic Monthly Press.
Lacquer, T. (1992). *Making Sex*. Cambridge, MA: Harvard University Press.
Nation, The. (2000). Editorial, October 9, p. 3.
Rhodes, R. (1999). *Why They Kill: The Discoveries of a Maverick Criminologist*. New York: Knopf.

Science. (2000). Editorial July 28.
Whyte, W. (1956). *The Organization Man.* New York: Simon & Schuster.
Wrangham, R., and Peterson, D. (1996). *Demonic Males: Apes and the Origins of Human Violence.* Boston: Houghton-Mifflin.
Young-Bruehl, E. (1996). *The Anatomy of Prejudies.* Cambridge, MA: Harvard University Press.
——— (1997). The anatomy of prejudices. *Journal for the Psychoanalysis of Culture and Society* 2(2):13–21.

11

Homophobias: A Diagnostic and Political Manual

THE RECENT HISTORY OF STUDYING HOMOPHOBIA

After the Second World War, when social scientific study of prejudice entered into its growth era and Gordon Allport published his encyclopedic *The Nature of Prejudice* (1954), concerned Americans who wanted to combat prejudice shared the idea that their campaigns should begin by demonstrating that the targets of prejudice are constituted by the prejudice. That is, they realized that step one in the operation of a prejudice is to create the target, to seize upon some sort of difference and turn that difference into a group definition. So, step one in combating prejudice was to show how the target had been created. Such educating would, it was hoped, stop the prejudice process and return the seized-upon difference to its proper proportion. The educational therapy went along with liberal social policies that were integrationist and assimilationist. Such policies said to prejudiced people, "If you will share neighborhoods and schools with that group, you will find that their difference does not mean they are not human beings like you."

For example: In 1950, a group of prominent natural and social scientists called together by the United Nations Educational, Scientific and Cultural Organization (UNESCO) issued a statement called "The Race Concept." The scientists hoped that their statement would stop the common misuses of the term "race" for all kinds of religious, geographic, linguistic, and cultural groups, to which all kinds of characteristics were then attributed. Further, if people understood what "race" properly denotes, and if they used only the precise physical and physiologically oriented definition of "race," they would then realize that scientists who speak of "races" do not include mental characteristics in their definition. There is an "essential similarity in mental characters among all human groups," and those differences of intelligence that intelligence tests measure are not essential or race specific. Further, the writers went on to teach, science has shown that race mixture has no bad results from the biological point of view, and its social results are all traceable to social factors, not "race" differences.

"The Race Concept" very effectively addressed the two key claims of mid-century racists: that there are mentally superior and mentally inferior races, and that racial intermarriage is debilitating to the superior races. The hope was to confine the concept of race to a narrow sphere and strip away all the accretions that have been heaped upon it by racism. Similar kinds of efforts were made to strip "the Jews" of a plethora of distorted and false historical claims about them, as well as to expose claims that they are a race, "the Semites," of different "blood" or origin than, say, "the Christians." Among feminists, too, much work was done to acknowledge that there are two sexes, biologically, and then to combat the piling up of other claims of difference on top of the fact of sexual-biological difference. There are two sexes, but one of them should not be "the second sex," in Simone de Beauvoir's famous phrase. If there had been a public group working to combat prejudice against homosexuals in the 1950s, it might have taken its instruction from the 1905 edition of Sigmund Freud's "Three Essays on the Theory of Sexuality," where he optimistically stated that "the pathological approach to the study of inversion has been displaced by the anthropological" (p. 139). Homosexuality, that is, exists as a practice everywhere, but different cultures understand it differently and only some designate it an illness or a deviation from a norm.

Homophobias: A Diagnostic and Political Manual / 273

The standard anti-prejudice operation of the 1950s, in which objective and impartial science or social science was the main instrument of education and correction, was to strip away evaluations that had been projected upon differences, to get down to the essential difference. In the late 1960s and early 1970s, this strategy was replaced by two others, which often conflicted. The first was to question very radically the scientific study of differences and any form of "essentialism," and the second was to re-evaluate evaluations or to offer alternative evaluations—a maneuver that sometimes ended up right back in essentialism. For example, the word "race," referring to the division of the world's peoples into three major groups, Caucasoid, Mongoloid, and Negroid, was exposed as not a useful tool of impartial and objective science, but, rather, as a category indebted to racism. At the same time, evaluations made on the basis of such partial science were appropriated and reworked. So, Frantz Fanon could urge upon people of color that they turn the tables on white imperialists, celebrating what had been despised, making a poetry of negritude. American readers of Fanon then made the powerful slogan "Black is beautiful." Similarly, second-wave feminists called into question scientific ideas about sex differences, and, using the new concept of gender, re-evaluated all of the ways in which gender difference has been socially and culturally built up on top of alleged sex differences. Specifically, great debates were waged over the nature of the female orgasm—which stood for the nature of female sexuality generally—and over all kinds of gender characteristics held to reflect female sexuality. Simone de Beauvoir had announced, "woman is not born but made," to which the next generation of feminists replied both that "woman" had been constructed with sexist science fictions and also that women and their ways can be made beautiful and powerful.

Both of the strategies of this period were designed to seize control of the definition-making process—to reject old definitions and make new ones—not to combat prejudice as such. In terms of political action and social policy, the strategies had mixed implications. The critiques of science and the conceptual deconstructions provided the theoretical underpinning for tolerance-promoting diversity counseling and workshops in schools and communities, but the cultural re-evaluations often supported either separatist movements or, eventually, what came to be known as "the politics of identity." As the ideal of the melting pot—the pot in which differences melted down to nothing prejudicial—faded, it became difficult to rationalize the social programs, like affirmative action, that were to do the melting.

While this mixed result was unfolding in the 1970s, the Gay Liberation Movement emerged, both a product of the definition-seizing strategies and a major contributor to them. The prejudice the Gay Liberation Movement tried to combat, named "homophobia" in 1972, was understood as a prejudice that constituted a group. It created the target "the homosexuals," a group held to be defined by their homosexual practices, essentially tied to same-sex partners. Science that was certainly not objective or impartial had been deployed for defining the homosexual group and for emphasizing its pathology relative to the heterosexual majority. So the Gay Liberation Movement set its sights right on this science and its definitions, which, practically, implied doing things like urging the American Psychiatric Association to stop classifying homosexuality as a pathology.

The homophobic science wielded by the American Psychiatric Association was certainly a long way away from the Sigmund Freud who had instructed very clearly in a 1915 note to his "Three Essays": "Psychoanalytic research is most decidedly opposed to any attempt at separating off homosexuals from the rest of mankind as a group of special character" (p. 145, n 1). But homophobic science could make appeal to a Sigmund Freud who was not so unprejudiced in his approach to homosexuality—namely, the one who considered homosexuality a deviation from the normal heterosexual outcome of development, and thus abnormal. This Sigmund Freud—Sigmund the Prescriptive, we might call him, as opposed to Sigmund the Descriptive—was a pioneer who had one theoretical foot in the late nineteenth century, when human sexuality was moralistically considered by most people to be at the service of human reproduction, and one foot in the twentieth century, when human sexuality was coming to be understood, with Freud's help, as ruled by the Pleasure Principle. Human sexuality was only divided up into homosexual sexuality and heterosexual sexuality at the insistence of those who held to the ideology of sex-for-reproduction, the Monogamists, we might call them, people who felt their hegemony giving way to forces supporting sex-for-pleasure, the camp of Hedonists. "The homosexual," like "the heterosexual," was created in a rear-guard action of tremendous intensity by people who were not just homophobic, but sex-phobic, or sex-for-pleasure phobic.

The Gay Liberation Movement theorist-activists who laid siege to the American Psychiatric Association understood very well that people who fear their own drives will characteristically try to locate those fearsome drives outside of themselves—and for this they need others. And a category, "the other." But in the early 1970s, a powerful critique of the category "homosexual" that did not rely on such psychoanalytic concepts—because this heritage was felt to be too tainted—was launched by radical lesbian-feminists, like Monique Wittig in France and Adrienne Rich in this country. They identified the Monogamists as the chief supporters of heterosexuality as a norm, and they concluded that sex-for-pleasure had been assigned to the homosexuals, who were classified as outlaws from the norm. But they stressed that normative heterosexuality is part of the general oppression of women by men; it is the key ingredient of sexism. The term "heterosexism" came into common use on the basis of this analysis, and for a time it was more common than "homophobia" as a designation for prejudice against homosexuals. But the tide turned back to "homophobia" in the 1980s as the AIDS epidemic brought into sharper focus prejudice against gay men. At the same time, radical lesbian-feminism receded before prejudice against lesbians within the Women's Movement. The Women's Movement and the Gay Liberation Movement, which had been intertwined as sexual liberation movements, were on different paths in the era of the politics of identity assertion. When, for example, lesbians were more newsworthy as "the Lavender Menace" within the mainstream Women's Movement than they were as objects of male rage for taking over male roles with women, the meaning of "heterosexism" got too complicated for the purposes of self-defense.

There is a general rule about the operation of prejudices in this history that I have been sketching. The rule is that prejudices intensify when the targets that they have called into existence threaten to undermine the rationale of the prejudice, and thus destroy the prejudiced person's defense. If a group called "the Semites," created by antisemitism out of "the Jews" is perceived to be out there in the world gathering financial power to infiltrate governments and take over the world, then the defense that created "the Semites" is not working; it must be shored up, new methods for it discovered, violence resorted to, and so forth. If a "race" group like "the blacks," constructed as unintelligent—and primitive and lazy as well—is perceived to be out there in the world moving up, being successful, marrying into the white race, then new methods for dealing with these uppity people must be found. As the group designated "the homosexuals" became more delineated as a group, while they were becoming more politically active and self-assertive, they needed to be contained, and thus the group definition of them was reinforced.

As homosexuals have become a more and more visible presence in America, prejudice against them has intensified and found new forms: the level of violence has increased, and ghettoizing policies have been designed to keep homosexuals out of "normal" institutions or, at most, closeted in them (as currently in the military). But this intensification is also partly a backlash against a great attitudinal shift in the direction of tolerance, a shift that has been fostered by sex-for-pleasure becoming more and more the dominant ideology, which has meant that typical heterosexual and homosexual sexual behaviors are coming to be more and more alike. As monogamy has declined as an ideal (except among fundamentalists) and an institution, divorce rates have risen, and as all kinds of families alternative to the mid-century nuclear model have appeared, those designated heterosexuals and homosexuals are less "other" to each other. Among the more tolerant heterosexuals, homosexuals are not now viewed as opening the gates to sexual anarchy or sexual redefinition. However, even among the more tolerant, a great deal of prejudice remains, and I would like to discuss that situation psychologically in what follows, as well as to try to characterize homophobia in relation to the other prejudices I have been mentioning: anti-Semitism, racism, and sexism. Then I want to note a third strategy of response to homophobia that is, I think, emerging in this era of changing attitudes toward sexuality and sexual expressions, this era when "homosexuals" as they have been designated for a hundred years or more, are disappearing—like an endangered pseudo-species.

THE PECULIARITIES OF HOMOPHOBIA AMONG AND ACROSS THE PREJUDICES

After the Second World War, in the heyday of prejudice studies and anti-prejudice natural and social science-led campaigns, an assumption prevailed that has ever since made compassing the prejudices in their specificities very difficult. That assumption was that all prejudices are alike because they are all manifestations of one prejudiced personality, the authoritarian personality. All prejudices are variations of "ethnocentrism," prejudice of an in-group against out-groups—all out-groups. A white Protestant person prejudiced against Jews will be prejudiced against Catholics and African Americans, and so forth, sweeping across all kinds of out-groups, even imaginary ones made up by social scientists trying to study prejudice. One of the reasons targeted groups emerged in the 1970s asserting their identities in re-evaluated terms is that this "ethnocentrism" thesis added to the insult of their being targeted the injury of being targeted for no special reason, only for being an "out-group."

In the context of this large "ethnocentrism" assumption, psychological study of prejudice was and remained rudimentary. It was hardly possible for the idea to arise that different kinds of people have—or, better, need—different kinds of prejudice. Nor was it possible to recognize that different out-groups or different targets of prejudice are quite different and serve quite different purposes. The realization did not arise that prejudices are like mechanisms of defense against groups constructed differently via projection and then experienced differently as sources of anxiety and threat. These mechanisms of defense differ from those familiar to psychoanalysts by being social, that is, by operating upon external objects rather than upon intrapsychic wishes and objects.

Working with the idea that prejudices are social mechanisms of defense, we can note that each person has his or her unique blend of the different sorts, although most people have a characteristic dominating defense or defense cluster, employed to varying degrees of rigidity or pathology. Analysts have long noticed that those different defenses support, or crucially shape, different character types. The different character types target—that is, construct—groups that fulfill their particular needs, and one of the most important things to note about homophobia is that it can serve all kinds of character types. Using a scheme of three character types derived from Freud's work, let me briefly show what I mean.

Obsessionals, who characteristically defend themselves with great rigidity against their own sexual and especially their aggressive desires, sustain and make thicker their defenses with images of objects who are trying to penetrate their defenses, undermine them, infiltrate them. Their prejudices are against people whom they conceive of as, on the one hand, dirty and polluting, and, on the other hand, shrewdly able to accumulate wealth. Their victim groups are commercial and educated peoples, in one way or another clannish, who exist among them as "strangers" or interlopers or itinerants or middlemen. The Jews are the archetypal victim group of obsessionals, but homosexuals (including Jewish homosexuals) can be hated in this way, too. When homosexuals are thus hated, their "degeneracy" is emphasized. They debilitate everything and everybody they touch, which can mean, as far as male homosexuals are concerned, that they feminize (by anally penetrating) or castrate. Money power is attributed to them. They bankroll politicians because they are supposedly more affluent as a group, they buy up media, promulgate "The Homosexual Agenda" guiding liberal politics, infiltrate political parties and government agencies, gain control—if admitted—over military men, and, worst, they teach, transmitting their way of life to innocent children. Now, they carry AIDS and they are being punished by that disease for their diseased state, a punishment that should proceed apace because they have begun to infect the heterosexual community. Ultimately, obsessional homophobes want the homosexuals eliminated; there should be some kind of Final Solution for them.

Hysterics, who characteristically split themselves into (at least) two "selves," one higher, more intelligent, more chaste, usually more feminine, and one lower, less intelligent, primitively sexual, and usually more masculine, need objects of prejudice who help sustain their split. They make the best racists: their lower objects are darker, associated with the night and with the dark colors of feces, pubic hairs, body orifices. But hysterics also make good homophobes: they keep homosexuals (including, of course, dark-skinned homosexuals) "in their place," which means, fundamentally, making them available for actual or fantasy debased sexual service. The most common service homosexuals are needed for is acting out the oedipal desires that those prejudiced against them will not admit in themselves or cannot act upon for themselves. Homosexuals provide a masquerade. "They" can love people of the same sex, and "we" (the heterosexuals) can punish them for it. "They" can do what is forbidden, and "we" can be the good ones by signing over our forbidden wishes to them. But meanwhile "we" can enjoy their loving vicariously, watch them on pornographic films, imagine ourselves as their lovers, even perhaps sojourn or experiment with them, and then return to our world, "forgetting" that we ever left or that we did what we did. It is very important, then, that "they" live nearby, not of our world but in it; they should have the servants' quarters of a subculture, say a bar culture, where they can be a secret. Homophobes of this sort do not want to eliminate homosexuals; they want to use them, enslave them.

Narcissists seize upon various marks of difference, depending on which difference is most charged and meaningful and threatening to them. For very many narcissists, the key difference is anatomical sexual difference, but this elemental difference can also be displaced into the realms of, for example, mental difference or cultural difference. At one and the same time, narcissists deny this difference and accentuate it. They need to be with people whom they consider like themselves, who can mirror them and reinforce the lineaments of their identities, but they also say these people are not-me. Women are for narcissistic men both phallic women—that is, like men—and castrated beings of inferior capacity. Homosexuals can be the same: like and less. In both homophobic and nonhomophobic cultures, men also form same-sex peer groups that are as crucial to their identities and their social orders as their families are—often more crucial—but in homophobic cultures, such groups are additionally structured by being defined as nonhomosexual. Men's groups, teams, clubs, military units, and so forth allow their members safe homoeroticism if they can be demarcated clearly from homosexual groups; their groups can even contain homosexual activity if there is a border, "not like them." Psychologically, what the same-sex peer groups give their members might be called genital supplementing. Men feel their sexual potency, their phallic power, augmented when they are with buddies; more than one penis is necessary to men whose ambitions are large but whose self-esteem is not secured inwardly, who suffer great castration anxiety. They expand, so to speak, to be the equals of their fathers; they disidentify with their mothers. Women, too, feel supplemented and defined as nonhomosexual in their groups, but they also tend to merge with their mothers through such groups as much or more than they use them for individuating from their mothers. For narcissistic mother-bonder women, lesbians are an allure but also a disrupting menace.

Distinctions made along characterological lines provide a particular lens on the forms homophobia takes at any given historical and cultural moment. The American debate during the course of 1993 over homosexuals in the military can be seen, for example, as resulting in a compromise psychologically happier for hysterical homophobes than for any other type. Homosexuals are to be admitted into the military, so they are available for actual or fantasy sexual service, but still they are secret, closeted, they don't tell. For obsessionals, this compromise is a horrible opening of the door to infiltrators, an invitation to rapists, and for narcissists it is a dreadful blurring of boundaries, a defeat for the project of establishing self-definitional spheres. Differently fantasized homosexuals were at issue in this debate. There were the homosexuals who were going to rape straight men in their beds or cruise them in the showers, seduce them. These are the primitively sexual ones who need to be kept in their place like people of color. Then there were the homosexuals who were going to infiltrate the military like a conspiracy, taking power away from the straight men, sapping fighting morale and making everyone vulnerable to the enemy, making the real men into women like a corrupting disease. Then there are the ones who would blur boundaries by looking and acting just like straight men, by being so virile and soldierly that straight men might not be able to distinguish them or be distinct enough from them—a narcissistic wounding.

To this way of thinking, homophobia is the hardest prejudice to study systematically, as well as being the one that is hardest to combat or deconstruct, because it is the prejudice that is character syntonic to the most character types. And this is not even taking much into account that homophobia is a prejudice cluster that involves variants for men and women, and for masculinity and femininity, in the prejudiced and in their targets. However, pointing up the complexity of homophobias does not mean that there are not common features among obsessional homophobia, hysterical homophobia, and narcissistic homophobia. One common feature can be seen by noting that homophobia shares character syntonicity to all character types with another form of prejudice that is only slowly coming to be recognized as prejudice: prejudice against people of a different developmental stage. Of these, prejudice against adolescents—who were given the name "adolescents" at the turn of the last century just as "the homosexuals" came into currency—is the most like homophobia, for it involves targeting a group that is held to be sexually anarchical, although in the case of adolescents the anarchy is charged up explicitly to developmental immaturity; they are "arrested." But, at any rate, sexual immaturity or deviation from heterosexuality is the common denominator charge; that is, for all the prejudiced character types homosexuals are like adolescents, or they are adolescents. This link, too, goes in the other direction: behind the rhetoric of hatred at "Generation X" lies the notion that the X'ers are not heterosexual enough; they are promiscuous and averse to marriage commitments, selfish and pleasure-driven, and so forth. In short, gay.

BEYOND HOMOPHOBIAS

For those who would dedicate themselves to combating the homophobias, what directions might follow from the history of efforts to fight prejudice and the understanding of prejudices in general and the homophobias in particular that I have sketched? This is a large question to take up, and I can do no more here than stay in the quick-sketches mode.

First, I think that it is important to recuperate the 1950s goal of combating prejudice itself, but to do so without returning to the idea that there is only one prejudice, ethnocentrism, or one type of prejudiced personality. I think that the duplex strategy of the 1970s and 1980s, combining deconstruction and identity politics, is not an effective combination for Gay Liberation in the present moment, although it was necessary at that time both to break down the monolithic assumptions about prejudice and to give victimized gays and lesbians encouragement and means to fight back.

Identity assertion now perpetuates group definitions that are the legacies of prejudices and the legacies of defenses against prejudices, tools of resistance. Such identity assertion makes continued sense for African Americans, who share a long group history and traditions that can be valuable in the way that the traditions of an ethnic or religious group are; similarly, it makes sense for women, whose biological and reproductive difference from men does distinguish them as a group to some degree (a degree quite variable with circumstances). But it does not make much sense for a group carved out of the general population at a particular moment as "the homosexuals" were, for they would be better off if the difference that has been asserted about them disappeared. I am not saying that the homosexuals would be better off being absorbed into the *heterosexual* majority, assimilated or converted, or anything of the kind. I am saying that they would be better off if the artificial difference heterosexual/homosexual receded and it became common to say: all humans are sexual in one way or another, or in more than one way, or in one way now and another way later; all humans are sexually quite labile and make more than one sexual object choice. Group assertion keeps in place the problem, which is the difference that was historically constructed and then elaborated with all kinds of pseudoscientific theorizing and cultural representing. An identity politics that reevaluates, asserting that "Gay is good," and doing so with Gay Pride, was necessary to help many closeted and persecuted people live more openly and more freely, but it has been difficult within that mode to say what I think needs saying, namely: "We are fighting to make ourselves unnecessary as instruments of other people's defensive needs; we are looking forward as we assert ourselves as a group to the time when we will not be forced to be one."

To keep the goal of disappearing in mind and help attain it, there needs to be a revival and continuation of the early 1970s critique of science and deconstruction of group concepts, that is, a critique aimed right at the binary heterosexuality/homosexuality and its history since the end of the nineteenth century. This critique can draw upon not only the radical feminist-lesbian work of the early 1970s that I mentioned, but the volumes of Foucault's *History of Sexuality* (1978), many works of "Queer Theory," the very important insights of Denis Altman's *The Homosexualization of America* (1982), and very recently the excellent survey in Jonathan Ned Katz's *The Invention of Heterosexuality* (1996). Katz's book is the first I know of that strongly and clearly notes the historical signs that normative heterosexuality is fading as definitions of heterosexuality fail more and more to fit the facts of the way people who qualify as heterosexuals actually organize their sexual lives, their families, and their social needs.

I think that differences between designated heterosexuals and designated homosexuals are growing less for the reason that Katz emphasizes: that sex-for-pleasure has replaced sex-for-reproduction as the ruling ideology of the moment and ways of pursuing pleasure do not divide up along hetero/homo lines. But there is also a reason that Katz does not note: both heterosexuals and homosexuals in the sex-for-pleasure era are more and more conscious of the human need for relatedness that is developmentally prior even to the libidinal need apparent in the Oedipus complex. This need, which is for cherishing affection, is not tied to love objects of either the same or the opposite sex, although it usually arises first in the mother–child dyad (which makes it opposite sex for males, same-sex for females); neither is it tied to reproduction. This elemental need for tender loving affection, for caretaking, for attachment, is the focus of study in most contemporary schools of psychoanalysis, and it has become so in a time when the absence of such affection and care is manifest in the character disorders (rather than symptom neuroses) that bring so many people to contemporary therapy settings.

On another level, the motivational study launched in the 1950s but not really continued in the 1970s and 1980s, needs to be revived and redirected. That tradition of motivational study was aimed at delineating a prejudiced personality—the authoritarian personality—and then considering how authoritarianism as a personality configuration could be reduced or ameliorated by different family and social structures, different ways of raising children and distributing society's goods, integrating institutions. Motivational study in our moment needs to be, I think, pluralized, that is, founded on the recognition that there are many motivations for prejudices and many sorts of prejudiced personalities or character types for whom prejudices are life organizing (as defenses are intrapsychically organizing). And this study needs to be keyed to the elemental human needs exposed, by their unsatisfaction, in the character disorders, the disorders subtending the most extreme and often violent manifestations of prejudice.

One of the key reasons for taking this venue is that it shows where antiprejudice work that goes beyond the cognitive-behavioral needs to be directed. It can be directed at people of the various character types who have become rigid and locked in by their traits, who have stopped growing, become mechanical, and it can be directed at people with character disorders. Further, it follows from this revised vision of antiprejudice work that no one who wishes to combat the homophobias should do so without also combating all the sorts of prejudices. Homophobia should no more be singled out of the field of prejudices than "the homosexual" was out of the field of human sexuality. Or, to say the same thing another way: as long as there is hysterical racism, for example, there will be hysterical homophobia; as long as there is obsessional anti-Semitism, there will be obsessional homophobia; as long as there is narcissistic sexism or heterosexism, there will be narcissistic homophobia. The task of combating homophobias has to be aimed, ultimately, at the roots of the prejudices in characters and character pathologies, and thus aimed, too, at all the social conditions that promote those characters and pathologies. The psychology behind such work cannot be merely cognitive-behavioral; it has to be psychoanalytic, I think, because only psychoanalysis has a characterology in any way adequate to the task.

REFERENCES

Allport, G. (1954). *The Nature of Prejudice*. Reading, MA: Addison-Wesley.
Altman, D. (1982). *The Homosexualization of America: The Americanization of Homosexuality*. New York: St. Martin's.
Foucault, M. (1978). *The History of Sexuality*. New York: Pantheon Books.
Freud, S. (1905). Three essays on the theory of sexuality. *Standard Edition* 7:123–245.
Katz, J. N. (1996). *The Invention of Heterosexuality*. New York: Plume-Penquin.
UNESCO (1961). *The Race Question in Modern Science*. New York: Columbia University Press.

12

Psychoanalysis and Characterology

INTRODUCTION

In his *Basic Theory of Psychoanalysis* (1960), Robert Waelder reminisced about a discussion Sigmund Freud had with some members of the Vienna Psychoanalytical Society in 1926.[1] Paul Schilder had presented a characterology, an attempt to systematize all the Freudian insights into character formation and structure. Although Freud was very interested and appreciative of Schilder's classifying effort, Waelder remembered, he was also hesitant. It seemed to Freud inevitable that younger theoreticians would want to sail out on the vast open sea of characterology, but he was not going to follow them. "I am an old hand in the coastal run and I will keep faith with my blue inlets."

---

1. Waelder repeated the story in an essay entitled "Neurotic Ego Distortion" (1958).

Freud's first followers and the next generation—Waelder's generation—made many brilliant contributions to Freudian characterology, most of them elaborating on the version of that characterology for which Freud's libido theory provided the organizing principle. They wrote about oral, anal and phallic characters, learning much about the oral from seminal papers by Karl Abraham, about the anal from Ernest Jones, and about phallic characters from Wilhelm Reich's enormously influential first edition of *Character Analysis* (1933). After Anna Freud's *The Ego and the Mechanisms of Defence* (1936) was received as a kind of summa of the mechanisms by which Freudians thought character is derived from defenses against libidinal drives, against superego commands, and against the claims of reality, her work became the orthodoxy to be both reckoned with and questioned. But original characterological study in the mid-century was done only with patients who presented with a "character neurosis" or "neurotic character" rather than the traditional psychoneuroses. Considering patients whose neuroses were so woven into the fabric of their characters that they served self-preservative goals meant that theory-building attention was given less to types of character neurosis (and thus characterology) than to the phenomenon of character neurosis per se.

In Freudian thought after the War, characterology never regained its association with the open sea where psychoanalytic adventurers would go, which was by that time called (in Ernst Kris's phrase) "the widening scope of psychoanalysis." Like diagnostics, characterology fell into neglect while theoretical battles were being waged among psychoanalytic schools over almost every one of the ingredients that had made up Freud's various approaches to characterology. Then the academic tendency called postmodernism, with its many and complicated questions about whether it makes any sense to speak of a self, lapped over onto characterology, making it seem almost as archaic and unsophisticated as biography writing. The only counter-tendency to the relative disappearance of characterology was in social psychology, where interpersonalist theorists of the trend called "Culture and Personality" explored relations between types of characters and types of societies, hoping to join social scientists in describing how societies and prejudices shape individuals.

Outside of the mainstream of Freudian psychoanalysis, turbulent as that was, there did, however, arise two streams of characterological thought, both of which developed research traditions. The first began with Carl Jung's *Psychological Types* (1921) and grew into the Myers-Briggs Type Inventory and various associated empirical instruments of character study. The second stream came from John Bowlby's postwar work on attachment, and it has grown into Attachment Theory, which involves assessment instruments and a typology of attachment "styles" (the word character is not used).

In the pages following, I am going to revisit certain key moments in the history of Freudian characterology, showing how this history brings up most of the major questions about what character is and how it develops. After that, I consider the Jungian empirical tradition and contemporary work on attachment styles. I want to suggest that these three forms of characterology, which were built up on such different foundations, by such different methods, complement each other, pointing in the same direction. But I also have a second purpose, which is to put these three approaches, with their similarities noted, in the framework of a reflection on characterology itself, its history, and the characterological roots of its forms. These two projects suggest, I think, several hypotheses about character and several directions in which characterology might develop in current psychoanalytic theory and practice.

CHARACTEROLOGY TYPES

Whatever else may be said definitionally about character, most contemporary theorists of all persuasions agree that character is a blend of biologically rooted ingredients—ingredients that are collectively called temperament—and influences written upon a person after birth, throughout life, cumulatively, with the earliest influences determining how later influences will be received. The Greeks, who supplied the vocabulary of character to the European tradition, also supplied the two basic metaphors that capture the blend of nature and nurture (or "second nature") in character. The noun *charakter* refers to a letter or mark impressed or engraved upon a clay tablet; it is the intersection of determining actions and a receptive material that has its own qualities. Similarly, the noun *tropos*, one of the most common words for character (along with *ethos*), points to the metaphor of cultivation: a person with a character is like a plant that is raised (the verb *trephein*) rather than one that has grown wild. The Romans translated *trephein* with *colere*, the verb from which *cultura* comes. A person's character is his or her individual culture added to his or her individual nature.

Although there has never been any agreement among characterologists about what "nature" or "temperament" compass, or about the ingredients of individual culture, there have nonetheless been recurrent types of characterology. In the European characterological tradition, which begins in Greece of the classical period, three basic forms of characterology have recurred. First, characterologists have repeatedly appeared who insist that there are but two character types, offering what might be called a dyadic characterology. Others have argued that all of humankind is, like Gaul, divided into three parts. These triangular characterologies might be described as oedipal, for they always involve one type that emerges as the superior type, besting at least one of the other two types, a rival. And, finally, there have been characterologists who assert a fourfold division, beyond the Oedipus complex. I think it can be argued that people of different character types produce dyadic, oedipal, and fourfold characterologies; that is, each of the typological variants is a projection of a different character type—and I will come back to this hypothesis later.

In addition to these three systematic modes, the European tradition includes many character studies (not typologies) that do not presume a characterological scheme or typology, but simply indicate that this person is dominated by this trait and that other person by that other trait. Here, the number of characters is theoretically unlimited, the portrait gallery unending. Aristotle's disciple Theophrastus was the father of this mode, and the thirty sketches in his book, although they were based upon Aristotelian teachings, were unsystematic. Theophrastus simply took up, one by one, the stupid man, the superstitious man, and so forth, presenting the salient trait, not really the character, of each. Among psychoanalysts, those who proceed in this way produce lists of character types—the impulsive character, the depressive character, the masochistic character, the obsessional character, the schizoid character, and so forth—but no principle for determining the types or their number.

In contrast to the unsystematic trait-list-makers, the European tradition includes many, many examples of characterologies built upon the foundation of a binary opposition. Carl Jung made a study of this history in his *Psychological Types*, where he noted how many modern thinkers, from Goethe and Schiller through Nietzsche to William James, saw variations on the opposition he himself sponsored, extroverts vs. introverts. But because he focused his attention on cognitive characteristics, Jung did not note that at the base of many dyadic schemes there is an affect theory about the mother–child dyad and how it produces happy or unhappy beginnings to life, thus making the foundation for pessimistic or optimistic characters. William Blake worked in this way, for example, as he wrote poems and made the prints for his *Songs of Innocence and Songs of Experience*. In Japan, the analyst Takeo Doi (1971) has argued for an elementary division of people into those whose instinctual "expectation to be sweetly and indulgently loved" (*amae* in Japanese) has been satisfied and those who are frustrated in different ways, which underlie different characterological forms.

Frequently, the opposition femininity vs. masculinity operates as a magnet for other pairs of characteristics. Freud associated the gender couple with passivity and activity, and also with narcissism and object-relatedness; similarly, he made femininity and masculinity central to hysteria and obsessionality, respectively. Among contemporary non-Freudian characterologists, femininity is frequently associated with concrete, relational thinking and masculinity with abstract, categorical thinking. In characterologies focused less on cognitive style and more on affective style—like the currently popular Type A vs. Type B—masculinity is assertive and aggressive, femininity more laid back, caring, and calm. The corollaries to these types in organizational psychology are Douglas McGregor's Theory X managers and Theory Y managers. The former are tyrannical people who begin from a negative theory of human nature and the latter are good ones who begin from a positive theory (and go on to advocate Abraham Maslow's goal of self-actualization).

Dyadic characterologies are the ones that most easily translate into cultural clichés and stereotypes because they most easily serve prejudices, which are structured as "we vs. them." Thus, for example, Men are from Mars and Women are from Venus. Meanwhile, on more methodological grounds, it should be said that many dyadic characterologies involve a category error. They mistake characteristics for character, or what might be called secondary characteristics for primary ones. Put another way: people of various character types can have masculine and feminine characteristics, just as people of different sexes can have masculine or feminine characteristics (gender). Character and sex are not the same sorts of categories as masculinity and femininity (the categories of gender).

Like dyadic characterologies, triangular characterologies often present characteristics, not characters, but these characteristics are not postulated on the "we vs. them" grounds. While dyadic characterologies relate more to experiences of splitting, and specifically splitting into an active masculine and a passive feminine part, triangular characterologies seem, rather, to relate to experiences of rivalry and to contain hypotheses about where control arises, about who should win the triangular oedipal battle. The *locus classicus* in the European tradition for a triangular characterology is Plato's vision in *The Republic* of controlling philosopher-kings with their male guardian auxiliaries, who police the potentially disruptive artisans or laborers (whom Plato associates with femaleness and with the domestic or nonpolitical sphere). The philosopher-kings are like sons who have triumphed over and made allies of their fathers to subdue their threatening mothers.[2]

In contrast to the triangular oedipal (and negative oedipal) characterologies, it seems to me, fourfold characterologies express a desire to be or to go beyond conflict, whether of the "we vs. them" dualistic sort or of the triangular oedipal sort. A fourfold characterology reflects experiences of differences among people and the search for a position that says "people differ, none is better." Or, it may hold that one type has a wide view that can compass all types and say, from such a position, that none is better.

The most influential philosophical characterologist of the fourfold sort was Aristotle, who based his scheme on the idea that there are four types of causes in the world and four sources of happiness. The vast

---

2. In one part of *The Republic*, Plato divided the philosopher-king group into two subtypes, called noetics and dianoetics, the latter much rarer than the former. But the fourfold characterology resulting from this subdivision seems like a refinement, not a fundamentally different scheme than the basic triangular one that dominates *The Republic* and appears again, for example, in the *Timaeus*. There, the whole of existence is made up of the Demiurge, the ideal forms and recalcitrant matter, and each individual has in his psyche a portion of each: the superior are more demiurgic, the guardians more associated with the forms, and the artisans are more material.

majority of men find their happiness in sensual pleasure or in acquiring material goods—these are the *hedone* and the *propraietari*. A smaller number find happiness in exercising their moral virtue (the *ethike*), and an even smaller number in exercising their intellects (the *dialogike*). The sages who exercise their intellects are the most self-sufficient or independent of external conditions and other people's behavior. It is this Aristotelian characterology that Tolstoy took as his model in *War and Peace*, where he described the four classes of the Freemasons lodge membership as those concerned most with social connections and their pleasures, those to whom the lodge's forms and ceremonies and possessions most appealed, those ethical types seeking a righteous path, and, finally, those intellectuals occupied only with the scientific secrets of the order.

In classical Greece, fourfold characterology emphasizing nature more than culture had its origins in Hippocratic medicine. The Hippocratic physicians, who were also, like all physicians in the ancient world, cosmologists, agreed with the pre-Socratic philosophers that there are four elements in the cosmos: water and earth, air and animating fire (*pyr*). Similarly, in the microcosmos of a human there are four humors, one of which dominates in each of the character types. Optimists are made sanguine and activist toward the future by their water-based blood, while melancholics are heavy with earthy black bile or gall as they are pulled by the past. (These are Aristotle's pleasure-seekers and goods-acquirers.) Passionate, quick-tempered people are dominated by fiery yellow bile or choler, while calm, rationalistic, or intellectual people are dominated by phlegm. (These are Aristotle's ethical men and dialogic philosophers.)

This Hippocratic scheme, elaborated in cosmology chiefly by the Stoics, was developed in Roman medicine by Galen (in the second century A.D.), and then, on the basis of Galen's texts, revived all over Europe during the Renaissance. In the sixteenth century, it had an especially great appeal among playwrights, whose stage characters exemplified the character types (so Shakespeare's contemporary Ben Jonson, for example, developed a genre called "Comedy of Humors"). Among the most influential Renaissance revivalists was a Viennese, Paracelsus, who symbolized the four character types: Salamanders are impulsive and changeable; Gnomes slow, industrious, and guarded; Nymphs passionate and intuitive; and rationalist Sylphs calm and curious.

FREUD'S CHARACTEROLOGIES

Freud's declaration in 1926 that he had no desire to go with Paul Schilder onto the wide sea of characterology came just as he was making the third of his momentous revisions of psychoanalysis. Like the structural theory and the second instinct theory, the new theory of anxiety that Freud was offering could, he knew, provide an organizing characterological principle. So it was clearer than ever to him that characterology can be constructed on many different principles and elaborated in many ways, as he admitted explicitly a few years later in a retrospective and synthetic paper called "Libidinal Types" (1931).

Although Freud characteristically—that is, as a matter of his own richly narcissistic character—never abandoned completely a theory that he had advanced, there are nonetheless three distinguishable phases in his thinking about character. I will sketch these briefly, emphasizing the principles on which his different approaches were founded.

In his early writings, before the "Three Essays," Freud did not yet speak of character types. As a typologist, he focused solely on psychopathology. He began his psychoanalytic work, of course, with hysterics and with the problem, which he and Breuer tackled together, of how to describe hysteria psychodynamically. But he also prided himself on his originality in the domain of obsessional neurosis. "I was obliged to begin my work with a nosological innovation," Freud explained. "I found reason to set alongside hysteria the obsessional neurosis as a self-sufficient and independent disorder, although the majority of the authorities place obsessions among the syndromes constituting mental degeneracy or confuse them with neurasthenia" (1896, p. 146). He did for obsessional neurosis what Charcot had inspired him to do for hysteria.

So, Freud was a typologist of the psychoneuroses, but his bent was to find the common denominator behind the types, the common cause. The isolation of obsessional neurosis had been exhilarating in and of itself, but also because it gave such support to his theory of the traumatic origins of hysteria, the so-called "seduction theory" postulating that a childhood sexual experience was causal in all hysterias. He noted (1896):

> The obsessional neurosis arises from a specific cause very analogous to that of hysteria. Here too we find a precocious sexual event, occurring before puberty, the memory of which becomes active during or after that

period . . . There is only one difference which seems capital. At the basis of the aetiology of hysteria we found an event of passive sexuality, an experience submitted to with indifference or with a small degree of annoyance or fright. In obsessional neurosis, it is a question on the other hand of an event which has given pleasure, of an act of aggression inspired by desire (in the case of a boy) or of a participation in sexual relations accompanied by enjoyment (in the case of a little girl). The obsessional ideas . . . are nothing other than reproaches addressed by the subject to himself on account of his anticipated sexual enjoyment, but reproaches distorted by an unconscious psychical work of transformation and substitution. [p. 155]

I have quoted this passage at length because it shows so clearly the trend in Freud's thought that inhibited him as a typologist, and thus also as a characterologist: he was looking for the single cause behind diverse phenomena and distinct conditions. There was to be a master key, playing the role that natural selection played in Darwin's theory. So, although he viewed the psychoneuroses as distinct conditions, he did not want to see them arising out of distinct matrices of factors.

Generally, stress on sameness in conditions, pathological or normal, eventually defeats typology. And Freud only ventured into typology again when his first sameness hypotheses failed to withstand clinical scrutiny. He abandoned the seduction theory as a universal etiology for the psychoneuroses, and he repudiated the solution he had given to the vexing problem to which he had given the title "choice of neurosis" (1905, pp. 112, 275, 319). Instead he turned to the possibility that there is a universal libidinal development, through different stages, out of which both the psychoneuroses and character come. Freud's first excursion into characterology, which was based on this libido theory, was expressed in papers like "Character and Anal Erotism" in 1908.

Developing his libido theory, which he thought was far more universal than the seduction theory, Freud emphasized passive sexual experience and active sexual experience, but not just in relation to traumatic events. He spoke of the (passive) orality in hysteria and the (active) anality or anal-sadism in obsessional neurosis. And, generally, he based his revised characterological thinking upon the idea that the pleasures associated with the various erotogenic zones can be sublimated into character traits or repressed by means of reaction formations. People who have been particularly excited for constitutional or environmental reasons by their anal functioning substitute a more acceptable excitement or defend against the original one strongly enough to make it disappear. A feces hoarder becomes a money hoarder, messmakers become clean freaks or control freaks, as they are now known thanks to the popularization of Freudian ideas. Parsimony, cleanliness, and obstinacy always go together, Freud thought, a cluster of traits making up "the anal character."

Although the anal character was and still is the staple of Freudian characterology, and the feature of it most widely woven into popular culture, Freud also hypothesized that there are oral characters and a third type, later called the phallic or phallic-narcissistic character, which was not studied per se by Freud himself, but became quite a specialty of Wilhelm Reich's, featured in his *Character Analysis*. In Freud's own work, all elaborations of narcissism became very complicated because of the shift in his work that took place before and during World War I, a shift that provided the foundations for what was later known as "Ego psychology."

In the early years of his collaboration with Jung, Freud began to emphasize that defenses he had long studied, like repression, involve conflict between two instincts or groups of instincts, which were familiar in Darwinian theorizing: the sexual instincts (ultimately aimed at reproduction) and the ego instincts (aimed at self-preservation). He admitted that his own work, including his second character theory, had been built on investigations focused on the sexual instincts, and that the ego instincts were less well known, despite a pioneering paper by Sándor Ferenczi "Stages in the Development of a Sense of Reality" (1913). But character, he speculated (Freud 1916–1917), is connected to the ego instincts and their neurosis-inducing conflicts with the sexual instincts: "for a neurosis to break out, there must be a conflict between the libidinal desires of a person and that part of his being which we call his ego, the expression of his instinct of self-preservation, which also contains his ideals of his own character" (p. 351). Forecast in this passage is the importance that the notion of ideals came to play in Freud's characterological thinking as it got associated with the concept of "the ego ideal" and later with "the superego."

It was from this line in his thought that Freud's emphasis on character as the ego's defensive structuration and as the history of the ego's object relations came. During this ego psychological period in his work,

Freud, like all characterologists in the European tradition, made character studies focused on a single trait or complex defining a person's character. This kind of focus, which had produced many literary variations on the Shrew, the Curmudgeon, the Ingenue, the Rascal, and on and on through centuries of plays and stories and portraits, had a quite specific meaning for Freud. For him, the definitional element was a desire or fantasy, usually unconscious, and opposed by the ego, like, for example, the fantasy of possessing the opposite-sex parent that Freud called the Oedipus complex. Out of the central oedipal fantasy flowed certain specific and typical narratives, so Freud made character studies of those wrecked by success, those who felt themselves to be exceptions, those committing criminal acts out of a sense of guilt. But he also studied people dominated by a fantasy derived from an experience of "the primal scene" (the Wolf Man's primal scene fantasy is the most elaborate example) or created in the course of masturbatory activity (the masochistic character's "a child is being beaten" fantasy, for example).

Generally, in this phase of his work, unlike in the second phase with its focus on transformations of eroticism, Freud put more and more emphasis on childhood experiences and object relations in the development of the ego and the formation of the ego's character. As he did so, he returned to his early question about the relation between the psychoneuroses and character and gave it a new answer. Rather than trying to link the psychoneuroses and character, he distinguished them (1913):

> In the field of the development of character we are bound to meet with the same instinctual forces which we have found at work in the neuroses. But a sharp theoretical distinction between the two is necessitated by the single fact that the failure of repression and the return of the repressed—which are peculiar to the mechanism of neurosis—are absent in the formation of character. In the latter, repression either does not come into action or smoothly achieves its aim of replacing the repressed by reaction-formations and sublimations. Hence the processes of the formation of character are more obscure and less accessible to analysis than neurotic ones. [p. 323]

This sharp distinction has often been questioned, but it is important to note for assessing Freud's attempt to move character study away from symptom study. In the same paper, "The Disposition to Obsessional

Neurosis," he described the difference between the ego-alien quality of a symptom and the ego-syntonic quality of a character trait, which makes a trait much harder to approach analytically.

While this third phase of Freud's characterological thinking was under way, and leading him toward "The Ego and the Id" and the synthetic formulation called "the structural theory," he introduced another line of inquiry. In the years just before and just after his tremendously important 1914 essay "On Narcissism," Freud frequently drew a fundamental contrast between those who love in a predominantly narcissistic manner and those who love in a more object-related manner. This contrast came from postulating that the libido has two fundamentally different objects: other people (object-libido) and the ego itself (ego libido). There are, thus, characters in which ego-libido dominates and those in which object-libido dominates.

These two types became identified with femininity and masculinity in the 1914 essay—to the consternation of generations of female readers—and the types acquired thereby the association of femininity with passivity and masculinity with activity that had developed over the years in Freud's thought. However, it is obvious in the qualifications Freud kept generating that he realized he was creating theoretical tensions and contradictions. Narcissism in men had been central to Freud's earliest gendered characterology, and he had always stressed the male's investment in the phallus and phallic activity and the male's fear of castration, so his 1914 judgment that males are more object-related—more inclined to loving than being loved—than females was problematic. (The phallic character was tied to narcissism and masculinity in Wilhelm Reich's elaboration, too, so he had to override Freud's 1914 association of narcissism and femininity.)

Freud's thoughts on narcissism were part of his effort to understand what he called the "narcissistic neuroses," as distinguished from hysteria and obsessional neurosis, the two psychoneuroses that were known as the "transference neuroses." Freud had become alarmed and then incensed as Jung, who had so distinguished himself as an interpreter of the psychoses, repudiated the libido theory and postulated a vague "psychic energy"—confusingly called libido—instead of the sexual instincts as the moving force in human beings. Responding, Freud considered the psychoses as "narcissistic neuroses," conditions in which a person is unable to form a transference or to be object-related. In a narcissistic neurosis, development from dominance by ego-libido or narcissism to object-relatedness has not taken place or has been undone. Viewing the narcissistic neuroses and psychoses in terms of fixations in or regressions to narcissism (see Freud 1913, p. 318), Freud had a theory that differed from Jung's emphasis on two positions, introversion and extraversion, the basic contrast of his characterology. Extreme introversion is, in Jung's view, psychosis.

This phase of Freud's characterological thinking culminated with the ideas offered in "The Ego and the Id" (1923) and elaborated over the next half dozen years in various subsequent texts. Freud began noting at the end of the First World War that he had become aware of the importance in mental life not just of object-relations but of identifications that are formed as object-relations are lost or left behind (to varying degrees). Identifications, he realized (Freud 1923, section III), make "an essential contribution towards building up what is called [the ego's] character.... The character of the ego is a precipitate of abandoned object-cathexes and contains the history of those object-choices" (p. 29). From the abandoned objects, set up in the mind as identifications, the ego acquires ideals, and comes to love its identifications and ideals as it once loved the objects. Freud thus offered a psychodynamic understanding of the process of influence, which had been held to be central to character-building by all characterologists and writers of treatises on the education of the young long before Freud.

In the final phase of his thinking about characterology, Freud abandoned his coastal run and sailed out on the wide sea himself with the brief 1931 paper "Libidinal Types." The paper is obviously a synthetic effort: it brings together the first approach to character, in terms of transformations of erotism, and the second, in terms of ego formation. Freud speaks of allocations (not transformations) of libido to the mind's agencies—id, ego, and superego—and then of relations of dominance among the mind's agencies. He no longer speaks of character as ego-character, but views the mind as a whole of which the ego is a part, attributing character to the whole mind. Even though "Libidinal Types" was not much cited after it was published, this notion of character as equivalent to the mind as a whole or the whole person or the self prevailed in later psychoanalysis over the notion of the ego-character.

In "Libidinal Types," Freud wrote as a triangular, oedipal characterologist, but he also gestured toward a fourth type. There are erotics, obsessionals, and narcissists, each characterized by a particular allocation of libido in one area of the mind. Among erotics, the libido concentrates in the id; among obsessionals, in the superego; and among narcissists, in the ego. But there is also a fourth, ideal type in which libido is evenly distributed.

Erotics, Freud said, are people whose main interest is focused on love, and specifically on being loved, so that they are marked by dependency on those who love them and by fear of losing that love. Obsessionals are people whose dominating superegos are in tension with their egos, and they suffer from anxiety of conscience more than from fear of loss of love. "[They] exhibit, we might say, an inner rather than an outer dependence; they develop a high degree of self-reliance, from the social standpoint they are the true upholders of civilization, for the most part in a conservative spirit" (1931, p. 218).

Freud presented the third, narcissistic type in words that echo the "On Narcissism" essay, but that also seem to contain the late fruits of his self-analysis in them, as a self-description:

> The characteristics of this [narcissistic] type are in the main negatively described. There is no tension between ego and superego—indeed, starting from this type, one would hardly have arrived at the notion of a superego; there is no preponderance of erotic needs; the main interest is focused on self-preservation; the type is independent and not easily overawed. The ego has a considerable amount of aggression available, one manifestation of this being a proneness to activity; where love is in question, loving is preferred to being loved. People of this type impress others as being "personalities"; it is on them that their fellow-men are specially likely to lean; they readily assume the role of the leader, give a fresh stimulus to cultural development or break down existing conditions. [1931, p. 218]

In "Libidinal Types," Freud raised the question—his now forty-year-old question—of the relation between these character types and pathologies, and again he distinguished neuroses from characters, this time emphasizing that a neurosis can arise from the breakdown of a character-formation. (Earlier, his key example of this process was [Freud, 1913] the "old dragon," the type of woman who, after menopause, deteriorates into anal sadism, obsessional neurosis.) It seems likely, he suggested, that erotics, if they became neurotic, would be hysterics, and obsessionals would be obsessional neurotics, as it seems likely that narcissists would have a predisposition to psychosis (or what later came to be known as a borderline condition). But he preferred to leave these possibilities open to investigation, along with the possibility that "pure types marked by the undisputed predominance of a single psychical agency seem to have a better chance of manifesting themselves as pure character-formations, while we might expect that the mixed types [erotic-obsessional, obsessional-narcissistic, erotic-narcissistic] would provide a more fruitful soil for the conditioning factors of neurosis" (1931, p. 219). The most harmonious character type, least susceptible to breakdown into a neurotic type, would be the theoretically possible fourth type, erotic-obsessional-narcissistic, a type in which none of the three agencies of the mind predominated.

After writing "Libidinal Types," which, as noted, seems to have had very little impact on the Freudian group, Freud did not again write a theoretical paper on character, but in occasional remarks he did continue to emphasize the superego and the object-relations story. "New Introductory Lectures on Psycho-Analysis" (1933) contains a summary:

> You yourselves have no doubt assumed that what is known as "character," a thing so hard to define, is to be ascribed entirely to the ego. We have already made out a little of what it is that creates character. First and foremost there is the incorporation of the former parental agency as the superego, which is no doubt its most important and decisive portion, and, further, identifications with the two parents of the later period and with other influential figures, and similar identifications formed as precipitates of abandoned object-relations. And we may now add as contributions to the construction of character which are never absent the re-action formations which the ego acquires—to begin with in making its repressions and later, by a more normal method, when it ejects unwished for instinctual impulses. [p. 91]

THE JUNGIAN PSYCHOLOGICAL TYPES

By the time Freud had evolved through his periods of characterological theorizing, he had catalogued many of the ingredients that a synthetic approach to characterology would need to take into account: instinctual drives, identifications, object relations. But he had not concerned himself with cognitive development or with early environmental or parenting influences.

Cognitive development was Carl Jung's special interest. From his earliest work on association, he was interested in how different people think. His characterological quest, which began during the tumult and crisis of his separation from Freud and was written out in his *Psychological Types* (1921), was provoked, he said, by his bewilderment at how differently Sigmund Freud and Alfred Adler understood human beings. But it seems very clear in his autobiographical writings that this contrast served Jung as a displacement site for his overwhelming interest in how differently Sigmund Freud and Carl Jung understood human beings.

Jung suggested that Freud put *eros* at the center of his world-view, while Adler focused on power; Freud saw human beings trying to satisfy their desires with other human beings, while Adler saw them struggling to overcome subjective conditions, feelings of inferiority. Jung chose to call the Freud type an extrovert and the Adler type an introvert. Extroverts are characterized by an "outgoing, candid and accommodating nature that adapts easily to a given situation, quickly forms attachments, and, setting aside any possible misgivings, will often venture forth with careless confidence into unknown situations," while introverts are characterized by a "hesitant, reflective, retiring nature that keeps itself to itself, shrinks from objects, is always slightly on the defensive and prefers to hide behind a mistrustful scrutiny" (1921, pp. 333, 373).

Although Jung emphasized the extrovert-introvert opposition, he also recognized that his typology was too simple, and he brought to it a fourfold scheme, which could be viewed biographically as representing his desire to be beyond the conflict he had had with Freud, to reach a more encompassing view. He cataloged four types of introverts and four types of extroverts, differentiated by the predominance in them of one of four "orienting functions"—thinking, feeling, sensation, and intuition. People in whom sensation is strong are "fact-minded," in contrast to thinking types who subsume facts under their thoughts and judgments. Feeling types adapt to reality in the medium of the "feeling value" they assign to things and people, while for intuitional types "reality counts only in so far as it seems to harbor possibilities which then become the supreme motivating force, regardless of how things actually are in the present" (p. 354).

It was this complex, cognitively oriented characterology that became the basis for the Myers-Briggs Type Indicator, the work of a daughter–mother team, Isabel Myers and Catherine Briggs, who developed it into a scheme of sixteen character types. In each of their types, summarized in Myers's *Gifts Differing* (1980), there is a particular weighting of the four universal axes of Extroverted-Introverted (E-I), Sensory-Intuitive (S-N), Thinking-Feeling (T-F), and Judging-Perceiving (J-P). But Myers also suggested that the sixteen types reflect four underlying temperament types, an idea that has been developed by David Kiersey, who has been the most influential current adapter of the Jung-inspired Myers-Briggs approach.

Kiersey (1998) coded the four basic temperament types in the manner of Paracelsus as impulsive and changeable Foxes (SP), industrious and guarded Beavers (SJ), calm, curious, rational Owls (NT), and passionate and intuitive Dolphins (NF); later he also used the shorthand Artisans, Guardians, Rationalists, and Idealists. Like Myers, Kiersey stressed that no one of the types is superior to any of the others; they are different, and specifically different in terms of what they "have in mind." The types identify people; they do not explain individuality or offer any genetic insight. Neither psychodynamically nor relationally oriented, they are rigorously unpsychoanalytic.

Unfortunately, Kiersey's acquaintance with Freud was startlingly superficial. He noted that the Hippocratic legacy, with its assumption that four types of humoral constitution are the foundation for four characters, was generally accepted in European philosophy and science from the Renaissance through the nineteenth century. But then he blamed its relative neglect in the twentieth century on the influence of Pavlov and Freud (Kiersey 1998). "Freud reduced mankind to mere animal, nothing more than a creature of blind instinct. Similarly, Pavlov reduced mankind not to animal, but to machine, its actions nothing more than mechanical response to environmental stimulation." Both Pavlov and Freud "suggested that all human beings are fundamentally alike and only superficially different," banishing to the dustbin of history the "ancient idea of the human as a vital organism animated by four different spirits" (p. 25).

Because he had this dismissive view of Freud, which he shared with all the psychologists of the so-called Third Force or Human Potential Movement (Abraham Maslow), who positioned themselves apart from

Freud and from Pavlov, Kiersey was not prepared to notice that his four temperament types are remarkably similar to the types Freud summarized in "Libidinal Types." The Fox or Artisan (SP), who resembles Freud's hysterical type, is alert to surroundings, aesthetically tuned, adaptable, activist, interested in facts and information more than concepts or theories, impressionistic, gifted for working with things, ready to meet and use (even exploit) people. Freud's obsessional is Kiersey's Beaver Guardian (SJ), who is also alert to surroundings, but for purposes of scheduling activities, attaining efficiency, and keeping control. "For SJs, everything should be in its proper place, everybody should be doing what they are supposed to do, everybody should be getting their just deserts, every action should be closely supervised, all products thoroughly inspected, all legitimate needs promptly met, all approved ventures carefully insured."

Freud's narcissistic type is Kiersey's Owl Rationalist (NT), who is introspective, intellectual, theoretical, independent, competent, and very tough-minded and objective in figuring out the way things and people are. Insisting that they have a rationale for everything that they do and say, rationalist researchers love system and order, but, above all, they love to have the answer—and they believe there is an answer to everything. (Interestingly, NT was Kiersey's own type, and it seems very likely that it was also Freud's. NTs are not likely to be great appreciators of theoretical systems not their own.)

Freud did not go further than gesturing at his fourth type, but it is not difficult to imagine the inclusive hysterical-obsessional-narcissist as Kiersey's Dolphin Idealist (NF), who is introspective, but concerned mostly with finding the meaning of things and people, with giving meaning and wholeness to people's lives. Idealists are intuitive, insightful, subjective, humane, sympathetic, creative, often religious or philosophical. And they want to be, as Kiersey (1998, p. 19) clearly understood, beyond conflict, so they make excellent producers of fourfold characterologies, which are beyond the triangular oedipal characterologies. (Isabelle Myers had identified herself, on her own Inventory, as an NF.) "Conflict in those around them is painful to NFs, something they must deal with in a very personal way, and so they care deeply about keeping morale high in their membership groups, and about nurturing positive self-image in their loved ones."

JOHN BOWLBY AND ATTACHMENT THEORY

John Bowlby became the director of the unit he named the Department of Children and Parents at the Tavistock Clinic in 1946 and began the research that resulted in *Attachment* (1969), *Separation* (1973), and *Loss* (1980). In this trilogy he argued that human attachment does not stem from any more fundamental instinctual drive like search for pleasure and avoidance of pain, but is itself the fundamental human capacity. He pointed to five instinctual responses—sucking, clinging, following, crying, and smiling—that serve the function of attaching a child to its mother. In Bowlby's view, which is very like Doi's view noted above, all pathology stems from interference with these reactions and from "inability to make and sustain confident, friendly, and cooperative relations with others" (1953, p. 109). Pathology is inability to exercise the capacity for relationships with which a child is born.

The first generation of researchers who followed Bowlby's lead gathered data in experimental situations like the Strange Situation, in which a child's parent leaves it in a room with a stranger and then, after a period, returns. This data was correlated with interview data about the same children's family lives and typical modes of relating to their parents. The researchers noted a pattern called secure attachment, and two basic types of insecure attachment. So, initially, three types arose out of empirical research, not out of any preconceived characterology.

The first insecure type, called "avoidant attachment," can be observed in a child who neither protests the parent's departure in the Strange Situation, nor is reassured by the parent's return. The child appears affectless, dulled. As a style, this avoidant attachment develops in context of parental rejection of attachment behaviors: it reflects the child's efforts to suppress the attachment system by eliminating emotional expression of distress. The second insecure pattern, called "ambivalent/resistant attachment," can be observed in a child whose response to the Strange Situation is to be upset by the parent's departure and unable to calm down after the parent's return. As a style, this insecure attachment develops over time in the context of inconsistent parental response to the child's attachment behaviors. Usually, the inconsistency means that the parental response is governed by the parent's needs, not the child's needs. The child then attempts to activate the attachment system by maximizing emotional expressions of distress, but it achieves no satisfactory resolution and cannot be soothed or calmed down.

These two insecure modes were posited by Bowlby's followers as styles or patterns, not as character types. But this raises the question whether, if the styles or patterns persist over time, if they become the consistent mode of response, they become characterological. Even a child who is ambivalent/resistant with one parent and avoidant with the other, given different parental response styles, might, over time, settle into a predominance of one mode or the other. And these modes are the modes characteristic of Freud's obsessional and hysterical characters, the first a thrower of scenes to get attention and the second a retreater into rigid, fixed behaviors in order not to have painful feelings. Freud's erotic-obsessional-narcissist, the one whose libidinal commitments are evenly distributed across the psychic agencies, could be described as securely attached.

Interestingly, as attachment researchers continued to collect data from experimental settings and from interview study of children in their families, the question about whether there are insecurely attached children who do not settle into one or the other of the insecure attachment types was answered as a third insecure type was isolated and described. A child with "disorganized-disoriented attachment" exhibits contradictory behaviors simultaneously or in rapid succession, and this is understood to reflect a breakdown in a consistent strategy for managing attachment motivation. The child attempts to forge a resolution through the adoption of more or less severe distortions of self. This is the behavioral pattern known in the Freudian nosology as the narcissistic neurosis.

A next generation of researchers explored these child types further by developing an Adult Attachment Inventory which allowed them to assess an adult's attachment style, make a prediction about how that adult's children would turn out, and then correlate the prediction with a study of the adult's children, who had been independently classified as secure, ambivalent/resistant, avoidant, or disorganized-disoriented types. Four adult types and four correlations emerged from this work (see Coates 1998).

First, "autonomous" adults were easily able in the interview situation to recall their early experiences and relationships, to provide illustrations for their generalizations about their relationships with their own parents. They were reflective about their relationships, not over-idealizing. Their style of regulating affect was flexible, not encumbered by pervasive defensive processes. They had "autobiographical competence," and a capacity to consider and reflect, called "metacognitive monitoring." And they raised securely attached children.

By contrast, in their interviews, "dismissive" adults minimized the importance of their early experiences and relationships, tended to describe relationships in idealizing, positive terms, vaguely, without illustration; that is, they recounted their relationships without affect. The interviewers could see that this dismissive style had developed in the context of parental rejection and functioned to obscure that rejection, minimize the disappointment. When painful memories did emerge in the interview, dismissive adults minimized or disavowed them, compromising their capacity for intimacy. Children of dismissive parents are avoidant, acting hyper-independent in the Strange Situation, refusing to seek comfort from the returning parent, although they are highly stressed. (Freud had always noted that obsessional children are often precociously mature and intellectual.)

The parents who produce ambivalent/resistant children are described as "pre-occupied/enmeshed." In their interviews they revealed themselves as preoccupied with their own parents and memories of them, still struggling to please them or struggling against them. They produced incoherent narratives, maximally affective, being unable to put affect-laden memories in any perspective. Interviewers experienced this type of person as drowning in feelings, ambivalently attached to their own memories. This style develops in context of intense but highly inconsistent parental attunement, dictated by the parent's needs, not the child's needs.

Adults who fostered disorganized/disoriented attachment in their children were "unresolved" with respect to their own traumas and losses. They were unable to prevent breakdown in their attempt to maintain a coherent strategy vis-à-vis their attachment experiences. In the interview, they either showed lapses of memory or unusual absorption in relation to questions about loss, abuse, trauma. They seemed to disappear, often talking of dead parents as though they were alive, or eulogizing them. They were dissociative, and then quickly regained their composure.

CONCLUDING REMARKS: BACK TO THE FRAMEWORK

One of the main reasons Freudian characterology did not develop much beyond the point where Freud left it in "Libidinal Types" is that his followers did not provide it with a reflective turn. Unlike Jung, they did not inquire into the subjective factor (or countertransferential factor) in characterology production, and they paid no attention to Freud's own awareness, expressed in "Libidinal Types," that their own characters determine how people understand character, and thus make characterologies. In a passage I quoted above, Freud had noted, for example, that a narcissistic person in whom there was little conflict between superego and ego would not be likely to discover the superego. Freud himself, a strong, bold narcissist, had, for many years, discussed conflict in terms of ego and drive, or, later, ego instincts and sexual instincts, and he had been slow to come to the concept of the superego, or to the claim that the superego is central to character formation.

I think that Freud could make this self-reflection in his last years because he was shifting characterologically, and, correspondingly, shifting theoretically away from his early emphases on dyadic and triangular (or structural theory) characterologies toward his last effort, the fourfold characterology. He was evolving—like many gifted narcissists in their old ages—toward the erotic-obsessional-narcissistic balance, beyond oedipal conflict; he was becoming the more securely attached type: the NF Idealist. Further, Freud's shift shows a key feature of character, which should be registered in any reflective characterology: human growth and change do not cease with adulthood.

People's characters are not carved on the clay tablets of their natures unalterably, or, to put the matter another way, the more unalterable a person's character is (and thus the less susceptible the person is to psychoanalysis) the more it should be described as a character disorder, or a neurotic character. A neurotic character is one that has stopped evolving, either because it has been cut so deep that it cannot change or because it has fragmented the substance into which it has been carved.[3]

---

3. This, of course, is not the postmodernist denial of the self, but a statement that the self or character is not an immobile entity or a steel scaffolding, but more like a pattern of forces, an electromagnetic field—or what is sometimes meant by a style.

It is even possible for a secure attachment style to emerge in adulthood after an insecure childhood, if the external and internal conditions for change are present and the original damage was not too great.

People's characters, further, are usually mixed, and different layers or different parts predominate at different developmental moments, prompting, among other manifestations, different characterological theories. It is worth considering, as I implied at the beginning of this essay, that people whose characters build up on multiple experiences of splitting—classically, hysterics—see opposition as the basic human phenomenon, and produce dyadic characterologies. People who are fixated in their oedipal stage struggles, tending toward what used to be called regression into anal-sadism, build up obsessional defenses, and produce three-part schemes. More narcissistic characters, embracing and even grandiose, go for fourfold characterologies. And one might hypothesize that narcissists who have in themselves elements of hysteria and obsessionality—Freud's balanced types—make fourfold characterologies in which they are the all-observing intuitive type.

Psychoanalysis has come to the juncture in its history when, with one hundred years of exploration to draw upon, it can take a comparativist perspective on a topic like character and characterology. We can ask what developments have taken place within the Freudian tradition and alongside it, and set out hypotheses. This is the time to investigate widely—to sail the blue sea empirically, biographically, and by gathering clinical data from many analytic situations.

APPENDIX

CHARACTEROLOGIES REFERRED TO IN "PSYCHOANALYSIS AND CHARACTEROLOGY"

Dyadic characterologies (usually based on a masculine/feminine axis, involving hysterical projection)

Masculine = active	Feminine = passive
Freud's object-related masculine type	Freud's narcissistic feminine type
Jung's extroverts	Jung's introverts
Theory X managers	Theory Y managers
Men are from Mars	Women are from Venus

Triadic characterologies (usually on an oedipal basis, perhaps involving obsessional-narcissitic projection)

```
              Plato's philosopher-kings
              Freud's narcissists
                    / \
                   /   \
   Plato's guardians   \   Plato's artisans
   Freud's obsessionals ∠ _ _ _ ∆ Freud's hysterics
```

Fourfold characterologies (involving a "post-oedipal" projection)

Hippocratic thoughtful phlegmatics	Hippocratic activist cholerics
Aristotle's dialogic people	Aristotle's ethical people
Paracelsus' Sylphs	Paracelsus' Nymphs
Freud's narcissist-obsessional-hysterical mixes	Freud's narcissists
Kiersey's intuitive NF Dolphins	Kiersey's rationalist ST Owls
Securely attached people	
Hippocratic melancholics	Hippocratic sanguine hedonists
Aristotle's acquisitive people	Aristotle's hedonists
Paracelsus' Gnomes	Paracelsus' Salamanders
Freud's obsessionals	Freud's hysterics
Kiersey's conservative SJ Beavers	Kiersey's changeable SP Foxes
Avoidantly attached people	Ambivalently/resistantly attached people

REFERENCES

Bowlby, J, (1953). *Child Care and the Growth of Love*. Harmondsworth, UK: Penguin.
——— (1969). *Attachment and Loss: Volume I*. New York: Basic Books.
——— (1973). *Attachment and Loss: Volume II*. New York: Basic Books.
——— (1980). *Attachment and Loss: Volume III*. New York: Basic Books.
Coates, S. (1998). Having a mind of one's own and holding the other in mind. *Psychoanalytic Dialogues* 8:115–148.
Doi, T. (1971). *The Anatomy of Dependence*. New York: Kodansha, 1973.
Ferenczi, S. (1913). Stages in the development of the sense of reality. In *First Contributions to Psychoanalysis*, New York: Brunner/Mazel, pp. 213–239.
Freud, A. (1936). *The Ego and the Mechanisms of Defence*. New York: International Universities Press, 1974.
Freud, S. (1896). Heredity and the aetiology of the neuroses. *Standard Edition* 2:142–156.
——— (1905). Three essays on the theory of sexuality. *Standard Edition* 7:125–248.
——— (1908). Character and anal erotism. *Standard Edition* 9:167–176.
——— (1913). The disposition to obsessional neurosis. *Standard Edition* 12:311–326.
——— (1914). On narcissism: an introduction. *Standard Edition* 14:67–104.
——— (1916–1917). Introductory lectures on psychoanalysis. *Standard Edition* 15/16:1–481.
——— (1923). The ego and the id. *Standard Edition* 19:3–66.
——— (1926). Inhibitions, symptoms and anxiety. *Standard Edition* 20:75–172.
——— (1931). Libidinal types. *Standard Edition* 21:215–222.
——— (1933). New introductory lectures on psycho-analysis. *Standard Edition* 22:1–182.
Jung, C. (1921). *Psychological Types. Collected Works of C. J. Jung*, volume 6. Princeton, NJ: Princeton University Press, Bollingen Foundation, Series XX, 1970.
Kiersey, D. (1998). *Please Understand Me II*. Del Mar, CA: Prometheus Nemesis Books.

Maslow, A. (1998). *Maslow on Management.* New York: Wiley.
Myers, I. B. (1980). *Gifts Differing: Understanding Personality Type.* Palo Alto, CA: Davies-Black.
Reich, W. (1933). *Character Analysis.* New York: Farrar, Straus & Giroux, 1949.
Waelder, Robert. (1958). "Neurotic ego distortions." *International Journal of Psycho-Analysis* 39:240–259.
———. (1960). *Basic Theory of Psychoanalysis.* New York: International Universities Press.

13

Amae in Ancient Greece

PREFACE

This essay is an archaeological report from a semantic site that students of Greek language and thought have overlooked. The oversight is surprising, given the richness and extensiveness of the field, but understandable, given the fact that the conceptual tools needed to explore the field have been missing.

Our site is a network of words representing the cherishing and nurturing activities that create and sustain affectionate bonds between children and parents, families and communities, citizens and cities. This word network spreads out from the verb *trepho* (to cherish, to nurture) and its cognate nouns and adjectives, and extends to such complementary verbs as *stergo* (to care for mutually) and *atitallo* (to rear as a surrogate parent).

The conceptual tools we have been using for our dig come from psychoanalytic theory, but from a variant that originated in a syncretism of Eastern and Western psychoanalysis rather than from the traditional theory developed by Freud and his first followers, As our guide to the semantic field of *trepho*, we have used the "*amae* psychology" of the Japanese psychoanalyst Takeo Doi, which centers on cherishing and nurturing human activities. By starting off our archaeological report with the story of how our tools developed from "*amae* psychology," we can offer, as we go, an explanation of why the semantic field of *trepho* has never before been deeply explored.

FINDING THE TOOLS: AMAE PSYCHOLOGY

Our preparatory story begins soon after the end of the Second World War, when the young Japanese psychiatrist, Takeo Doi, spent two years on a fellowship at the Menninger Clinic in Kansas. Several years after that, he traveled to America again and began his training as a psychoanalyst in San Francisco. After returning to Japan in 1956 to finish his training, Doi wrote about his America sojourns, considering them as turning points in his life, central to the best-selling books about "*amae* psychology" that eventually made him one of the most important intellectuals in postwar Japan.[1]

Far from home, out of his Japanese element, Doi had become aware that he could not find satisfactions for his *amae* and that he could not *amaeru*. And he also found that he could not translate these everyday Japanese words, *amae* and *amaeru*, into English. The usual translation of *amae* as "dependency" was too indistinct and unemotive to catch Doi's feeling that his American hosts, despite their good intentions, could not fulfill—or even recognize—his need to *amaeru*, which means to presume upon someone's benevolence, expecting to be cherished and nurtured. At parties, Doi's American hosts had asked him what he wanted to eat and drink, while he was accustomed at home to receiving what he wanted without asking, without having to choose. Choosing made him weary, while the Americans seemed to relish choosing and to place enormous value on having choices. Doi settled on a phrase

---

1. Doi's best-known book is *The Anatomy of Dependence* (New York: Kodansha, 1973, from the Japanese original of 1971), which is cited in our text with page references. Also available in English is *The Anatomy of Self: The Individual vs. Society* (Tokyo: Kodansha, 1986).

to describe his desire and to translate *amae*: "the expectation to be sweetly and indulgently loved." But the phrase did not catch a crucial allusion in *amae* to an infant's primary, preverbal relation with its mother, a passive yearning; nor did it indicate how positively the Japanese felt about *amae*, how essential to all later relationships it seemed to them to be.

The noun *amae* is closely connected to the intransitive verb *amaeru*, which, as we noted, means to presume upon another's benevolence and cherishing love. A remarkable variety of English vernacular verbs have been proposed by Doi and by others as equivalents to *amaeru*: to wheedle, to coax, to be indulged, to act like a spoiled child, to ask for favors, to be babied or to play baby.[2] But Doi was always careful to note that the sweet quality suggested by the Japanese verb, which he thinks reflects the derivation of both *amae* and *amaeru* from the adjective *amai*, "sweet," is not reflected in these English expressions. More generally, he thought that Western languages do not have a word for the expectation to be sweetly and indulgently loved because Western cultures put great value on outgrowing "being a baby," while they think of indulgence as spoiling. Independence, not dependence, is privileged.

In the conceptual vocabularies of psychiatry and psychoanalysis, Doi argued, independence, autonomy, and self-reliance are intertwined to constitute the goal of treatment. After observing the clinical practice of his colleagues in America, Doi reflected that those who subscribed uncritically to this goal of independence neglected their patients' need for indulgent love and thus "tended in effect to abandon the patient to his helplessness and even make it impossible to understand the patient's true state of mind" (p. 22).

When Doi was first writing about *amae*, he found only one Western psychoanalyst who did recognize in *amae* a familiar concept. This was the Hungarian émigré to England, Michael Balint, who acknowledged Doi's articles in *The Basic Fault* (1968). Balint thought that all patients—all people—were once dependent infants experiencing "primary love," a phrase that had been proposed by his teacher in Budapest, Sándor Ferenczi. But this "primary love," which people continue to

---

2. For a list of translation suggestions, see Frank Johnson, *Dependency and Japanese Socialization: Psychoanalytic and Anthropological Investigations into Amae* (New York: New York University Press, 1993).

experience throughout their lives and to bring into therapeutic relations, did not, Balint acknowledged, imply the passivity that is a feature of Doi's *amae*, which is an expectation to get loved, not to love actively. Balint remarked that "all European languages fail to distinguish between active love and passive love," and Doi often cited Balint's agreement to announce his own "conviction that the existence of an everyday word for passive love—*amae*—was an indicator of the nature of Japanese society and culture" (p. 20).

After Doi published the major work from which these quotations come, *The Anatomy of Dependence* (1971; 1973 in English), a huge literature on "*amae* psychology" grew up, which was focused precisely on the nature of Japanese society and culture and how Japan differed from the West. Anthropologists and sociologists have made "*amae* psychology" the centerpiece of studies of Japanese child-rearing and family structure, Japanese business methods, Japanese national consciousness, and so forth. But the larger question of whether *amae* is a universal condition has gone largely unconsidered until quite recently, when psychoanalytically trained infant researchers have begun to explore Doi's description of the preverbal infant–mother bond.

A shift within psychoanalytic theory has made this attention to Doi's work possible. As long as psychoanalysts were taking for granted that infants are psychologically unable to come into relationships with their caregivers, neither Balint's "primary love" nor Doi's *amae* could receive much attention in infant study. The idea that infants are initially unable to form mental representations of the people around them (their objects), and thus have no representations to invest with so-called "object libido," was encapsulated in Freud's conviction that the infant's condition was "primary narcissism" not "primary love." He held that a child's libido is initially invested in its emerging ego, as "ego libido." Slowly, after children have become capable of forming object representations and using language to name the representations, they develop from being narcissistically "autoerotic" to being "alloerotic." Similarly, they move from having omnipotent thoughts, unchecked by reality, to having reality-tempered or realistic thoughts connected to the object world.

"Primary love," on the other hand, implies that an infant loves instinctually, from the beginning of life, and that a child is in a relationship with its parents or caregivers from the beginning of life. Doi thought of this instinctual drive for love (or to get love) as an "ego instinctual drive" because it is essential to bringing the ego into being and on into its mature form, which is only possible if the ego is cherished and nurtured, if the drive for love is met with love. Doi did not, however, think of *amae* as the sexual or libidinal instinctual drive for pleasure; rather, he thought that the ego instinctual drive was for nurture, affiliation, affection, cherishment.

With his reference to "ego instinctual drive," Doi was making an allusion to Freud's first instinct theory, which Freud replaced in the 1920s with a second theory involving the controversial distinction between "the life instincts" (*Eros*) and "the death instinct" (*Thanatos*). Before this second formulation, Freud had assumed a contrast between sexual instincts and ego instincts, or, as he often put it, species preservative or reproductive instincts and self-preservative instincts—or, even more abruptly, Sex and Hunger. When he moved to the second theory, "the life instincts" compassed both sexual and ego instinctual drives, and this is one reason the ego instincts were largely occluded in later psychoanalysis. The sexual instincts, always Freud's focus, obscured them. No theorist since Freud has really explored the ego instincts, so Doi's suggestion that *amae* is an ego instinct fell into a conceptual vacuum.[3]

But, as we noted, psychoanalysis has begun to shift, repudiating Freud's notion of primary narcissism and focusing on the primary relatedness of infants to their caregivers. Rich empirical study has propelled the shift.[4] For example, right after the Second World War, while Doi was making his first trip to America, another Hungarian-trained émigré psychoanalyst, René Spitz, made film studies of infants who were in hospitals while their mothers were unavoidably absent because of death or illness. These children were quite adequately cared for by the hospital staff, but they nonetheless failed to thrive; they sank into a kind of depression, which Spitz called "anaclitic depression," that is, depression of the developmental stage of dependency (technically: *anaclisis*). In Doi's terms, the children's expectation to be sweetly and indulgently loved was frustrated. Similarly, in England, John Bowlby studied what he called

---

3. See Elisabeth Young-Bruehl and Faith Bethelard, *Cherishment: A Psychology of the Heart* (New York: Free Press, 2000), p. 56, and "The Hidden History of the Ego Instincts," in this volume.

4. The empirical studies mentioned in this paragraph are described in *Cherishment* (footnote 3) and some are mentioned in Johnson's book (footnote 2).

"attachment behavior," noting that children are behaviorally organized for attachment from birth. The English pediatrician-psychoanalyst D. W. Winnicott spoke about infant "ego-relatedness." The Swiss psychoanalyst Daniel Stern wrote a pioneering book with a title that summarizes the psychoanalytic shift: *The Interpersonal World of the Human Infant*. And, against this background, psychoanalytic infant researchers like René Spitz's American student, Robert Emde, have now turned directly to Doi's work and begun studying *amae* empirically. In their book *Cherishment: A Psychology of the Heart* (2000), Elisabeth Young-Bruehl and Faith Bethelard showed how Doi's work has begun to have an influence in the West, while they proposed that we use the old English word, "cherishment" for the sweet and indulgent love, ego-instinctually based, that Doi was describing. This word "cherishment" also has the merit of working in both an active and a passive sense.

HOW TO USE THE TOOLS WE HAVE FOUND: A METHODOLOGICAL INTERLUDE

We can say summarily that Takeo Doi has given us two tools for digging in the semantic field of the Greek verb *trepho*: the idea that human beings have an instinctual expectation to be loved—that is, that they are innately social or relational beings—and the idea that their experiences of being loved in infancy make a template in them for all their future relationships, including their therapeutic relationships. But before we show what these tools allowed us to discover, we want to consider briefly how the absence of these tools meant that the *trepho* semantic field went unexplored.

Working from his personal and clinical experience, and reflecting on his "culture shock" in America, Doi arrived at a complex position. On the one hand, he maintained that *amae* is peculiarly Japanese, in the sense that Japanese has a richly elaborated vocabulary for the *amae* states he studied. Western languages, he thought, lack *amae* vocabulary and, as Balint noted, make little distinction between active and passive love, getting love and getting loved. On the other hand, he assumed that *amae*, as an ego instinct, was universal, a human and not just a Japanese reality. He was also fond of telling a story about a psychiatrist in Tokyo who reframed the question of how universal *amae* is by remarking "Well, even puppies do it!" A universal instinct should have an expression in all languages—even puppytalk—to one degree or another, in one form or another.

The unresolved problem in Doi's analysis—how to reconcile the fact that all cultures share universal essentials with the perceived difference between Japanese and Western culture—is very much like the question that has preoccupied a series of eminent Classical scholars regarding the "otherness" of the Greeks. Classical Studies since the formulations of Nietzsche have experienced pendulum swings back and forth between theories that emphasize how unique and distinct from modern Western cultures ancient Greek culture was, and theories that emphasize the similarities among cultures, stressing the commonality of universal human experience. When Oxford's Regius Professor of Greek, Sir Hugh Lloyd-Jones, published his 1971 book, *The Justice of Zeus*, based on his Sather Lectures at Berkeley, he was highly aware of how different his view of the Greek mind was from that presented by several of his distinguished predecessors. They had emphasized the otherness, often the "primitiveness," of early Greek conceptions of mind, and the tendency for that mind to be "taken over" by irrational and demonic forces. Lloyd-Jones saw far less difference between the archaic Greek and the modern view of human and divine nature. Referring to his disagreement with E. R. Dodds's (1958) *The Greeks and the Irrational*—a highly influential book that had taught a previous generation of Hellenists to view the Greeks as extremely different from us—Lloyd-Jones quotes correspondence from Dodds that says, "I stressed the element of change in Greek beliefs, you stress the element of continuity; we are both of us right, though both of us at times exaggerate the partial truth we are stressing" (p. 24). And recently another Sather Lecturer, Bernard Williams, following in this tradition, explicitly defines his task as seeking a balanced assessment that evaluates fairly both the differences and the similarities.[5] It is

---

5. Bernard Williams, *Shame and Necessity*, Berkeley, 1993. See especially pp. 1–20, "The Liberation of Antiquity." Williams also effectively notes Nietzsche's complex attitude of identification with and detachment from Hellenic culture (pp. 4, 9–11). As Williams summarizes, "the ancient Greeks . . . are among our cultural ancestors, and our view of them is intimately connected with our view of ourselves. That has always been the particular point of studying their world" (p. 3).

318 / *Character Theory and Its Applications*

clear, then, that declarations about the particularity of one culture—be it Japanese or Greek or any other—run the risk of mapping the world in ways that obscure its full reality, while declarations about the universality of human experience can obscure the distinctive and idiomatic ways that cultures represent the world.

If we find ourselves turning again to ancient Greece as a testing ground for theories about present-day psychological and social realities, it is because the Greeks offer, in their rich body of literature and philosophy, not just a wealth of material but the direct antecedents to the intellectual culture of the modern West. Doi's claim that there is no vocabulary for *amae* in "the West " referred only to the contemporary West, where he had been a traveler. We think that turning to the ancient West will show that Doi was half right and half wrong. He was wrong, we think, in that the Western tradition does have its own richly elaborated version of *amae* vocabulary, but he was right in the sense that it is not easy to dig that vocabulary out from under layers of language and thought that do privilege independence in human relations and that do understand infants as isolates, not in relation to their caregivers. Modern Westerners who do privilege independence and speak pejoratively of dependence have not been able to see clearly into cultures where dependence is celebrated and where the cherishing interactivity of infants and their caregivers is assumed.

Within Classical Studies, we want to note another form of privileging of independence (at the expense of interdependence). Dictionaries of classical Greek inevitably privilege the study of the independent word, as though it were a freestanding entity, an isolate. Accordingly, classical philology has evolved a tradition of *Geistesgeschichte* that focuses on key words that represent ideas central to Greek intellectual history; these words are usually nouns. Thus "big concept" nouns like *paideia, dike, moira, hybris, nomos, metis, ate,* and *psyche,* for example, have all received one or more book-length treatments, and other nouns like *physis, hamartia,* and *nous* are repeatedly emphasized. All of these words are certainly deserving of the extensive study they have received. They name complex and abstract ideas that cannot be properly understood outside of the cultural context within which they were developed, as Doi had argued about the word *amae* and the Japanese cultural context. But we think it very significant that the vocabulary that presents the closest equivalent to "*amae* psychology" in ancient Greek is not one of nouns; it is a verb-based system, presenting actions. One reason, we suggest, that what we call the "*trepho*-system" has not been noticed, much less studied comparatively, is that it is not centered on an abstract noun. It is not about concepts, it is about action, specifically interaction.

There is a homology here: as psychology in the modern West (until recently) has concentrated on the individual, the tradition of classical *Geistesgeschichte* has concentrated on the individual word, particularly the noun. As psychoanalysis has concentrated on the individual infant, born into its primary narcissism and only slowly coming into relation with its caregivers, so *Geistesgeschichte* has concentrated on words in their lexical distinctness and dictionary definability. This methodological limitation, which was particularly marked at the end of the nineteenth century, at the moment when Freud was developing psychoanalysis, has been progressively overcome under the recent influence of the sociolinguistic approach, which insists that words have their full meaning only in contexts of usage. *Geistesgeschichte* has begun to reform itself accordingly, just as psychoanalysis has become more relational (and psychotherapy in general more concerned with groups and families). But it is still the case that nouns are privileged in Classical Studies.

As a verb denoting action or process, *trepho* involves doing and being done to. Hence, on the basis of grammar alone, an important difference arises, whose implications are huge. With *trepho* we are looking at an entirely different realm of experience, not abstract principles that govern society or the cosmos, but the intimate connection between two living creatures—a cherishing one and one being cherished. This realm has not been much studied by philologists generally, as their attention has seldom been on infants and mothers (or even on child rearing) and they have not been much concerned with the psychoanalytic insight that people carry over the effects of their infant–mother bonds into their adult intimacies and adult relationships generally.

THE SITE: *TREPHO'S* SEMANTIC FIELD

Let us repeat by way of introduction to *trepho*'s semantic field that the verb in all its many meanings presents the dynamic interaction between a nurtured being and a nurturer. Like the Japanese with their "*amae* psychology," the ancient Greeks assumed that all living beings desire and expect nurturing. They had well-developed linguistic resources for expressing this, especially rich in the earliest stage of recorded Greek, the world of the Homeric epics, where even ocean waves may be viewed as living beings, as we shall see. This desire is innate, instinctive; in human beings it is ego instinctual, meaning self-preservative (to use the psychoanalytic terms Doi adopted). If living beings do not receive the nurture they desire, then they do not undergo the development that their inborn developmental plan calls for. But even more than the Japanese (as Doi represents them), the ancient Greeks stressed that nurturing beings are also driven by their natures to nurture: they do as has been done unto them. The unfolding of their desire to nurture is shaped by their experience, which includes the effects upon them of the beings they nurture. There is always reciprocity, interactivity, and interdependence in the nurturing process that *trepho* represents.

The relational semantics of the verb *trepho* seems to represent an idiosyncratic development within the Greek language, as we can see by viewing the verb against its Indo-European background. In his *Dictionnaire Etymologique de la Langue Grecque* (*s.v. trepho*), Pierre Chantraine stressed that the verb has "a root with a very concrete meaning, used in a technical and familiar way (cf. *trephein turon* [to make or curdle cheese]) that then took on the sense 'make grow' [*faire grandir*], from which [we get] 'to nourish.'" We believe that this process by which *trepho* "took on" an expanded sense is of the utmost importance. The Indo-European cognates of *trepho* retain this same very concrete root meaning: to form a solid or sediment out of a liquid medium. Germanic, Slavic, and Celtic all have cognates that refer to sediment forming in brewed beverages like beer (including the English word "draff" and possibly "dregs"). The process is purely physical. But only the Greek *trepho*, in Chantraine's words, exhibits the "special innovation" of a semantic development toward "making grow" in the sense of "nourish, foster, or cultivate."[6]

---

6. For further discussion of the unusual semantics that connects "congeal" to "foster," see E. Benveniste, *Problèmes de linguistique générale*, Paris, Gallimard, 1966, pp. 2192–2194.

That is, in Greek—and uniquely in Greek within the Indo-European family of languages—the verb *trepho* evolved to turn a physical process into a relational process between an agent and a recipient, a nurturer and something or someone nurtured. Cheese-making was viewed as an improving process, one in which a caregiver purposefully brings a product into being. This apparently was the starting point for the other meanings of *trepho* to expand to human recipients of the action.

In our earliest Greek texts, Homer and Hesiod, the original meaning of *trepho*, "to thicken," is still present in descriptions of milk turning into cheese (*Iliad* 5.903, *Odyssey* 9.246), as well as moisture forming into ice (*Od.* 14.476–7) and brine condensing on the human body (*Od.* 23. 237). A step in the direction of relationality is apparent in the wording of *Od.* 14.410, referring to fodder that "thickens" or "nurtures" the "blossoming fat" of pigs. But by far the most common meaning of *trepho* in these early poems is the fully relational one: "make grow," "nurse," "care for," applied to any caretaking activity from agriculture to animal husbandry to child-rearing. Hesiod in *Works and Days* (781) uses the verb *entrephomai*, the middle-voice form of *trepho* compounded with prefix *en-*, to describe a farmer tending his plants.[7]

The most fully realized interactional contexts for the meaning "rear, raise, foster" show child-rearing in which the child-rearer is also affected by the child-rearing process. A clear example is the goddess Thetis's poignant address to her son Achilles in *Il.* 1.414:

> *O moi, teknon emon, ti nu s' etrephon, aina tekousa*
> Ah me, my child, why did I raise you, giving birth to bitterness?

As Achilles' mother and his nurturer, Thetis is inevitably affected by his destiny, which is to die young—and not live to care for her.

A host of nouns was derived from this verbal sense of "nurture, raise." They compass the caregiver, the one who receives care, and the

---

7. The meaning is not fully clear, and in fact the learned commentary of M. L. West (Hesiod, *Works and Days*, Oxford, 1978) suggesting we may have here the older implication of *trepho*, "make firmer," leads him to translate "get them bedded in." While this is possible, the passage, in contrasting the worst time for sowing new seeds with what we should do for existing plants, could easily support our meaning "give special care to."

care or nurturing or cherishing itself. A nurse is *trophos* or *tropheus*. A nursling, that is, a child who has not yet been weaned, is *trophimos*. *Trophe* is food, generally, or nurture in both a physical and a more spiritual sense, but *trophe* also means way of life or livelihood, that is, the way in which people sustain the nurturance they have received.

It is important to observe that the nouns in this semantic field can switch reference among the three elements in the nurturing process: the caregiver, the cared for, and the care. The noun *trophe*, which, as we just noted, means food can also refer to those fed, including a group of those fed—a brood, or a group of young people. When Oedipus the King speaks in the first line of Sophocles' play to the petitioners who have come to him to beg his help and fatherly care as they confront the plague upon their city, he addresses them as *tekna* (sons) and as *nea trophe*, which means "latest offspring" but also carries the sense "those who have been fed."

The same easy switching of referent can be seen in the noun *tropheia*, which can refer to food or care given—mother's milk—or to payment for care given—nurse's wages. Among adjectives, *trophimos* can mean nourishing (active, referring to care given) or well-nourished (passive, referring to the recipient of care). Thus the semantics of both nouns and adjectives in what we have designated as the "*trepho*-system" confirm our view that the Greeks viewed the caregivers, the care receivers, and the care as an interactive system or a reciprocal process.

One noun in particular presents the care system very clearly. *Threptra* or *threpteria* is the "return owed to parents for nurturance." It shows that the nurtured child is the one who grows into an adult who can nurture, and is obliged to.[8] The child switches roles. And it is a disaster—as Thetis laments—when a child does not live to become the caregiver.

A range of adjectives offer meanings from "well-nourished" (*trophimos*, which as we noted, can be active or passive) to "well-formed" (*tropheros*) to "cresting/peaking" (*trephoenta, trophis*). In Homeric epic, the latter two words were apparently reserved for special use in describing large ocean waves, so the vocabulary for describing waves is unexpectedly significant in showing the full semantic reach of the *treph-* root.

---

8. See Nancy Felson (2002), "*Threptra* and Invincible Hands: The Father-Son Relation in *Iliad* 24," *Arethusa* 35(1):35–50.

The normative epic view of waves is that they are large, and so we find the stock phrase "big wave," *mega kuma*, 17 times (13x *Il.*, 4x *Od.*), plus the (less metrically convenient) reversed word order *kuma mega* (2x *Il.*). For the plural "waves" (*kumata*), less commonly mentioned, we have *kumata makra*, "long waves" (1x *Il.* and 4x *Od.*). But, in an occasional passage of special excitement or emphasis, when the poet wishes to call attention to the threatening mass of the waves, he does it by emphasizing that the waves' bigness is a fully developed quality, the end-point of the process of nurturing and growth that has brought the waves to their final perfected form. There are three such passages: *Il.* 16.621, *Od.* 11.307, and *Od.* 3.290.

The first of these, *Il.* 16.621, names *kumata te trophoenta*, which Lattimore translates "the waves that grow to bigness," suggesting the inherent nurturance metaphor but not being able to capture its full meaning: the idea that the growth has been fostered. The second passage, *Od.* 11.307, has the synonymous *trophi kuma*. The adjective *trophis* ("fully grown") is a relatively rare one, appearing only here and in a passage in the fifth century Herodotus (4.9) that describes the point at which three sons of Heracles reach their full growth as men. In the third passage, *Od.* 3.290, we seem to find (the text has been disputed) the third person plural imperfect passive, *tropheonto*, of a rare verb *tropheomai*.[9] The full implied meaning again defies complete translation:

> *kumata te tropheonto peloria isa oressin,*
> waves were nourished to fullness, enormous, equal to mountains

The idea that the waves have been *nurtured* to their bigness is carried by the adjectives (and the possible verb *tropheo*mai) in these passages; it is also supported in another passage in which the nurturer is named—a wave is *anemo-trephes*, "wind-nurtured" (Il. 15.625).

To complete our inventory of adjectives, we should note the closely related *tarphus* (*tarph-* a linguistically standard variant of the root *treph-*, with *a* for *o* substitution and *rho* + vowel sequence reversed). This

---

9. So reads the Oxford Classical Text. If we follow the more recent edition of H. Van Thiel, *Homeri Odyssea* (New York: Hildesheim 1991), the true reading is not *tropheonto* but *trophoenta*, making this phrase identical to (and probably a formulaic repeat of) *Iliad* 16.621.

324 / *Character Theory and Its Applications*

word is used in Homer and archaic poetry to mean "thick" in the sense of "close together, crowded," used physically of wooded thickets and metaphorically of frequently repeating events. There is a similar semantic perspective in the related noun *thrombos* (*th-* aspiration replacing *ph-* aspiration), meaning granule or small lump (the source of the English word thrombosis). Both *tarphus* and *thrombos* offer a totally different view of the nurturing relation. It is seen from outside; the process of congealing or bringing together or growing is presented as a product—a lump, a group, a cluster, a crowd.

With these nouns and adjectives in mind, we can return to the verb *trepho* and consider an instance where it is curiously repeated and other instances where it is linked to related verbs of nurturing and cherishing. In the famous description in Hesiod's *Theogony*, 192–7, of the birth of Aphrodite from the severed genitals of Ouranos, the poet played on the passive form of the verb, (*e*)*threphthe*, and its range of possible meanings:

> A white foam from the god-flesh
> Collected around them, and in that foam a maiden developed
> And grew (*ethrephthe*). . . .
> Aphrodite is her name . . . since it was in foam
> She was nourished (*threphthe*)
> (190–2, 195–7, trans. Lombardo)

In the first use, the foam thickens into a young woman; in the second, the woman is "nurtured into being" within the foam. The first use presents a physical process, the second presents the foam as the caregiver of the maiden, like a parent, after whom she is named. No literal translation could possibly unite the two meanings that are combined successfully in the single Greek verb (here as aorist passive third person singular *ethrephthe*). Lombardo ingeniously resorts to three different English verbs—develop, grow, and nourish—using the first two in combination, to translate *ethrephthe*, and yet the parenting by the foam that is present in the Greek cannot be fully captured in his English version.

As the Greeks continued to use the verb *trepho* in its distinctly relational sense, they made subtle distinctions by linking this word with others. A specialized verb, *atitallo*, implies cherishing done by someone who is not the regular nurturing parent. There is an Iliadic passage

(16.191–2) that perfectly represents the relation and difference between *trepho* and *atitallo* by using them together. Eudorus is being described, son of the mortal girl Polymede and the god Hermes. After bearing Eudorus, Polymede had been taken in marriage by Echekles, and the divine bastard was given to the old man Phylas to raise:

> And the old man Phylas took the child,
> brought him up (*etrephen*) kindly
> and cared for him (*atitallen*), wrapping him in love (*amphagapazomenos*)
> as if his own son.

With its verbs, this passage presents the complex idea that parent–child nourishing is the basic nourishing, the template; a foster parent must not only replace that care but give a special care that makes the child feel like a true son or daughter (*amphagapazomenos* literally means circling 'round with *agape*, which is a nonsexual, ego instinctual love).

One remarkable feature of Greek culture was the emphasis put on making sure that no child (especially no male child) went uncherished, unfostered. When a child was orphaned, in ideal circumstances a parent figure stepped in and assured the child that he would be treated like a son. The Greeks had a special verb, *orphaneuo*, which meant to take care of orphans. And the language had specific names to designate types of fostering figures: an *orphanophylax* was a guardian for an orphan whose father had been lost in battle, for example.

When the dimension of cherishing that was to be stressed was ethical and concerned obligation of parents to children and children to parents (the domain of *threpteria* as we noted above), the cherishing relationship was often shown by still another verb, *stergein*. This verb was not used in the Homeric period, but it was commonly used in the Classical period to refer not only to the reciprocal nurturing love between family members, but also to that between citizens and their state, between colonies and their mother-country, and so on. *Stergein* was frequently used by Aristotle, as in a characteristic passage from the *Nichomachean Ethics* (VIII, xii, 2): "Parents love (*stergousi*) children as part of themselves, whereas children love parents as the source of their being." It may well be that *stergein*, with its formalism, was used for what *trepho* had conveyed in an earlier time, prior to formal adjudication of family obligations.

WEST DOES MEET EAST

It may be, as Takeo Doi argued, that in the cultures of "the West," where independence is valued highly, there is no vocabulary for *amae*. But in the ancient West, we have been arguing, there is the wide-ranging system formed by *trepho* and its related terms. The *trepho* system afforded Aristotle a basis for his philosophical portrait of parent–child relations, a portrait that shows, on a level more theoretical than any reached in the epic tradition, how similarly the Greeks and Doi thought about "the expectation to be sweetly and indulgently loved." Aristotle, however, because he always stressed the end (the *telos*) toward which human relationships naturally tend, and, indeed, toward which the whole cosmos as a living being is tending, paid greater attention than Doi to the consequences of a child's expectation of love being fulfilled. As a clinician, Doi looked more to what happens if the child is thwarted— a concern often expressed in cultures of dependency, as we noted in considering the well-developed Greek vocabulary for orphans and for adoption.

In his *Nichomachean Ethics*, Aristotle emphasized that parents are lovable to the child because they are the source of its being and of the cherishment that the child needs. Reception from the parental source entails an obligation: "The parent gives the child the greatest of gifts— its being—but also cherishment and education or culturation (*trophes kai paideias*); and because the child receives, it owes the parent honor and service" (VIII. xi. 2). Similarly: "Children love their parents because the parents have bestowed on them the greatest benefits as the cause of their being (*einai*), their cherishment (*trephenai*) and later their education."[10] Well-cherished children will impart to their parents what Aristotle names (IX. ii. 8) *trophe*—a word that is usually very blandly and misleadingly translated "maintainence," but which, as our exploration has shown, has a much fuller meaning. It is, Aristotle says (IX. ii. 8), more beautiful (*kallion*) to impart cherishment to those who gave us our existence than it is to take care of ourselves.

---

10. Aristotle makes it clear that children love their parents by nature, instinctually, but he also indicates (VII. xii. 2) that they need to have "understanding or at least perception" to show this love fully.

In Aristotle's philosophy, the basic Greek conviction that people are born for relatedness was most fully articulated. Speaking of human happiness, he famously said, "no one would choose to have all possible good things on the condition that he must enjoy them alone, for humans are sociable beings [dwellers in the *polis*], and designed by nature to live with others" (IX. ix. 3). The most elementary form of human sociability is the relationship between parent and child, and this is the form that subtends all later developments of relatedness—that is, it is the form that subtends adult private relationships and all public life. The cherishment that we receive as children prepares the way for how we are able to be cherished as adults and for how we are able to cherish others—our children, our peers, our fellow citizens.

But it is also in Aristotle's philosophy that we can see the emergence of an emphasis on independence—termed autarky—as a value that would have seemed quite strange to the Homeric Greeks. For Aristotle, however, there was no tension between appreciating the naturalness of human sociability and praising the autarky of the rarest of human beings, the philosopher, who can live—and desires to live—in a condition of self-sufficiency. "What is called self-sufficiency is characteristic of contemplation" (X. vii. 4). The philosopher's way of life is a *telos* that presupposes earlier cherishment and education among other people; it is a natural final, superior step in human development. But in later European and then American cultures in which independence (or individualism) and self-sufficiency were highly valued in and of themselves, this autarky element of Aristotle's philosophy was often invoked without the developmental context he assumed.

By contrast, from within a culture like that of the Homeric Greeks in which interdependence was completely valued, it would have been as difficult to speak of autarky as it would have been for a Japanese of Takeo Doi's generation. In such cultures, people who move outside of the dependency system, whether by their own choice or because they are being punished, are extremists by the culture's norms. Achilles, the most famous Greek example, challenged the existing system of reciprocity and care by refusing to receive gifts as compensation for a breach of care and hospitality that he had suffered at the hands of Agamemnon. He becomes a paradigm of thwarted expectation to be sweetly and indulgently loved, and an entire epic poem is needed to describe the consequences of his frustrated wrath and his final restoration to a caregiving order. In Book XXIII, Achilles joins his fellow chieftains in bestowing prizes on the winners of the funeral games for his friend Patroclus, helping to restore a social care-giving order among peers. Then, in the final XXIVth Book, he shows his completed reintegration in an intimate, emotional, domestic sharing of grief and compassion with the king of his enemies. At the beginning of the poem, a father-king, Agamemnon, had offended a son figure, Achilles, and by the end an elderly father-king figure, Priam, whose own son has died at Achilles' hands, restores Achilles to the full, natural order of interdependence and reciprocity—on a symbolic level one might say Priam "adopts" him back into the community of the compassionate. This restoration, as our archeology of *trepho* and its network of related words has shown, is an assertion in adult, social terms of the caring and nurturing that is natural between parents and children.

Index

Abraham, K., 9, 52, 129, 141, 172, 286
Adler, A., 45, 51–52, 53, 55, 62n9, 65, 171, 300
Affection, Freudian theory, 28–30
Aggression
  Adler, 52
  civilization and, 26, 34–35
  frustration, 54
AIDS epidemic, 190, 275, 278
Ainsworth, M., 132, 145
Alexander, F., 132
Allen, W., 179
Allport, G., 271
Altman, M., 282

Amae psychology, 311–328
  characterology types, 289
  cherishment culture and, 31–35
  ego ideal, 106, 110–111
  integration of, 326–328
  love, 9–10
  methodology, 316–319
  overview, 311–312
  tools for, 312–316
  trepho's semantic field, 319–325
  wise baby dream, 84–85
American Psychiatric Association (APA), 188, 219, 274, 275
American Psychoanalytic Association (APA), 250, 251

Amphitheater of terror dream case, wise baby, 90–94
Anaclitic object, 10
Andreas-Salomé, Lou, 170–171, 172, 175
Antiquity. *See* Greco-Roman antiquity
Antisemitism, prejudice, 272, 275, 278
Anxiety
　ego ideal, 104
　ego instincts and, 61–64, 67
　Freudian theory, 28
Arendt, H., 36
Aries, P., 36
Aristotle, 288, 291, 325, 326–327
Athens, L., 251n2
Attachment, passion and, 5
Attachment theory. *See also* Bowlby, J.
　Amae psychology, 315–316
　characterology, 287, 303–305
　Darwinism, 50
　ego ideal, 107
　libido theory, 46

Balint, A., 130, 137–139, 140, 142n9, 147
Balint, M., 30, 61, 69, 83–84, 130–131, 137–138, 140, 142, 144–147, 171, 175, 313–314
Bayer, R., 219n7
Beauvoir, S. de, 173, 272–273
Benedek, T., 132
Beneviste, E., 320n6
Bergman, A., 71n16
Bethelard, F., 316
Bibring, E., 47n1
Biology
　bisexuality, 191–194
　gender differences, 158–159
Biphobia, 179

Bisexuality, 179–212. *See also* Female homosexual; Homosexuality; Lesbianism
　categorical challenges, 190–206
　　biology, 191–194
　　object choice, 200–206
　　psychology, 194–200
　contemporary perspective, 187–190
　definitional issues, 179–180
　Freud, 162, 169, 182–185
　Kinsey and sex research perspective, 185–187
　psychoanalytic situation, 206–210
　sexologist perspective, 180–182
Blake, W., 289
Bloch, 218n5
Blos, P., 101, 116, 117
Bowlby, J., 32n6, 69, 107, 130–132, 145, 175, 287, 303–305, 315–316. *See also* Attachment theory
Breuer, J., 292
Briggs, C., 301
Bright, S., 189
Budapest School, 129–153
　Mother–child dyad, 140–145
　Oedipus complex, 168
　overview, 129–133
　psychosis, 145–149
　transference and countertransference, 133–140
　Winnicott and, 150
　women, 175
Buhle, M. J., 220n8
Burkhardt, 23
Burlingham, D., 130, 139n4
Bush, George W., 250

Castration anxiety, ego instincts and, 63

Chantraine, P., 320
Character
 homophobia, 276—281
 violence, 259—264
Characterology, 285—310
 attachment theory, 303–305
 Freudian, 285, 292–299, 306
 Jungian, 299–302
 overview, 285–287
 problems of, 306–307
 summary chart, 308
 types, 287–291
Charcot, J.-M., 164, 292
Chasseguet-Smirgel, J., 100, 101, 102–103, 104
Cherishment culture, 23–43
 ego instinct *amae* and, 31–35
 Freudian theory, 25–31
 humanity's growth principle, 39–42
 modernism and, 35–39
 overview, 23–25
Child-centeredness, cherishment culture and, 35–36
Chodorow, N., 197, 221
Chomsky, N., 136
Chromosomes, bisexuality, 192–194
Civilization. *See also* Cherishment culture
 aggression and, 26
 instinct and, 25, 29
Clairvoyants, 134
Clinging, 144–145
Clitoris, 195
Coates, S., 304
Columbine High School tragedy, 250
Communication, transference and countertransference, Budapest School, 133–140
Confucius, 99–100, 113
Countertransference, transference and, Budapest School, 133–140

Culture. *See also* Cherishment culture
 bisexuality, 201–203, 205–206
 female homosexual, 217–224
 homophobia, 279–280
 violence, 264–268

Darwin, C., 49–50, 181
Darwinism
 bisexuality, 181, 192
 characterology, 293, 294
 ego instincts, 47, 49–50, 52
 instinct, 5
Death instinct
 Amae psychology, 315
 ego instincts and, 66n12
 Ferenczi, 143–144
 Freudian theory, 25
 libido theory, 46
 object splitting, 80
Dependency
 amae psychology, 32–33, 312
 Budapest School, 140–145
 love, 10–11
 self-preservative, 83–84
 wise baby dream, 84–85
De Saussure, R., 214n1
Deutsch, H., 216, 217
Developmental perspective
 bisexuality, Freudians, 184
 characterology, Jung, 300
 ego ideal, 109–117, 122–127
 ego instincts, 6
 female homosexual, 230–236
Devereux, G., 112, 139n4, 168
Dissociation, hysteria, 260
Dodds, E. R., 317
Doi, T., 9–10, 25, 32–33, 39, 70n15, 83–84, 106, 228, 289, 312–318, 320, 326–327
Domenici, T., 223

Dora case (Freud), 133
Dream analysis
    amphitheater of terror dream case, wise baby, 90–94
    end of analysis dream case, wise baby, 95–97
    Freud, 168
    lobster dream case, wise baby, 87–89
    wise baby, Ferenczi, 75
    wise baby dream, 84–87
Drive theory, ego instincts, 48
Dualism, Freud, 26–27

Ego ideal, 99–128
    case example, 117–121
    Confucius, 99–100
    confusions and clarifications, 104–108
    development of, 109–117
    formulation of, 100–104
    psychopathologies, 121–127
    superego and, 19–21
Ego instincts, 45–74. *See also* Instinct theory
    amae psychology, 31–35, 315
    anxiety and, 61–64
    Darwinism, 5
    developmental perspective, 6
    dual instinct theory, 64–68
    ego ideal, 104–106
    instinct theory, 25–31, 170
    love, 10, 11–12, 14
    narcissism, 58–61
    overview, 45–47
    post-Freudian innovations, 68–71
    psychopathologies, 47–58
    wise baby dream, 86
Ego psychology, ego instincts, 25–26, 69

Ellenberger, H., 52n5
Ellis, H., 49, 182
Emde, R., 316
Empathy, Budapest School, 139
End of analysis dream case, wise baby, 95–97
Environmental movement, 37–38
Erikson, E., 112n5
Eros
    aggression and, 26
    sexual instincts, 66
Erotophobia, 180
Ethnocentrism, prejudice, 277
Evolutionary psychology, love, 3–6
Evolution theory. *See* Darwinism

Fairbairn, W. R. D., 30n4, 131, 227–228
False self
    true self and, 70, 75, 81–82
    wise baby dream, 85
Fanon, F., 267, 273
Fausto-Sterling, A., 193n10
Federal Bureau of Investigation (FBI), 252–253
Federn, P., 133
Felson, N., 322n8
Female homosexual, 213–245. *See also* Homosexuality; Lesbianism
    case example, 236–243
    contemporary views, 217–224
    developmental perspective, 230–236
    instinct theory, 224–230
    psychoanalysis, 213–214
    stereotyping, 214–217
Feminist movement, 37–38, 173–174, 196, 220–222, 264, 272, 273, 275

Fenichel, O., 113
Ferenczi, S., 30, 52–53, 55, 56n7, 61, 75–79, 80–81, 83–86, 89, 91, 103, 129, 130–150, 168, 170, 175, 184, 214n1, 227, 294, 313. See also Budapest School
Firestein, B., 182, 199, 202
Firestone, S., 173
Fisher, H., 4
Fliess, W., 183
Fonagy, P., 132
Foucault, M., 188, 218–219, 282
Freud, A., 7n3, 69, 108, 129, 130, 131, 139n4, 140n6, 150, 258–259, 286
Freud, S., 5–10, 19–20, 23–35, 45–58, 59–68, 70, 83, 100–101, 103–106, 108, 109–110, 113, 116, 122, 129–131, 133–136, 138, 140, 142, 144–150, 158–159, 162–172, 176, 181, 182–185, 186, 191, 196–197, 203–205, 214–216, 218, 221, 223, 224–230, 232–233, 235, 257–258, 259, 262, 263n7, 272, 274, 285–286, 289, 292–299, 300–301, 302, 304–305, 314–315
Friendship, self-inhibition, 29
Fromm, E., 261n6
Frustration
  aggression, 54
  infancy, 11

Gagnon, J., 189n8
Galen, 291
Gay and Lesbian Liberation Movement, 188–190, 219, 222, 274, 275, 281–282

Gender differences. See also Women
  biology, 158–159
  characterology, 289–290, 296
  psychoanalysis, 161–164
Genetics
  bisexuality, 192–194
  violence, 251
Gindorf, R., 182n5, 198n13, 201n18, 202n19
Goethe, J. W. von, 23, 289
Good enough mother concept, 69–70
Greco-Roman antiquity. See also Amae psychology
  amae in, 311–328
  bisexuality, 201, 202, 206
  characterology types, 287–288, 290–291
  love, 6–14
Greenacre, P., 141n7
Growth principle
  cherishment culture and, 31–35, 39–42
  ego instincts, 47, 68
Guilt
  ego ideal, 112–113
  sexuality, 17–18
Guntrip, H., 131

Haeberle, E., 182n5, 198n13, 201n18, 202n19
Hall, G. S., 62n8
Harnik, J., 130
Hartmann, H., 25, 26n2, 69, 102
Hendrick, I., 62n8, 114n6
Herdt, G., 201n18, 202n19
Hermann, I., 130, 132, 142n7, 144, 145
Hermaphroditism, bisexuality, sexologist perspective, 181

Herodotus, 323
Hesiod, 321, 324
Hippocratic medicine, 291, 301
Hirschfeld, M., 184–185, 203
HIV/AIDS epidemic, 190, 275, 278
Hockenos, P., 266
Holder, A., 109n2
Hollos, I., 130, 140n6
Homer, 12, 36, 321, 324
Homophobia, 220, 271–284
  combating of, 281–284
  current studies in, 271–276
  peculiarities of, 276–281
  violence, 268, 276
Homosexuality. *See also* Bisexuality; Female homosexual; Lesbianism
  bisexuality, 181–182, 201–202
  ego instincts, 59–61
  evolutionary psychology, 5
  Ferenczi, 143
  politics, 188–190
  psychoanalysis, 206–210
Hooker, E., 219
Hormones
  bisexuality, 192–194
  instinct theory, 34n8
Horney, K., 32n6, 169, 173–174, 228, 261n6
Hunger, psychopathologies, 47–58
Hysteria
  characterology, 292–293
  Freud, 164–168
  homophobia, 278–279
  Jung, 56–57
  repression, 259–260
  violence, 262

I Ching, 40–42
Identification, Budapest School, 137–138

Identity politics, 282
Ignotus, H., 140n6
Infancy. *See also* Mother–child relationship
  Amae psychology, 314–315
  love, 9, 10–11
Instinct
  civilization and, 25
  Darwinism, 5
Instinct theory. *See also* Ego instincts
  Amae psychology, 315
  dual, ego instincts, 64–68, 170
  ego ideal, 104–106
  ego psychology, 25–26
  female homosexual, 224–230
  Freud, 25, 26–31
  hormones, 34n8
  violence, 257–258
  wise baby dream, Ferenczi, 76–77
International Psychoanalytic Association, 53

Jacobson, E., 102, 114
Jagger, M., 203
James, W., 289
Janet, P.-M.-F., 56
Jaspers, K., 36
Johnson, F., 313n2, 315n4
Jones, E., 53n6, 135, 149, 169, 215, 216n4, 286
Jonson, B., 291
Jung, C. G., 45, 51–53, 56–59, 66, 133–134, 135n1, 171–172, 228, 287, 289, 294, 297, 299–302

Karr-Morse, R., 251
Katz, J., 219n6, 282
Kernberg, O., 222
Kessler, 50n4

Khantzian, E. J., 62n8
Kierkegaard, S., 23
Kiersey, D., 301–302
Kinsey, A., 186–187, 188–189, 195, 198, 200, 203, 206–207, 219
Kirk, S., 188n7, 219n7
Kirkpatrick, M., 219
Klein, F., 200
Klein, M., 9, 30, 61, 69, 79–80, 129, 141, 142n8, 150, 169, 170, 215, 216n4, 226n10
Kohut, H., 132
Krafft-Ebing, R. von, 181–182, 183, 188, 189, 198
Kris, E., 286
Kropotkin, P., 50n4
Kutchins, H., 188n7, 219n7

Lacan, J., 158, 172–173
Lacquer, T., 159
Lattimore, 323
Le Doux, E., 64n11
Lesbianism. See also Female homosexual
  bisexuality, 201–202, 206
  psychoanalysis, 207–210
Lesser, R., 214n2, 223
Levy, K., 140n6
Levy, L., 140n6
Libido theory
  characterology, 286, 293–294, 297–299
  dual instinct theory, 66
  ego instincts, 45–47
  Ferenczi, 142–143
  post-Freudian innovations, 69
Lieberman, Joseph, 250
Lloyd-Jones, H., 317
Lobster dream case, wise baby, 87–89

Lombardo, 324
Love
  Amae psychology, 312–315 (See also Amae psychology)
  culture of, 23–43
  evolutionary psychology, 3–6
  expectation of, true self, 82–84
  Freud, S., 9
  Greek antiquity, 6–14
  infancy, 9, 10–11
  narcissism, 7, 9
  psychoanalysis, 133–134
  psychology of, 3–21
  psychopathologies, 47–58

Mack, J., 62n8
Magee, M., 223, 233n16
Mahler, M., 31, 70, 71n16, 111, 132, 175, 230–231
Main, M., 132, 145
Malthus, T., 49, 51
Manic defense, mourning and, 9
Marx, K., 23, 26
Maslow, A., 301
Mastery, ego instincts, 67
McGregor, D., 289
Miller, D., 223, 233n16
Millett, K., 221
Milrod, D., 114n7
Mitchell, J., 174, 221
Modell, A., 32n6
Modernism, cherishment culture and, 35–39
Mondimore, F. M., 192n9
Money, J., 198n13
Morgan, C., 219
Mother–child relationship. See also Infancy
  amae psychology, 32–33, 314–315
  Budapest School, 140–145
  Freudian theory, 28–29

Mother–child relationship (*continued*)
    good enough mother concept, 69–70
    object relations theory, 30
    Spitz and, 69
    Winnicott, 81
Mourning, love and, 9
Myers, I., 301, 302
Myers-Briggs Type Inventory, 287, 301

Narcissism
    characterology, 295–296, 298
    ego instincts, 58–61
    homophobia, 279
    love, 7, 9
    primary
        ego ideal, 101–103, 106
        gender differences, 162–163
    rejection hypersensitivity, 14–18
    romantic ideal, 12, 14, 18–19
    violence, 263
Native Americans, bisexuality, 201
Nature/nurture controversy
    bisexuality, sexologist perspective, 181
    violence, 252
Neurasthenia, characterology, 292
Neuroses, ego instincts, 47–58
New Age psychology, unconditional love, 11
Nietzsche, F., 23, 289, 317
Nunberg, H., 101–102, 133

Object choice, bisexuality, 200–206
Object relations theory, 30
    Budapest School, 131
    ego ideal, 107
    ego instincts, 60, 61, 68
    women, 175–177

Object splitting, death instinct, 80
Obsessional neurosis
    characterology, 292–293, 295–296, 299
    homophobia, 280
    hysteria, 165–167
Occult
    Ferenczi, 133, 136
    Freud, 135
Oedipus complex
    bisexuality, 197
    Budapest School, 168
    characterology, 295
    ego ideal, 117
    female homosexual, 215
    Freudian theory, 28n3
    preoedipal phase and, 31
Ovid, 12

Palos, G., 134
Paracelsus, 291
Parental seduction, ego instincts, 54–55
Passion, attachment and, 5
Pathologies. *See* Psychopathologies
Patriarchy
    bisexuality, 205
    homosexuality, 220
Pavlov, I., 302
Peterson, D., 252
Piers, G., 112n5
Pine, F., 71n16
Plato, 289
Plaut, E., 32n6, 62n8
Pleasure, sexuality and, 5
Pleasure principle, reality principle and, 46, 47, 52–53
Politics
    feminist movement, 37–38, 173–174, 196, 220–222, 264, 272, 273, 275

Gay and Lesbian Liberation
    Movement, 188–190, 219,
    222, 274, 275, 281–282
  homophobia, 271–284 (*See also*
    Homophobia)
  homosexuality, 188–190
  violence, 250
Post-coital sadness, 9
Power, modernism, 38
Prejudice
  bisexuality, 179–180
  female homosexual, 217–224
  homophobia, 271–284 (*See also*
    Homophobia)
  violence, 259–264 (*See also*
    Violence)
Preoedipal phase
  ego ideal, 101
  Jung, 57–58
  Oedipus complex and, 31
  Winnicott, 81
Primary narcissism, 30–31
  ego ideal, 101–103, 106
  gender differences, 162–163
Psychoanalysis
  bisexuality, 182–185, 194–200,
    206–210
  Budapest School, 129–153
  characterology, 285–310 (*See also*
    Characterology)
  cherishment culture, 23–25
  female homosexual, 213–214
    (*See also* Female
    homosexual)
  love, 133–134
  repetition and, 67
  women and, 157–178
Psychopathologies
  ego ideal, 121–127
  ego instincts, 47–58
  Ferenczi, 137

psychoses, Budapest School, 145–
    149
  Winnicott, 81
Psychoses
  Budapest School, 145–149
  ego instincts, 47–58
  Ferenczi, 137

Racism
  prejudice, 272, 273, 275–276
  violence, 266–267
Rado, S., 131, 140n6
Rapprochement subphase, ego ideal,
    111–112
Reality principle, pleasure principle
    and, 46–47, 52–53
Regression, Budapest School, 131,
    138, 147
Reich, A., 102, 110, 263
Reich, W., 138, 286, 294, 296
Reik, T., 32n6
Rejection, hypersensitivity to, 14–
    18
Repetition, psychoanalysis and, 67
Repression, violence, 259–260
Rhodes, R., 251n2
Rich, A., 219n6, 275
Riviere, J., 9
Robertson, P., 265
Roman antiquity. *See* Greco-Roman
    antiquity
Romantic ideal
  balance in, 14–19
  expressions of, 12
  superego and ego ideal, 19–21
Rudnytsky, P., 130

Schilder, P., 285, 292
Schiller, F., 5, 49, 289
Schizophrenia, Budapest School,
    146, 148

Schoenberg, E., 214n2
Schreber case (Freud), 146n11
Script theory, 189
Searles, H., 132
Sechehaye, M. A., 82
Seduction. *See* Parental seduction
Seduction theory, hysteria, 165, 167–168
Self-inhibition, friendship, 29
September 11, 2001 terrorist attacks, 250, 251, 253
Severn, E., 136n2, 147–148
Sexism
  Freudian theory, 29–30
  homophobia, 275
  prejudice, 272
Sexologist perspective, bisexuality, 180–182
Sexual instincts
  Amae psychology, 315
  Darwinism, 5
  dual instinct theory, 64–68
  ego ideal, 109
  ego instincts and, 48, 57–58, 170
  Ferenczi, 143
  instinct theory, 25–31, 34–35
  wise baby dream, Ferenczi, 76–77
Sexuality
  disconnection in, 18–19
  ego instincts, 10, 11–12
  narcissism, 17–18
Shakespeare, W., 15–18
Shame, ego ideal, 112–113, 117–121
Sherfy, M. J., 174
Simon, W., 189n8
Singer, M., 112n5
Sober, E., 50n4
Socarides, C., 216–217
Social Darwinism, 50, 52
Solnit, A., 24n1

Sophocles, 322
Spielrein, S., 52, 134
Spitz, R., 31, 69, 105, 109n2, 132, 143, 315, 316
Split-off self, wise baby, dream analysis, Ferenczi, 76–79
Stekel, W., 183
Stendhal (Marie-Henri Beyle), 23
Stereotyping
  female homosexual, 214–217
  racism, 276
Stern, D., 31, 316
Stoics, 291
Stoller, R., 174, 191, 195, 197, 198, 199, 222
Strachey, J., 25, 108
Sullivan, H. S., 132, 173, 228, 233
Sulloway, F., 49, 191n2
Superego
  ego ideal, 100–101, 109
  ego ideal and, 19–21
Suttie, 131

Telepathy, Ferenczi, 140
Temperament, characterology, 301
Terrorist attacks, 250, 251, 253
Theophrastus, 288
Therapeutic action, libido theory, 46–47
Thompson, C., 132
Tocqueville, A. de, 23
Tolstoy, L., 291
Totalitarianism, 36–37
Transference, countertransference and, Budapest School, 133–140
Transitional objects
  ego ideal, 111
  good enough mother concept, 70
Transsexuality, bisexuality and, 198–200

Trauma
  anxiety, 62
  Budapest School, 131, 140–145, 148–149
  Ferenczi, 75
  repetition of, psychoanalysis and, 67
  Winnicott, 81
  wise baby dream, Ferenczi, 77–79
Trepho's semantic field, *amae* psychology, 319–325
True self
  expectation of love, 82–84
  false self and, 70, 75
  Winnicott, 79–84
  wise baby dream, 85

Ulrichs, K. H., 182, 198
Unconditional love, New Age psychology, 11
Unconscious, transference and countertransference, Budapest School, 133–140
United Nations Educational, Scientific and Cultural Organization (UNESCO), 272

Van Thiel, H., 323n9
Violence, 249–270
  case examples, 253–259
  character and prejudice, 259–264
  current perspectives on, 249–253
  homophobia, 268, 276
  types of, 264–268

Waelder, R., 45, 285, 286
Weinberg, G., 220
West, M. L., 321n7
White, R., 62n8
White, W. A., 132

Whyte, W., 261n6
Wiley, M., 251
Williams, B., 317
Wilson, D. S., 50n4
Winnicott, D. W., 10, 31, 69–71, 75, 80–84, 85, 105, 107, 111, 130, 131, 147, 150, 171, 175–176, 316
Wise baby, 75–98, 146
  amphitheater of terror dream case, 90–94
  dream analysis, Ferenczi, 75–79
  dream of, 84–87
  end of analysis dream case, 95–97
  lobster dream case, 87–89
  true self, Winnicott, 79–84
Wittig, M., 219n6, 275
Wolf Man case (Freud), 60–61, 166, 232, 295
Women, 157–178. *See also* Female homosexual; Gender differences; Lesbianism
  difference theory, 167–170
  Freudian theory, 29–30
  gender differences, 161–164
  late Freudian thought, 170–172
  nosology, 164–167
  object relations theory, 175–177
  overview, 157–161
  post-Freudian thought, 172–174
  violence against, 262–264
Women's Liberation Movement. *See* Feminist movement
Wrangham, R., 252

Young-Bruehl, E., 117, 158, 259n5, 315n3, 316

Zeldin, T., 38–39, 41
Zetzel, E., 150